2ND EDITION

MECHATRONICS MATTERS

ENGLISCH FÜR MECHATRONIK

von
Georg Aigner
Michael Benford
Jan Richter
Isobel Williams
Wolf-Rainer Windisch

unter Mitarbeit der Verlagsredaktion

Cornelsen

MECHATRONICS MATTERS

Verfasser/in:	Georg Aigner, Landshut; Michael Benford, Bochum; Jan Richter, Freiberg; Isobel Williams, Berlin; Wolf-Rainer Windisch, Freiburg
Verfasser KMK-Seiten:	Michael Benford, Bochum; Jan Richter, Freiberg; Manfred Thönicke und Jörg Trabert, Hamburg; Wolf-Rainer Windisch, Freiburg
Berater/innen:	Antje Baehr, Essen; Annette Fauth, Freiburg; Nils Krämer, Düsseldorf; Jan Richter, Freiberg; Wolf-Rainer Windisch, Freiburg
Projektleitung:	Simone Conrad
Außenredaktion:	James Abram
Redaktionelle Mitarbeit:	Christine House
Bildredaktion:	Gertha Maly, Christina Scheuerer
Layoutkonzept:	finedesign, Berlin
Gesamtgestaltung und Technische Umsetzung:	vitaledesign, Berlin
Umschlaggestaltung:	vitaledesign, Berlin
Coverfoto:	Fotolia/Mopic
Illustrationen:	Oxford Designers & Illustrators

Erhältlich sind auch:
Handreichungen für den Unterricht mit MP3-CD und Online-Zusatzmaterialien
ISBN 978-3-06-451521-5

www.cornelsen.de

1. Auflage, 1. Druck 2017

Alle Drucke dieser Auflage sind inhaltlich unverändert und können im Unterricht nebeneinander verwendet werden.

Druck: Mohn Media Mohndruck, Gütersloh

ISBN 978-3-06-451519-2
ISBN 978-3-06-451520-8 (E-Book)

PEFC
PEFC/04-31-1033

PEFC zertifiziert
Dieses Produkt stammt aus nachhaltig bewirtschafteten Wäldern und kontrollierten Quellen.
www.pefc.de

Vorwort

Mechatronics Matters 2nd edition ist die vollständige Neubearbeitung des bewährten Englisch-Lehrwerks für Mechatroniker/innen, die am Berufsschulunterricht oder an betrieblichen Fortbildungen teilnehmen.

Das Lehrwerk setzt Englischkenntnisse voraus, die dem Niveau A2 des Europäischen Referenzrahmens *(Common European Framework of Reference)* entsprechen. Es deckt die Themen der aktuellen Lehrpläne der Bundesländer für Englisch in der Berufsschule konsequent ab.

Mechatronics Matters 2nd edition besteht aus zwölf Units, die flexibel einsetzbar sind. Jede Unit umfasst vier abgeschlossene Lernsituationen, die jeweils in einer Doppelstunde bearbeitet werden können. Eine Unit ist wie folgt aufgebaut:

Foundation: Diese Doppelseite bietet Ihnen mit technischem Grundwissen und elementarem Themenvokabular einen Einstieg in das Thema der Unit.

Part A/B: Diese stark technisch ausgerichteten Module können je nach Umfang der Inputmaterialien jeweils zwei oder drei Seiten umfassen. Hier werden fachspezifische Schwerpunkte der Unit mithilfe authentischer und aktueller Materialien behandelt.

Communication: Berufliche Kommunikation steht im Fokus des abschließenden *Communication*-Teils. Ein „Das kann ich"-Kästchen – eine Checkliste zur Selbstevaluation – rundet die Unit ab und ermöglicht es den Lernenden, über ihren persönlichen Lernerfolg zu reflektieren.

Alle Lernsituationen sind so konzipiert, dass sie ausgelassen oder zu einem anderen Zeitpunkt behandelt werden können. Somit berücksichtigt die Modulstruktur einer jeden Unit die organisatorische Vielfalt des Englischunterrichts und schafft größtmögliche Flexibilität im Unterricht.

Besonderer Wert wird in diesem Lehrwerk auf **Handlungsorientierung** und direkten Berufsbezug gelegt: Jedes Modul beginnt mit einer branchenspezifischen *Situation* und führt über handlungs- und kompetenzorientierte Lernschritte zu einem Handlungsprodukt. Dieses Lernziel ist jeweils zu Beginn des Moduls mit einem Pfeil gekennzeichnet und ermöglicht so eine schnelle Orientierung.

Unterschiedliche Aktions- und Sozialformen ermöglichen zudem den Einsatz von kooperativen Lernformen und fördern **eigenverantwortliches Lernen**.

Um der Heterogenität der Auszubildenden gerecht zu werden, finden sich zahlreiche Aufgaben zur **Binnendifferenzierung** in den Units. Diese sind mit einem Strich unter der Aufgabenziffer gekennzeichnet und verweisen auf editierbare Kopiervorlagen in den Handreichungen, die alternative Bearbeitungsmöglichkeiten für die jeweilige Aufgabe zur Verfügung stellen.

Zur Vorbereitung auf die **KMK-Prüfung** für Niveau A2 und B1 werden anhand von sechs Unterrichtseinheiten und einer kompletten Musterprüfung prüfungsrelevante Materialien und Aufgaben angeboten und so eine systematische Prüfungsvorbereitung ermöglicht.

Grundlegende grammatikalische Strukturen werden durchweg im **situativen Kontext** vermittelt, ergänzt durch eine systematische Grammatikübersicht im Anhang. Zur Erweiterung des berufsrelevanten Wortschatzes wird schwieriges **Fachvokabular**, das zum Verständnis der Materialien notwendig ist, in jedem Modul in einer *Toolbox* gesondert hervorgehoben. Eine umfangreiche *Unit word list* mit allen neuen Wörtern in chronologischer Reihenfolge wie auch eine *A-Z word list* mit allen neuen Wörtern in alphabetischer Reihenfolge befinden sich im Anhang, ebenso wie berufsbezogene *Useful phrases*, die eine effektive berufliche Kommunikation erleichtern.

Sämtliche Audiomaterialien finden Sie in den Handreichungen für den Unterricht. Typische Sprachhandlungssituationen im Berufsalltag werden multimedial mit visueller Unterstützung trainiert: Diese visualisierten Hörtexte sind mit ▶ gekennzeichnet und schulen effektiv das Hör- und Sehverstehen. Ein Webcode, mit dem Sie die visualisierten Hörtexte aufrufen können, befindet sich ebenfalls in den Handreichungen.

Der Verlag, die Autoren sowie die Berater und Beraterinnen wünschen Ihnen viel Erfolg und Freude mit *Mechatronics Matters 2nd edition.*

Table of contents

1 My company

FOUNDATION: A company profile

Situation: You are an apprentice with a German company that also has lots of trainees from abroad.
→ **You write a short profile of your company in English for the apprentice file.**

1 Reading a company website

Before you write the profile, you read another company's English profile online.

AT Adler Technology Group – a global player

A The Adler Technology Group is a German producer of cables and connectors. Its head office is in Duisburg in North Rhine-Westphalia. The company was founded in July 1948 by Hans-Joachim Adler and his wife, Luise. Today, Adler Technology Group is still a family business. It is run by Wolfgang and Suzanne Adler and their two children, René Adler and Mareike Adler-Schmidt.

B The structure of the company looks like this:
Wolfgang Adler – Chairman of the Board, General Partner
Mareike Adler-Schmidt – General Partner, Senior Vice President Finance and Purchasing
René Adler – General Partner, Senior Vice President New Technologies
Suzanne Adler – Partner, Senior Vice President Sales and Marketing

C Although it is a family business, Adler is also a global player. There are 11 factories, located in Germany, the Netherlands, France, Great Britain, Romania, the USA and China. Forty-seven sales companies look after Adler's customers worldwide. The company employs around 6,000 people, including over 500 engineers and research scientists.

D Adler Technology Group develops, manufactures and sells electrical and electronic cables and connectors. Our products are used in mechanical engineering, factory automation, power generation and distribution as well as industrial electronics and telecommunication.

E Vocational training and apprenticeships for young people play a central role in the company.

A Match the headlines 1–6 to the paragraphs A–E. There is one headline more than you need.

1 Company structure
2 Interesting information for trainees
3 About Adler
4 Adler's customers
5 Introduction to Duisburg
6 Adler worldwide

TOOLBOX

apprentice – *Lehrling, Auszubildende/r*
apprenticeship – *Lehre, Ausbildung*
customer – *Kunde/Kundin*
electrical/electronic – *elektrisch/elektronisch*
engineer – *Ingenieur/in*
vocational training – *Berufsausbildung*

B Say if the following statements are true or false according to the text. Correct the false statements.

1. Adler Technology Group is a multinational company.
   False: Adler Technology Group is a family business and is well known abroad, but it is not a multinational.
2. Adler's head office is in Germany.
3. The company was founded in 1948.
4. No one from the original family works for the company any longer.
5. All production is done in Germany.
6. Adler has an international sales team.
7. The company sells to customers in many different sectors.
8. There are no training possibilities at Adler.

2 Introducing a company

A group of young people are introducing themselves and the companies they work for.

2 **Copy the grid below into your exercise book. Then listen and complete the grid.**

Name of company	Sector	Head office	Size
BCC Electronics			*medium-sized*
International Solutions			*start-up*
Nilsson Construction	*building*		
Han Gao			
Jahn Services			
Aikon			

3 Making notes about your company

A Make notes that you can use to give a short description of your company. Cover the points below:

- name of the company
- sector
- location
- number of employees
- what the company does
- target group/customers
- some competitors

Asking for information

Who do you work for?
What is the name of your company?
Where is the company located?
How many employees does your company have?

› *Grammar: Questions and short answers, page 158*

B Talk with a partner. Your partner will ask you questions about your company. Use the notes above. You have three minutes to answer. › *Useful phrases: Describing your company, page 149*

4 Writing the company profile

Now it is time to write the company profile for the apprentice file.

On your own, or with your partner, write a short profile of your company. Structure your information under the headings you used for exercise 3A above. Present your company to the class and be prepared to answer questions from the audience. › *Useful phrases: Describing your company, page 149*

TOOLBOX

automotive sector – *Automobilbranche, -industrie*
electronic equipment – *elektronische Geräte/Ausrüstung*
medium-sized company – *mittelständischer Betrieb*
multinational company – *multinationaler Konzern*

PART A: The structure of a company

Situation: You work for Mech-On, a German mechanical engineering company. Today is your first day at the British subsidiary of Mech-On in Newcastle. Your supervisor, Martin Foster, describes the structure of the UK branch.
→ **You describe the structure of your training company in Germany.**

1 Understanding an organization chart

First of all, Martin Foster shows you an organization chart of the UK branch of Mech-On.

A **Work with a partner. Study the chart and make sure you understand all the words in the list below.**

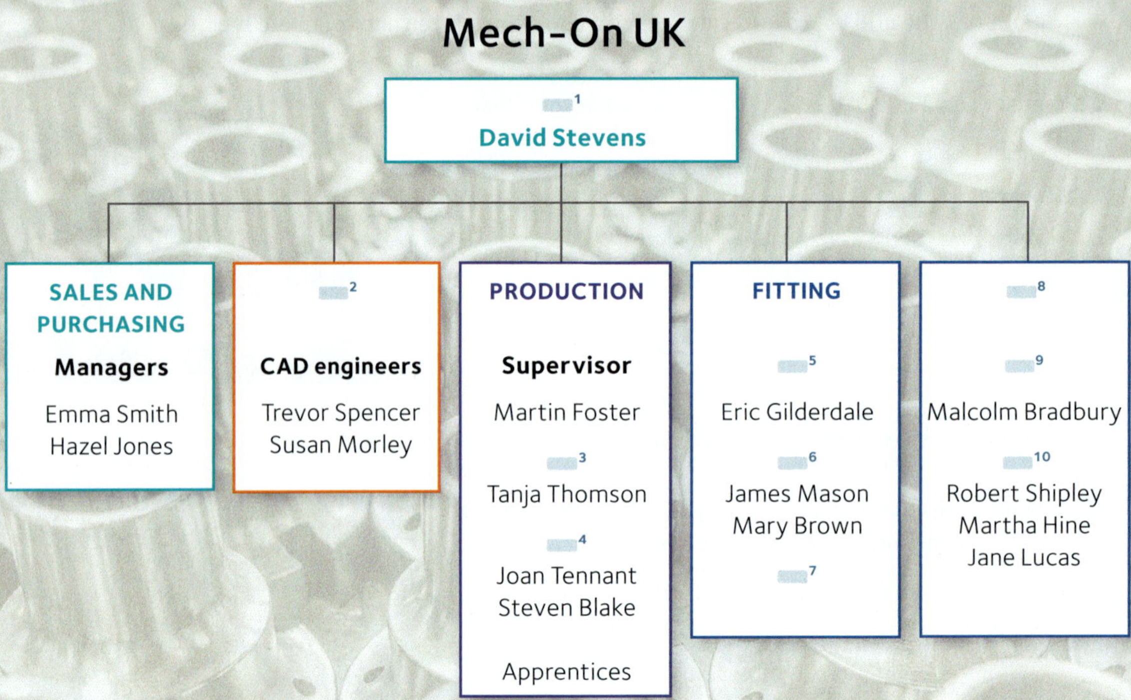

B 3 **Now listen and complete the chart with words from the list.**

Apprentices · Construction · Fitters and turners · Foreman · Head of division · Line manager · Quality control · Quality control manager · Skilled workers · Test technicians

Describing responsibilities

Tanja **is** in charge of two skilled workers.
Mr Stevens **supervises** all the processes here.

› *Grammar: Simple present, page 158*

TOOLBOX

CAD engineer – *Technische/r Zeichner/in*
fitter – *Monteur/in*
fitting – *Montage*
foreman/-woman – *Vorarbeiter/in, Meister/in*
head of division – *Bereichsleiter/in*
quality control – *Qualitätskontrolle*
skilled worker – *Facharbeiter/in*
turner – *Dreher/in*

2 Reading emails to Mech-On

Martin Foster would like to test your understanding of the organization of the Newcastle branch. He gives you excerpts from five emails to Mech-On.

Work with a partner. Decide together which department they should go to.

To:

Subject:

1 As we had a problem with a shaft that was 7 micrometres too small in diameter we checked the whole batch you delivered and found out that although the shafts had a quality label on them, about 30% of them were out of tolerance.

2 The flywheel you delivered is too heavy. We would like to send it back to you and ask you whether you could drill holes around the outer ring to reduce the weight. There should be 30 holes altogether, each of them with a diameter of 18 mm.

3 We need to make changes to the lifting system because the hydraulic piston does not fit properly. Could you please email me the drawing with all the tolerances mentioned as we are not sure where the problem is.

4 The cable system was connected to the lift cabin with a screw with a special head which we cannot work with. I know that the purpose is to keep the screw tightened but we have to take the cabin out of the lift shaft so need to have the correct tool.

5 Thank you very much for your offer. We accept the price of the connecting pipes. As far as the flanges are concerned, we have been offered a better price by a different supplier. As our cooperation has been going on for more than 7 years now, we would like to ask you whether you could make us a better offer for the flanges.

3 Describing the Mech-On head office

Now Martin Foster wants to know about the structure of the Nuremberg head office.

Work with a partner. Partner A: Look at File 1 on page 134. Partner B: Look at File 9 on page 138.

4 Describing the structure of your training company

A **Work in groups with students from your own company. Decide together what you are going to include on your organization chart before you draw it. Make sure you include the names of the main departments and the names and positions of people in important positions.**

B **Explain the company to someone from another group.**

› *Grammar: Simple present, page 158*

PART B: Visitors to the company

Situation: You work for Ritter Starkstromtechnik, an electrical engineering company in Dortmund.
→ **You prepare a presentation for English-speaking visitors to your company.**

1 Presenting products and services

You are part of the team that is preparing a presentation to show what Ritter has to offer.

A Match the headings in the list to the slides (1–4).

Automation · Installation · Switchgear · Switching devices

Slide 1
- Industrial and domestic (re-)wiring
- Trunking and tray work with sleeves up to 36 kV
- 24-hour emergency service

Slide 2
- Low and medium voltage panels
- Standard systems
- Customized solutions
- Official certification

Slide 3
- Control technology
- Process visualization
- Remote systems
- Industrial and wireless communication

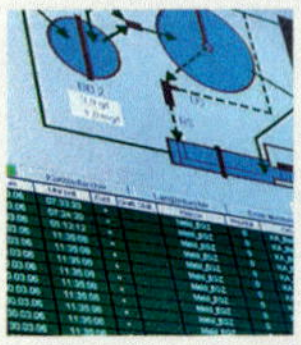

Slide 4
- Medium voltage and high current circuit breakers
- Rail technology
- Compact construction
- Low maintenance

B Work with a partner. Use the words in the list to complete the gaps in the commentary below.

available · final · move · offer · overview · range · see · shows · specialize · start

Good morning, ladies and gentlemen and welcome to Ritter. My name is Thomas Keller and I'm the sales director. This morning I'll ___[1] our short presentation of the company with our four main fields and then look at each field in more detail. Here at Ritter we ___[2] in installation, automation, switchgear and switching devices. Our company has many household names as customers and we operate all over the world.
[Slide 1] The first slide ___[3] you that we have state-of-the-art mobile equipment for our installation work. No job is too large or small, simple or complicated for us and we are ___[4] 24/7.
[Slide 2] As you can ___[5] from this slide, we manufacture low and medium voltage switchgear to guarantee fail-safe power distribution. We ___[6] a complete service from design to operation, including certification.
[Slide 3] Let's now ___[7] on to automation. We can install a wide ___[8] of control technology systems, and our customers include the heavy and chemical industries, power stations, data centres and hospitals.
[Slide 4] Now let's look at the ___[9] slide about our switching devices. Electrical switches are a vital component in industrial systems and transportation, and this shows a high current circuit breaker used in rail technology.
That was a brief ___[10] of Ritter Starkstrom. Many thanks for listening. If you have any questions, I'll be delighted to answer them.

C 4))) Now listen and check your answers.

TOOLBOX

circuit breaker – *Leitungsschutzschalter, Sicherungsautomat*
control technology – *Leittechnik*
customized – *maßgeschneidert*
sleeve – *Muffe*
tray work – *Installation in Kabelpritschen*
trunking – *Leitungsführung*
wireless – *drahtlos*

2 Taking visitors on a guided tour

Stig Lindqvist, a Swedish customer, visits Ritter Starkstromtechnik and Thomas Keller takes him on a guided tour.

A 5 **Listen to the conversation and label the locations on the diagram (1–12) using the list below (a–l).**

a Assembly, Wiring and Training	d Copper Workshop	g Final Assembly	j Sales
b Break Room	e Design	h Metal Workshop	k Showroom
c Conference Room	f Electrical Design	i Pre-assembly	l Storeroom

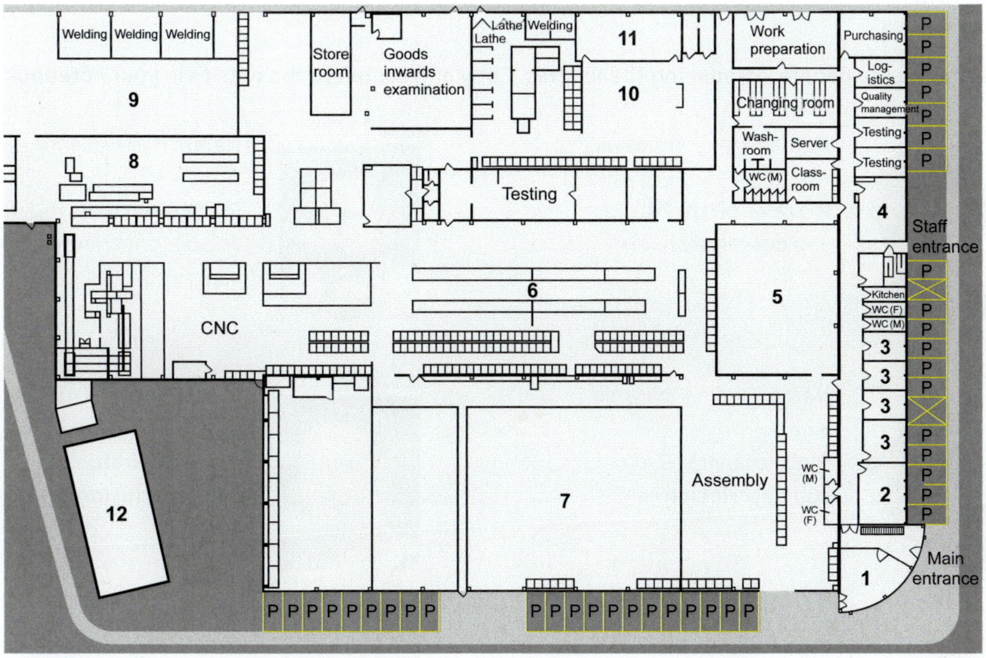

B 5 **Listen to the dialogue again and complete the sentences below.**

1 Let's ___ in the showroom here by the main entrance.
2 Here you can ___ some examples of our products.
3 Let's walk down the corridor ___ the big conference room on our right.
4 ___ the conference room you can see our sales offices.
5 Here on our ___ is the storeroom. We keep our components here.
6 It's next ___ to the copper workshop …
7 ___ there on our left you can see the lathes and some more welding equipment, …
8 Our last ___ is the break room.

3 Showing visitors around your company

You are now ready to describe your company's products and services to English-speaking visitors.

Work on the following tasks in small groups from the same training company.

1 Prepare a presentation about your company consisting of 4–5 slides. Give the presentation to the other members of your group first, then to your class. The audience can ask questions.
2 Make a large poster of the layout of your company, label the most important locations in English and hang it up on the wall. Take it in turns to show visitors around your company and answer their questions.

› *Useful phrases: Describing your company, page 149; Showing visitors around the company, page 149*

COMMUNICATION: Introductions and small talk

Situation: You work at Mech-On, a Nuremberg-based mechanical engineering company.
→ **You look after a visitor from England until your supervisor, Ms Müller, is ready to meet him.**

1 Introducing yourself and others to colleagues

The Human Resources department at Mech-On stores information about its employees on computerized personnel files.

A 6 **Listen to the people introducing themselves. Copy and complete the entries in your notebook.**

Name: Martyna Nowak
Age: ___ [1]
Place of birth: Poland
Job description: ___ [2]

Name: Halil Özdemir
Age: ___ [3]
Place of birth: ___ [4]
Job description: Training supervisor

Name: Deema Mansour
Age: ___ [5]
Place of birth: Syria
Job description: ___ [6]

Name: Robert Klein
Age: 21
Place of birth: ___ [7]
Job description: ___ [8]

Name: Canan Tolon
Age: ___ [9]
Place of birth: Turkey
Job description: ___ [10]

Name: Alexei Melnyk
Age: 39
Place of birth: ___ [11]
Job description: ___ [12]

B **You have three minutes to introduce yourself to the other people in the class.**

My name is …

I'm … years old.

I was born in …

I'm a/an …

> **Talking about jobs**
>
> What **do you do**? – I'm **a** trainee. / I'm **an** energy engineer.
> What **is** your job? – I'm **a** mechanic. / I'm **an** electrical engineer. (NOT: ~~My job is …~~)

C **Introduce one of the people you met to the rest of the class.**

This is …

He's/She's … years old.

He/She was born in …

He's/She's a(n) …

2 Making formal introductions

A **Work with a partner. Introduce yourself in a formal way to your partner (a visitor).**

B **Now formally introduce your partner to another pair.** › *Useful phrases: Making introductions, page 149*

3 Making small talk

A **In groups, choose suitable topics for small talk in business. Say which topics you should avoid.**

holidays · your city/town · religion · the journey to the meeting place · illnesses · sport · politics · the weather · pay · where someone works

B **Match the questions (1–6) to the possible responses (a–f).**

1 Is this your first time in Berlin?
2 How is your hotel?
3 It's lovely weather, isn't it?
4 How was your journey?
5 Where are you based?

a Yes. It's fantastic. We've been very lucky this year.
b Very nice. I travelled by train this time.
c Yes. I've heard that it's a very interesting city.
d Fine. I have a good view from the window in my room.
e In Scotland. In Edinburgh, in fact.

4 Meeting and greeting the visitor

Now it is time to meet the visitor. You know that the person Ms Müller is expecting is called Mr Brown.

A **Work in groups of three. Complete the dialogue. Then close your books and practise the dialogue.**

You	*Excuse*[1] me. *Are you*[2] Mr Brown?
Visitor	Yes, I am.
You	I'm (own name). ___[3] do you do? ___[4] to Mech-On.
Visitor	Thank you. It's ___ ___ ___ ___[5].
You	I'm afraid Ms Müller has been held up, but she'll be here in a few minutes. ___ ___ ___[6] your coat?
Visitor	Yes, thank you. Here you are.
You	___[7] you like something to drink?
Visitor	Yes, please. I'd like a cup of coffee with milk and sugar.
You	Here you are. Is this your ___ ___[8] in Germany?
Visitor	No. I've been here before, but only on holiday.
You	Oh. Here's Ms Müller now. Mr Brown, ___ ___[9] Ms Müller.
Ms Müller	___[10] morning, Mr Brown. Sorry to keep you waiting.
Visitor	No problem. Your assistant has been looking after me very well.

Offering help/refreshments

Can I take your coat?
Would you like something to drink?
Would you like some tea or coffee?

› *Useful phrases: Showing visitors around the company, page 149*

B **Write your own dialogue and practise it in your group.**

DAS KANN ICH (Unit 1)

- Ein kurzes Firmenprofil meines Ausbildungsbetriebs auf Englisch erstellen. (Foundation)
- Die Struktur meines Ausbildungsbetriebs auf Englisch beschreiben. (Part A)
- Meinen Ausbildungsbetrieb englischsprachigen Besuchern/Besucherinnen präsentieren. (Part B)
- Eine/n englischsprachige/n Besucher/in empfangen und jemandem vorstellen. (Communication)

2 My workplace

FOUNDATION: Health and safety in the workplace

Situation: An accident happened in your company recently, so all the apprentices are sent on a safety training course.
→ **You make a safety poster for your workshop.**

1 Talking about hazards at work

The trainer gives a short talk about dangers at work before she asks you to discuss your own ideas.

Soldering, testing, routine maintenance checks – these are just three of the jobs you might be doing in the workshop. We all enjoy what we're doing there, but there could be some dangers attached to the work. Take soldering for example. The tip of a soldering iron is at a temperature around 300 to 350 degrees and can burn your skin. Apart from that, the soldering process gives off fumes and these fumes can be harmful if you're soldering for a long time. Safety in the workshop is very important. …

A 7 **Listen and answer as many of these questions as you can.**

1 What protective clothing does the trainer mention?
2 What examples of messiness on the floor are given?
3 What is the safety rule for emergency switches?
4 How should you fill a shelf?
5 How can you make sure you have enough ventilation in the workshop?
6 What problems related to guards and screens does the trainer mention?
7 What advice does the trainer give about tools?
8 What tools does she give as examples?

B **When you have finished, work in groups and compare your answers.**

TOOLBOX

emergency cut out switch – *Not-Aus-Schalter*
guard – *Schutzvorrichtung*
hard hat – *Schutzhelm*
maintenance – *Wartung, Instandhaltung*
protective clothing – *Schutzkleidung*
screen – *Schutzschirm*
soldering – *Weichlöten*
soldering iron – *Lötkolben*
ventilation – *Belüftung*
ventilator – *Abzug, Ventilator*

2 Reading safety guidelines

Complete the safety guidelines with imperative forms of the verbs in the list.

~~keep~~ · make sure · not distract · ~~not smoke~~ · not wear · not work on · open · shut down

1 *Keep* your workplace clean. *Do not smoke* in the workshop.
2 ___ jewellery around machines.
3 ___ another employee while he/she is working.
4 ___ electrical appliances while they are plugged in.
5 ___ machinery before cleaning or maintenance.
6 ___ the windows so there is enough air in the workshop.
7 ___ you know the safety rules.

> **Giving orders and instructions**
>
> **Do not block** emergency exits.
> **Keep** emergency stop buttons free.
> **Switch off** machinery before you remove the safety cover.

› *Grammar: Imperatives, page 158*

3 Describing accidents and emergencies

Work in groups. Describe an accident or emergency you know of that happened due to dangers in the workshop. Report to the class.

› *Grammar: Simple past, page 159; Past progressive, page 159*

I was standing on a ladder. A colleague bumped into the ladder and I fell off.

4 Recognizing safety signs

A

B

C

D

E

F

G

H

I

J

Match the signs (A–J) to the meanings (1–10). What do the different colours of the signs mean?

1 danger: high voltage
2 fire extinguisher
3 emergency exit
4 wear gloves
5 acid
6 highly flammable
7 no entry
8 no naked lights
9 first aid
10 wear safety goggles

5 Making a safety poster

Now it is time to make a poster for your workshop showing how to stay safe at work.

A **Work in groups. Think of a headline for your poster and draw safety signs. Make a short list of safety rules in English (use imperatives).**

B **When you have finished your poster, pin it on the wall and do a gallery walk. Rank the posters using the categories below. Give points from 1–5 for each category.**

headline · design · correct signs · instructions/imperatives · overall effect

TOOLBOX

acid – *Säure*
emergency exit – *Notausgang*
fire extinguisher – *Feuerlöscher*
first aid – *Erste Hilfe*
flammable – *brennbar*
high voltage – *Hochspannung*
naked lights – *offene Flammen*
safety goggles – *Schutzbrille*

PART A: Describing your job

Situation: You work as an electrician for a large international company, the Everlight Corporation.
→ **You create a job profile for the company website to help recruit more electricians worldwide.**

1 Showing what you do

You and your colleagues are asked to choose photos of your jobs for the website.

A Match the job descriptions below with the photographs of electricians at work (1–4).

panel builder · installation electrician · machine maintenance technician · powerline technician

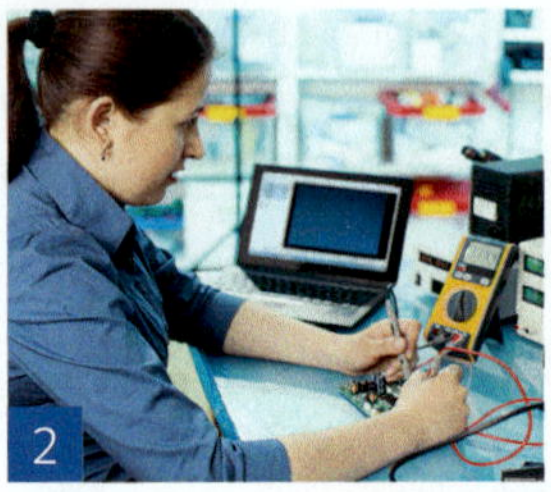

B Who says what? Pair the speech bubbles with the jobs.

A My work basically involves wiring and rewiring houses, flats and commercial premises.

B My work consists of installing, checking, maintaining and repairing machinery in a factory.

C I spend my time assembling and testing the electrical panels used in machinery.

D My job means maintaining and repairing the national grid, which transmits electricity all over the country.

2 Preparing a job profile

Everlight wants to post video job profiles with voice-over commentaries on its website.

A Martin Cheung, an American panel builder, writes the following key facts. Use them to complete his commentary. Sometimes there is more than one word missing.

Martin Cheung					
Town/City	**Profession**	**Tasks**	**Workplace**	**Working hours**	**Why I like my job**
Seattle, USA	panel builder	understanding schematics; putting together control panels; soldering components onto circuit boards	factory; workshop	37 hours per week; Monday–Friday	working with my hands; regular hours; time for hobbies

Hi, I'm Martin Cheung and I work in the Everlight ___[1] in Seattle. I trained as a ___[2] and now at Everlight I use ___[3] to assemble the electronic ___[4] used for heating, ventilation and air-conditioning systems, which basically means soldering ___[5] on circuit boards. I work indoors in a well-equipped ___[6] for 37 hours ___[7] week from Monday to Friday. I enjoy working with my hands and I like the ___[8] hours because it gives me time for my hobbies in the evening.

B **Copy the table headings into your exercise book then read Sarah Clark's text and note down her key facts.**

My name's Sarah Clark. I'm an installation electrician for Everlight in Liverpool in the UK. My job is basically wiring and rewiring buildings. I spend a lot of time putting in conduit in preparation for the wiring and also attaching electrical equipment, such as electric cookers and water-heaters. I work in houses, flats or commercial premises. I have a five-day, 40-hour week and I like my work because travelling from place to place means there's a lot of variety and I never work anywhere for very long.

C 8 **Now listen to Jarek Król's voice-over commentary and note down his key facts. Listen to the recording twice if necessary.**

D **With a partner, write out Jarek Król's voice-over commentary again using his key facts and your memory. How close can you get to the original?**

E **Now use Jean-Luc Delon's key facts below to write his voice-over commentary.**

Jean-Luc Delon		
Town/City	**Profession**	**Tasks**
Calais, France	powerline technician	maintaining and repairing the national grid; repairing and replacing overhead power cables; laying underground cables to connect electricity substations to the grid
Workplace	**Working hours**	**Why I like my job**
outdoors; high up on pylons; on the ground	35 hours per week; standby day and night for emergencies	working outdoors in the fresh air

3 Creating a job profile

Now it's your turn to create a job profile and commentary to be posted online for your employer.

A **Work with a partner. Use the headings in the examples above to make a list of the key facts for your own job. Add or take a photograph of yourself at work.**

B **Use your key facts to create your own job profile. Write a text or voice-over commentary.**

- If you want, record it on a smartphone and play it to the class.
- If possible, make a video of yourself at work accompanied by your voice-over commentary.
- Show it to the class and discuss it.
- Does it make other people want to do your job?

› *Useful phrases: Describing your job, page 149*

Describing your job

My job involves **being** on standby.
My work consists of **installing** machinery.
Travelling from place to place means there's a lot of variety.

› *Grammar: Gerunds, page 161*

TOOLBOX

to assemble – *montieren, zusammenbauen*
to install – *installieren, einbauen*
to maintain – *warten, instand halten*
to repair – *reparieren*
to replace – *ersetzen*
to (re)wire – *neu verkabeln*
to solder – *löten*
to test – *prüfen*

PART B: The dual system of vocational training

Situation: You are working at the British subsidiary of your company.
→ **You give a short presentation about vocational training in Germany to your British colleagues.**

1 Reading about the dual system

Your supervisor suggests you use information from the following text for your presentation.

Learning by doing in Germany

Most students in Germany complete their high school education between the ages of 15 and 18. After that, some of them enter a dual training scheme at a vocational college.

The dual system combines hands-on learning with classroom learning. This means that the apprentice gets job experience at work and a deep knowledge of their trade at school.

One company that offers apprenticeships is Mech-On, a medium-sized company in the metal trade based in Nuremberg. Mech-On offers apprenticeships in mechanics, electronics and mechatronics.

Gaining a vocational college qualification in trades like these gives young workers good chances in their future lives. The qualification standards are the same throughout the whole of Germany, which means that the degree is recognized by every company.

Taking on an apprentice costs a lot of money but, at the end of the day, the company often benefits. By training their own expert staff, businesses of every kind create the next generation of workers. Apprentices who are offered a permanent position at the end of their apprenticeship are already familiar with the structure of the company and the way things work. Another advantage of keeping on apprentices is that a company reduces recruitment costs.

Learning by doing is an important part of the German education system. Whether someone is a mechanic or a workshop manager, he or she has probably gone through the dual education system at some time in their life. Even though the German degree is not recognized in some countries, the fact that someone has trained in Germany is often enough to get them a good position abroad.

A Say if the following statements are true or false. Correct the false statements.

1 Vocational college training is only for students who have been to university.
2 Apprentices must have job experience before they can get a place at a college.
3 Mech-On trains people for different types of jobs in the metal industry.
4 A vocational school qualification is accepted by every German firm.
5 Training young people doesn't cost a company anything.
6 There are no advantages for a company that trains young people.
7 A lot of qualified workers have attended vocational college.
8 German dual system qualifications are recognized all over the world.

B Find the words in the text that match the following definitions.

1 a school that teaches the skills that are necessary for particular jobs
2 learning by doing
3 an exam that you have passed
4 particular areas of business
5 advantages
6 a long-time job
7 finding new people to join a company
8 completed

C Work with a partner. Note down information in the text that you can use in your presentation.

German students complete high school between 15 and 18.
dual system = hands-on learning + classroom learning

2 Making a mind map

You continue with your preparation, brainstorming and making a mind map.

A Work with a partner. Describe your working/training situation in Germany using the points below. You can add more points if you like. Make notes.

- what you are training for
- what you like / don't like about your training: breaks, canteen, noise in workshop, …
- how many weeks you spend in the company
- weekly/daily working hours, overtime work, pay, holidays
- working alone/supervised
- how many days/weeks you spend at vocational college
- what you learn at college

Talking about what you do regularly

We **usually** work for … hours a week.
We **sometimes/never** have to work overtime.
We **always** have a break for 15 minutes at 9 o'clock.

German vocational schools

The following are the official terms for German vocational schools:

Berufsschule	vocational college
Berufsfachschule	technical college of vocational education
Technikerschule / Meisterschule	technical college of further education
Fachoberschule / Berufsoberschule / technisches Gymnasium	technical college of higher education

B Use your notes to make a mind map. The ideas on the right should start you off. Add more branches if you need to.

3 Giving a presentation

It is time to write up and give your presentation.

A Continue to work with your partner. Use the notes you made for exercise 1 C and the mind map you produced for exercise 2 to write up your presentation.

B When you are ready, take turns to give your presentation to the class.

› *Useful phrases: Giving a presentation, page 150*

COMMUNICATION: Telephoning

Situation: You are working in the UK subsidiary of Hamm Maschinenbau GmbH.
→ **You call a client and leave a voicemail message. Later, you take a message.**

1 Making a telephone call

Your supervisor has left you a note asking you to call a customer, Mr Dalton.

First, check the phrases for making a call. Put them in the order you will use them when you call.

a Could you ask … (*name*) to call me back?
b Good morning/afternoon.
c I'd like to speak to/leave a message for … (*name*).
d I'm calling on behalf of … (*name*).
e It's about the …
f My number is …
g Thank you. Goodbye.
h The details are as follows: …
i This is … (*name*) from Hamm Machines Ltd.

- *Phone Esher Engineering to confirm the service checks on their lathes.*
- *Say that you're calling on my behalf.*
- *Ask to speak to Roger Dalton. He's the factory manager.*
- *Tell him that two maintenance technicians will be at the factory at 8.30 on Tuesday, 7 June.*
- *All checks should be completed by 12.30 at the latest.*
- *If you only get voicemail, ask for Mr Dalton to call you back to confirm the date and time.*
- *Give him your mobile number. Thanks.*

2 Leaving a voicemail message

When you call Esher Engineering, you only get voicemail, so you have to leave a message for Mr Dalton.

Work with a partner. Use the phrases in exercise 1 and the note above to complete the voicemail message. Each gap represents one word.

"Good morning. This is ___ ___[1] from Hamm Machines Ltd. I'm calling ___ ___ ___[2] my supervisor, John Hall. I'd like to ___ ___ ___ ___[3] Mr Dalton, the ___ ___[4]. It's ___ ___[5] service checks on your lathes. The ___ ___ ___ ___[6]: We'll be sending ___ ___ ___[7] to your factory at 8.30 on Tuesday, 7 June. All checks should be completed by 12.30 ___ ___ ___[8].
___ ___ ___[9] Mr Dalton ___ ___ ___ ___[10] to confirm the details? My ___ ___[11] 0177 58412503. ___ ___[12]. Goodbye."

3 Preparing to take a call in English

Match the English sentences (1–10) to the German equivalents (a–j) on page 21.

1 I'm sorry, I didn't understand. Could you repeat that, please?
2 I'm afraid the line is engaged.
3 I'm sorry, … (*name*) is unavailable at the moment.
4 Please hold the line.
5 Who's calling, please?
6 Would you like to speak to someone else?
7 Would you like to leave a message?
8 I'm trying to connect you.
9 I'll put you through.
10 Could you spell your name, please?

TOOLBOX

to be unavailable – *nicht zu sprechen sein*
to connect sb – jdn *verbinden*
engaged – *besetzt*
extension – *Durchwahl*

a Bleiben Sie bitte dran.
b Der Anschluss ist besetzt.
c Ich stelle Sie durch.
d Ich habe nicht verstanden. Bitte wiederholen Sie.
e Buchstabieren Sie bitte Ihren Namen.
f Möchten Sie mit jemand anderem sprechen?
g Ich versuche, Sie zu verbinden.
h Möchten Sie eine Nachricht hinterlassen?
i Die Person, mit der Sie sprechen möchten, ist im Moment nicht da.
j Wie ist Ihr Name, bitte?

4 Taking a message

Your colleague, Julie Matthews, takes a call from a supplier.

9 **Before you listen to the call, complete the dialogue using phrases from exercise 3. Then listen and check.**

> **Giving telephone numbers**
> Say each digit separately, except for double digits, e.g. 01233455 = "oh (*AE*: zero) one two double-three four double-five".

Julie Hamm Machines Ltd. Julie Matthews speaking.
Liam Can I speak to Martin Brown in the workshop, please?
Julie *Who's calling please* [1]?
Liam This is Liam Donnelly.
Julie I'm sorry, ___ ___ ___ ___ ___, ___ [2]?
Liam It's L I A M D O double-N E double-L Y. I'm calling from Machine Tools in Manchester. It's about the drills Mr Brown ordered.
Julie Thank you, Mr Donnelly. I'll try Mr Brown for you. Please ___ ___ ___ [3].
Liam Thank you.

...

Julie Mr Donnelly. I'm sorry, Mr Brown is ___ [4] at the moment. Would you like to ___ ___ ___ ___ [5]?
Liam Yes. All right. Anyone in the workshop will do.
Julie Thank you. I'll ___ ___ ___ [6].

...

Julie I'm sorry, Mr Donnelly. I'm afraid the line ___ ___ [7]. Would you like to ___ ___ ___ [8] for Mr Brown?
Liam Yes, please. Would you tell Mr Brown that the drills he ordered aren't available and ask him to call me to discuss an alternative. My telephone number is 161 839 5005 and the extension is 822.
Julie ___ ___ [9]. I didn't ___ [10]. Could you ___ ___ [11], please?
Liam Sure. It's 161 839 5005, extension 822.
Julie Thank you, Mr Donnelly. I'll make sure that Mr Brown gets the message.

5 Role-play: A telephone call

Work with a partner. Partner A and Partner B: Look at File 3 on page 135.

› *Useful phrases, Telephoning, page 150; Taking telephone calls, page 151*

DAS KANN ICH (Unit 2)

- Ein Plakat mit Sicherheitsvorschriften für die Werkstatt gestalten. (Foundation)
- Mich und meine Arbeit in einem Tätigkeitsprofil auf Englisch beschreiben. (Part A)
- Eine kurze Präsentation über die duale Ausbildung auf Englisch halten. (Part B)
- Eine Nachricht auf einer Mailbox hinterlassen; eine Nachricht weiterleiten. (Communication)

TOOLBOX

mobile phone (*AE*: cell phone) – *Handy*
to put sb through – *jdn durchstellen*
voicemail – *Mailbox*

KMK Exam practice 1

1 Hörverstehen

Im Rahmen der Projektwoche Ihrer Berufsschule besucht Ihre Klasse die Hannover Messe. Jede/r Auszubildende soll ein Profil eines in Europa tätigen Elektrobetriebs erstellen. Sie besuchen den Stand eines großen amerikanischen Unternehmens und hören eine Präsentation in englischer Sprache über die Aktivitäten der Gesellschaft in Deutschland.

10 **Kopieren Sie die Tabelle und füllen Sie sie während der Präsentation aus.**

Name des Unternehmens	
Sitz	
Standort(e) in Europa	
Geschichte des Unternehmens	
Produkte	
Umsatz	
Zahl der Mitarbeiter	

Grobhandtaster

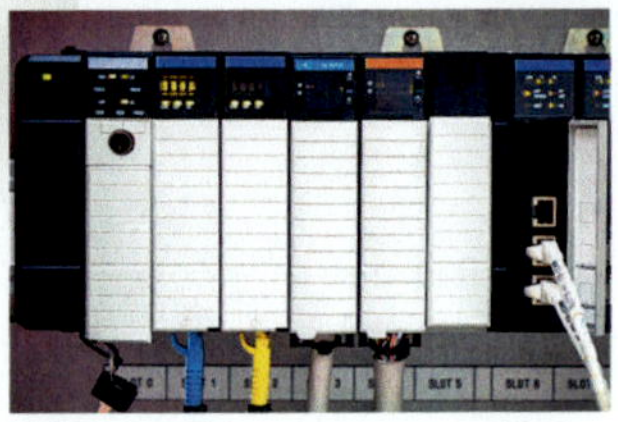

Speicherprogrammierbare Steuerung

2 Interaktion

Sie befinden sich am Stand eines Unternehmens auf der Hannover Messe.

Erstellen Sie in Partnerarbeit einen Dialog aus folgenden Rollenkarten.

Jack/Jill Lawrence
von Power Incorporated aus Delaware in den USA

Sie suchen englische Verkaufsliteratur von verschiedenen deutschen Firmen.
Sie stellen Fragen zu:
- der Qualität der Produkte
- Lieferzeiten bzw. Installation bzw. Wartung
- Problemlösung/Troubleshooting
- der Garantie

Sie geben dem/der Mitarbeiter/in Ihre Visitenkarte.
Sie bitten um ein Angebot für … (Produkt/Dienstleistung).

Eigener Name und Position in Ihrem Betrieb
die Person, die gerade Standdienst macht

Sie nutzen diese Gelegenheit, Ihre Firma kurz zu präsentieren.
Sie beschreiben:
- die Produkte Ihres Unternehmens
- die Dienstleistungen (z. B. Installation, Wartung, Reparatur)
- den/die Standort(e)

Sie geben dem/der Besucher/in:
- Verkaufsliteratur
- Ihre Visitenkarte

TOOLBOX

8-pole flat cable – *achtpolige Flachleitung*
assembly line production – *Fließbandfertigung*
ground fault circuit interrupter – *RCD*
three-phase oil contactor – *Drehstrom-Ölschütz*

3 Leseverstehen

Sie arbeiten im Ausland bei einem Unternehmen für elektrische Installation und erhalten als neue/r Mitarbeiter/in eine Broschüre über Sicherheit am Arbeitsplatz.

Beantworten Sie die Fragen zu dem Ausschnitt auf Deutsch.

HSE Health and Safety Executive

Electrical safety and you – A brief guide

Assessing the risk

The risk of injury from electricity is strongly linked to where and how it is used. The risks are greatest in harsh conditions, for example:

- in wet surroundings – unsuitable equipment can easily become live and can make its surroundings live;
- outdoors – equipment may not only become wet but may be at greater risk of damage; and
- in cramped spaces with a lot of earthed metalwork such as inside a tank – if an electrical fault developed it could be very difficult to avoid a shock.

Some items of equipment can also involve greater risk than others. Extension leads are particularly liable to damage – to their plugs, sockets, connections and the cable itself. Other flexible leads, particularly those connected to equipment which is often moved, can suffer from similar problems.

Reducing the risk

- Choose equipment that is suitable for its working environment.
- Electrical risks can sometimes be eliminated by using air, hydraulic or hand-powered tools which are especially useful in harsh conditions.
- Make sure that equipment is safe when supplied and that it is then maintained in a safe condition.
- Provide an accessible and clearly identified switch near each fixed machine to cut off power in an emergency.
- For portable equipment, use socket outlets which are close by so that equipment can be easily disconnected in an emergency.
- The ends of flexible cables should always have the outer sheath of the cable firmly clamped to stop the wires (particularly the earth) pulling out of the terminals.
- Replace damaged sections of cable completely.
- Use proper connectors or cable couplers to join lengths of cable. Do not use strip connector blocks covered in insulating tape.
- Some types of equipment are doubly insulated. These are often marked with a 'double-square' symbol ⧈. The supply leads have only two wires – live (brown) and neutral (blue). Make sure they are properly connected if the plug is not moulded.
- Protect light bulbs and other equipment which could easily be damaged in use.
- In potentially flammable or explosive atmospheres, only special electrical equipment designed for these areas should be used. You may need specialist advice.

Source: http://www.hse.gov.uk/pubns/indg231.htm

1 Unter welchen Umgebungsverhältnissen drohen besondere Gefahren für Elektriker/innen?
2 Welche elektrischen Betriebsmittel sind besonders anfällig?
3 Wie kann man die Notwendigkeit umgehen, elektrische Betriebsmittel zu verwenden?
4 Welche Rolle spielt die Nähe des Speisepunktes bei der Versorgung elektrischer Betriebsmittel mit Strom?
5 Worauf ist beim Anschließen der Leiter eines flexiblen Kabels an die Kontakte eines Steckers bzw. einer Steckdose zu achten und warum?
6 Wie sollen Kabellängen verbunden werden und wie nicht?
7 Worauf ist bei doppelt isolierten Betriebsmitteln ohne Schutzleiter zu achten?
8 Unter welchen Bedingungen sollte man fachmännischen Rat einholen?

3 Tools for mechatronics technicians

FOUNDATION: Favourite tools

Situation: You work at an international technology company in Germany which employs technicians from all over the world.
→ **You make a list of expressions for tools in English.**

1 Using the right tools

Three employees talk about some of the tools they like to use and what they use them for.

A 11 **Read what the employees say and decide who is talking. Then listen and check.**

a I enjoy working with my vernier callipers. They're used for measuring thicknesses, inside diameters, outside diameters and depth. It's the best measuring tool ever. It's much more accurate than a normal ruler. That can only measure down to 1 millimetre, or maybe 0.5 millimetres if you have a good one. Good vernier callipers can measure within 0.1 millimetres. The second tool I like is my inspection mirror. I use it when I'm working on machines to check for screws and things that might have become loose during vibration testing.

b I spend a lot of time on the factory floor, checking and repairing machinery and devices. If something's not working properly, I have to diagnose the problem – find out what's wrong – then I have to fix it. In this case, I use a multimeter that measures voltage, current and resistance or one that can measure the capacitance, inductance and current gain of transistors. That one's a very advanced, high-tech tool. At the other end of the scale, I often have to use a soldering iron which is a very simple tool. My father taught me how to use a soldering iron when I was a kid.

c I like working with the centre punch I made myself. Basically, you use a centre punch to mark the centre of a hole when drilling holes. A drill can wander if it doesn't start in a hole, so you use the punch to form a dent to guide the tip of the drill. You place the tip on the point where you want the hole, then hit it hard with a hammer. An automatic centre punch operates without the need for a hammer, but I really prefer the one I made. It's just a metal rod with a shaped tip on the end that has been hardened.

B Look at the close-up photos of tools from the text. With a partner, try to guess which tools they are.

1

2

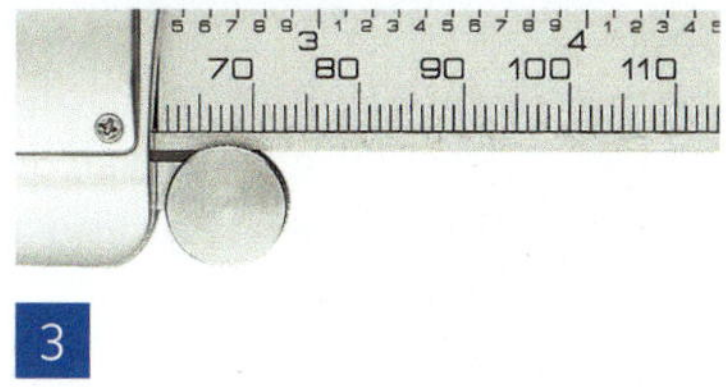

3

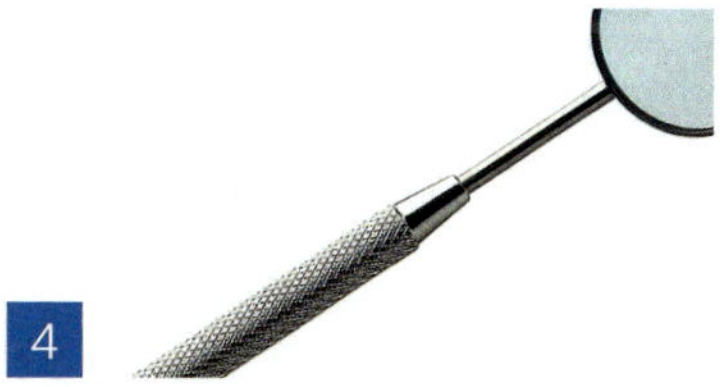
4

5

6

2 Naming tools in English

You are working in the tool store. As your supervisor can't speak English and some of the technicians don't speak German, he asks you to make a list of the tools for him in English.

A Work with a partner. Make two columns in your exercise book. Copy the English words for tools you have learned on these pages in the second column. Find the German expression in the wordlist and write it in the first column.

Handwerkzeuge	Hand-held tools
Messschieber	*vernier callipers*
	inspection mirror

B Add the German expressions for other tools you know. Check your dictionary for the English words. Keep adding to this list.

› *Part A, exercise 1, page 26*

3 Game: What's in my toolbox?

Twenty questions is a game to test your knowledge of the English names for tools.

A Choose two tools that you like working with or tools that you and your colleagues use every day. (Use your dictionary if you don't know the English word.) Do not show your list to anyone.

B Now work in groups of four. Take turns to ask and answer yes/no questions to find out what tools your partners are thinking of. Who has most points when the game is over?

Twenty questions: Rules

1. *You are only allowed to ask yes/no questions.*
2. *You are only allowed to ask 20 questions. Someone should keep a note of how many questions have been asked.*
3. *The person who names the tool first gets one point.*
4. *If all 20 questions have been asked and no one has guessed the name of the tool, then the person thinking of the tool gets the point.*

Asking and answering questions

Do you use this tool in the workshop?
– Yes, **I do**. / No, **I don't**.
Did you make this tool yourself?
– Yes, **I did**. / No, **I didn't**.
Can you carry it in your pocket?
– Yes, **you can**. / No, **you can't**.
Is it small? – Yes, **it is**. / No, **it isn't**.

I'm thinking of a small tool that I use a lot.

Is it a centre punch?

Yes, that's right. / No, it isn't.

› *Grammar: Questions and short answers, page 158*

PART A: Hand tools and test equipment

Situation: Your vocational college is taking part in an exchange programme for apprentice mechatronics technicians from all over Europe. There is also a "buddy" system as part of the exchange programme.
→ **You write a report about a day at work as part of the buddy system.**

1 Describing tools

To prepare for the exchange, you go to the mechatronics workshop at your college and make an English list of some of the tools and equipment that mechatronics technicians often use.

A Label the tools (1–20) using the words from the list.

Allen keys • angle grinder • clamp meter • combination pliers • crimping pliers • electric drill • extension reel • flat-bladed screwdriver • hacksaw • infrared camera • multimeter • open-ended spanner • Phillips screwdriver • portable digital oscilloscope • ring spanner • side-cutters • soldering iron • vernier callipers • voltage tester • wire strippers

B With a partner, describe the tools using the table on page 27.

It's a tool for making holes. What is it?

It's a (power) drill. ... OK, my turn. It's a tool for tightening and loosening nuts and bolts. What is it?

It's a(n) ...

Describing tools

A(n)	Allen key	is	a tool	for	breaking	bolts.
	multimeter		a device		checking	brick(s).
	…		an instrument		connecting	channels.
Pliers		are			cutting	chisels.
Side-cutters					gripping	components.
…					hitting	concrete.
					holding	distances.
					joining	electrical.
					loosening	circuits.
					making	holes.
					measuring	metal.
					stripping	nuts.
					testing	screws.
					tightening	stone(s).
					turning	wire(s).

C **Work in small groups and talk about these topics:**

- which tools you use, how often you use them and what jobs they are for
- what other tools and equipment you use and for what jobs

Start like this: *I often/sometimes/occasionally use a(n) … when I …*

2 Choosing the best tools for the job

Aleksi Mäkinen from Finland is your "buddy" in the exchange programme. Today, you and Aleksi are on a building site. Your task is to install the wiring for several sensors at an assembly line. Parts of the wiring harness can be laid in cable ducts, one longer cable has to be laid in the concrete floor. Peter, your supervisor, explains the best way to cut a channel in the floor to lay a cable.

A 12 **Listen to the dialogue and list all the tools and equipment they talk about, including the power tool in the photo.**

B 12 **The next day your supervisor asks you to tell him about the cable-laying job on the building site. Listen to the recording again, take notes and then summarize what you did the day before.**

Start like this: *We had to lay a cable in the floor, so Peter first showed us where to lay it. Then … . After that … . Next … . Finally, …*

Talking about the past

I **talked** to the boss yesterday.
He **told** me where to lay the cable.
He **didn't say** anything else.

› *Grammar: Simple past, page 159*

TOOLBOX

bolt – *Schraube (ohne Spitze für eine Mutter vorgesehen), Bolzen*
nut – *Mutter*
screw – *Schraube (mit Spitze)*
wall chaser – *Mauerfräser*
washer – *Unterlegscheibe*

screw

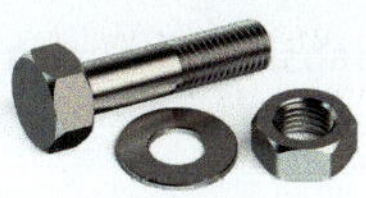
bolt, washer, nut

cable duct – *Kabelkanal*
chisel – *Meißel*
inductive proximity sensor – *induktiver Abstandssensor*
mallet – *Hammer*
wiring – *Verkabelung*
wiring harness – *Kabelbaum*

3 Helping apprentices from abroad

As part of the exchange visit, you look at the tools and test equipment you use and practise talking about them.

A Do the following tasks, using your toolbox from work.

- Arrange the hand and power tools in the order in which you most frequently use them.
- Draw up a list of German and English terms.
- Present the five most frequently used tools to your class and explain what they are for.

B Work with a partner. You and your "buddy" Aleksi are working together on a building site. Use the prompts below to act out a role-play with him.

You

Sagen Sie, dass Aleksi und Sie gemeinsam die Fehlersuche in einem Schaltschrank durchführen sollen und zunächst überprüfen wollen, ob in den einzelnen Leitungen elektrischer Strom fließt.

Aleksi Mäkinen

Fragen Sie, ob Sie das Multimeter holen sollen.

You

Sagen Sie, dass ein Multimeter nicht ideal geeignet sei. Besser wäre hier eine Strommesszange für Wechselstrom.

Aleksi Mäkinen

Sagen Sie, dass Sie in Ihrem finnischen Betrieb keine Strommesszange im Werkzeugkasten haben und daher nicht wissen, wie man sie benutzt.

You

Sagen Sie, dass eine Strommesszange einfach zu benutzen ist, indem man sie einschaltet und um die zu prüfende Leitung klemmt.

Aleksi Mäkinen

Sagen Sie, dass dabei ein großer Vorteil ist, dass man den Stromkreis nicht auftrennen muss!

You

Sagen Sie, dass es mit einer Strommesszange außerdem möglich ist, sehr große Stromstärken zu messen.

Aleksi Mäkinen

Fragen Sie, was man beim Arbeiten mit Strommesszangen sonst noch beachten muss.

You

Sagen Sie, dass man bei Strommesszangen für Gleichstrom die Stromrichtung beachten muss.

Aleksi Mäkinen

Sagen Sie, dass es in einem Kabelbaum sicher nicht einfach ist, immer nur die Leitungen in die Strommesszange zu nehmen, die man messen will.

You

Sagen Sie, dass das stimmt und dass Sie den Schaltplan haben, um jetzt die richtigen Leitungen über ihre Kabelfarben herauszufinden.

C Work with a partner and describe a job you did using hand or power tools.

- Describe what you had to do.
- List the hand and power tools you used.
- Explain step by step how you used them, first to your partner then to the class.

› *Grammar: Simple past, page 159*

D Now describe a whole day at work for your company's website. Choose a day last week or month and describe what you did.

› *Grammar: Simple past, page 159*

PART B: Machine tools for production

Situation: You are doing work experience at RoboCron Ltd, a large machine manufacturer in York.
→ **You explain how one of the machines works to a new colleague.**

1 Identifying machine tools

A Match the machine tools (1–7) with the names from the list.

bandsaw · drilling machine · grinding machine · milling machine · off-hand grinder · power hacksaw · turning machine

1

2

3

4

5

6

7

B 13)) Listen to the sounds of five machine tools. Which ones can you see in the photos?

2 Describing three different machine tools

Your supervisor shows you three of the machine tools that are used at RoboCron. He gives you three different tasks to test your knowledge of the machines.

A Work with a partner. Complete the text with words from the list.

column · chuck · dial · head · motor · swivelled · vice

A **drilling machine** is composed of a base that supports a ___[1], which in turn supports a table. Workpieces can be supported on the table with a ___[2] or hold down clamps, or the table can be ___[3] out of the way to allow tall workpieces to be supported directly on the base. The column also supports a ___[4] containing a ___[5] which turns the spindle at a speed controlled by a variable speed control ___[6]. The spindle holds a drill ___[7] to hold the cutting tools.

TOOLBOX

bandsaw – *Bandsäge*
chuck – *Spannfutter/Bohrfutter*
clamp – *Klemme*
column – *Säule*
drilling machine – *Bohrmaschine*
grinding machine – *Schleifmaschine*
milling machine – *Fräsmaschine*
off-hand grinder – *Handschleifmaschine*
spindle – *Spindel*
to swivel – *schwenken*
turning machine – *Drehmaschine*
vice – *(Maschinen-) Schraubstock*

B Read the description of the milling machine. Then complete the vocabulary card with English words and expressions from the text.

The **milling machine** is a frequently-used workshop machine tool. Milling machines are usually used to machine flat surfaces, but can also produce irregular surfaces. They can also be used to drill, bore and produce slots. The most common type is a vertical spindle machine with a swivelling head. A milling machine removes metal by rotating a multi-toothed cutter that is fed into the moving workpiece. Most milling machines are equipped with a power feed for one or more axes. The power feed can produce a better surface finish because it is smoother than a manual feed.

Milling machine

a ebene Flächen bearbeiten ▬
b unebene Flächen erstellen ▬
c schwenkbarer Kopf ▬
d Fräswerkzeug mit mehreren Zähnen ▬
e automatischer Vorschub ▬
f manueller Vorschub ▬

C Read the description of the turning machine. Then use your dictionary to write your own vocabulary card. Keep your card safely. You will need it for exercises 3 and 4.

Turning machine

The **turning machine** is another very common machine tool in the workshop. A turning machine rotates a workpiece against a tool whose position it controls. It is used to manufacture parts and features that have a circular cross section. The spindle, which is driven by an electric motor through a system of gear trains, is the part of the turning machine that rotates. The tailstock can be used to support the end of the workpiece with a centre, or to hold tools for drilling, threading, or cutting tapers.

TOOLBOX

axis, axes – *Achse*
to bore – *innendrehen*
centre – *Reitstockspitze*
cross section – *Querschnitt*
to drill – *bohren*
gear train – *Getriebe*
slot – *Schlitz*
swivelling head – *schwenkbarer Kopf*
tailstock – *Reitstock*
taper – *Kegel*
to thread – *Gewinde schneiden*
vertical spindle machine – *Maschine mit senkrechter Spindel*

3 Understanding how a turning machine works

Your supervisor shows you the turning machine and gives you a list of parts.

A Work with a partner. Match the following parts to the turning machine on page 30. Add new words to the vocabulary card you made for exercise 2C.

a apron
b bed slideways
c chuck
d compound slide
e control unit
f headstock
g protective hood
h rack
i tailstock
j tool holder

B What does each part of the turning machine do? Match these descriptions to the parts of the turning machine in exercise 3A.

1 This part makes sure that the workpiece which has to be machined is held right in the centre.
2 This serves as housing for the driving pulleys, back gears, headstock spindle, live center and the feed reverse gear.
3 This is located between the headstock and tailstock and supports, guides and feeds the tool against the workpiece during operation.
4 This protects the lathe operator from flying chips or coolant during operation.
5 This slides along the bed to accommodate different lengths of workpiece between the centers.
6 This is fastened to the compound slide and it houses the gears, clutches and levers required to move the cross slide.
7 The working parts of the lathe, such as the headstock and tailstock are mounted on this heavy, rugged casting. It provides a base for the carriage assembly which carries the tool.
8 Here you can type in all the data necessary for manufacturing a workpiece. There is also the emergency-stop switch.
9 This is located below the headstock and contains a number of different sized gears to change speed and direction of rotation.
10 This is mounted on the compound rest and it rigidly clamps the cutting tool at the correct height.

4 Explaining how the turning machine works

Your supervisor asks you to explain how the turning machine works to a new colleague.

A Work with a partner. Use your vocabulary card from exercise 2C and phrases from exercise 3 to make notes. Make sure you cover all the parts of the turning machine mentioned in exercise 3.

You can start like this:

A turning machine is a machine tool which holds the workpiece rigidly between two rigid and strong supports called centres or in a chuck which revolves. The cutting tool is held and supported in a tool holder which is fed against the revolving workpiece. The cutting tool is normally fed either parallel or at right angles to the axis of the workpiece.

B Work in groups. Use your notes to explain the different parts of the turning machine.

TOOLBOX

apron – *Schlosskasten*
bed slideways – *Maschinenbett*
compound slide – *Längsschlitten*
control unit – *Steuergerät*
headstock – *Spindelkasten*
protective hood – *Schutzhaube*
rack – *Zahnstange*
tool holder – *Werkzeughalter*

COMMUNICATION: Emails

Situation: You work at Technical Tools, a supplier to the technical trades, where your supervisor asks you to take care of a customer enquiry.
→ **You write an email to a customer.**

1 Giving email addresses over the phone

You check the English for some of the symbols that appear in email addresses.

A Match the symbols (1–6) to the words (a–f).

1 +	**4** -	**a** at	**e** plus
2 _	**5** .	**b** dot	**e** number
3 @	**6** 3	**c** hyphen	**f** underscore

B 14)) Listen to your supervisor and a customer on the phone. Which email addresses are correct?

1
a tm.martin@technical-tools.de
b tmmartin@technical_tools.de
c tm.martin@technical_tools.de

2
a maryannbrown@5+5_services.net
b mary-anne-brown@5+5services.net
c maryann-brown@5+5services.net

C Work with a partner. You are going to dictate email addresses to each other.

Partner A: **Look at File 2 on page 134.**
Partner B: **Look at File 10 on page 138.**

Can you spell that, please?

Could you repeat that, please?

2 Writing a subject line

The first indication of what is in an email is the subject line. This must state clearly what the email is about.

A Work with a partner. Study the subject lines (1–6) below and find an email which …

1 is a request for information.
2 gives information about a meeting.
3 asks for assistance.
4 contains new information.
5 announces a change of plan.
6 is a covering letter for a brochure.

a **Subject:** Need your help with English
b **Subject:** New venue for event on Saturday
c **Subject:** Flyer (attached)
d **Subject:** Meeting 25.03. Starting time?
e **Subject:** Update on project
f **Subject:** Agenda

B With your partner, write suitable subject lines for the following emails (1–6).

1 Sorry, I would like to change the date of the meeting to Friday 12 July.
2 Could you send me information about the presentation, please?
3 I am on holiday from 21.03 till 04.04 inclusive and will answer emails when I return.
4 I am writing to confirm your application for a stand at the Technical Trades Fair. The stand number is C208.
5 As promised, here is the link to the website www.tipsformails.com.
6 This is just to let you know that I am interviewing a new technician at 12.30.

TOOLBOX

hyphen – *Bindestrich, Minus*
underscore – *Unterstrich*

3 Writing a reply to an email enquiry

Your supervisor gives you the enquiry below and asks you to reply by email.

Dear Sir/Madam

We have studied your catalogue on the internet and are interested in your Phillips screwdrivers (catalogue number SP 492876) and your slotted screwdrivers (catalogue number SS 8592201).
We would like to order 100 of each type of screwdriver.
We would also like to order 1,000 boxes of Phillips screws and 1,000 boxes of slotted screws.
Please let us know if you have these items in stock.

Yours faithfully
Robert Johnson

Robert Johnson Building Ltd

Use a suitable greeting and subject line and reply to Mr Johnson. Include the following points:

- Thank him for his enquiry.
- Say that the screwdrivers and the screws are in stock.
- Say you will dispatch them next week.
- Say that you look forward to doing business with him in the future.
- Use the correct complimentary close.

› *Useful phrases: Writing emails, page 151*

Using polite language in emails

Could and *would like* are more polite than phrases with *can*, *need* or *want*.
~~Can~~ you let me know by Monday? → **Could** you let …
I ~~need~~ the information today. → I **would like** the …
We ~~want~~ to have a meeting. → We **would like** to …

Salutation and complimentary close in emails

If you do not know the name of the person you are writing to, begin your email with *Dear Sir/Madam*.
If you do not know your business partner well, use a formal salutation and complimentary close.

	Salutation	Complimentary close	
Formal (to unknown person)	Dear Sir/Madam	Yours faithfully	
Formal (to person whose name you know)	Dear Ms/Mr Smith	Regards Best regards	Best wishes Yours sincerely
Less formal	Dear Paul / Hi Paula Good morning, Paul	Regards Best regards	Best wishes All the best

DAS KANN ICH (Unit 3)

- Eine Liste der englischen Bezeichnungen für Werkzeuge erstellen. (Foundation)
- Einen kurzen Bericht über einen normalen Arbeitstag auf Englisch verfassen. (Part A)
- Die Bestandteile einer Drehmaschine auf Englisch benennen und beschreiben. (Part B)
- Die E-Mail eines britischen Kunden auf Englisch beantworten. (Communication)

TOOLBOX

Best regards / Regards – *Schöne Grüße*
complimentary close – *Grußformel (am Briefende)*
salutation – *Anrede*
subject line – *Betreff*
Yours faithfully – *Mit freundlichen Grüßen*
Yours sincerely – *Mit freundlichen Grüßen*

4 Materials for mechatronics

FOUNDATION: The right materials for the job

Situation: Your company is taking part in an international trade fair.
→ **You give a short presentation at the fair about the materials your company uses.**

1 Classifying materials

Your supervisor suggests that you start your presentation with an overview of materials the company uses.

> **Aluminium or aluminum?**
> *BE:* alu**min**ium: the stress is on the third syllable
> *AE:* al**u**minum: the stress is on the second syllable

A Copy and complete the grid with materials from the list.

carbon fibre · cast iron · glass · glass fibre · lead · magnesium · stone · titanium · wood · zinc

Metals		
ferrous metals	non-ferrous metals	
e.g. *steel* ___[1]	heavy metals e.g. *copper* ___[2] ___[3]	light metals e.g. *aluminium* ___[4] ___[5]
Non-metals		
natural materials	artificial materials	compounds
e.g. ___[6] ___[7]	e.g. ___[8] plastics	e.g. ___[9] ___[10]

B Make a mind map showing the materials your company works with.

TOOLBOX

aluminium/aluminum – *Aluminium*
cast iron – *Gusseisen*
copper – *Kupfer*
lead – *Blei*
steel – *Stahl*
titanium – *Titan*
zinc – *Zink*

2 The mechanical properties of materials

You decide to check what you know about the properties of metals.

A Combine the words and phrases to make sentences describing the mechanical properties of materials.

1 Elastic 2 Flexible 3 Hard 4 Hard-wearing 5 Light-weight 6 Malleable 7 Resilient 8 Tough	material	can will is able to	**a** absorb energy when it is deformed elastically. **b** bend or deform in response to an applied force. **c** deform under compressive stress without developing defects. **d** reduce weight while preserving strength. **e** withstand shock and plastically deform without fracturing or rupturing. **f** withstand surface indentation and scratching. **g** last a long time and remain in good condition. **h** resist a distorting influence or stress and return to its original size and shape when the stress is removed.

B With a partner, choose two materials. Decide together what type of material they are and describe their properties. Make notes.

C When you are ready, find another pair and take turns to describe the materials you have chosen. Ask them to guess the materials.

It's a silvery-grey metal. It's light-weight and flexible.

I think it's aluminium.

Describing properties

Carbon fibre is a **good** material for crash helmets.
Plastic is a **useful** material for household goods.
Steel is **hard**.
The metal feels **rough**.

› *Grammar: Adjectives and adverbs, page 161*

3 Presenting the materials

It is time to prepare, structure and give your presentation.

A Work with a partner. Decide together what materials you are going to talk about. Use your mind map from exercise 1B and add the qualities of the materials to it.

B Use your mind map to make a vocabulary handout that you can give your audience.

C Now make notes about what you are going to say in your presentation. The structure below will help you.

Introduction:
- Greet the audience.
- Give a very short introduction about yourself. Say where you work and what you do.
- Say what you are going to talk about and distribute your handout.

The main part of the presentation:
- Classify the types of materials you work with.
- Describe the qualities of the materials and how these qualities are necessary for the jobs you do.
- Refer to your handout when necessary.

Conclusion:
- Summarize what you have said in the main part of the presentation.
- Ask and answer questions from the audience.
- Thank everyone for coming and say goodbye.

D When you are ready, give your presentation.

› *Useful phrases: Giving a presentation, page 150*

PART A: Materials in electronics

Situation: You are an apprentice at TEC Elektronik, a producer of electronic devices. Your company sends you on a training course about materials in electronics to their Irish subsidiary in Dublin.
→ **You mediate information from an interview for your German supervisor.**

1 Looking at a printed circuit board

Your first task on the training course is to read an English text about printed circuit boards (PCBs).

A **Some words are missing from the text. Complete the gaps using the words from the list.**

components · copper · electric circuits · electronic device · insulating · interconnections

Cross-section through a populated multi-layer PCB (SDRAM-module)

Printed Circuit Boards (PCBs) are found in every modern ___[1]. In order to enable the ___[2] of the device to function properly, conducting ___[3] are needed between the various ___[4] of the circuit.
Many modern devices often require very complex multilayer structures consisting of ___[5] conductor patterns and ___[6] materials.

B **Now read the following descriptions and match them to the labels (A–G) in the picture.**

1 **Component(s):** The basic passive or active devices in electronic circuits, such as resistors, capacitors, diodes, transistors, or integrated circuits. Components are mounted to PCBs either as *surface-mount devices* (SMD) in a reflow soldering process or as *through-hole devices* (THD) in a wave soldering process.
2 **Plated through hole (PTH):** In order for the components to make contact with inner conductive layers, drilled holes are plated with a conducting material. Plated-through holes are also used for making interconnections between the layers. They are then called vias.
3 **Glass fibres in epoxy resin:** An insulating composite material that uses layers of glass reinforcement fibres bonded by an epoxy resin.
4 **Copper traces on internal layer:** Conductive layers of thin copper foil that make up the inner connections between the plated through holes of a PCB.
5 **Copper trace on external layer:** The surface conductive copper traces of a PCB.
6 **Solder pad:** A small copper area that is not covered by a solder mask and is used as a solder point.
7 **Solder mask:** A polymer coating that can be applied to the surface copper traces of a PCB for protection against oxidation and to prevent solder from forming unwanted connections between closely spaced solder pads.

TOOLBOX

component – *elektronisches Bauelement*
populated PCB – *eine (mit Bauelementen) bestückte Leiterplatte*
composite material – *Verbundwerkstoff*
solder – *Lot*
reinforcement – *Verstärkung*
polymer coating – *Kunststoffbeschichtung*
copper traces - *Leiterbahnen*

2 Describing the layout of a modern PCB

Next, you create simple applications using the BBC micro:bit.

> **The BBC micro:bit**
>
> The BBC micro:bit is a very popular single-board microcomputer that contains all the necessary components of a small control computer. For example, a processor, USB and Bluetooth interfaces, power supply, sensors, inputs and outputs are all combined on a single PCB that measures only 4 cm x 5 cm.

Front

Back

A **Work with a partner. Study the photos of the micro:bit and the list of components below. Describe the position of the electronic components on the micro:bit.**

1 programmable front buttons A and B
2 3V power port
3 ground port
4 Micro USB connector
5 5 x 5 LED matrix
6 Reset button
7 accelerometer and compass chipset
8 Bluetooth antenna
9 processor
10 battery connector
11 3 digital and analogue I/O connectors (labelled 1, 2, 3)

B **Work in small groups. Talk about your experiences using single-board computers. Use these ideas to help you:**

- Which single-board computers do you know?
- What are these boards capable of?
- What applications have you used a single-board computer for?
- Explain how you programmed the board.
- What's the advantage of having accelerometer and magneto-meter sensors on board?
- Which other sensors/actors would you like to connect? Why?
- Which applications could you imagine using boards with these sensors/actors for?

> **Describing where something is**
>
> The USB-connector is **on the back** of the board **next to** the Reset button. The LED matrix is located **in the centre** of the PCB's front side **between** the programmable buttons.

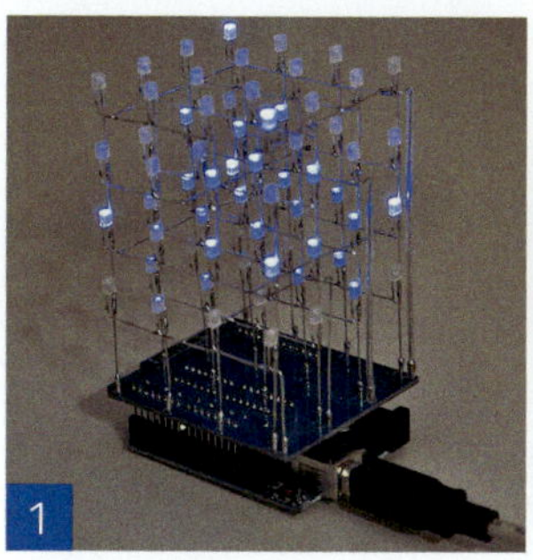
1

2

3

1 Arduino UNO board driving an LED cube shield
2 custom single-board computer controlling a 3D printer
3 ODROID-U3 board running a Linux desktop operating system

TOOLBOX

interface – *Schnittstelle*
accelerometer – *Beschleunigungssensor*
magnetometer – *Magnetfeldsensor (Kompass)*
I/O connector – *Anschluss, nutzbar als Eingang oder Ausgang*

3 Talking about lead-free soldering

In the next part of your course, you look at alloys used in soldering.

Examples of leaded and lead-free solder alloys

In traditional electronic assembly tin-lead-based solders with tin-lead compositional ratios of 60 : 40 or 63 : 37 were used. These alloys melt at a temperature of approximately 183 °C. Since lead is very toxic, it is no longer allowed in solders. Consequently, several new lead-free solders have been developed and are now widely used for both reflow and wave soldering.

	Alloy type	Composition	Melting Point
1	bismuth-tin	Bi58/Sn42	139 °C
2	tin-lead	Sn60/Pb40	183 °C
3	tin-lead	Sn63/Pb37	183 °C
4	tin-indium-silver	Sn77.2/In20/Ag2.8	187 °C
5	tin-silver-copper-antimony	Sn96.1/Ag2.6/Cu0.8/Sb0.5	211 °C
6	tin-silver-copper	Sn95.5/Ag3.8/Cu0.7	217 °C
7	tin-silver-copper	Sn96.5/Ag3.0/Cu0.5	220 °C
8	tin-copper	Sn99.3/Cu0.7	227 °C

Work with a partner. Study the table and contrast the types of solder alloys.

› *Grammar: Comparatives and superlatives, page 162*

Comparing things

Alloy 2 has a **lower** melting point than alloy 4.
Alloy 6 contains **less** tin than alloy 5.

4 Listening to a talk about materials

At the end of your course, you listen to an interview with an expert in the field of materials in electronics.

A 15 **Listen to the interview and match items from the lists to make true statements.**

1 Materials for electronic devices …
2 Conductors are materials …
3 Materials which don't allow electricity to flow easily …
4 Semi-conductors can behave …
5 Silicon needs to be doped …
6 The RoHS directive …
7 Electronic components can …
8 Lead-free solders with lower melting points …

a before it can be used in components.
b are called insulators.
c can be distinguished into three basic categories.
d prohibits the use of leaded solders in electronics.
e contain significant amounts of bismuth or indium.
f like both, insulators and conductors.
g which don't prevent the free flow of electrons.
h be destroyed by higher soldering temperatures.

B 15 **Listen again and take notes on the following topics:**

- Leiterplatten bestehen aus …
- als Beschichtungen werden verwendet …
- die RoHS-Richtlinie legt fest …
- die verfügbaren bleifreien Lote verursachen …
- die hohen Verarbeitungstemperaturen können …
- …

5 Mediation: Materials used in PCB production

After the course, your supervisor asks you to give him a summary of Professor Bassford's talk.

Use your notes from exercise 4B to give a talk (in German) about the materials used in PCB production.

PART B: A metal workpiece

Situation: You work for a metal engineering company that produces specific workpieces for customers.
→ **You describe workpieces and draw a workpiece according to a customer's specifications.**

1 Adding dimensions to a drawing

Your supervisor calls an English customer because some dimensions on a sketch of a workpiece are missing.

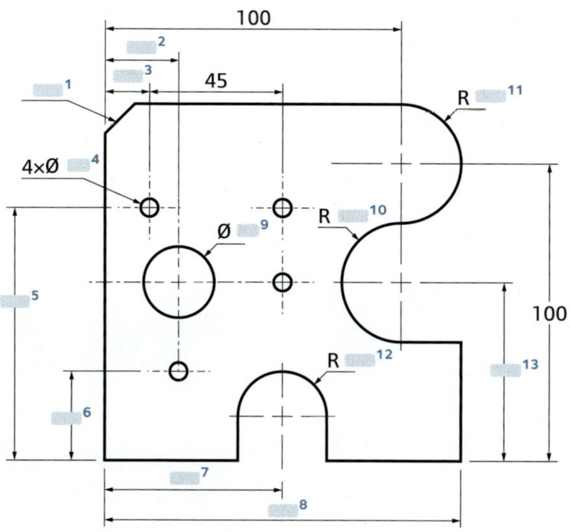

A **16)) Listen to their conversation and note down the missing dimensions.**

B **Where can you see the following information on the drawing? What do these lines mean?**

continuous line · thin chain-dotted line · dimension line

C **16)) Close your books. Listen again and draw the full workpiece on a separate piece of paper.**

2 Describing shapes

Your supervisor asks you to write a list of English expressions for describing workpieces. You label some sketches so that she can keep them by his phone.

A **Copy and complete the drawings with the following information.**

chamfer · circumference · concave · convex · diameter · groove · radius

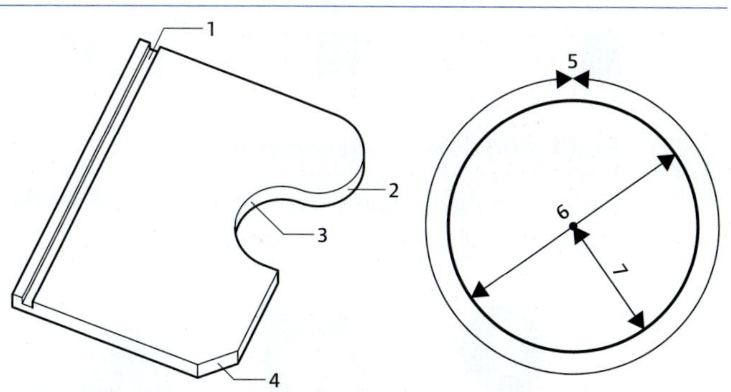

TOOLBOX

chain-dotted line – *strichpunktierte Linie*
chamfer – *Fase*
continuous line – *durchgezogene Linie*
edge – *Kante*
groove – *Nut*

B Complete this word families table with the missing adjectives. Use your dictionary if necessary.

2D shapes			3D shapes		
shape	noun	adjective	shape	noun	adjective
	square	*square*		cube	*cubical*
	rectangle			rectangular solid	
	triangle			cylinder	
	circle			sphere	
	semi-circle			hemisphere	*hemispherical*
				cone	

› *Grammar: Adjectives and adverbs, page 161*

C Match the drawings (1–10) to the words in the list.

bar · block · casting · film · plate · rod (circular bar) · sheet · strip · tube · wire

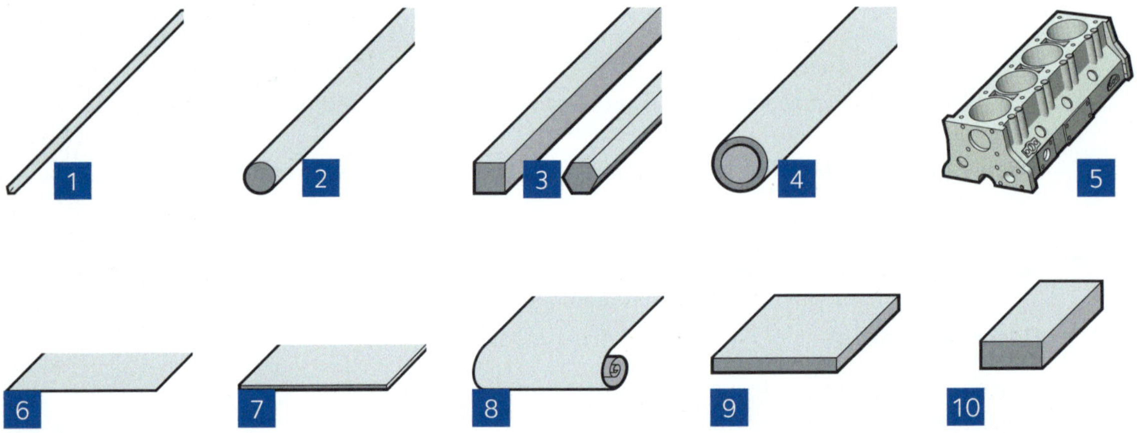

3 Practising describing workpieces

Part of your in-company training programme is a monthly test. You prepare for this month's test by checking descriptions of workpieces.

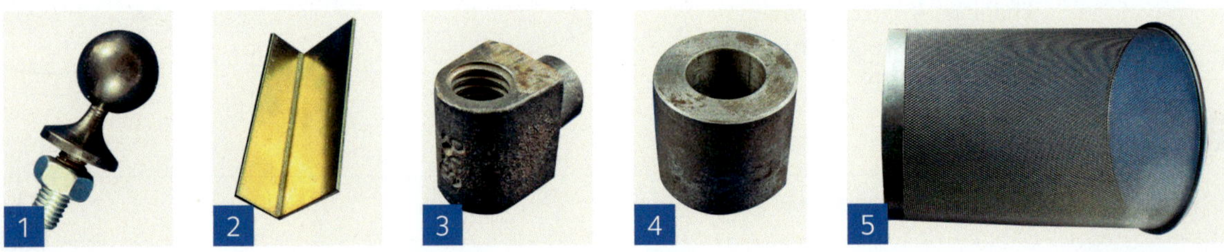

A **Match the workpieces (1–5) to the descriptions (a–e).**

- **a** This workpiece is a rectangular solid with a radius on the left, a cylinder on the right and a thread through it. It is machined from a casting.
- **b** This workpiece has a thread with a nut on the left and a sphere on the right. It is made from a rolled rod.
- **c** This workpiece is cylindrical and is made from rolled steel.
- **d** This workpiece is conical and is made from sheet metal.
- **e** This workpiece is an L-shaped rectangle and is made from sheet metal.

B **Work with a partner. Say what you think the workpieces are.**

4 Describing workpieces to your partner

It is time to draw a workpiece according to a customer's specifications.

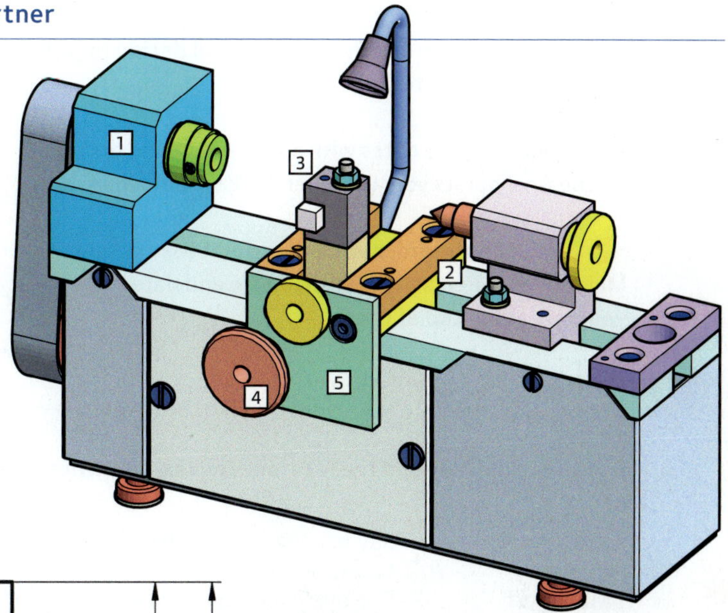

A **Work with a partner. Look at the drawing of an apron together, then complete the description with the missing dimensions. Which part (1–5) of the turning machine does the drawing match?**

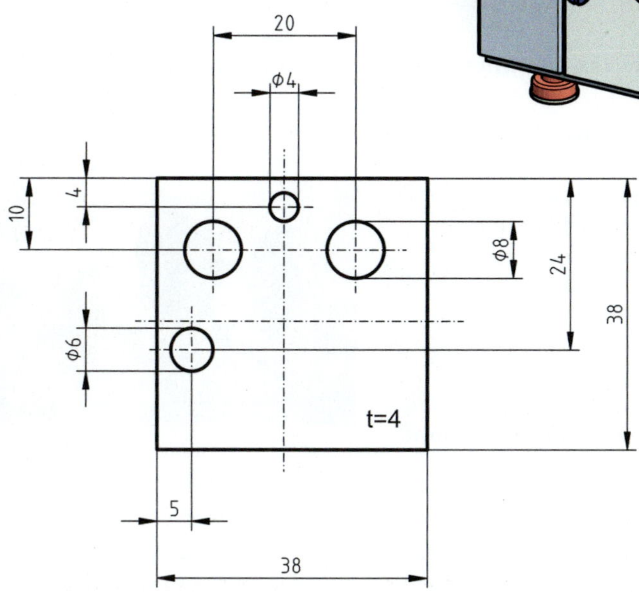

The apron is a square plate which is 38 mm long and ___[1] wide and ___[2] thick. There are four boreholes in the plate. The first has a diameter of ___[3] and it is ___[4] down from the top side of the plate. The next two boreholes are symmetrical, they are ___[5] from the top and ___[6] apart. Their diameter is ___[7]. The fourth borehole is ___[8] down from the top side and ___[9] from the left edge. It has a diameter of ___[10].

B **Work with a partner. Partner A: Look at File 6 on page 136. Partner B: Look at File 14 on page 140.**

Sit back to back and take turns to describe workpieces from the turning machine.

› *Useful phrases: Describing size and dimensions, page 152*

TOOLBOX

thread – *Gewinde*

COMMUNICATION: A short presentation

Situation: Some apprentices from the UK are soon going to start work at your company.
→ **You give a short presentation to the new apprentices about your work.**

1 Thinking about the contents of a presentation

Your supervisor gives you a list of points you should include in your talk.

what the company does · your department · what you do

A **Work with a partner. Read the list and decide together what you would like to add to your supervisor's list above. Make notes.**

B **Compare your notes with another pair and decide on the final points you will cover. Make a mind map.**

C **Agree on the order you will present the contents. Make a numbered list. Write the name and date of your talk at the top of the list.**

Presentation to new trainees: 08.07.20..
1 *Introduction (self/the company)*
2
3

2 Writing the presentation

A **Use your mind map and the list from exercise 1 to write your text. Follow this structure.**

Introduction	– Say in a few words what you are going to talk about.
Main part	– Use one paragraph for each topic. – Use signposts to move from one subject to the next.
Conclusion	– Summarize the main ideas. – Invite questions from the audience.

B **Check the text together for clarity and correctness as follows.**

- Is the information in the text correct? If not, correct it.
- Is the spelling and grammar correct? Use your dictionary and the list of phrases on page 43.

3 Making a prompt card

A presentation comes across best when the presenter looks at the audience and speaks naturally. As it is difficult to do either of these things when you read from a text, you should make yourself a prompt card.

A **Follow the steps below.**

- Highlight important words and phrases in your text.
- Copy the words and phrases onto an index card.
- Include signposts to structure the ideas.

- manufacturing company
- workshop
- apprentice ...

B **Practise your presentation in your group, using only your prompt card.**

Structuring a presentation

Introduction
My name is … and this is my colleague, …
We are … apprentices at … (*name of company*) in Germany.
This morning/afternoon I'm / we're going to give a short talk/presentation on …
I/We will be happy to answer any questions at the end of the talk.

Main part
I've/We've divided the talk/presentation into … parts.
First/Firstly … / Second/Secondly, … / After that … / Finally …

Signposts
To begin with … / Next …
Now … / I would also like to mention …

Conclusion
To conclude, … / To sum up, …
I'd/We'd be happy to take questions now. / Does anyone have any questions?
Thank you for listening.

4 Giving your presentation

It is time to give your presentation and to give each other feedback.

A **Decide who is going to speak first in your group. When it is your turn, stand up, look directly at the audience and smile. Then speak freely and clearly using your prompt card. Ask for questions at the end.**

B **Give each other feedback using this feedback sheet. Give points from 1 to 3.**
(1 point = needs improvement,
2 points = good,
3 points = very good)

› *Useful phrases: Giving a presentation, page 150*

Presentations feedback		Points
Content	you covered all the necessary points	
	you used examples to support your points	
Structure	your talk was easy to follow	
	you used useful phrases to structure your talk	
	you summarized the main ideas in your conclusion.	
Presentation	you smiled and looked friendly	
	you spoke clearly and freely	
	you looked at the audience when you spoke	
Dealing with questions	you dealt with questions in a friendly manner	
	you answered all the questions clearly	
Overall score for the presentation		/30

DAS KANN ICH (Unit 4)

- Eine kurze Präsentation über die Materialien halten, die meine Firma verwendet. (Foundation)
- Die wesentlichen Informationen eines englischen Vortrags auf Deutsch wiedergeben. (Part A)
- Ein Werkstück auf Englisch beschreiben sowie nach einer englischen Beschreibung skizzieren. (Part B)
- Eine kurze Präsentation über meine Arbeit für neue Auszubildende halten. (Communication)

KMK Exam practice 2

1 Leseverstehen

Sie haben ein neues Multimeter gekauft. Die folgende Gebrauchsanweisung ist auf Englisch geschrieben.

Überlegen Sie, welche der Aussagen 1 bis 4 richtig oder falsch sind. Beantworten Sie anschließend die Fragen 5 bis 7 auf Deutsch. Notieren Sie sich die Lösungen in Ihrem Heft.

The DigitalPlus Multimeter – better design, best quality!

Follow these suggestions about how to care for your multimeter and enjoy many years of use.

The meter should be kept dry at all times. Liquids can contain minerals which will corrode the delicate electric circuits. So wipe the meter dry of moisture as quickly as possible.

The meter should be stored and used in environments with normal temperatures. Use of the device in extreme temperatures can crack plastic components, deplete the battery and shorten the device's life.

Keep the meter in good condition by regularly wiping it clean with a damp cloth. The use of cleaning products including harsh solvents and strong detergents is to be avoided at all times. These will damage your device.

Do not open your device or attempt repairs on its internal components. This can cause the device to malfunction and may invalidate the warranty. If your meter is not working properly, return it along with your receipt of purchase and warranty to your retailer.

REPLACING THE FUSE

CAUTION: AVOID ELECTRIC SHOCK BY DISCONNECTING THE TEST PROBES BEFORE REMOVAL OF THE BATTERIES OR FUSE. REPLACE ONLY WITH SAME TYPE OF BATTERIES OR FUSE. THIS DEVICE DOES NOT CONTAIN USER-SERVICEABLE PARTS. SERVICE SHOULD BE CARRIED OUT BY QUALIFIED PERSONNEL ONLY.

Replace the fuse safely by following these steps. Your meter comes complete with a spare fuse, which is located at the back of the battery compartment.

1. Before disconnecting the test leads, turn off the power.
2. The battery compartment cover should now be opened.
3. Pull the green ribbon which will cause the fuse to eject.
4. Insert a replacement fuse on the ribbon ring. Use only a fuse of the following type/ rating: 0.315A, 250V, 5 x 20 mm miniature fuse.
5. Snap the battery compartment cover closed.

1 Es ist wichtig, das Messgerät trocken zu halten.
2 Die Batterien im Multimeter sind hitzebeständig. Hohe Temperaturen verkürzen nicht ihre Lebensdauer.
3 Die Garantie erlischt, wenn Veränderungen am Multimeter vorgenommen werden.
4 Das Multimeter wird ohne Ersatzteile geliefert.
5 Wie sollte das Multimeter gesäubert werden?
6 Was ist zu tun, um einen Stromschlag zu vermeiden?
7 Wo befindet sich die Ersatzsicherung?

2 Interaktion

Sie arbeiten für die Firma Secu Industriesteuerungen GmbH an der Installation einer Steuerung für eine neue Fertigungslinie im Presswerk eines Automobilherstellers. Gerade sind Sie mit der Verschraubung von Trägerplatten am Maschinenbett beschäftigt.

Verwenden Sie die Rollenkarten, um ein Gespräch zwischen einem Mechatroniker / einer Mechatronikerin und einem Praktikanten / einer Praktikantin aus Großbritannien als Rollenspiel durchzuführen.

Mechatroniker/in

Aus den Montageunterlagen haben Sie die geforderte Schraubenfestigkeitsklasse (10.9) und das Anzugsdrehmoment (70 Nm) entnommen.

- Sie fragen den Praktikanten / die Praktikantin, ob er/sie Schrauben der Festigkeitsklasse 10.9 und passende Muttern geholt hat.
- Sie sagen, dass die Muttern nicht passen.
- Sie fragen ihn/sie, ob er/sie die Bedeutung der Festigkeitsangaben kennt.
- Sie erklären ihm/ihr, dass die Sicherheit einer Schraubverbindung von der Verwendung der richtigen Werkstoffe abhängt. Sie weisen den Praktikanten / der Praktikantin auf die Festigkeitsangaben auf den Schraubenköpfen hin und erklären ihm/ihr, wie daraus die Größe der Mindestzugfestigkeit und Mindeststreckgrenze ermittelt werden: Erste Zahl multipliziert mit 100 ergibt Zugfestigkeit in N/mm^2 und erste Zahl multipliziert mit zweiter Zahl und Faktor 10 ergibt Streckgrenze in N/mm^2.
- Sie erklären, dass immer auch die Festigkeitsklasse der Mutter zur Schraube passen muss und dass es wichtig ist, das Anzugsdrehmoment zu beachten.

Praktikant/in

Sie haben gerade Schrauben, Muttern und Sicherungselemente aus dem Lager geholt.

- Sie sind sich nicht sicher. Auf den Schraubenköpfen ist die Angabe 8.8 eingeprägt, auf den Muttern die Zahl 10.
- Sie fragen den Mechatroniker / die Mechatronikerin, worin sich die Schrauben unterscheiden.
- Sie sagen, dass Sie noch nie von Festigkeitsklassen gehört haben.
- Sie haben die Berechnung der Festigkeitswerte verstanden und erklären, wie man die Werte für die beiden abgebildeten Schrauben ermittelt.
- Sie erinnern sich an eine Schulung und erklären, dass man niemals eine Schraubverbindung bis an die Streckgrenze belasten darf, sonst verformt sich der Schraubenwerkstoff plastisch und die Sicherheit ist nicht mehr gewährleistet. Fragen Sie, warum auch auf den Muttern Zahlen eingeprägt sind.
- Sie sagen, dass Sie bereits den passenden Drehmomentschlüssel mitgebracht haben.

TOOLBOX

Schraubverbindung – *bolted assembly*
Mindestzugfestigkeit – *minimum tensile strength*
Mindeststreckgrenze – *minimum yield strength*
Festigkeitsklasse – *strength class*
Anzugsdrehmoment – *tightening torque*
Drehmomentschlüssel – *torque wrench*

5 Manuals and safety instructions

FOUNDATION: Numbers and measurements

Situation: Your company wants to order a number of aluminium platform trolleys, ladders and scaffolds from a British supplier.
→ **You clarify the details of one of the products with the supplier.**

1 Talking about numbers

Before the phone call, you check your knowledge of the English terms for mathematical operations.

A 17 **Listen and match the symbols to the English mathematical terms.**

1 is approximately equal to
2 degree
3 divided by
4 is equal to / equals
5 is greater than
6 is less than
7 minus
8 multiplied by / times
9 per cent
10 squared
11 plus or minus
12 is not equal to

a	≠	b	–	c	>	d	=
e	x	f	≈	g	<	h	°
i	%	j	x^2	k	±	l	÷

› *Talking about numbers, page 227*

B **Work with a partner. Partner A: Look here. Partner B: Look at File 4 on page 135.**

Read out these mathematical statements. Partner B will write them down. When you have finished, check that Partner B has written them correctly.

1 A > B
2 3 x 6 = 18
3 x ≠ y
4 0.65 ÷ 5 = 0.13
5 3% of 1,387,669 = 41,630.07
6 10 ± 0.3

2 Describing dimensions

You now check the words for describing dimensions.

A **Copy and complete the drawings with the words from the list.**

depth/deep · diagonal · height/high · ~~length~~/long · thickness/thick · width/wide

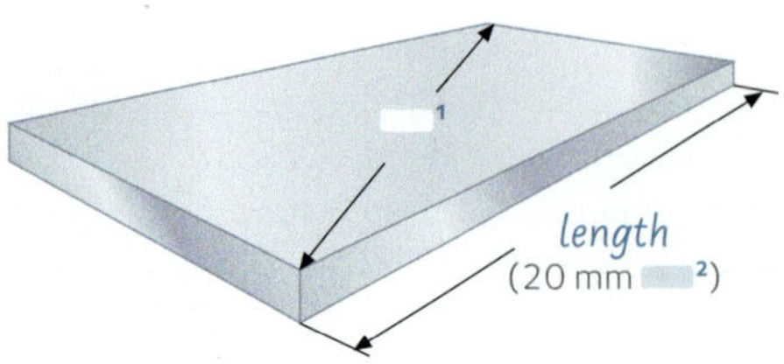

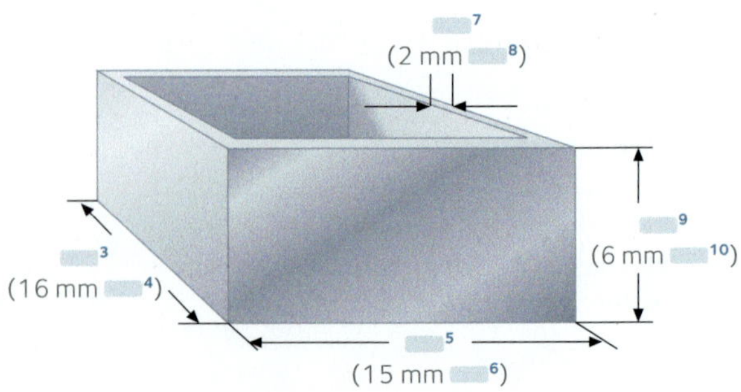

B Describe these boxes to your partner.

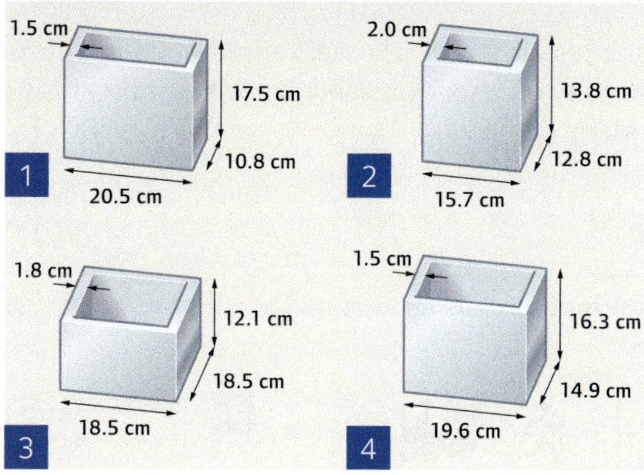

Giving dimensions

The box is 15 mm **wide** / has a **width** of 15 mm.
The metal plate is 2 mm **thick**. / The **thickness** of the metal plate is 2 mm.

Dimensions or measurements of rectangular solid shapes are given in reverse alphabetical order – **width** (side to side), **height** (top to bottom), **depth** (front to back):
The box is 20.5 cm **by** 10.8 cm **by** 17.5 cm.

› *Useful phrases: Describing size and dimensions, page 152*

3 Role-play: Giving specifications on the phone

You have received an email from Walker Aluminium (UK) Ltd with information about a platform trolley you are interested in. Unfortunately, some of the information is incorrect. The company calls you to correct the mistakes.

Work with a partner. Partner A: Look here.
Partner B: Look at File 11 on page 139.

Take the call from Partner B (Walker Aluminium Ltd) and ask about the correct information.

Clarifying details

Asking about and giving dimensions
What are the dimensions of the ... ?
It says here that the ... measures ... by ... .

Confirming information
The trolley is made of ... .
The castors are made of ... .
Could you repeat that, please?

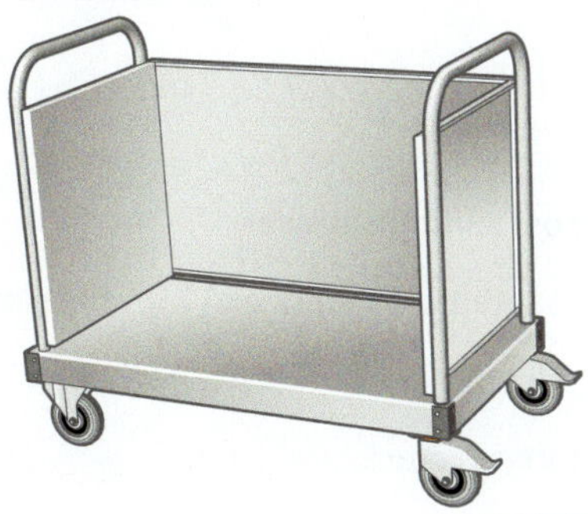

PLATFORM TROLLEY / aluminium
1500 x 700 x 670 mm

Other information:
Four castors on the bottom made of steel.
They measure approximately 170 mm in diameter and 65 mm in width.
All wheels are fitted with wheel brakes.

When you have finished, check your information with Partner B.

TOOLBOX

brake – *Bremse*
castor – *Laufrolle*
depth – *Tiefe*
height – *Höhe*
length – *Länge*
rubber – *Gummi*
thickness – *Dicke, Stärke*
width – *Breite*

PART A: Installation instructions

Situation: Your company has to install an alarm system in a warehouse. You are working with Märta Bengtsson, a Swedish apprentice who is in Germany on work experience but who speaks little German.
→ You discuss the installation of a smoke alarm system.

1 Understanding diagrams

First you read the installation instructions for the motion detectors to find out where to mount them.

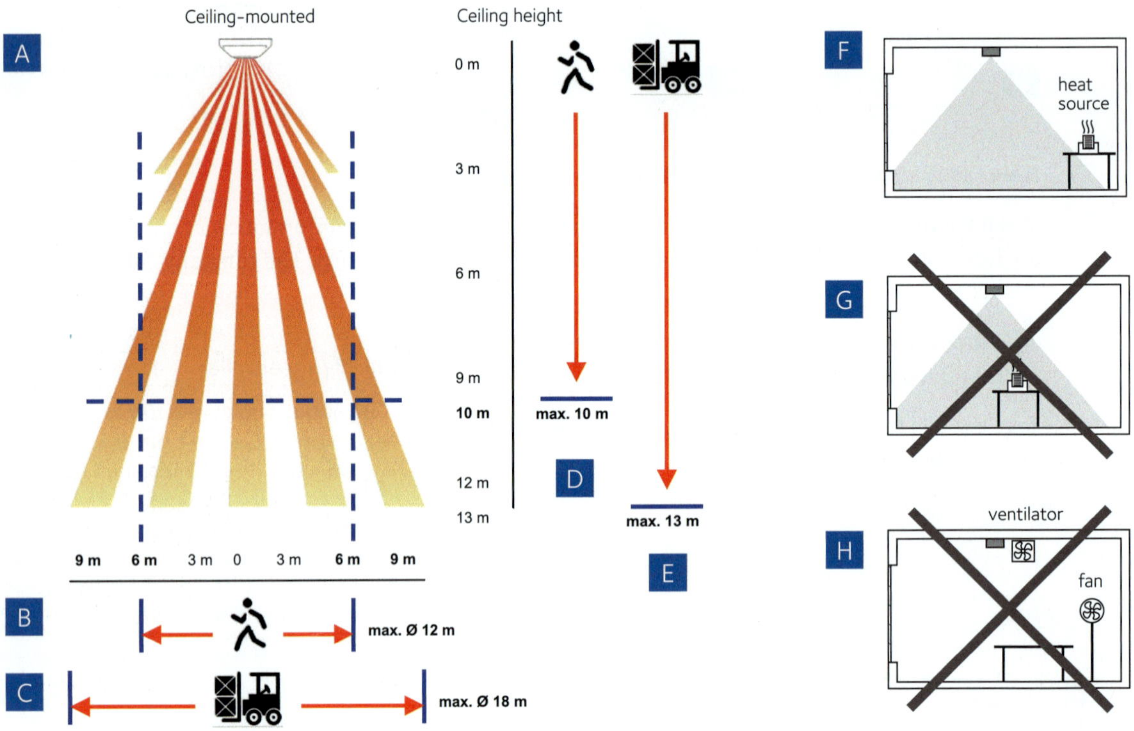

High Bay Motion Detector – installation instructions

Source: www.osram.com

Study the diagram and complete the statements below with the most suitable answer.

1 The device only detects …
a large machines.
b moving objects.
c people using machines.

2 It is designed to be mounted …
a at eye-level.
b on a wall.
c on the ceiling.

3 The detection zone is …
a bigger for vehicles.
a the same for people and vehicles.
c bigger for people.

4 If the alarm is mounted at a height of 12 m, it can detect …
a a fork-lift truck.
b a person.
c a person and a fork-lift truck.

5 A heat source in the detection zone …
a makes no difference.
b will trigger the detector.
c should not be directly under the detector.

6 The motion detector trips when the air around it is …
a hot.
b cold.
c moving.

2 Discussing the installation

In the warehouse, your supervisor discusses the job with Märta and they decide where to put the motion detectors.

18 Copy the diagram, then listen to the dialogue and complete your diagram with the following information:

- the dimensions of the warehouse
- how many motion detectors you need
- where to install the motion detectors

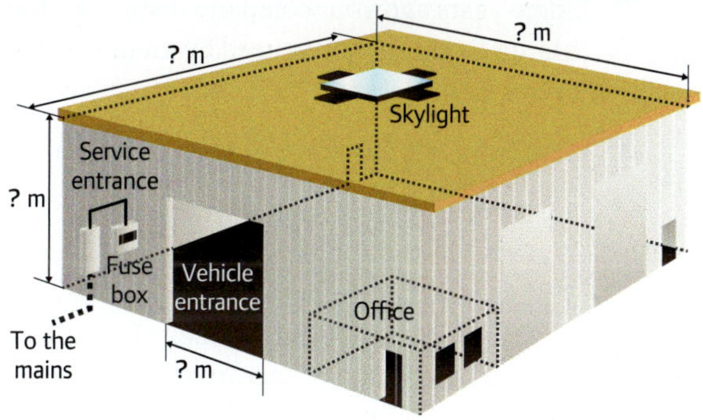

3 Connecting the motion detectors

Your next task is to decide how to connect the motion detectors so that any one of them will trigger the warehouse lights and alarm if tripped.

A **Work with a partner. Study the wiring diagrams 1 and 2 and decide which one is suitable in this case and why.**

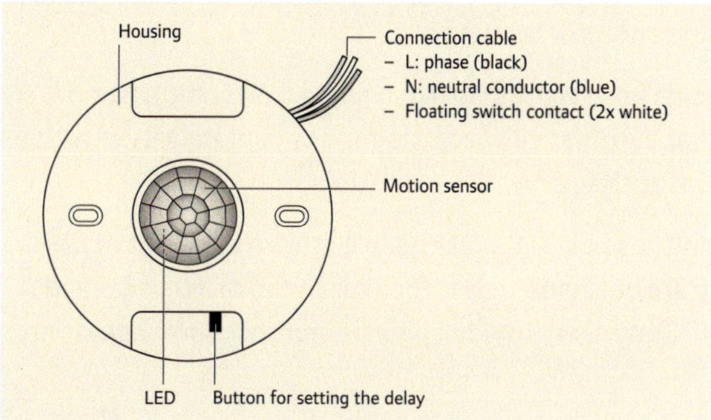

High Bay Motion Detector: Design

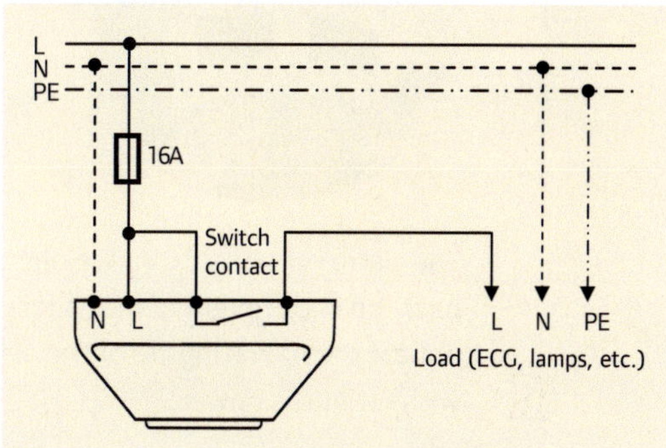

Wiring diagram 1: Mains voltage switching

B **Report your ideas to the class.**

> **Talking about consequences**
>
> If it **trips**, it **switches** on the alarm.
> If it **is tripped**, it **switches** on the lights.

› *Grammar: Conditional sentences, page 160*

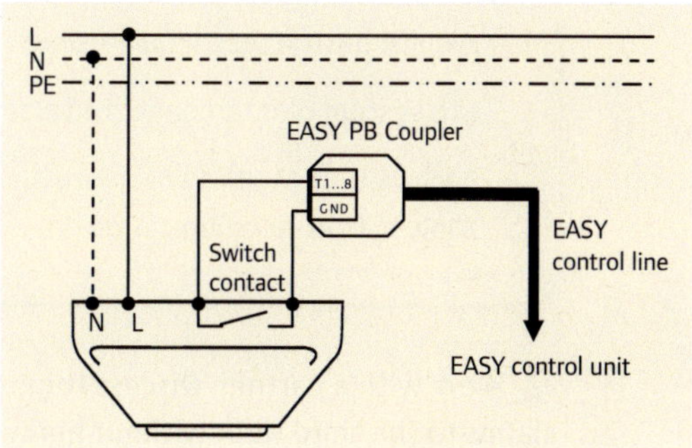

Wiring diagram 2: Floating (potential-free) switching

TOOLBOX

to detect – *erkennen, wahrnehmen*
fork-lift truck – *Gabelstapler*
fuse box – *Sicherungskasten*
heat source – *Wärmequelle*
to mount – *montieren, anbringen*
service entrance – *Hausanschlusskasten*
skylight – *Dachluke*
to trigger – *auslösen*
to trip – *auslösen, ausgelöst werden*

4 Extending an alarm system

Some years ago your company installed a hardwired heat and smoke alarm system on the first two floors of a large, 3-storey house used by an international company. The firm has now expanded to the top floor and needs more alarms.

A Study the information below on the alarms that are currently fitted and then do the following tasks.

1. List the hazards the alarms react to.
2. Describe their response to dust.
3. Explain what happens if there is a power outage.
4. Give the life span of the lithium batteries and explain why it is so long.
5. Explain the significance of a flashing amber (yellow) light.
6. Explain how the functionality of an alarm can be tested.
7. Describe what happens when one of an interconnected set of alarms sounds.

FireGuard:
Multi-Sensor Optical Smoke and Heat Alarm

The **FG911 Multi-Sensor Fire Alarm** has two separate sensing elements – optical and heat – and responds to all types of fire, e.g. fast flaming and slow burning.

It also avoids false alarms with its unique dust compensation feature that automatically adjusts for any contamination within the optical sensor chamber.

The alarm runs on 230V AC mains power and has built-in rechargeable lithium cells that act as a back-up in the event of mains failure. They are designed to last for a minimum of 10 years and outlast the operating life of the alarm itself. They also provide up to six months' alarm operation without mains power.

The FG911 self-checks its sensors, battery voltage and internal circuitry approximately every 40 seconds. If a fault is found, a combination of red/amber LEDs flash and/or a signal tone beeps.

A quick button test simulates high temperatures to check the optical chamber, electronics and horn.

In a system of interconnected alarms, when one unit senses fire, all the alarms sound.

Each FG911 Multi-Sensor Fire Alarm can also be fitted with an add-on FG611RL radio link module to allow hybrid communication between hardwired and wireless alarms.

B Work with a partner. Discuss together if it is possible to expand the current system of interconnected alarms to the third floor without hardwiring.

TOOLBOX

compensation feature – *Ausgleichsfunktion*
dust – *Staub*
fast-flaming – *schnell brennend*
hazard – *Gefahr*
horn – *Hupe*
optical – *optisch*

PART B: Safety at work

Situation: You work for PowerGen in Berlin, an international electronics company. The theme of the company's training day this year is *Safety first!*
→ **You make a video clip describing how you follow safety rules at work.**

1 Discussing safety procedures

The trainer first gives your seminar group some warning signs and pictures to discuss.

A Match the explanations (A–E) below to these signs.

1

2

3

4

5

A This equipment will not stop electrical equipment or installations from burning.
B There is no insulation on these conductors. If you touch them, you will get a shock.
C You mustn't block this door because someone might need to open it quickly.
D Electricity enters this building underground, so you must be careful when using earthmoving machinery or tools.
E You mustn't switch this circuit back on again. Only the person who switched it off is allowed to switch it back on again.

B With a partner, make a list of the signs you see at your own workplace and explain them to each other in English.

C With a partner, look at the situations below and say what the people should/ shouldn't do.

Expressing obligation, prohibition and permission

You **must** be careful when using tools.
You **mustn't** block this door.
Only the person who switched it off **is allowed to** switch it back on.

› *Grammar: Modal verbs and their substitutes, page 162*

D Explain to your partner what will happen if they aren't careful.

If the workman touches the overhead power cable, he will ...

› *Grammar: Conditional sentences, page 160*

TOOLBOX

(electric) shock – *Stromschlag, elektrischer Schlag*
live – *unter Spannung*

E **PowerGen wants to make sure the five German safety rules are used throughout the company, so you discuss them in English at the seminar. With a partner choose the correct statement to complete each rule.**

5 Sicherheitsregeln

Vor Beginn der Arbeiten
- freischalten
- gegen Wiedereinschalten sichern
- Spannungsfreiheit feststellen
- erden und kurzschließen
- benachbarte, unter Spannung stehende Teile abdecken oder abschranken

Rule 1: Before you work on electrical equipment or a circuit, you must …

a switch it off.
b turn it off.
c disconnect it.

Rule 2: The next thing you must do is …

a tell your workmates that you're working on the circuit or equipment.
b lock and tag it so no one turns it back on again.
c test the circuit to see if it's still live.

Rule 3: If, for example, the multimeter reading for the circuit is zero, …

a you still mustn't start work on it.
b it's safe to start work on it.
c you can be sure the circuit isn't live.

Rule 4: You short-circuit a circuit by touching the …

a black conductor against the blue conductor.
b blue conductor against the green-yellow conductor.
c black conductor against the green-yellow conductor.

Rule 5: If there are live electrical components near where you're working, …

a don't start work until you've disconnected them.
b make it impossible to touch them if you can't disconnect them.
c be careful not to touch them.

2 Reading about electrical hazards

The trainer now gives you a text about electric shocks.

A **Read through the text and find expressions in English for the German words in the list.**

Brustkorb • Dauer • erstarren • Herzkammerflimmern • Herzstillstand • Kribbeln

How dangerous is an electric shock?

Electricity can kill: most deaths result from a current entering the body and passing through the chest or the head. In all cases, the voltage (V) is less important than the strength of the current (A – amperage) and the duration (how long it flows through the body).

An electric shock of 1 mA isn't dangerous or painful to most people. You may feel a slight 'tingle', if anything. A 5 mA shock is unpleasant, but not usually dangerous.

With slightly higher currents, there is a danger that your muscles will 'freeze' and you won't be able to let go of the electricity source. This reaction greatly increases the duration of the shock and happens somewhere between 6 mA and 30 mA. Most adults can still let go at 15 mA AC (or 70 mA DC), and this value is known as the 'let go' or 'freezing' current. Higher currents than this are extremely painful and may cause death.

Currents of 1–4 amps disturb the rhythm of your heartbeat, causing ventricular fibrillation (uncoordinated heart function). Nerve damage is also likely. A shock of this strength may even stop your heart (cardiac arrest) and cause death.

A current of over 10 amps causes serious internal and external burns and will almost certainly cause death by cardiac arrest.

B **Read the text again, then copy the table below and complete it with expressions a–l.**

	Strength of AC current	Reactions
1	1 mA	*tingling (k)*
2	5 mA	
3	6–30 mA	
4	50–150 mA	
5	1–4 mA	
6	>10 A	

a cardiac arrest possible
b cardiac arrest likely
c death likely
d death possible
e extreme pain
f freezing of muscles
g mild pain
h strong pain
i nerve damage
j severe burns
k tingling
l ventricular fibrillation

3 Applying the safety rules

You are back at work in Germany now and Vasil Vankov, an apprentice from PowerGen's Bulgarian branch, is with you for a month's work experience. Today your supervisor wants you to diagnose a fault in the transport system of a production line.

A 19 **Listen to Vasil and your supervisor and answer the questions.**

1 Why do the tumble dryers sometimes bump into packaging stations?
2 Why doesn't the supervisor want to check the sensors first?
3 Why do they decide to replace the power supply unit?
4 What safety measure doesn't Vasil understand?
5 How does he test the AC voltage range of the multimeter?
6 Why does Vasil touch two of the conductors against each other?

B **Work with a partner and discuss other possible causes of the problem.**

4 Preparing a video clip

Now it is time to prepare a video clip, describing how you follow safety rules at work.

Work in small groups. Think of a recent job you did at work. Use the following prompts to create a short video clip showing safety rules.

- Write notes on what you did for the job.
- Note down how you followed the safety rules at each stage of the job.
- Use a smartphone or video camera to make a short video clip explaining the safety rules you followed.
- Present your video clip to the class.

› *Useful phrases: Talking about health and safety, page 152*

TOOLBOX

burn – *Verbrennung*
(to) damage – *Schaden; beschädigen*
to disconnect – *vom Netz trennen*
painful – *schmerzhaft*
safety rule – *Sicherheitsvorschrift*
sporadic – *gelegentlich, vereinzelt*
to tag – *kennzeichnen*
to touch – *berühren*

COMMUNICATION: Graphs and charts

Situation: Your union representative is speaking at an international conference next week.
→ **You prepare notes on some graphic information that he can use in his talk.**

1 Describing graphs

You refresh your knowledge of the English expressions for describing graphs.

A Match the names in the list to the graphs (a–c). There is one name more than you need.

bar chart · line graph · pie chart · table

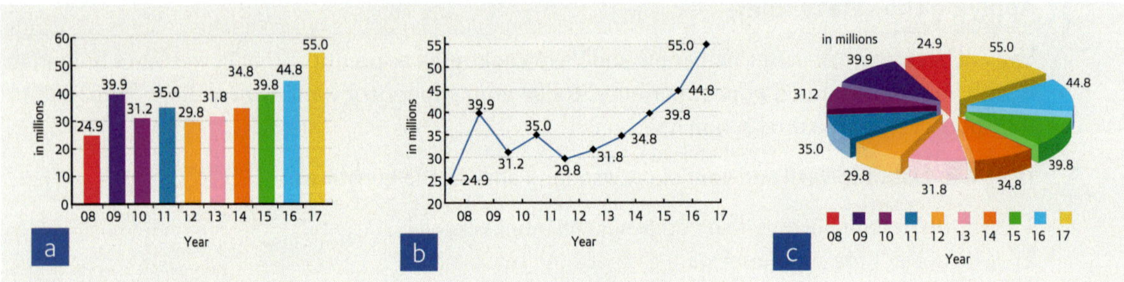

B Match the words/phrases (1–15) to the graphs (a–h). For some graphs, several expressions can be used.

1 to remain constant / stay the same
2 to go up / down
3 to increase / the increase
4 to hit a maximum / minimum
5 to flatten out / to level off
6 to decrease / the decrease
7 to drop / the drop
8 to rise / the rise
9 to fluctuate / the fluctuation
10 to fall / the fall
11 to climb / the climb
12 to peak / the peak

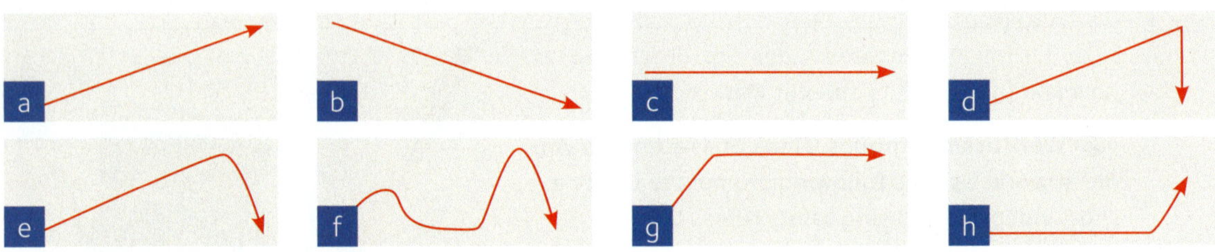

C Work with a partner. Partner A: **Look here.** Partner B: **Look at File 5 on page 136.**

Describe this line graph to Partner B. Partner B will draw it. Check Partner B's graph when you have finished. › *Useful phrases: Describing graphs, page 152*

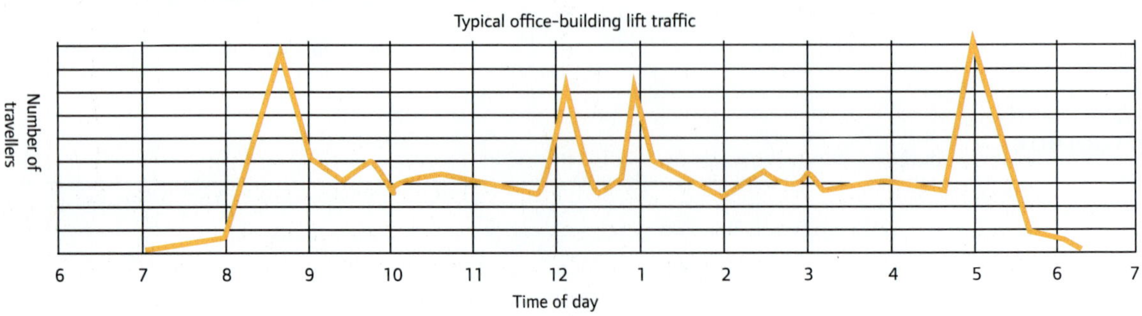

2 Talking about figures

At the conference, your union representative uses a table to describe sales of technical products worldwide in the last financial year.

A 20)) **Listen and decide which of the tables is being presented.**

A

Quarterly sales (millions of euros)				
Area	Q. I	Q. II	Q. III	Q. IV
UK	10.3	11.4	8.2	10.5
Germany	8.9	9.3	8.6	7.1
E. Europe	0.2	0.8	1.7	3.6

B

Quarterly sales (€ m)			
Q. I	Q. II	Q. III	Q. IV
10.3	11.4	8.2	10.3
8.0	8.3	8.1	6.2
0.3	0.9	3.8	4.5

C

Quarterly sales (€ m)			
Q. I	Q. II	Q. III	Q. IV
10.3	11.4	8.2	10.7
8.2	7.4	8.0	9.5
0.5	1.6	2.3	2.3

B **Work with a partner. Choose one of the tables and describe the sales figures for Germany or Eastern Europe. Your partner should say which table you are describing.**

3 Describing a table

Your union representative would like to compare and contrast average working hours in Germany with conditions in other countries. You have found the following table.

	Working hours per week	Working day*	Lunch break
Germany	41.1	07.30/08.30–16.00/17.30	30–45 mins 12.00–13.30
France	37.9	08.00–18.00	60 mins 12.00–14.00
GB	41.4	08.00/09.00–17.00/18.00	60 mins 12.00–14.00
Scandinavia	39.1	08.00–16.00	30 mins 11.30–12.00
USA	40+	08.00–17.00+	30 mins 12.00–13.00

* The working day: Blue collar workers in some countries begin work one hour earlier than white collar workers.

Work with a partner. Study the table and write notes, using the following headings:

Introduction
The table shows information about … .

A **Working hours per week**
The shortest working hours per week are to be found in … .

B **Working day**
In Germany, most people begin work between 7.30 and 8.30 and finish … .

C **Lunch breaks**
People in France and Great Britain have the longest … .

DAS KANN ICH (Unit 5)

- Maße und andere Produktdetails am Telefon auf Englisch erklären. (Foundation)
- Einen Rauchmelder nach einer englischsprachigen Bedienungsanleitung installieren. (Part A)
- Ein kurzes englisches Video über Sicherheitsvorschriften vorbereiten. (Part B)
- Notizen anhand einer Grafik auf Englisch erstellen. (Communication)

PART A: An electric door-operating system

Situation: Your company, Lorenz Automation GmbH in Hildesheim, manufactures doors and door-operating systems for factories and warehouses.
→ **You identify a customer's requirements and recommend a suitable product.**

1 Preparing for the visit

Before you visit the customer, you review the presentation you have prepared on your tablet computer.

A Match the descriptions of the doors (A–D) with the illustrations (1–4).

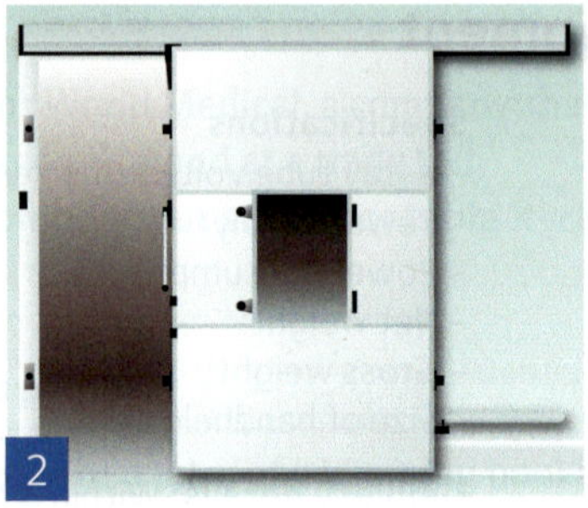

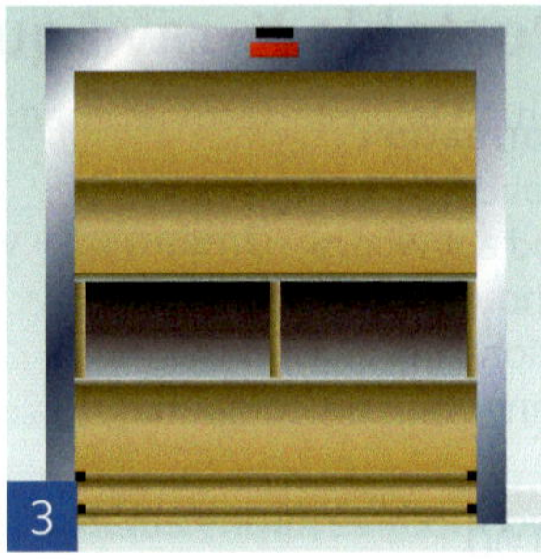

- **A** A durable, fully insulated, power-assisted sliding door is the ideal solution for cold storage applications. Premium, non-corrosive materials as strong as steel but 30% lighter, guarantee perfect performance and efficiency at extreme temperatures for many years.
- **B** A fast, fully automatic, PLC-operated rollup door is the robust space-saving solution of choice in an internal, rapid transit environment. Tight seals optimize temperature control, and inbuilt window panels guarantee excellent visibility.
- **C** A strip door is an excellent secondary barrier. It is a cost-effective way of reducing refrigerated air loss from coolers and freezers, and protecting against noise, wind, dust and pollution while ensuring easy access and maximum visibility for vehicles and pedestrians.
- **D** Swing doors are a fast and efficient solution in a high-traffic work space. Our robust, fully automatic doors are PLC-controlled and have bumpers to protect against impact damage. Tight seals also reduce thermal loss in temperature-controlled environments.

B With a partner discuss which of the doors above are most suitable for the situations below. (More than one answer may be possible.)

- frozen food storage
- frequent transport by fork-lift truck, power-assisted and/or manual trolleys
- preventing a sharp rise in temperature when a freezer or cooler door is opened
- regular use in a narrow doorway by pedestrians, trolleys and small vehicles

TOOLBOX

bumper – *Stoßfänger*
durable – *strapazierfähig*
impact – *Aufprall*
insulated – *(wärme)isoliert, isolierend*
non-corrosive – *korrosionsbeständig*
power-assisted – *Servo-*
robust – *widerstandsfähig*
seal – *Dichtung, Verschluss*
vehicle – *Fahrzeug*
visibility – *Sicht*

2 Using programmable logic controllers

Many of your company's products use PLCs, so you find an English description of them on the internet.

A PLC (programmable logic controller) converts input signals into output commands. Its central processing unit (CPU) reacts to data received from sensors, switches or buttons and sends commands to its output section, for example to actuators, motors or lights. The CPU is accessed and programmed via its communication ports. Program commands and data are stored in its non-volatile memory. PLCs are used by industry in many situations where automation is required and they can be quickly and easily re-programmed to meet changing conditions.

Programmable Logic Controller

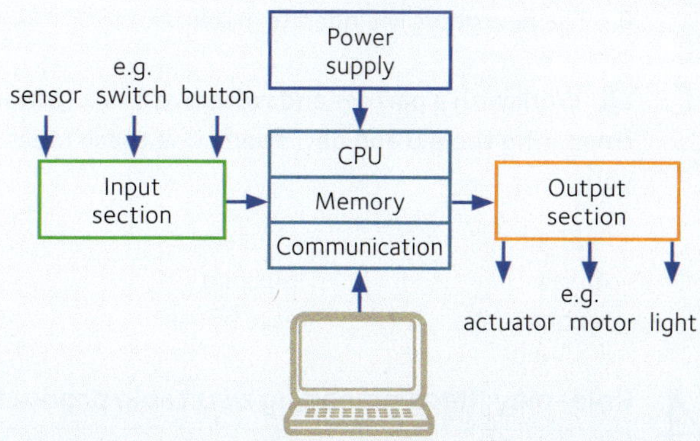

A **Match the highlighted English words in the text with the German terms in the list.**

Aktor • Bedingungen • Befehl • nichtflüchtig • reagieren • speichern • umwandeln • zugreifen auf

B **Your presentation includes a description of the PLC unit. With a partner, use the diagram above to discuss how doors 1 and 3 would be programmed to operate automatically. Give a short presentation to your class.**

Begin like this: *First of all, we would ... . Then ... . After that, ... Next ... . Finally, ...*

› *Unit 4, Communication, page 42; Useful phrases: Giving a presentation, page 150*

3 Identifying requirements

You go with your supervisor to visit a Danish company, Olsens Frugthave a/s. Your supervisor talks to Ebba Olsen, the managing director, about the company's requirements.

A 22 **Listen to the dialogue and make notes on these aspects:**

- the current door
- its location
- its dimensions
- power supply
- temperature(s) at location
- traffic
- operating mode(s)
- your recommendation
- the next step

TOOLBOX

3-phase current – *Drehstrom*
data sheet – *Datenblatt*
electrically operated – *elektrisch betrieben*
lighting – *Beleuchtung*
mechanisch – *mechanical*
to rewire – *neu verkabeln*

B 22)) **Listen again and complete the sentences below with words from the dialogue. Sometimes there are two words missing.**

1 We have a number of solutions, all of which are ___ to operate.
2 Must the new door be ___ big ___ this one?
3 I want something ___. This door is really ugly!
4 You need a door between room temperature and a much ___ temperature.
5 A PLC is a programmable logic controller. It's the ___ way of operating the door.
6 The new doors will operate much ___.

C **Work with a partner and write five or six sentences comparing the old and new doors. Use these ideas to help you:**

- weight
- noise
- appearance
- efficiency
- flexibility
- ease of use

Making comparisons

The new model is **as** big **as** this one but **easier** to use and **more efficient than** the old one. It operates **more quietly** and it's the **most flexible** solution.

› *Grammar: Comparatives and superlatives, page 162*

4 Role-play: Recommending a suitable product

Your company sends you to talk to Tamish Patel, the director of Indian Living Store, a furniture company in Cologne. Mr Patel, who speaks English better than German, wants an automated door for his warehouse.

Role-play the dialogue, using these prompts.

You

Stellen Sie sich vor (Vor-, Nachname und Firma).

Tamish Patel

Begrüßen Sie Ihren Besuch und stellen Sie sich vor.

You

Fragen Sie, wo die Installationsarbeit für das neue Tor durchgeführt werden soll.

Tamish Patel

Zeigen Sie ihm/ihr das jetzige Tor und erklären Sie, dass Sie ein neues, großes, elektrisch betriebenes Rolltor bekommen.

You

Fragen Sie, ob er ein Datenblatt zum Tor hat.

Tamish Patel

Geben Sie ihm/ihr das Datenblatt.

You

Fragen Sie, ob Drehstrom vorhanden ist.

Tamish Patel

Sagen Sie, dass Sie nicht sicher sind. Sie haben elektrische Beleuchtung im Lager, aber keine Maschinen dort.

You

Erklären Sie, dass Sie ein neues Kabel für Drehstrom verlegen müssen, denn 230 V sind nicht genug. Der Antrieb braucht 400 V Drehstrom. Sie empfehlen, das Lager komplett neu zu verkabeln.

Tamish Patel

Bedanken Sie sich für die Informationen. Sagen Sie, dass Sie etwas Bedenkzeit brauchen und bitten Sie um ein Angebot per E-Mail.

You

Versprechen Sie, dem Kunden ein Angebot zu schicken und schließen Sie das Gespräch höflich ab.

Tamish Patel

Sie bedanken sich und schließen das Gespräch höflich ab.

PART B: Installation of a new turning machine

Situation: You work at the British subsidiary of Mech-On. The company has ordered a NEF 400 V3 CNC turning machine and it will soon be delivered.
→ You solve a problem with the power supply.

1 Estimating the space requirements

Your supervisor asks you to help to find a suitable space for the new machine on the factory floor.

A Read the definitions of parts of the machine (1–8) and match them to the parts listed below the plan.

1 a device to transport small cut pieces of metal
2 the control centre for electric currents and functions
3 the connection for compressed oil
4 the device which pumps liquids to reduce temperature on cutting tools
5 machine for bulk production of round parts
6 the connection for compressed air
7 the electrical connection on the back of the machine
8 the area where you work in front of the machine

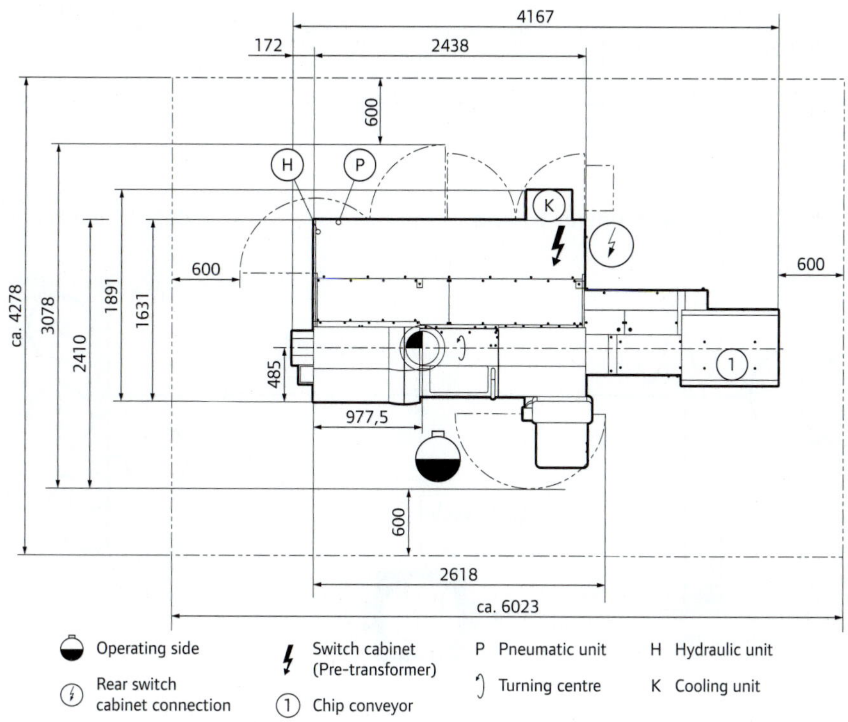

Source: DMG MORI

B Study the plans with your partner and answer these questions.

1 What's the length and width of the machine, including the chip conveyor and tank?
2 How much space does the machine require, including the necessary working space around it?
3 What's the approximate distance between the electric and the pneumatic connection?
4 What's the approximate distance between the pneumatic and the hydraulic unit?
5 What's the length of the chip conveyor?

2 Completing the electrical installation

Your supervisor asks you to email the electrician the electrical specifications of the NEF 400 V3.

Copy the table and complete it with information from the box.

10 mm² · 21 kVA · 31 A · 35 A · 400 V · 50 Hz · L1, L2, L3 · PE

Operating Voltage (U)	1
Phases	2
Protective earth	3
Main fuse (slow blow)	4
Nominal current (I)	5
Frequency (f)	6
Nominal apparent power (S)	7
Conductor cross section (A)	8

3 Troubleshooting

A test run of the new NEF 400 turning machine reveals a problem with the power supply.

A **Work with a partner and discuss the oscillogram. What does it tell us about the power supply? Write a few sentences to describe what is happening.**

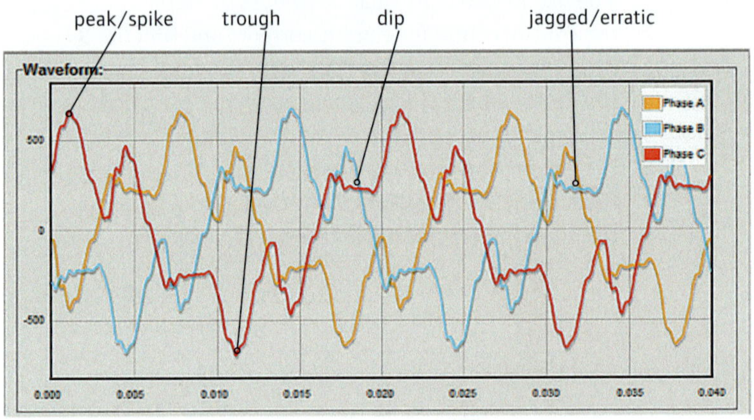

B **You decide to use an active dynamic filter (ADF) to fix the problem. Read the manufacturer's website on page 63 then label the diagram below.**

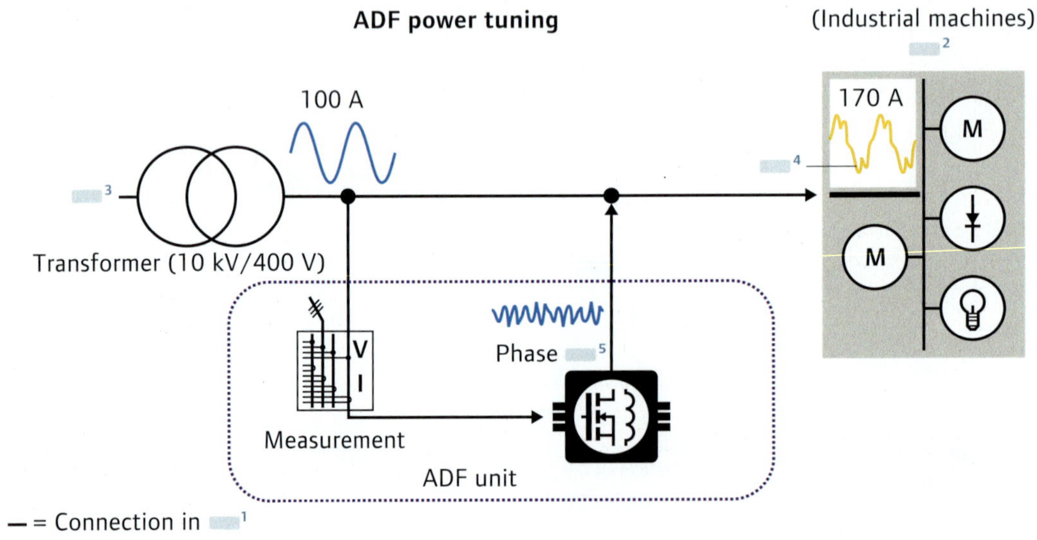

TOOLBOX

apparent power – *Scheinleistung*
conductor cross section – *Leiterquerschnitt*
fuse – *Sicherung*
nominal current – *Nennstrom*
operating voltage – *Betriebsspannung*
protective earth – *Schutzleiter*
slow blow – *träge*

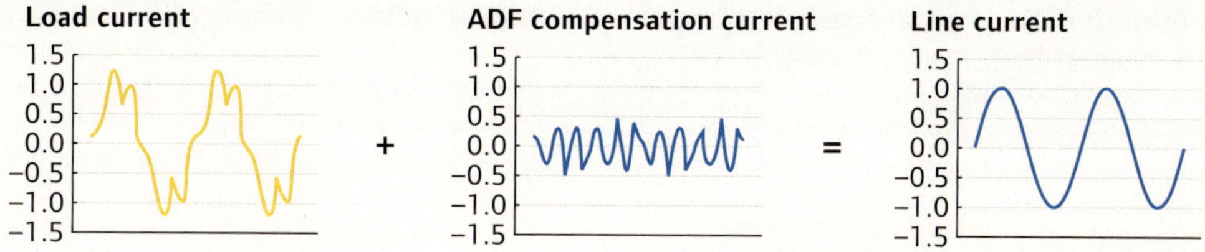

The ADF operational principle

An ADF module is basically a very advanced computer controlled current generator with the ability to produce any shape or form of current with little or no delay.

A simplified diagram of the operating principle is shown in the figure here. Each module is connected in parallel, in shunt, with the load that requires compensation. The power flows of electrical currents between the load and the network are measured and analysed to determine whether disturbances such as reactive displacement and/or harmonics are present.

If found, the ADF unit injects phase currents that are the exact opposite of, for example, the harmonics and/or reactive displacement. This is done in order to cancel out the load behaviour.

Source: www.adfpowertuning.com

4 Describing the solution

After the ADF has been installed in the circuit, you test the power supply and obtain the oscillogram below.

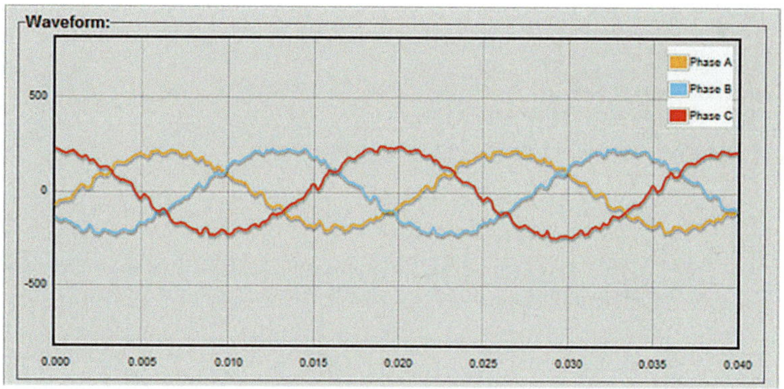

A **Work with a partner. What does the oscillogram tell us about the power supply now? Write a few sentences to describe what has changed.**

B **With your partner, use the three diagrams to prepare a short presentation to the class on how the problem with the power supply at the Mech-On plant was solved.**

C **Think of a technical problem that you have recently solved at work. With a partner, prepare a brief presentation on it and give it to the class. Use diagrams and other suitable aids wherever possible.**

› *Useful phrases: Giving a presentation, page 150*

TOOLBOX

dip – *Gefälle*
erratic – *unregelmäßig*
jagged – *zackig*
peak/spike – *Spitze*
regular/irregular sinus curve – *(un)regelmäßige Sinuskurve*
sinusoidal – *sinusförmig*
trough – *Tief(st)punkt*
waveform – *Kurve*

COMMUNICATION: Arrangements for meetings

Situation: You work at Juncker Anlagenbau GmbH in Dusseldorf. The company is taking part in the Ecological Trade Fair next week.
→ **You write three emails to make arrangements for meetings with customers.**

1 Setting up a meeting with a client

Paul Smith, the Chief Engineer at Juncker, asks you to arrange a meeting with a customer. He gives you the following instructions.

Pls. get in touch with Mary Doyle at Waste Water Solutions, Dublin; set up a mtg. to present our filter presses. Ms Doyle wants to discuss some details before ordering.
Suggest we meet at ETF in Glasgow: 26 April, morning any time until 12.30 p.m.; or 27 April, betw. 12.30 and 6.30 p.m. Need about 3 hrs.
Ask which day is suitable (pls. book room for mtg.).
Thanks. Paul

Telling the time in English-speaking countries

When telling the time in English, use the short forms, *a.m.* and *p.m.*
a.m. *(ante meridiem)* = between midnight and midday
p.m. *(post meridiem)* = after 12.00 noon
In English-speaking countries the twenty-four hour clock is generally only used for timetables.

Work with a partner. Complete the email to Ms Doyle using words and phrases from the notes above.

From: trainee@juncker_anlagenbau.de
To: m.doyle@wastewatersolutions.ie
Subject: **Meeting with Paul Smith to discuss filter presses**

Dear Ms Doyle

Paul Smith, Chief Engineer at Juncker Anlagenbau, has asked me ___[1] with you in order to ___[2] a meeting. Mr Smith would like to ___[3] our filter presses and ___[4] with you before you place your order.

Mr Smith will be at the Ecological Trade Fair in Glasgow next week so he ___[5] either of the following dates: 26 April at any time in the ___[6] until 12.30 p.m. or 27 April between 12.30 and 6.30 p.m.

He thinks that the meeting will take about ___[7].

Please let me know if either of these dates ___[8].

I hope to hear from you by tomorrow as I need time to ___[9] a room for the meeting.

Yours ___[10]

TOOLBOX

filter press – *Filterpresse*

waste water – *Abwasser*

2 Replying to the invitation to the meeting

Complete Mary Doyle's reply using words and phrases from the list.

An appointment · Best wishes · booked · invite · look forward · reserve · Thank you · We are in

___[1] for your email.

___[2] on Thursday, 26th at 9.30 a.m. would suit me best.

My company has ___[3] a stand with a small room attached, so you do not need to ___[4] a meeting room.

___[5] Hall 3, stand number 75. We would like to ___[6] Mr Smith for a working breakfast.

I ___[7] to seeing Mr Smith again.

___[8]

Mary Doyle

3 Changing arrangements

Because Paul has to set up a small presentation for Ms Doyle on Thursday morning, he postpones a breakfast meeting with his business partner, Ian Duncan.

Write Mr Smith's email to Ian Duncan to postpone the breakfast meeting. Explain the situation and use details from the itinerary below to suggest a new date and time for a meeting, e.g. for lunch or dinner.

Giving dates, days and times

at 6 p.m., **at** lunchtime
at night, **at** the weekend
on Monday, **on** 21 June
in the morning, in January, **in** 2017

ITINERARY – **Wed 25th – Sat 28th**			
Wed 25	Flight LH 134 07.20 → Glasgow (arr. 08.40)		Dinner: Hans Treder 19.00 (Wallace Restaurant)
Thur 26	~~Breakfast: Ian Duncan 7.30 – 9.00~~ Mary Doyle (presentation) 9.30 – 12.30	Meeting: SysMet 14.00 – 16.00	
Fri 27	Stand: 10.00 – 12.00	Meeting: KL Pipes 14.00 – 18.00	
Sat 28	Golf: Harry Jones 11.00		Flight LH 918 19.15 → Dusseldorf (arr. 21.25)

› *Useful phrases: Making arrangements, page 153*

DAS KANN ICH (Unit 6)

- Eine/n Kunden/Kundin beim Kauf eines technischen Geräts beraten. (Foundation)
- Eine/n Kunden/Kundin über automatische Torantriebe auf Englisch beraten. (PartA)
- Ein Problem bei der Stromversorgung für eine/n Kunden/Kundin lösen. (PartB)
- Treffen mit englischsprachigen Kunden/Kundinnen per E-Mail organisieren. (Communication)

KMK Exam practice 3

1 Mediation

Ihr Ausbildungsbetrieb erwartet in vier Wochen Besuch von drei Praktikanten/Praktikantinnen aus verschieden Ländern. Alle drei sprechen Englisch. Sie werden von Ihrem Ausbildungsleiter gebeten, die Praktikanten per E-Mail auf Englisch zu kontaktieren, um ihnen als erste Information die Sicherheitsbestimmungen beim Bedienen von elektrischen Werkzeugen zukommen zu lassen. Von Ihrem Ausbildungsleiter erhalten Sie die untenstehenden Sicherheitsbestimmungen auf Deutsch als Vorlage.

Übertragen Sie die untenstehenden Sicherheitsbestimmungen in Form einer Checkliste ins Englische. Es wird keine Übersetzung erwartet.

Sicherheit beim Bedienen von elektrischen Werkzeugen

- Um Verletzungen vorzubeugen, ist es wichtig, dass Sie mit schnelldrehenden elektrischen Maschinen wie z. B. Bohrern, Fräsen oder Schleifmaschinen stets konzentriert arbeiten. Das gilt nicht nur für Sie, sondern auch für andere Personen.
- Vergewissern Sie sich, wo der Not-Aus-Schalter ist, um die Maschine im Notfall zu stoppen. Sie müssen wissen, wo das Notfalltelefon ist.
- Geeignete Schutzkleidung und -schuhe sind unbedingt erforderlich. Denken Sie auch an passenden Augenschutz. Für manche Arbeiten ist das Tragen von Handschuhen Vorschrift. Generell ist es notwendig, bei längeren Haaren ein Haarnetz zu tragen.
- Befestigen Sie die Werkstücke und kontrollieren Sie Werkzeughalterungen gut.
- Lassen Sie eingeschaltete Geräte nie unbeaufsichtigt!
- Sollten Sie Reinigungsarbeiten an einem elektrischen Werkzeug vornehmen wollen, so trennen Sie es vorher vom Stromnetz.
- Säubern Sie Ihren Arbeitsplatz.

2 Produktion

Schreiben Sie nun die E-Mail an die Praktikanten/Praktikantinnen, in der Sie über sich berichten, in welchen beiden Abteilungen Ihres Betriebes Sie am liebsten waren und warum (oder welche beiden Tätigkeiten Sie am liebsten ausführten).

Erwähnen Sie den Grund Ihrer Mitteilung und weisen Sie auf die Wichtigkeit der Sicherheitsbestimmungen im Anhang hin. Gern stehen Sie für gemeinsame Unternehmungen nach Dienstschluss mit Rat und Tat zur Verfügung. Schließen Sie die E-Mail mit dem Satz, dass Sie sich auf den Besuch freuen.

3 Mediation

Sie arbeiten als Mechatroniker/Mechatronikerin bei einer Firma, die Steuerungen für Fertigungsanlagen entwickelt und installiert. Bei einem Ihrer Kunden soll ein S7-300 Modul ausgetauscht werden. Die Montagearbeiten werden von der Kundenfirma selbst vorgenommen, deren Techniker Sie per Hotline um Hinweise zur Installation der Anlage bittet. Ihnen liegt dazu das englischsprachige Handbuch (siehe Seite 67) vor.

Lesen Sie die Montagehinweise durch und fassen Sie die wesentlichen Aussagen stichpunktartig auf Deutsch zusammen.

SIMATIC

S7-300 Automation System

Installation Manual

Warning

You may come into contact with live wires if the power supply module and any additional load power supply units are connect-ed to the mains. You should therefore disconnect the S7-300 from the power supply before starting the wiring. Only use ferrules with insulating collars to press-fit onto the ends of the cables. Once you have wired the modules, close all the front panels. You can then switch on the S7-300 again.

Wiring

1. Open the front panels of the power supply module and *CPU.
2. Remove the strain relief clamp from the power supply module.
3. Strip the power cable to a length of approximately 11 mm and connect it to L1, N, and to the ground conductor terminal of the power supply module.
4. Screw-tighten the strain relief clamp again.
5. You can now wire your CPU: Insert the connection comb and screw-tighten it.
6. Close the front panel.

The figure on the right illustrates the procedures described above.

❶ Cable grip of the power supply

❷ Connection comb (accessory for power supply)

Source: Siemens.com

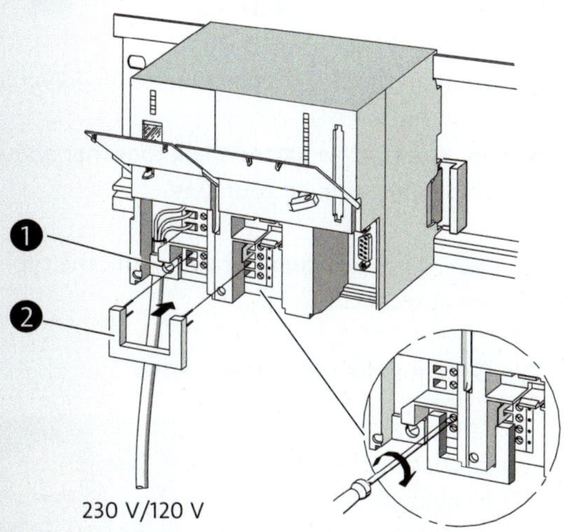

TOOLBOX

CPU (= central processing unit) – *hier: Rechenmodul*
ferrule – *Aderendhülse*
strain relief clamp – *Zugentlastungsklemme*

7 Communicating with colleagues

FOUNDATION: Internal communication

Situation: Your firm is carrying out measures to improve internal communication.
→ **You do a survey to find out which means of communication colleagues use and what improvements they would like.**

1 Talking about communication at work

A What method(s) of communication do you use most at work? Make a list.

B Work with a partner. Talk together about the advantages/disadvantages of the means of communication on your lists.

C Work with another pair. Rank the types of communication according to how useful they are when you are at work.

2 Getting the message across

Three trainees are discussing their company's decision to improve internal communication. (The discussion is in three sections.)

David
Construction mechanic

Marta
CAD engineer

Janek
Energy engineer

TOOLBOX

to access information – *auf Informationen zugreifen*
face-to-face meeting – *persönliches Treffen/Gespräch*
to share information – *Informationen teilen*
to synchronize files – *Dateien abgleichen/synchronisieren*

A 23 **Listen and say who expresses the following opinions.**

1 A face-to-face meeting is good when you want to make a quick decision.
2 When you want a quick decision in writing, it's better to send a text message.
3 It doesn't take long to write an email.
4 You need to be at work to access the intranet.
5 You can access cloud storage from anywhere.
6 Slides should only be used for graphic images and shouldn't have a lot of text.

B 23 **Listen again and complete the notes on the advantages and disadvantages of the different types of communication systems below.**

1 If the other person isn't around, you can't have a ___ .
2 Good options for making a ___ are using the telephone for a phone call or a message.
3 One of the things people really dislike about emails is that ___ .
4 The advantage of using the cloud is that the company can ___ with clients.
5 An intranet is ___ so it's easy to find the information you're looking for.
6 When they're full of writing, slides are ___ .

3 Carrying out a survey

You do a survey among your colleagues to find out their ideas about internal communication.

A **In class, brainstorm ideas for questions for your survey.**

Do you use … at work?

How often do you use … at work?

In your opinion, what are the advantages/ disadvantages of … ?

What type of communication would you like to use at work?

Talking about quantities

How many text messages do you get at work every day?
– I get **a lot**. **A lot of them** are instructions from my supervisor.
How much time do you spend answering emails?
– Too **much** time.

› *Grammar: Much, many, a lot (of), page 161*

B **Make two charts to record the results of your survey.**

1 Communication we use at work			
type of communication	How many people use this?	advantages	disadvantages
email	*HHH II*	*you can send attachments*	*too many emails every day*

2 Communication we would like to use at work	
type of communication	advantages

C **Use the results of your survey to make suggestions on how to improve internal communication in your firm.**

PART A: Schematics and data sheets

Situation: You join an internet forum for people who are interested in electronics.
→ You learn how to understand and use data sheets.

1 Identifying components

Many of your discussions are about electrical components and schematics (circuit diagrams).

A Match the words in the list to the electrical components (1–10).

capacitor · diode · full-wave bridge rectifier · glass fuse · integrated voltage stabilizer · mains input socket · resistor · transformer · transistor · tube

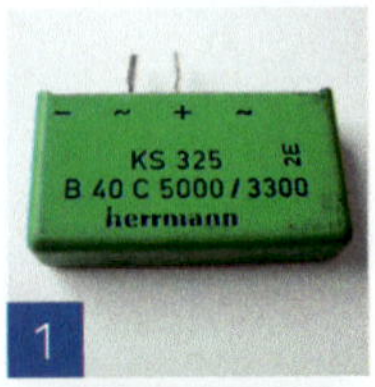

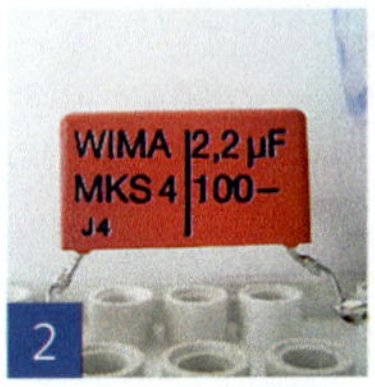

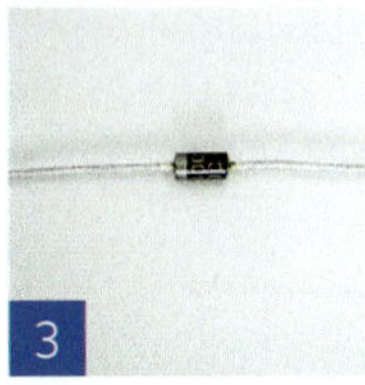

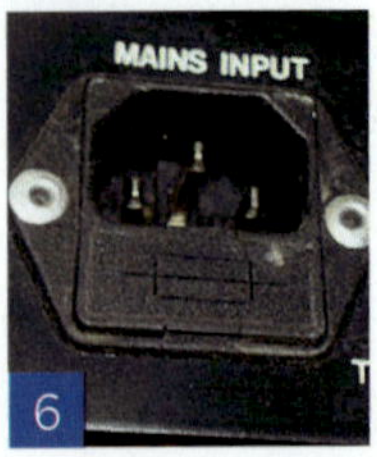

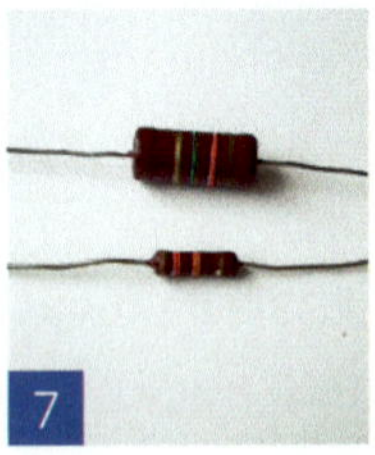

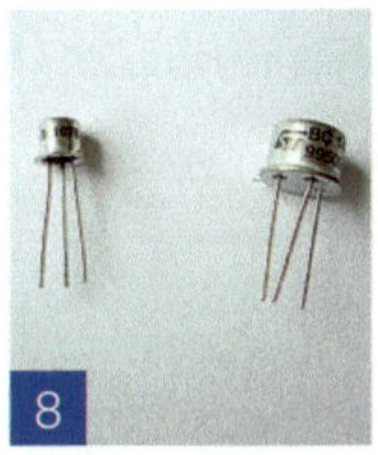

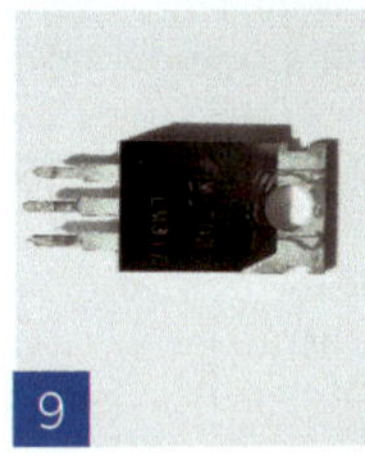

B Now find the correct symbols (a–j) for the components above.

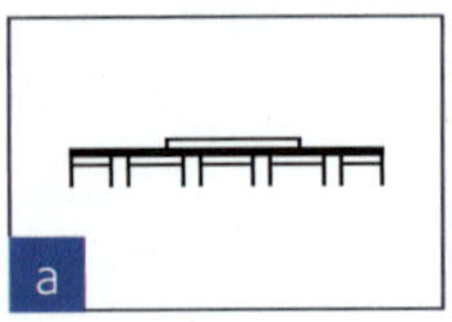

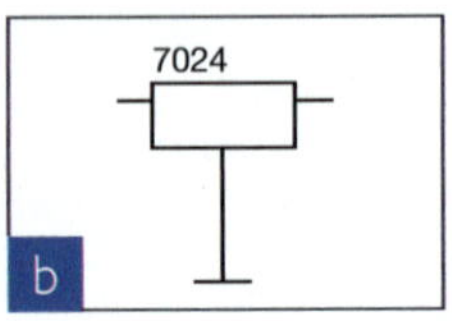

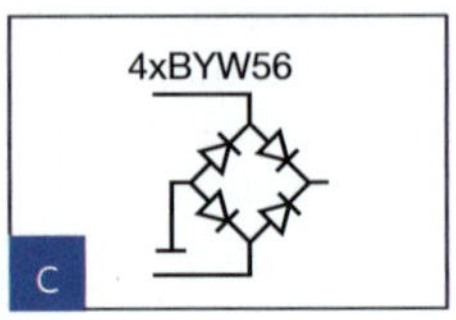

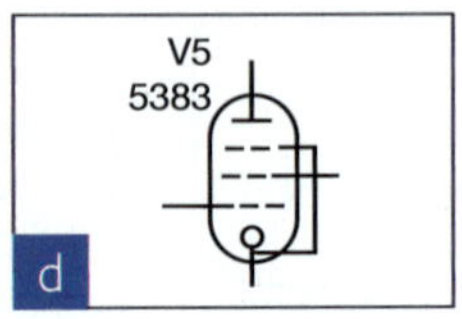

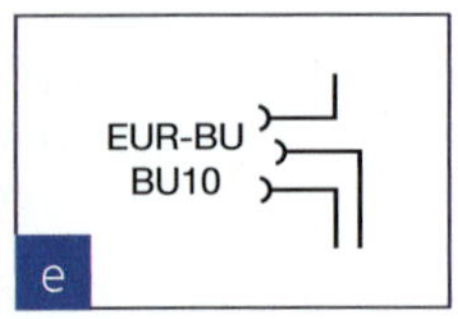

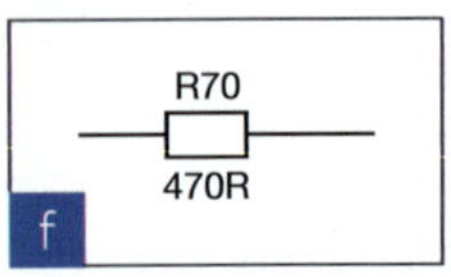

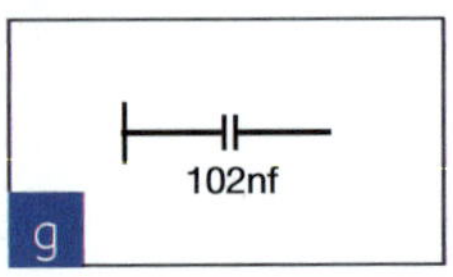

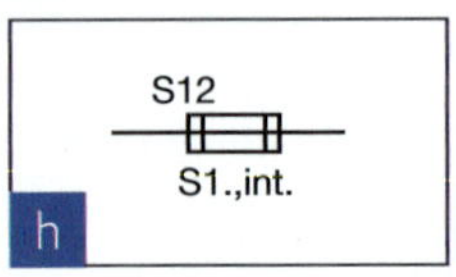

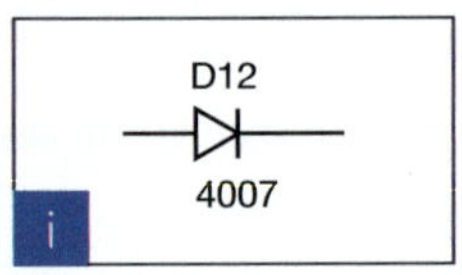

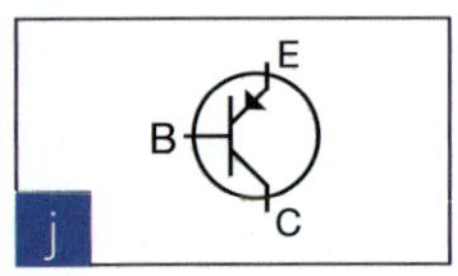

C Work with a partner. Partner A: **Look at File 15 on page 141.** Partner B: **Look at File 19 on page 144.**

Use the schematics in the Files to practise identifying electrical components.

D Work with a partner. Use the words in the lists to ask and answer questions about the components above.

amplify · energize · protect · raise or lower · rectify · reduce · smooth · stabilize · store

an electric charge · the circuit · the current · the voltage

What do you call a component that protects a circuit?

It's a(n) …

2 Tracing a fault

In today's webinar the host, Randy Martin, is helping Armin Feiertag to find out what is wrong with some electrical equipment.

24)) Listen to the dialogue and answer the questions below. Refer to the schematic while you listen.

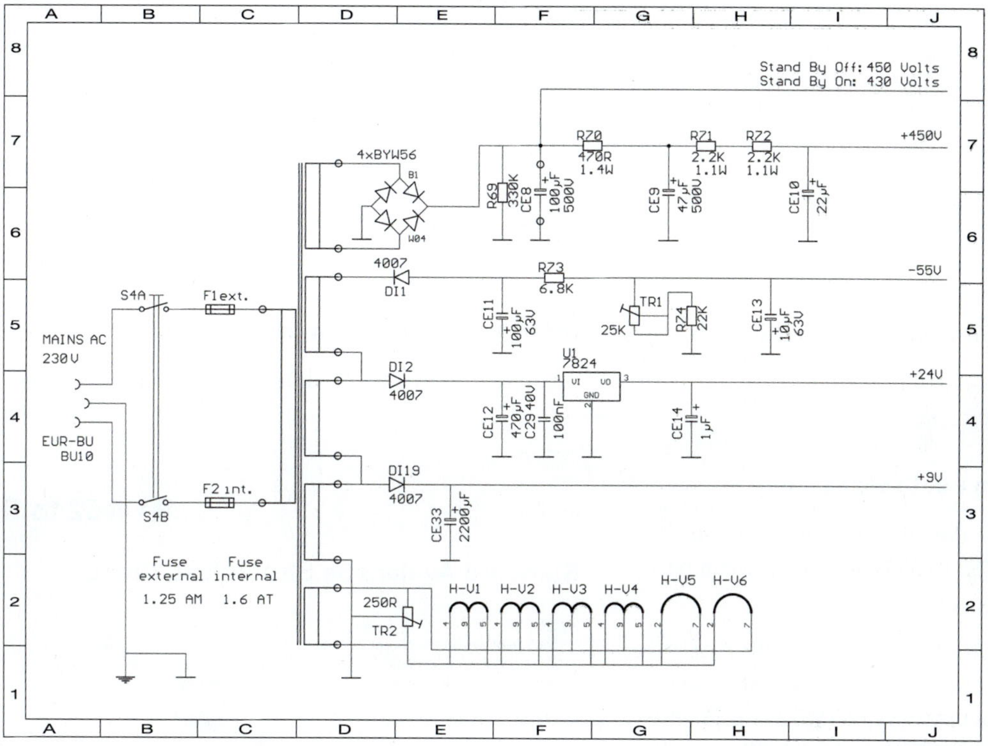

1 What sort of equipment is Armin working on?
2 What went wrong?
3 What tests has Armin carried out since the equipment failed?
4 What safety precautions has Armin taken?
5 Why is Randy optimistic that the equipment can be repaired?
6 What sensory checks has Armin carried out?
7 Which components do they talk about after Armin finds the schematic?
8 What does Armin do with the digital multimeter and what conclusions does he draw?

Talking about finished and unfinished time

Yesterday it suddenly **cut out**.
I **had** a problem like that last year.

Since then **I've replaced** one of the glass fuses.
Three fuses **have blown** this month.

› *Grammar: Simple past, page 159; Present perfect, page 159*

TOOLBOX

to blow – *durchbrennen*
charred wires – *verkohlte Kabel*
to connect / disconnect – *anschließen / vom Netz trennen*
control light – *Kontrolllampe*
fuse – *Sicherung*
GFCI ground fault circuit interrupter *(AE)* – *FI-Schalter*
illuminated – *beleuchtet*
mains lead – *Netzkabel*
to measure – *messen*
sensory check – *sensorische Kontrolle*
smell of burning – *Brandgeruch*
tracing a fault – *Fehlersuche*
tube *(AE)* / valve *(BE)* – *Röhre*

3 Understanding technical advice

Further tests show that the four BYW56 diodes in the bridge rectifier have to be replaced. Armin has four BYW52 diodes and wants to know if he can use them, so he posts a question online and gets this reply:

Hi Armin,
You have to be very careful with diodes because you could blow the equipment with the wrong ones if they can't handle a surge.
The diodes you need have to be able to handle a peak forward surge current of 50 amps for a maximum time of ten milliseconds. This is given as "t_p (time/peak) = 10 ms half sine wave" on a data sheet. "Half sine wave" refers to AC. They have to have an average forward current of 2 amps, and a repetitive peak reverse voltage of 1,000 volts.
Good luck!
Kimberly

With a partner study Kimberly's answer and find the English equivalents of these German terms.

1 starker Anstieg
2 Spitzendurchlassstrom
3 Sinuskurve
4 Wechselstrom
5 durchschnittlicher Durchlassstrom
6 wiederkehrende Spitzensperrspannung

4 Using a data sheet

Armin downloads a data sheet on BYW52 to BYW56 diodes to compare their characteristics.

A **With a partner study this data sheet then draw up a list of the important characteristics of BYW52 and BYW56 diodes using the advice in Kimberly's post.**

Characteristics	BYW52	BYW56
Peak …		

B **Explain the following values from the data sheet.**

1 2 A
2 600 V
3 12 A
4 10 ms
5 1000 W
6 175 °C

C **Discuss the characteristics of the two diodes with your partner and decide whether the BYW52 is suitable or not. Share your ideas with the class.**

BYW52 to BYW56
Semiconductors

Standard Avalanche Sinterglass Diode

Features
- Controlled avalanche characteristics
- Glass passivated junction
- Hermetically sealed package
- Low reverse current
- High surge current loading

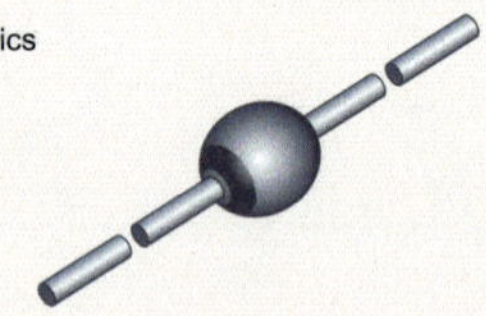

Applications
Rectification, general purpose

Mechanical Data
Case: Sintered glass case, SOD 57
Terminals: Plated axial leads, solderable per MIL-STD-750, Method 2026
Polarity: Colour band denotes cathode end
Mounting Position: Any
Weight: 370 mg. (max. 500 mg)

Absolute Maximum Ratings
T_{amb} = 25 °C, unless otherwise specified

Parameter	Test condition	Sub type	Symbol	Value	Unit
Reverse voltage = Repetitive peak reverse voltage	see electrical characteristics	BYW52	$V_R = V_{RRM}$	200	V
	see electrical characteristics	BYW53	$V_R = V_{RRM}$	400	V
	see electrical characteristics	BYW54	$V_R = V_{RRM}$	600	V
	see electrical characteristics	BYW55	$V_R = V_{RRM}$	800	V
	see electrical characteristics	BYW56	$V_R = V_{RRM}$	1000	V
Peak forward surge current	t_p = 10 ms, half sinewave		I_{FSM}	50	A
Repetitive peak forward current			I_{FRM}	12	A
Average forward current	φ = 180°		I_{FAV}	2	A
Pulse avalanche peak power	t_p = 20 µs half sine wave, T_j = 175 °C		P_R	1000	W

PART B: Relocation of production

Situation: You work for Schmidt Ltd in Cork, Ireland, a subsidiary of Schmidt AG in Dortmund. The company is relocating the production of thermal fuses from its factory in Cork to Bangkok in Thailand.
→ **You write a short memo about the preparations for the installation of machinery in the new factory.**

1 Reading about thermal cutoff fuses

You will be travelling to Thailand with the project manager, Kate O'Brien, to supervise setting up the machinery in Bangkok. Before you leave, you read the company's website to check your knowledge of the company's product.

a Thermal cutoff fuses are small devices that are integrated into the circuit boards of the many electrical appliances that are used in industry and in the home. The devices are designed to protect the appliances from overheating and catching fire.

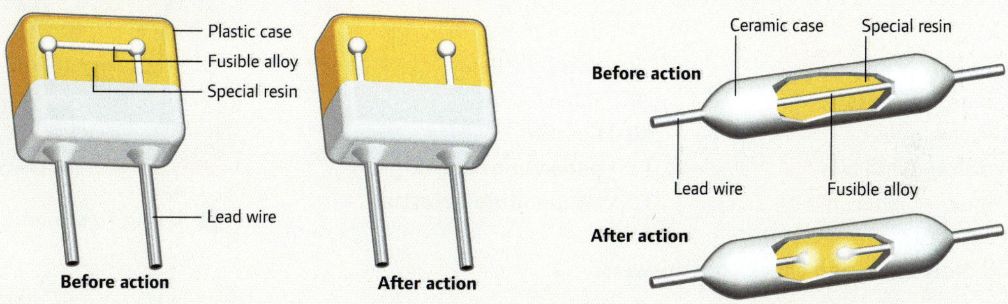

b Each device contains a thermal pellet made of an organic material or fusible alloy. In order to guarantee hermetic sealing, each device is resin-sealed. When the ambient temperature of the appliance containing the device reaches a specific temperature, the thermal pellet in the device will melt. As soon as this happens, the electrical current to the appliance is immediately interrupted to protect the appliance. <u>It should be noted that once thermal reaction has happened, the thermal cutoff device must be replaced.</u> Schmidt AG produces a broad range of thermal cutoff fuses to suit the operating temperatures and rated currents of each type of electrical appliance.

c Our thermal cutoff fuses conform to environmental standards and regulations. Due to their small size, they are extremely sensitive to abnormal temperatures. The fuses cover a wide range of operating temperatures (73°C – 240°C) and some versions are able to operate under large currents (0.5A – 15A range). The high-quality resin-seal guarantees the high reliability and accuracy of the thermal cutoff fuses.

d Our thermal cutoff technology is used in many domestic appliances and commercial applications. These include: domestic irons, hair dryers, refrigerators, electric kettles, coffee makers; air conditioners, ventilation fans, electric fans, gas boilers; transformers, adaptors; chargers, battery packs; photocopiers, laser beam printers.

A **Skim the information and match the headings (1–5) to the paragraphs (a–d). There is one more heading than you need.**

1 Advantages of Schmidt's thermal fuses
2 Applications
3 How they work
4 Installation instructions
5 Thermal cutoff fuses

B **With a partner, take turns to find the answers to the following questions.**

1 Where are thermal cutoffs used?
2 How is the cutoff fuse made waterproof and airtight?
3 How is the circuit interrupted?
4 Why must the thermal cutoff device be replaced after it has done its job?
5 What is the maximum current for the cutoff?
6 What is the maximum temperature for the cutoff?
7 Name at least three household devices that use Schmidt's thermal cutoff fuses.
8 Name at least three industrial or commercial uses for thermal cutoff fuses.

2 Skyping with a colleague abroad

A few days before your flight, Kate has a skype conference with Surat Meesang, the factory manager in Bangkok. They discuss the installation of the resin-sealing unit, which is vital for the production of the thermal fuses.

A **Work with a partner. Before you listen to the conversation, decide together which of the words below you might hear.**

1 crate
2 forklift truck
3 nuts and bolts
4 screwdrivers
5 drill and drill bits
6 glue
7 data cables
8 power cables
9 cable trunks
10 flooring
11 pneumatic hose
12 temperature detection

Using first names

If a person is in a higher position than you, you should always use their surname until they specifically ask you to use their first name. If you and a colleague are at the same level, you may suggest using first names if you wish.
Please call me Kate.
Thank you. My first name is Surat.

B 25 **Now listen and check your answers.**

C 25 **Listen to the conversation again and answer these questions.**

1 When will the resin-sealing unit arrive at the factory?
2 Why should it be left in its crate until you and Kate arrive?
3 How heavy is the machine?
4 What is the DFG 435 and why can it not be used for the installation?
5 What does Kate suggest instead?
6 How is the machine going to be fixed to the floor?
7 What equipment will the electricians use to fix the machine?
8 What is going to be laid under the flooring?

TOOLBOX

appliance – *Gerät*
cable trunk – *Kabelkanal*
circuit board – *Leiterplatte, Platine*
cutoff – *Abschaltung*
domestic – *Haushalts-*
electric circuit – *Stromkreis*
flooring – *Fußboden*
forklift truck – *Gabelstapler*
fusible alloy – *Schmelzlegierung*
hermetic sealing – *hermetische Abdichtung*
resin-seal – *Gießharzverguss*
thermal fuse – *Thermosicherung*

3 Role-play: Discussing what is going to happen

Before your write the memo for the files, you check some of the details with Kate O'Brien.

Work with a partner. Partner A: You are the apprentice at Schmidt Ltd in Cork. Partner B: You are Kate O'Brien. Discuss in English who is going to do what in the process of setting up the resin-sealer.

You	Kate O'Brien
Fragen Sie, wann die Versiegelungsanlage bei der Fabrik ankommen wird.	Antworten Sie: am 29. November.
Fragen Sie, wer die Kiste nun auspacken wird.	Antworten Sie, dass die Kiste bis zur Ankunft in Thailand nicht ausgepackt werden soll.
Fragen Sie, ob der richtige Gabelstapler bereitsteht.	Antworten Sie, dass Herr Meesang einen TFG 540 von einer Fabrik in der Nähe besorgen wird.
Fragen Sie nach den Bolzen und der Bohrmaschine.	Antworten Sie, dass die Bohrmaschine und die 18 mm-Bolzen schon am Arbeitsplatz sind.
Fragen Sie nach dem Kleber, mit dem die Bolzen in den Boden geklebt werden.	Antworten Sie, dass es den Kleber im Materiallager der Fabrik gibt.
Fragen Sie, ob Sie einen Kabelkanal für das Anschlusskabel und die Datenleitung legen müssen.	Antworten Sie, dass das Kabel unter dem Boden verlegt werden kann.
Fragen Sie, wann sie die Anlage in Betrieb nehmen möchte.	Antworten Sie: am 3. Dezember.

› *Grammar: Future with* will *and* going to, *page 159*

4 Writing a memo for the files

Now you write a short memo on the most important details of the skype call for the project files.

Look back at your answers to exercises 2B and 3 and use them to write the memo.

Schmidt Ltd, Cork, Ireland

Project no. 1603: Relocation of production of thermal cutoff fuses to Bangkok

Report update: 21/11 – Installation of resin-sealing unit

Project manager, Kate O'Brien, planning installation with Surat Meesang, factory manager, Bangkok

The following points were covered:

1 The resin-sealer has arrived at …

2 It will be delivered to the … on …

…

COMMUNICATION: Reports

Situation: You work in the maintenance department of a British factory.
→ **You prepare a report for your supervisor on a health and safety incident.**

1 Reading a notice

You are the first to arrive at the workshop this morning. You find the following notice on the door.

IMPORTANT NOTICE: NO ENTRY!

Maintenance Workshop 2.01

Fire damage: workshop closed.
Please go to the Quality Control Workshop (1.01) in the building opposite and report to Irene McCartney, QC Manager

Andy Murray, Workshop Manager
9 p.m. Tuesday, 13/07/20..

A Read the notice and answer the following questions.

1 Why is the workshop closed?
2 Which workshop do workers have to go to instead?
3 Where is the other workshop?
4 Who should workers report to when they get there?
5 Who wrote the notice?
6 When was the notice written?

B Write a short text message to your colleagues telling them not to come to the workshop. Explain the situation in a few words and tell them where to go instead.

2 Reading statements about the fire

Andy Murray gives you these statements to read so that you can write a short report about the fire.

A Who said what? Match the statements (1–4) to the names of the people who made them (a–d).

a Tommy Atkins, Construction Mechanic
b Andy Murray, Workshop Manager
c Jackie Stewart, Security/First-aider
d Angela Thomson, Welder

1 *It was just before 8 o'clock. I was working in the office when I heard shouting in the workshop next door. I ran in there and saw Tommy Atkins trying to put out a fire on the floor. Angela Thomson was using the fire extinguisher but the fire was spreading. I set off the alarm and went with Tommy and Angela to the assembly point outside the building.*

2 *I was welding. Suddenly, there was a crash and Tommy shouted. I smelled acetone so I turned off my welding equipment. It was too late. There was a flash and then the floor started to burn. Tommy started stomping on the flames but that didn't work. I got the fire extinguisher off the wall but the flames were everywhere. Acetone keeps on lighting even after you stomp on it. Andy got Tommy and me out of the workshop and took us to the assembly point. We were taken to hospital.*

TOOLBOX

ambulance – *Rettungswagen*
assembly point – *Sammelplatz*
emergency services – *Einsatzkräfte, Rettungsdienste*
fire extinguisher – *Feuerlöscher*
first aid – *Erste Hilfe*
first-aider – *Sanitäter/in*
incident – *Vorfall, Ereignis*
to spread – *sich ausbreiten*

3 *The fire alarm went off at 19.58. I could see the flames in the Maintenance Workshop from my window. I called the fire brigade. At the Assembly Point, I administered first aid to two colleagues and called an ambulance. (time: 20.05). Tommy Atkins had burns on his hands and legs and Angela Thomson was in shock. The emergency services arrived at 20.15. Mr Atkins and Ms Thomson were taken to hospital. The fire was extinguished by 20.40.*

4 *I finished repairing a tank. When I reached over to unplug the soldering iron, I knocked over a bottle. I didn't know it was there. As soon as the bottle broke, I realized it was acetone. Someone else must have left it on the bench after a job. The acetone spilled on the floor. It trickled across to where Angela was welding and caught fire. I stomped on the flames and tried to put them out but it was no use. My hands and legs were burned so Mr Stewart put something on the burns and called the ambulance.*

B **Work with a partner. Put the events above in chronological order to make a record of the incident.**

Tuesday 13.07.20..
Just before 8 o'clock: *Angela Thomson was welding in the workshop; Tommy Atkins was repairing a tank. Tommy Atkins knocked over ...*
19.58: ...
...
20.40: ...

3 Writing an incident report

It is time to write the incident report for the Administration department.

Work with a partner. Write a formal report about the fire, using the record you produced in exercise 2B and the following structure.

Report on fire incident

Introduction: Say where and when the incident happened. Give the names and job titles of the people involved.

Background: Describe the situation just before the incident happened; give the starting time.

The fire incident: Describe the events that took place in the workshop.

Dealing with the emergency: Describe what happened at the Assembly Point, when the emergency services arrived and how the fire was dealt with.

Describing an incident

We **were working** in the workshop. Angela **was welding**. I **finished** repairing the tank. I **tried** to put the flames out, but they **were spreading** quickly.

› *Grammar: Simple past, page 159; Past progressive, page 159*

DAS KANN ICH (Unit 7)

- Eine Umfrage über Kommunikationsmittel im Betrieb durchführen. (Foundation)
- Englische Datenblätter verstehen und verwenden. (Part A)
- Ein Memo über das Aufstellen einer Maschine in einer Fabrik schreiben. (Part B)
- Einen kurzen Bericht über einen Vorfall in einer Fabrik schreiben. (Communication)

4 Explaining the system

You and Sheila are in a meeting with Derek Ashborne. You discuss the construction drawing for the mat-washing system for Jinsibei.

A Match the words in the list to the numbers (1–7) on the construction drawing.

conveyor · filter · hot air blower · pallet · palletizer · rollers · water jets

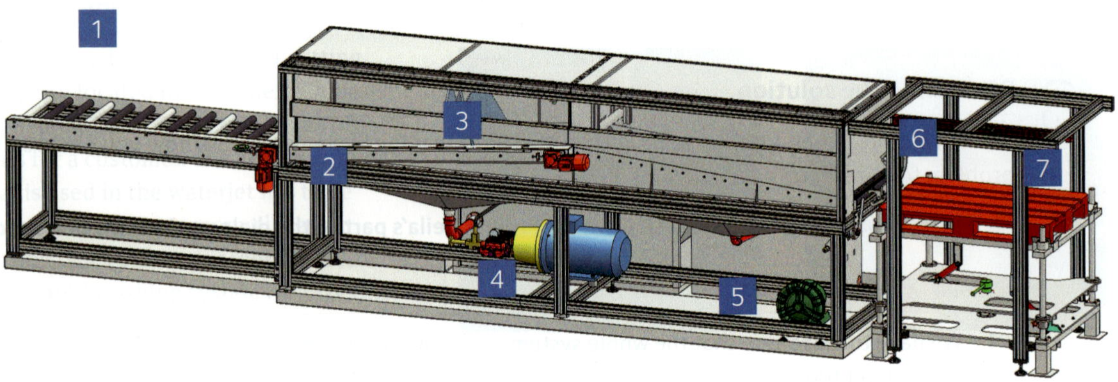

B Put the sentences in the correct order to describe how the mat-washing system works.

a A forklift truck takes away the pallets.
b A filter separates the sand from the water.
c Water jets wash the mats clean of sand.
d Hot-air blowers dry the mats.
e The conveyor transports the mats upwards.
f The operator puts the mats on the rollers.
g The conveyor rolls the mats onto the palletizer.

C Now explain to your partner how the system works.

Describing processes

Active: A forklift truck takes away the pallets.
Passive: The pallets **are taken** away **by** a forklift truck.

› *Grammar: Passive forms, page 160*

5 Talking about different applications

Derek Ashborne is pleased with the system that you have designed. He asks you to think of some other applications for the system.

Work in small groups. Think of some other items that could be cleaned using a similar system. Use the photos below or your own ideas.

Make any changes to the system that you think are necessary and present it to the class.

PART B: The presentation of the washing system

Situation: You work for Hilmer Cleaning Systems in the UK, and you have to plan an automated washing system for a customer in China. The system has now been constructed, and you fly to Shenzen to install and commission it and to train the operators.
→ **You prepare a presentation to explain the system to the customers.**

1 Describing the mat-feeding system

The first part of your presentation will deal with the mat-feeding system.

A **Look at the diagram and read the description. Then answer the questions below.**

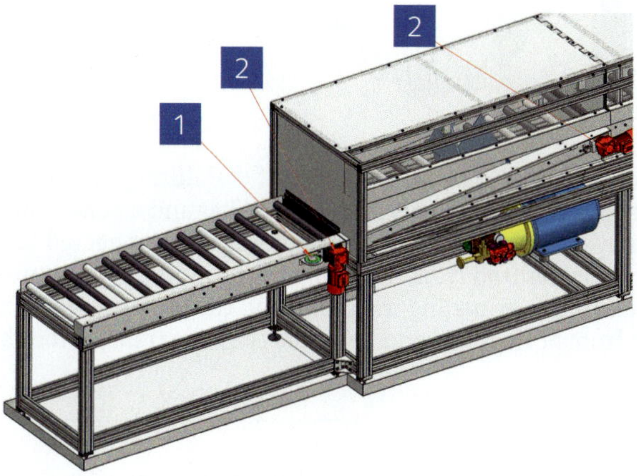

1: the mat-feeding system

After a worker has placed the mats onto the feeding system, he has to press the push-button (1). The motors of the feeding system and the interior transport system (2) start and the mat moves in the direction of the washing system. When the first ultrasonic sensor is activated by the mat, the pump starts and the washing system starts to wash the mats. Excess water drips into the floor tray.

1 How does the system start?
2 How does the mat move?
3 How does the pump start?
4 What's the purpose of the floor tray?

B **Now complete these prompts to create the first slide for your presentation. You can label the diagram if you wish.**

1: the mat-feeding system

- mats placed ___
- push-button ___
- motors of feeding system ___
- mats move ___
- ultrasonic sensor ___
- pump and ___
- excess water ___

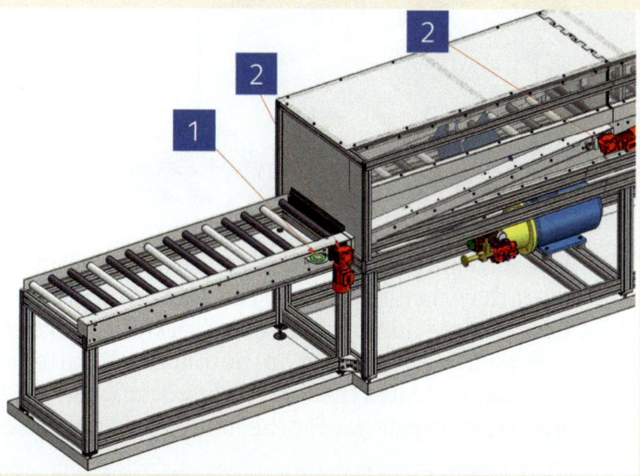

2 Explaining the washing system

You now prepare the next two slides for the presentation.

A Complete the explanation of the washing system with the words from the list.

140 · alternating · chemicals · coupling · hoses · minute · nozzles · plunger · pressure · valve

2: the washing system and high-pressure nozzles

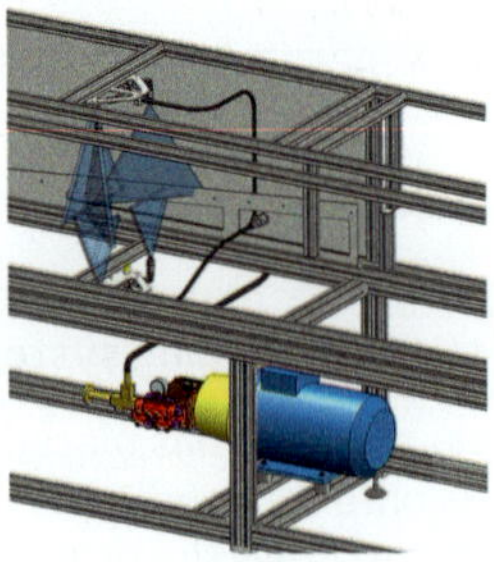

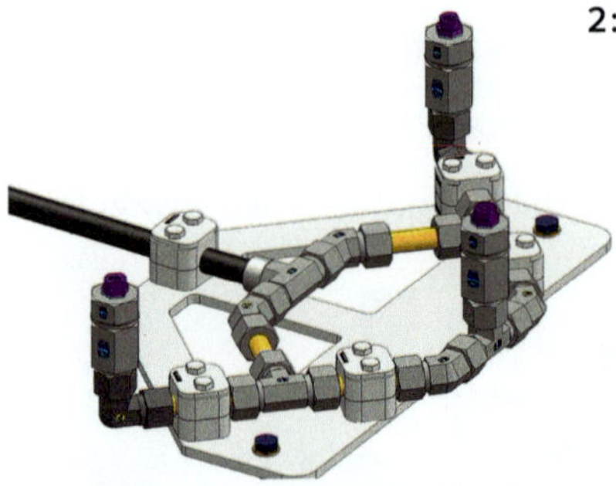

Water under high ___[1] is used to clean the mats, to avoid the usage of ___[2] during the washing process. The pressure is created by a ___[3] pump with a nominal pressure of ___[4] bar and a pump capacity of 48 litres per ___[5]. The pump is driven by a 15 kW ___[6] current motor which is connected to the pump by a Rotex-___[7] to avoid knocks being transmitted from the pump to the motor. A pressure-limiting ___[8] is integrated in the water hose to avoid overloading the pump and the pressure ___[9]. The mats are cleaned by three high-pressure ___[10] from both above and below as they are transported through the washing system.

B Replace the German words in the text below with the correct English words from the list.

activates · blower · drying area · feed · light barrier · nozzles · switches off · time lag

3: the washing process

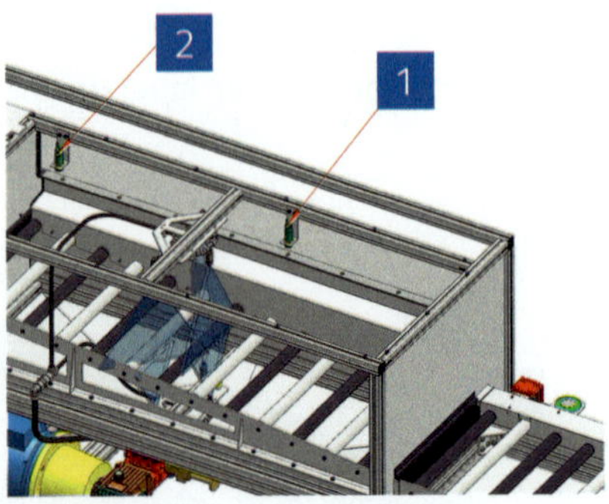

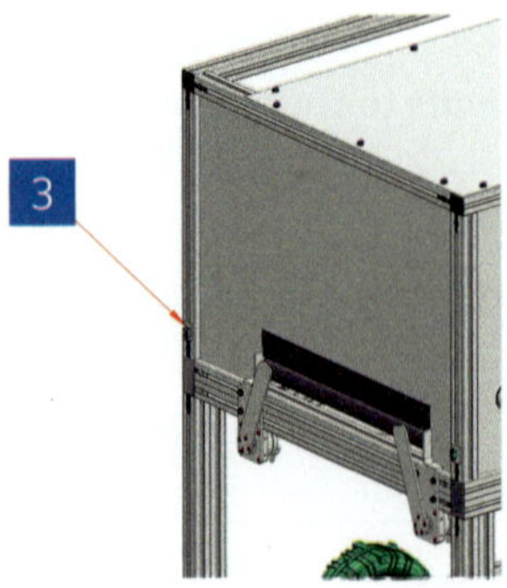

The incoming mat ___[1] (*betätigt*) the first ultrasonic sensor (1), the pump starts and the ___[2] (*Düsen*) start the washing process. The second ultrasonic sensor (2) starts the ___[3] (*Gebläse*). When the mat is at least two-thirds in the ___[4] (*Trocknungsbereich*), the ultrasonic sensor (1) is no longer activated. The pump ___[5] (*schaltet ab*) automatically after a short ___[6] (*Zeitverzögerung*) to avoid wasting water. The mat activates the ___[7] (*Lichtschranke*) (3) but because the second ultrasonic sensor is no longer activated, the motor for the mat ___[8] (*Einzug*) switches off while the blower remains on.

C Use words from the explanations to write prompts for the slides. Label the diagrams if you wish.

3 Explaining the drying and stacking systems

The fourth and fifth slides of your presentation will describe the drying system and the stacking system.

Use the diagrams and descriptions to write prompts and label the diagrams for the remaining slides of the presentation.

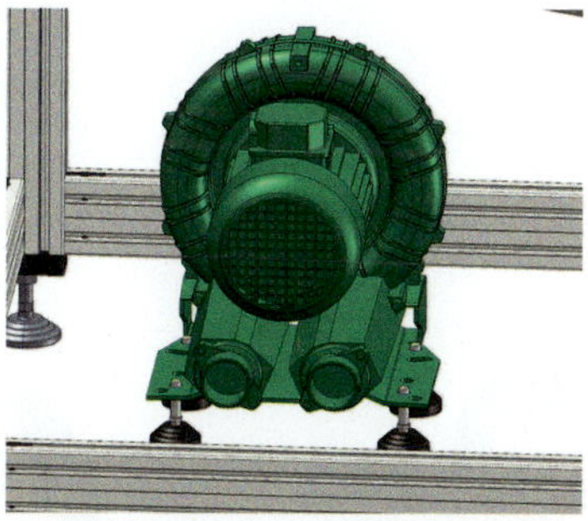

4: the drying system

The blower, which has an air-flow rate of approximately 3,900 litres per minute, stands on vibration-cushioned feet. The air is sucked in, compressed and then distributed through PVC-hoses into the nozzles. The air is blown on both sides of the mats to provide the optimum drying process.

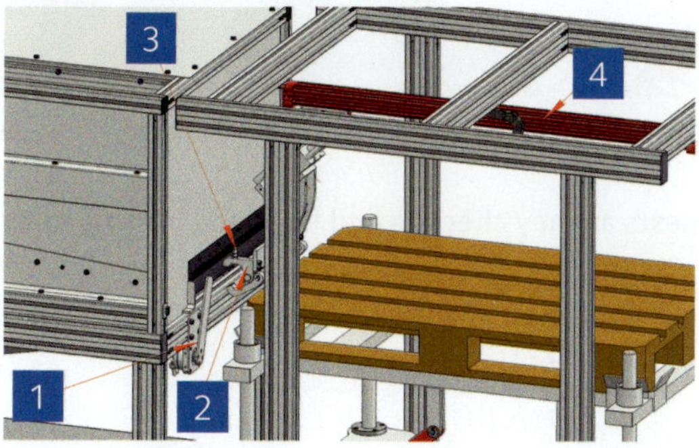

5: the stacking system

The endstops (1) are folded to the sides and the force of gravity pulls the mat into the gripper (2) of the palletizer. Both sensors (3) are activated, the gripper grabs the mat and pulls it slowly over the pallet. The end switch (4) of the linear unit is activated and the blower is switched off. The mat is placed on the pallet. The weight of the mats forces the pallet downwards.

4 Presenting the mat-washing system to Jinsibei

Now it is time to present the system to the customer.

A **Work in groups of five. Each person in the group is responsible for creating one of the slides and explaining what it shows to the audience.**

Slides:	Remember:
• mat-feeding system • washing system • washing process • drying system • stacking system	• give your presentation a suitable introduction and conclusion • don't fill the slide with text, just use short key words or prompts • don't read the text, use your own words • keep eye contact with the audience • be prepared to answer questions from the audience

B **Practise your presentation in your groups, then give your presentation to the class. (You can give each other feedback using the feedback sheet on page 43.)**

› *Useful phrases: Giving a presentation, page 150*

TOOLBOX

air-flow rate – *Luftdurchsatz*
beat – *Schlag*
to compress – *verdichten*
endstops – *Endanschläge*
feed – *Einzug*
gripper – *Greifer*
vibration-cushioned – *schwingungsgedämpft*

COMMUNICATION: Business trips

Situation: Your company has won an award as one of the four best European start-ups of the year. You are going to the prize-giving ceremony in Amsterdam, where you will stay at the International Hotel.
→ You do internet research to find information about people from other cultures.

1 Checking in and checking out at a hotel

When you arrive at the hotel, there are four guests in front of you at reception. You listen to the receptionist talking to them.

1 Giovanni Rossi

2 Mary McGregor

3 Yusuf Zuabi

4 Akira Banerjee

A 27 **Copy the table. Listen to the first three guests as they check in and fill in the missing information.**

	What questions do the guests ask?	What information does the receptionist give?
Giovanni Rossi	[1]	[2]
Mary McGregor	[3]	[4]
Yusuf Zuabi	[5]	[6]

B **Akira Banerjee is checking out. Read what she says to the receptionist. What do you think the receptionist said to the guest?**

1 Good morning. I'm very well, thank you.
2 I would like to check out.
3 I was in room 207.
4 It's been great. I love Amsterdam.
5 Yes, thank you. Everything was fine. I'll definitely be back.
6 Thank you. I'm flying KLM. They're very good.

C 28 **Now listen and check your answers.**

2 Role-play: At reception

Work with a partner and role-play a conversation at a hotel reception desk.

Partner A: You are the hotel receptionist. Greet the guest, welcome him/her to the hotel and take down his/her details. You begin.
Partner B: You are a guest who has just arrived. Use your own personal details to check in and answer the receptionist's questions.

After that, do a second role-play and practise checking out.

› *Useful phrases: Checking in and out at a hotel, page 153*

3 Chatting at breakfast

Next morning, the breakfast buffet is very full. You find a free seat at a table with another guest.

A **Work with a partner. Put the dialogues in order to produce a conversation.**

1 **A** Pleased to meet you, too. Where are you from?
B I'm from … . What about you?
A I'm from …

2 **A** I was here on holiday a few years ago.
B Where are the best places to go?
A If you have time, you should really go to …

3 **A** I'd better get ready to go now. Have a good day.
B Thanks. See you later.

4 **A** Good morning. Is this seat taken?
B No, it's not. You can sit here. Are you here for the prize-giving ceremony?

5 **A** Have you been to Amsterdam before?
B No, I haven't. What about you?

6 **A** Yes, I am. My name's …
B Pleased to meet you. I'm …

B **Find a new partner. Add your own details then close your books and practise the dialogue.**
› *Unit 1, Communication, page 12*

4 Cultural awareness

On the plane home, you read the following quiz about different cultures.

A **Work with a partner. Complete each sentence with the best ending. When you have finished, ask your teacher for the answers and discuss which answers surprise you.**

1 **Many Japanese people …**
- a always bow when they meet people for the first time.
- b bow when they meet each other, but they will shake hands with Westerners.
- c never shake hands with anyone.

2 **A lot of Irish people respect people who are …**
- a aggressive and dominant.
- b formal and quiet.
- c rich and powerful.

3 **In Italy, you should never ask people about their …**
- a families.
- b hobbies.
- c job or where they live.

4 **In the Netherlands, some people will think you are rude if you …**
- a eat cheese with a knife and fork.
- b leave a small amount of food on your plate when you've finished eating.
- c leave the table during a meal.

5 **Soon after you've been introduced, many British people will …**
- a invite you to visit them at home.
- b start to use first names.
- c want to know everything about you.

6 **Many people from the Middle East may ask to take a break during meetings so that they can …**
- a go for a walk.
- b phone home.
- c pray.

B **Work in a group of four. Find information about people from other cultures on the internet. Use the information to make up a quiz like the one above. Pin your quiz on the wall and do a gallery walk with your partners. How highly does your team score on the other groups' quizzes?**

DAS KANN ICH (Unit 8)

- Eine Liste von Normen erstellen, die meine Firma vertritt. (Foundation)
- Eine Beschreibung einer automatischen Waschanlage auf Englisch anfertigen. (Part A)
- Eine Präsentation der automatischen Waschanlage auf Englisch erstellen. (Part B)
- Quizfragen über kulturelle Unterschiede auf Englisch zusammenstellen. (Communication)

1 Leseverstehen

In Ihrem Betrieb gibt es häufig Probleme durch Stromausfall. Sie sollen für Ihren Ausbildungsleiter eine Präsentation über ausfallsichere Stromversorgung vorbereiten und stoßen auf folgenden Artikel im Internet.

Fault-tolerant power supplies

Why have redundant power supplies?

Imagine a 24VDC 10A power supply driving motors and sensors on a conveyor based production line. For two or three years everything works fine, then one Friday (always at the end of the month), the power supply fails causing the conveyor to stop. Even if a spare part is in stock, it could still result in 30 minutes of expensive lost production.

If two identical power supplies had been installed in a fault-tolerant, redundant mode, the remaining (good) unit would have continued to power the production line. The failed power supply could then be replaced at a more convenient time during routine maintenance.

The effectiveness of having a fault-tolerant power strategy was demonstrated after Hurricane Katrina hit the Gulf Coast in 2005. A television station interviewed the heads of two telecom carriers to find out when their telephone services would be operational again. The interview was very short – 'we never lost service' they replied.

Large industrial complexes have expensive and complex backup systems consisting of battery banks, generators and uninterruptible power supplies.

Frequently used terminology

Hot-swap

Some equipment is operated 24 hours a day, 7 days a week, allowing no time to bring the system down for maintenance. In this case, the failed power supply must be 'swapped' out and a new one inserted without disruption to equipment operation.

DLP-PU block diagram

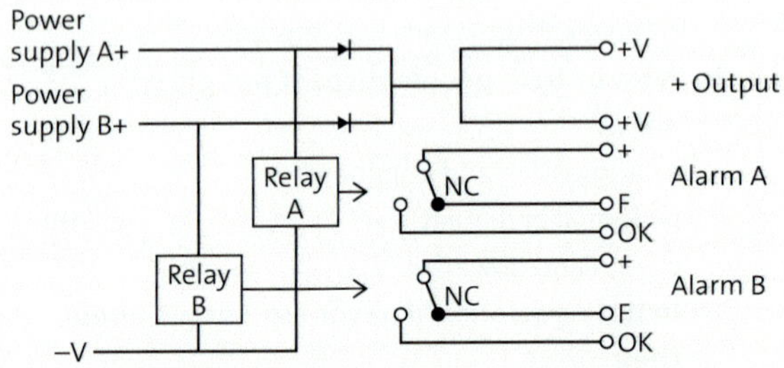

ORing diodes

In the rare event of a power supply failing with a shorted output, low-voltage-drop ORing diodes block that short from bringing down the system power. The diagram shows how a short circuit is flagged up by alarm relays to prevent a power failure from going unnoticed and bringing the whole system down.

Beantworten Sie die Fragen zum Text auf Deutsch.

1 Welche Produktionsart wird im ersten Beispiel beschrieben?
2 Warum ist in dem Beispiel eine schnelle Reparatur des Netzteils die schlechtere Lösung?
3 Welche Lösung wird stattdessen angeboten?
4 Welches positive Beispiel wird genannt?
5 Welche Lösungen für die ausfallsichere Stromversorgung findet man in großen Industrieanlagen?
6 Welcher Vorgang wird unter der Überschrift ‚Hot-swap' beschrieben?
7 Warum führt man einen ‚Hot-swap' durch?
8 Welche Funktion hat das ORing-Modul?
9 Wozu dienen die Alarmrelais?

2 Hörverstehen

Sie machen ein Praktikum in Irland bei der Firma Shanahan Electrical Services in Limerick und verbringen einen Tag mit Auszubildenden am Limerick Institute of Technology. Dort nehmen Sie am theoretischen Unterricht teil und besuchen eine Stunde über einfache Stromkreise. Heute stellt eine Auszubildende einen einfachen Berührungsschalter vor.

29 **Verfolgen Sie den Dialog zwischen dem Lehrer und der Auszubildenden und ergänzen Sie das Diagramm, indem Sie die Komponenten und ihre jeweiligen Bezeichnungen und/oder Werte eintragen. Sie hören den Dialog zweimal.**

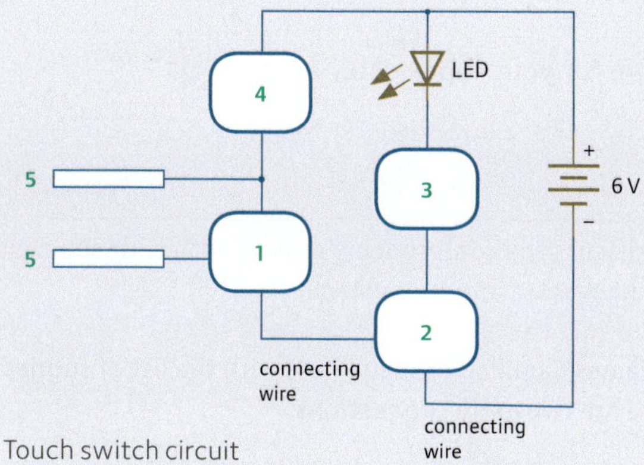

Touch switch circuit

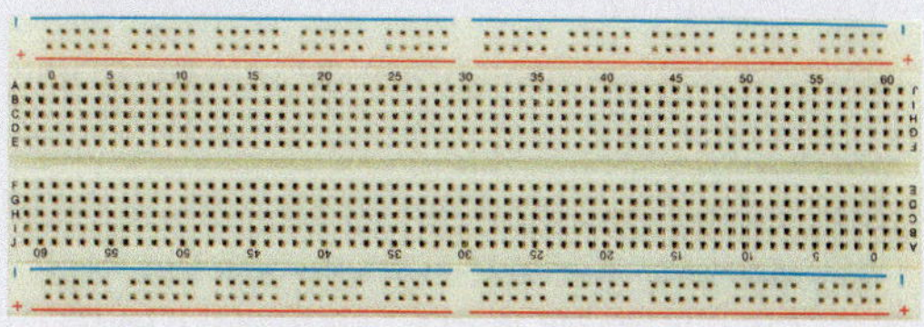

breadboard = *Steckplatine*

3 Produktion

Im Rahmen des theoretischen Unterrichts am Limerick Institute of Technology in Irland sollen Sie einen Bericht über einen Stromkreis schreiben. Nutzen Sie die Anweisungen und den Vordruck, um die Bestandteile und Funktionsweise des Berührungsschalterstromkreises zu beschreiben.

Anweisungen:

- Erstellen Sie eine Liste der benötigten Bauteile und Materialen.
- Beschreiben Sie, wie die Bauteile auf der Steckplatine miteinander verbunden sind.
- Erläutern Sie, wie der Stromkreis funktioniert.
- Nennen Sie ein weiteres Beispiel für die Anwendung des Stromkreises.

Name:	
Course:	*Electrical engineering*
Assignment:	*Simple electrical circuits*
Circuit:	*Touch switch*
Components and materials:	
Report:	

9 Enquiries and offers

FOUNDATION: A video conferencing system

Situation: You work for the German subsidiary of a Maltese firm that is interested in installing a video conferencing system.
→ **You write a report on a suitable system for your supervisor.**

1 Listening to a phone call

The owner of the firm in Malta would like to discuss the conferencing system with your supervisor, Claudia Weber. He has sent an email describing what he wants from the system.

A **Work with a partner. Match the items in James Camilleri's email (1–4) with the list of suggestions Claudia Weber would like to make (a–f). There are two extra suggestions.**

From: james.camilleri@maltech.com
To: claudia.weber@maltech.com
Subject: **video conferencing system**

Hallo Claudia

Just a quick note before our phone call.

Here's my list of what I would like from the video conferencing system. We should be able to

1 store data that everyone can access wherever they are
2 re-play the sessions later
3 access help when we need to
4 try out the system for nothing so that we can see if it's right for us.

Looking forward to our call.
James

a) calendar integration
b) cloud storage
c) free trial
d) multi-language support
e) user manual
f) video recordings

B 30 **Listen to the telephone conversation and check your answers to exercise 1A. Does James Camilleri agree or disagree to the extra items Claudia Weber suggests?**

Comparing items

This is **the cheapest** system.
This is **the most/least expensive** system.
good > **best** bad > **worst** little > **least**

› *Grammar: Comparatives and superlatives, page 162*

2 Comparing video conferencing systems

You find an overview of video conferencing systems online.

A **Study the chart below and choose the system you think is best.**

B **Work with a partner. Compare your ideas and agree together on the system which is best for the company. Make notes on the advantages of the system you have chosen. Make notes on the other systems so that you can argue against them.**

C **Work with another pair. Discuss all the options and decide on the best system for the company.**

www.TechMatters.com/review-of-video-conferencing-systems

	JOIN US	BUSINESS SCOPE	Let's Meet	TALK TO ME
	€15	€18.99	€12.99	€30
Free Trial	10 Days	14 Days	15 Days	30 Days
Operator-Assisted Meetings	✓	✗	✓	✗
Multi-Language Support	✓	✓	✗	✓
Calendar Integration	✗	✓	✗	✓
Phone Support	✓	✓	✗	✓
Cloud Storage	✓	✓	✓	✓
Audio Recordings	✓	✓	✓	✓
Video Recordings	✗	✓	✓	
Additional Support	Email, Forums, Chat	Email, Online Learning Centre, Webinars	Email, User Guide, FAQ	Online Help, Webinars

3 Writing a report

Now you write the report on the system you have chosen for Claudia Weber and James Camilleri.

Work with a partner. Write your report on the video conferencing system using the following structure.

Introduction	– State the purpose of the report. – Give a short description of your research.	*This report will explain how we ...* *We searched the internet and found ...*
Main part	– Give the names of the systems. (The system you are going to suggest should come last on the list.) – Say which system you have chosen and explain why.	*We have chosen the ... (name of the system) because ...* *The system features ...* *It does not feature ...*
Conclusion	– Sum up and make recommendations.	*For these reasons, we believe that ...* *In conclusion, we suggest ...*

› *Unit 7, Communication, page 76*

PART A: An enquiry for linear drives

Situation: You work in the Quality Assurance department of Findlay Engineering in Glasgow, a company that supplies components for the automotive industry.
→ **You write an enquiry to a manufacturer of linear drives.**

1 Reading about precision measuring equipment

Your department needs a new, custom-made precision measuring system to accurately measure the HGV axles that Findlay Engineering produces. While you are doing reseach online, you find the following website. Some words are missing.

Read the website and complete the text with the words from the list.

accurate · contours · deviation · integrated · probe · repetitive · requirements · results · robust · stationary

Kuiso Measuring Instruments

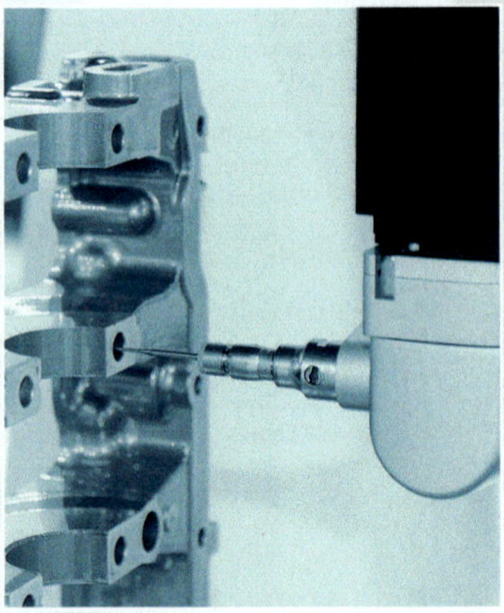

Kuiso measuring systems can be used for simple or complex measuring tasks, for example measuring either the surface roughness of a production workpiece or the ___ 1 of a workpiece such as angles, radii, distances and coordinates. We provide mobile versions that work in separate measurement runs and ___ 2 models that measure in a single step using a high-precision ___ 3.
Kuiso measuring systems are extremely precise and ___ 4. They can detect even the smallest ___ 5 from the standard, ensuring that your serially-produced components are of ___ 6 high quality.

Flexible measuring systems

Kuiso measuring instruments are based on a versatile modular design, so they can easily be added to or ___ 7 into existing measuring systems. You can configure your measuring station according to your own ___ 8.

The measurement ___ 9 can be compared on computer with the actual CAD profile. In this way, you can be sure that your production workpieces meet your specifications and are of the highest quality. Since the contour measurement systems are both compact and ___ 10, they can be used both in production and in the measuring room.

TOOLBOX

contour – *Umriss*
custom-made – *speziell angefertigt*
deviation – *Abweichung*
HGV (heavy goods vehicle) – *Lkw*
probe – *Sonde*
repetitive – *(sich) wiederholend*
stationary – *ortsfest*
versatile – *vielseitig verwendbar*

2 Reading about linear drives

To measure the lorry axles accurately, you will need to mount the measuring device on a linear drive made up of a guiding rail and slides.

A Read the following website and find out what these expressions are in English. They are in the same order as in the text.

1 Kugeln
2 Präzisionsstahlschiene
3 Schlitten
4 Reibung
5 Steifigkeit
6 Führung
7 gehärtet
8 geschliffen
9 Abstreifer
10 Verschleiß

RACE linear drives

RACE linear drives achieve an extremely precise linear motion with the help of ball bearings between the precision steel rail and the slide. The coefficient of friction in our slides is only one-fiftieth of conventional slides. The slides can accommodate vertical and horizontal direction loads because of the extreme rigidity of the guidance of the slide on the rail.

RACE linear drives are extremely efficient and accurate and can be used in machining centres, lathes, grinding machines, heavy cutting machines and measurement systems. Industrial applications include industrial automation systems, laser engraving systems, packaging machines and even lifting equipment.

Special features
- precision steel rails and slides, in sizes 20, 25, 30 and 35
- slides with four-row hardened and grounded roller bearings with wiper
- smooth running characteristics and low wear
- high accuracy and parallelism of the rails and slides
- standard length up to 4000 mm, special length on request

All our mechanical components are made of an aluminium-steel compound and are produced exclusively in our factory in Böblingen, Germany. The perfect gearing of all components ensures high flexibility, low costs and excellent work results.

Whether it is precision steel rails, drive units or slides, our components require only minor planning and minimal installation time.

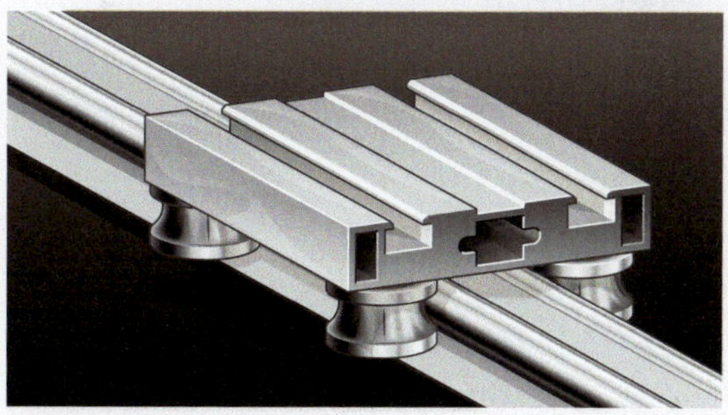

B Read the text again and answer the following questions.

1 Why is the friction of the linear drives so low?
2 Why can the slides accommodate vertical and horizontal loads?
3 Where are the components for the linear drives produced?
4 What materials are the components made of?
5 How are the ball bearings protected from wear?
6 What is the maximum length of the steel rail in metres?

TOOLBOX

to accommodate – *aufnehmen*
gearing – *Verzahnung*
slide – *Schlitten*

3 Understanding an online catalogue

You need to build three measuring systems for lorry axles with a length of 4.5 m. You check Race's online catalogue to get a rough idea of what the rails and slides cost.

A **Work in a small group and discuss which of the following rails and slides are most suitable for a measuring system for lorry axles.**

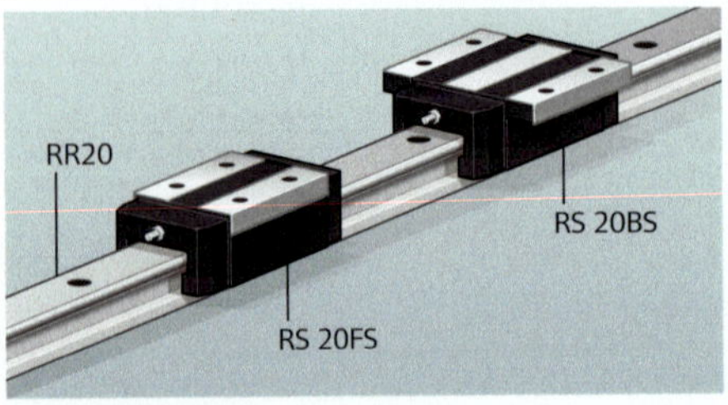

RACE linear drives: rail and slide combinations	
Characteristics	**Applications**
– two-point contact structure – large permissible load – high rigidity – high precision (under 0 μ gap) – can be pre-loaded	– machine centres – CNC lathes – heavy cutting machines – automation devices – measuring equipment

RACE LD20

Precision steel rail RR20	
length	3000 mm
width	20 mm
weight	2.5 kg
order code	RR20 3000
price:	€200.12
Slide RS 20FS	**Slide** RS 20BS
€ 33.18	€34.94

RACE LD25

Precision steel rail RR25	
length	4000 mm
width	25 mm
weight	2.5 kg
order code	RR25 4000
price:	€ 309.14
Slide RS 25FS	**Slide** RS 25BS
€40.24	€42.00

RACE LD30

Precision steel rail RR30	
length	4000 mm
width	30 mm
weight	5.1 kg
order code	RR30 4000
price:	€372.71
Slide RS 30FS	**Slide** RS 30BS
€50.82	€50.82

RACE LD35

Precision steel rail RR35	
length	5000 mm
width	35 mm
weight	5.8 kg
order code	RR35 5000
price:	€535.12
Slide RS 35FS	**Slide** RS 35BS
€81.00	€70.24

B **Report your ideas to the class. Do you agree/disagree on the most suitable system? Explain your answers.**

4 Writing an enquiry

Now it is time to write an enquiry for linear drives.

Work with a partner. Write an email to Race using the following prompts to help you.

- Use a suitable salutation and complimentary close.
- Use the addresses "sales@racegmbh.de" and "qadept@findlay.co.uk" and today's date.
- Ask for a quotation for three sets of the system you have chosen.
- As you are a regular customer, request a discount of 15%.
- Enquire about the date of delivery and the guarantee on the system.

› *Useful phrases: Writing enquiries, page 154*

PART B: A desktop CNC milling machine

Situation: You work for H&P Ltd, a company in Sheffield that produces hydraulic power units and pneumatic controllers.
→ **You search the internet for a desktop CNC milling machine and present it to your colleagues.**

1 Talking about desktop machines

You and the other apprentices learn about all the large machines that H&P Ltd uses, but you sometimes wonder if smaller machines might also be useful.

A **Think of some jobs you could do in your company with a small desktop CNC milling machine. Make a list.**

B **Work with a partner from the same training company. Compare your lists. Do you have the same ideas?**

C **Work with another pair from a different company. Are there any items on their list that surprise you? Report your ideas to the class.**

2 Producing labelling plates

The company is having problems with the labelling plates on its aggregates. Your supervisor, Sina Akrazi, is discussing the problem with the production manager, Harry Moore.

31)) **Listen to their conversation and answer the following questions.**

1 What has just happened to the labelling plates on the aggregates?
2 What problems did they have when Bensons supplied the labelling plates?
3 What would be the advantage of producing their own labelling plates?
4 Which materials could they use for the plates?
5 Where do they start to look for a suitable machine?
6 What features does the machine that they find have?

3 Reading about a desktop CNC milling machine

Sina Akrazi asks you to find out more about the Stepcraft 2/240 model. You find the text on page 96 on the company website.

A **Read the text then say whether the following statements are true or false. Correct the false statements.**

1 Stepcraft has its own CAD software.
2 You can machine S 135 steel with the Stepcraft 2/240.
3 The electronics are designed to provide enough power to the stepper motors in case of heavy tasks.
4 You can only buy the CNC machine as a DIY kit.
5 You don't have to read a lot of text to complete the installation.
6 You have to use Stepcraft tools with the CNC machine.
7 The maximum power for the spindles is 500 kW.
8 The Stepcraft is connected via a parallel interface to the computer.

TOOLBOX

aggregate – *Aggregat*
to engrave – *eingravieren*
gantry – *Portal*
labelling plate – *Typenschild*
model-maker – *Modellbauer/in*

Become an expert

Customize computer based workpieces to real models. With a suitable drawing program or a CAD software, you can create a work file which can be processed by the Desktop CNC/3D System: Accurate, efficient and reproduced as often as you want. The workpiece materials are virtually unlimited: Wood, thermoplastics and non-ferrous metals like aluminium, brass or copper, can be processed.

Excellent quality at a fair price

The STEPCRAFT aluminium profile series has been developed in order to ensure sufficient accuracy and stability of the machine. It consists of two different linear track profiles and the cover profile. All other connecting elements consist of aluminium or stainless steel and together with the profiled structure they ensure the required rigidity. The stepper motors from Nanotec® have been carefully selected and specifically adapted to exactly fit the machine. The electronics have been specially designed to match the characteristics of the motors so that sufficient power for a reliable operation of the 3D system is ensured.

DIY kit or ready built machine

The machine is available as a DIY kit or as a directly operational system. If you opt for the kit, you save money. The construction of the machine is designed so that you can simply set up the machine within a few hours without any special tools. Only screw together – done! The EasyBuild installation instruction needs (almost) no text. The step-by-step instructions are based on chronologically numbered instruction steps with graphic images of all intermediate steps. The last section always shows the finished assembly so that you can easily check your own result.

Compatibility

Due to the 43 mm collar a wide range of tools can be used. With optional adapters, you can also use Proxxon or Dremel tools as drilling-/milling spindles directly. Other drilling-/milling spindles up to a power limit of 500 watts can also be used. Other system-guided tools, such as a drag knife, engraving needle or hot cutting system can be used optionally.
With the parallel interface of the STEPCRAFT 3D System many CNC softwares, such as EMC2, Mach 3 and more, can be used.

Source: https://www.stepcraft-systems.com/en/cnc-3d-systems/stepcraft-2-420

TOOLBOX

collar – *Spannhals*
compatibility – *Kompatibilität*
drag knife – *Schleppmesser*
durability – *Langlebigkeit*
engraving needle – *Graviernadel*
hot cutting system – *Heißschneidesystem*
rigidity – *Steifigkeit*
stepper motor – *Schrittmotor*

B **Complete the gaps with suitable verbs from the list. Sometimes you have to change the form of the verbs.**

adapt · base · check · connect · control · ~~create~~ · operate · ~~process~~ · reproduce · use

Let me explain how this CNC milling machine works. First you *create*[1] a work file with a suitable CAD software on your computer and it is *processed*[2] by the machine's CNC/3D system. You can produce just one workpiece or you can ___[3] it as often as you need. The aluminium profiles ensure that the machine is rigid and ___[4] accurately and efficiently. The Nanotec® stepper motors have been specifically ___[5] to fit the machine exactly and the electronics are designed to ___[6] them precisely and reliably. The machine is available as a DIY kit or ready-assembled. The step-by-step assembly instructions are ___[7] on numbered graphic images. At the end of each section you can ___[8] your assembly against the pictures in the manual. Because of the large diameter of the toolholder, a wide range of tools can be ___[9]. You can ___[10] the CNC milling machine to your computer via a parallel interface.

› *Grammar: Passive forms, page 159*

4 Discussing the Stepcraft 2-420 system

Sina and Harry are discussing whether to buy the desktop CNC machine.

32)) **Listen to their conversation and answer the following questions.**

1. Which components are included in the package?
2. Why are the 6-point ball bearing cages necessary?
3. Why can the system be cleaned easily?
4. What is the minimum feed rate in mm/sec?
5. What's the maximum thickness of the processed materials?
6. What is necessary for the connection to the computer?
7. What is the operating voltage?
8. How long is the warranty?

5 Researching your personal CNC milling machine

Think about a project you have recently done at your company or at home, where a desktop CNC milling machine would have been helpful. If you have not done a project recently, you can use the workpiece below.

A **Think about the sizes of the workpieces and decide which machine would be appropriate.**

B **Research details, sizes and prices of desktop CNC machines on the internet. (If you do not have the internet available, you can look at File 8 on page 137.)**

C **Present the model you have chosen to the class. Describe the project you need it for and explain why you have decided on that particular model.**

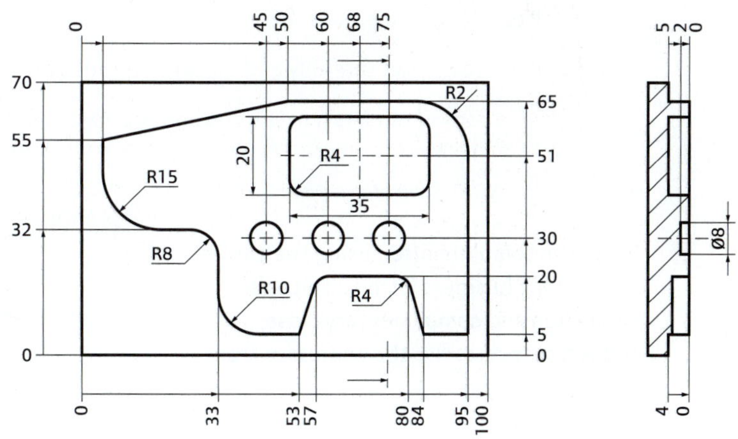

› *Useful phrases: Giving a presentation, page 150*

TOOLBOX

3-phase current – *Drehstrom*
6-point ball bearing cage – *6-fach kugelgelagerter Laufwagen*
to adjust – *einstellen*
assembly instruction – *Aufbauanleitung*
connecting cable – *Anschlusskabel*
to dismantle – *zerlegen*
feed rate – *Vorschub*
play-free – *spielfrei*

COMMUNICATION: The layout of business letters

Situation: You work at World Medical, a company that manufactures and repairs medical equipment. This week, you are helping out in the office.
→ **You write an offer to a new customer in the UK.**

1 Reading an English business letter

Your supervisor gives you a letter of enquiry from a new customer.

Study the layout and match the parts (1–11) of the letter on page 99 to the labels below (a–k).

a address	**d** copies	**g** inside address	**j** signature
b body of the letter	**e** date	**h** reference initials	**k** subject line
c complimentary close	**f** enclosure	**i** salutation	

2 Writing an English business letter

Your supervisor asks you to write an offer to Ms Lambert at the Dryden Medical Clinic.

A Complete the letter with suitable words and phrases from the list.

confirmation · deal with · delivery · discount · enclosing · enquiry · guaranteed · look forward to · offer · packed · price · this date

Thank you for your ___[1] about surgery lights. We are pleased to send you the following ___[2]:

One (1) ceiling light, WM 0076. ___[3]: €2700.00.

We can deliver within two weeks of ___[4] of your order. Terms of ___[5] are DAP.

This offer lasts for two weeks from ___[6]. If you place your order within one week, we can also offer a 2% ___[7]. All of our lights are ___[8] for 2 years.

We will ___[9] your order carefully and quickly. The light will be ___[10] in a wooden packing crate.

I am ___[11] a copy of our latest catalogue and price list and ___[12] future orders.

› *Useful phrases: Writing offers, page 154*

B Write the complete offer, using the correct layout for a business letter, a suitable salutation and complimentary close, today's date, etc. Use the addresses from the letter on page 99.

› *Useful phrases: Writing business letters, page 154*

Salutation and complimentary closes in letters

	Salutation	Complimentary close
to a firm	Dear Sir or Madam	Yours faithfully *(BE)*
		Yours very truly / Cordially yours *(AE)*
to a person	Dear Mr Brown	Yours sincerely *(BE)*
	Dear Sharon	Sincerely yours / Best personal regards *(AE)*

TOOLBOX

confirmation of an order – *Auftragsbestätigung*
terms of delivery and payment – *Liefer- und Zahlungsbedingungen*
trade magazine – *Fachzeitschrift*
trial order – *Probebestellung*

1 Dryden Medical Clinic
17 Dryden Street
London SE9 2BS
+44 (0)20 129546783
info@drydenclinic.com

2 29 April 20..

3 Our ref: LL/DC

4 World Medical
Rudower Straße 250
12489 BERLIN
GERMANY

5 Dear Sir or Madam

6 Enquiry about surgery lights

7 We have seen your advertisement in this month's editon of the trade magazine "Medical Business". We see that your company sells medical equipment.

We are an outpatient clinic in London. We are planning to add a new operating theatre and are interested in your surgery lights. We would like to place a trial order for one ceiling light. If the product is suitable, we will place a second order.

Please let us have details of your terms of delivery and payment. We would also like to know what type of packaging you use to protect the light during transport.

Barclay's Bank Head Office, London will be happy to supply references.

Many thanks for your attention to our enquiry.

We look forward to hearing from you soon.

8 Yours faithfully

9 *Linda Lambert*
Linda Lambert
Clinic Manager

10 cc Dr. Alice Black

11 Enc: Information pack "Dryden Medical Clinic"

DAS KANN ICH (Unit 9)

- Einen Bericht über ein neues Videokonferenzsystem auf Englisch schreiben. (Foundation)
- Eine Anfrage für Linearantriebe an eine englische Firma verfassen. (Part A)
- Eine Desktop-CNC-Fräsmaschine im Internet suchen und auf Englisch präsentieren. (Part B)
- Ein Angebot für eine englische Firma erstellen. (Communication)

10 Ordering technical products

FOUNDATION: Aluminium containers

Situation: You are getting some work experience at AluBox, a British company that makes aluminium containers.
→ **You call a customer and confirm his order by email.**

1 The product

The owner of a company that organizes events and festivals in Scotland, is interested in buying aluminium containers which he can use to transport electronic equipment to events. He has found this page on the AluBox website

www.AluBox.com/crates

Stackable Aluminium Containers – AB 56

Our AB 56 universal containers are made of light-weight aluminium. We use high-quality materials.

- The containers can be used for storage and for transport.
- They offer excellent protection of goods, materials, electronic equipment, etc.
- The AB 56 series comes in two colours: black and silver.
- Every container is fitted with two snap fasteners.
- The fasteners can be locked with a padlock.
- The AB 56 series is available in 3 standard sizes: small (2 handles), medium and large (4 handles).
- Same-sized containers can be stacked to save space in a warehouse or during transport.
- Every container in the AB 56 series comes with a five-year guarantee.

TOOLBOX

handle – *Griff* | padlock – *Vorhängeschloss* | snap fastener – *Schnappverschluss*

A **Read the description of the product on page 100 and answer the following questions.**

1 What are the containers made of?
2 What can they be used for?
3 What kinds of things can be stored in the containers?
4 How can the containers be carried?
5 How can the containers be closed?
6 How long is the guarantee period?

B **Talk to a partner. Discuss the advantages of the containers for transporting electronic equipment. Make notes that you can use when talking to the customer.**

> **Describing objects**
>
> These containers **are made by** AluBox.
> They **can be stacked** one on top of the other.

› *Grammar: Passive forms, page 160*

2 Role-play: A phone call with a customer

Your supervisor tells you that a prospective customer, Mr Young, would like some information before he places an order. He asks you to call Mr Young.

Work with a partner. Partner A: Look here. Partner B: Look at File 12 on page 139.

Read the website on page 100 again and prepare to answer Mr Young's questions.

- Ring Mr Young, introduce yourself and explain why you are calling.
- Answer Mr Young's questions using the information on the website.
- Suggest that he orders the medium-sized container (length: 800 mm; width: 600 mm; height: 610 mm).
- Say that you will confirm his order by email.

› *Useful phrases: Telephoning, page 150; Advising customers, page 152*

3 Confirming the order

Your supervisor asks you to confirm the order by email.

Work with the same partner as in exercise 2. Complete the email using words from the box.

catalogue · container · delivery · electronic equipment · guarantee · handles · list · medium · order · trial

Dear Mr Young

With reference to our telephone call of today, I would like to confirm your order. As agreed, AluBox will supply a ___[1] order as follows:

10 black Stackable Aluminium Containers – AB 56-suitable for transporting ___[2].

___[3]-sized (length: 800 mm, width: 600 mm, height: 610 mm) with four ___[4].

___[5] within 2 weeks.

Every ___[6] in the AB 56 series comes with a five-year ___[7].

We attach a copy of our latest ___[8] and price ___[9].

Thank you again for your ___[10]. We look forward to establishing regular business with you.

Yours sincerely

PART A: Types of electric motor

Situation: Your company has a contract to replace the motor of a conveyor belt at a food-processing factory in Ireland.
→ **You recommend an electric motor to meet the customer's requirements.**

1 Understanding the basic principles

Before you start to look for a suitable product, you review the basic theory of electric motors.

A **Use highlighted words from the text to complete the gaps (1–10) in the summary after the text.**

Simple DC motor

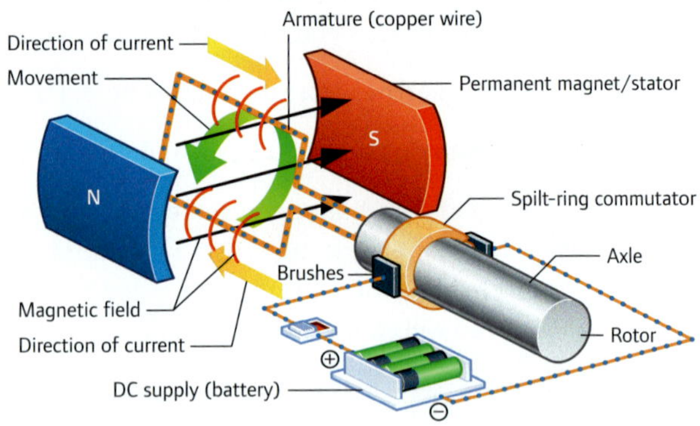

When an electric current travels through conductors (e.g. copper wire), it produces a magnetic field. If this magnetic field then passes through another magnetic field, e.g. between the two poles of a permanent magnet, the two fields interact and make the wire move. This is because the negative pole of the wire's magnetic field is attracted to the positive pole of the magnet's magnetic field. The negative pole of the wire's field is also repelled (pushed away) by the magnet's negative pole. If an electric current enters and leaves a magnetic field along a loop of copper wire (armature) attached to an axle, the forces of attraction and repulsion between the two magnetic fields make the armature rotate (green arrow). Normally, the armature would only rotate half a turn and stop but in a motor, the direction of the current in the armature is reversed again and again by using a split-ring commutator which makes contact with the DC supply through brushes. The alternating polarity of the magnetic field around the armature makes it turn continuously because it is constantly attracted to the magnetic fields of the permanent magnet. The moving part of an electric motor is called the rotor. The stationary, permanent magnet is the stator. The direction in which the rotor turns is explained by Fleming's left-hand rule (see diagram below).

The motor in the diagram is powered by a ___[1] current from a battery. The part of the motor which doesn't move is called the ___[2], and in this motor it is a permanent ___[3]. The moving part of the motor is the ___[4]. Metals like gold, silver and copper are good ___[5], and when a current passes through them, they produce a ___[6] field. The north pole of this field is ___[7] to south pole of the field around the stator. The polarity of the magnetic field in the armature is ___[8] by the split-ring ___[9]. It makes contact with the power supply through two ___[10].

B **Find out more about Fleming's left-hand rule on the internet and explain to your class how it can be applied in the case of the DC motor above.**

Fleming's left-hand rule

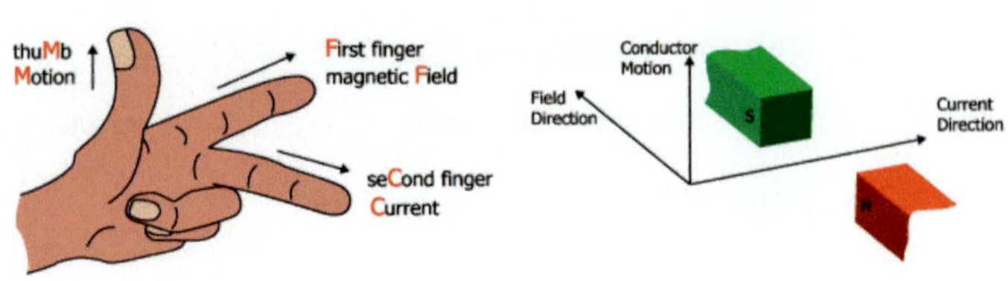

2 Comparing electric motors

You find companies selling a range of different motors on the internet.

A Read the table about five different types of electric motor. Match each motor (1–5) to the correct German term in the list below.

bürstenbehafteter Gleichstrommotor • bürstenloser Gleichstrommotor • Drehstrom-Asynchron-Motor mit Käfigläufer • einphasiger Spaltpolmotor • Universalmotor

Motor type	Characteristics	Applications
1 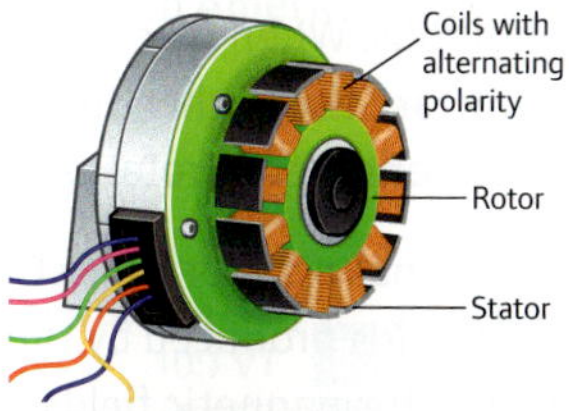	suitable for continuous use; very few moving parts; little wear and tear; compact; quiet	computer fans, DVD drives
2 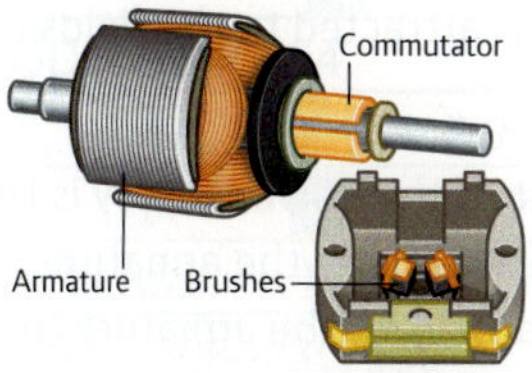	not suitable for continuous use; cheap to manufacture; many uses; battery-powered; cheap; brushes wear out; sparks from brushes	car windows and seats, toys
3 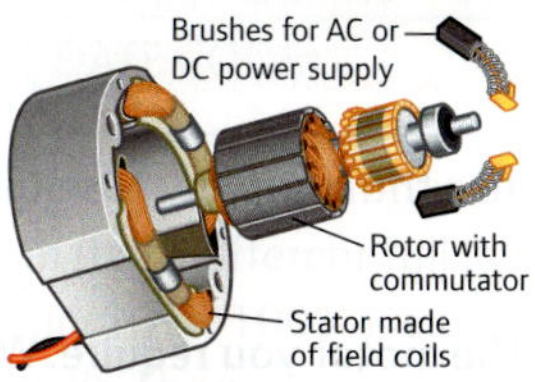	uses AC or DC power; powerful; many uses; not suitable for continuous use; brushes wear out; noisy	vacuum cleaners, food mixers, power tools; cranes; hoists
4 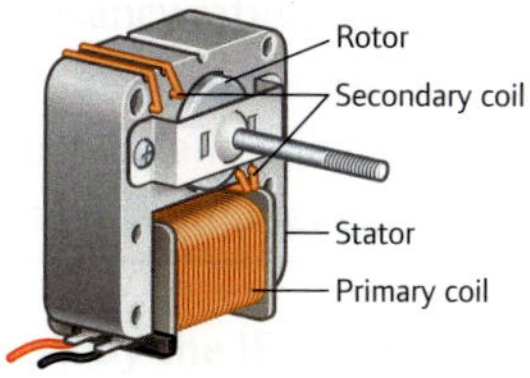	self-starting motor; suitable for low-power, continuous use	air conditioning, fans, hair dryers, refrigerators
5 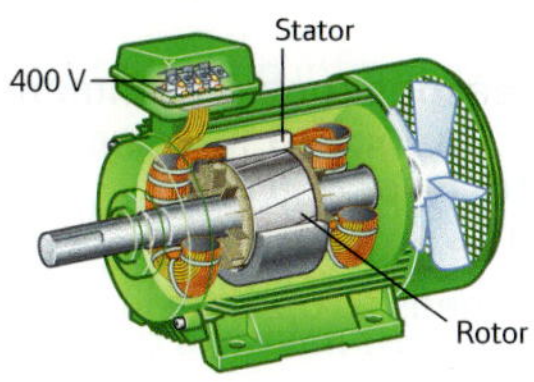	suitable for continuous use; few moving parts; little wear and tear; self-starting; high power and efficiency; quiet	used in industry, e.g. lifts, machine tools, pumps

TOOLBOX

armature – *Anker*
to attract, attraction – *anziehen, Anziehung*
to repel, repulsion – *abstoßen, Abstoßung*
to reverse – *umkehren*
split-ring commutator – *Stromwender mit Stromwenderlamellen*
stator – *Ständer*
wear and tear – *Verschleiß*

2 Understanding motor enclosure classifications

You research the IP (International Protection Code) and NEMA motor enclosure classifications.

Find the English expressions for the German terms in the list. (They are in the same order as in the text.)

Fremdkörper • Durchmesser • Tropfwasser • Sprühwasser • Spritzwasser • Strahlwasser • Staub • Motorgehäuse • Anwendung • mit Lüfterkühlung • wasserdicht • unbelüftet • feucht

IP codes

	1st numeral		2nd numeral
	Protection against solid objects		**Protection against liquids**
2	Protected against solid objects greater than 12 mm in diameter (e.g. fingers)	2	Dripping water (light rain); protected against the vertical drops of water
3	Protected against solid objects greater than 2.5 mm in diameter (e.g. tools and thick wires)	3	Spraying water; protected against drops of water falling at 60°
4	Protected against small objects greater than 1 mm in diameter (e.g. most wires, thin screws)	4	Splashing water; protected against splashing water
5	Protection against dust	5	Water jet; protected against water sprayed against the motor enclosure

Common NEMA classifications

ODP	Open Drip Proof	For indoor applications in clean, dry locations
TEFC	Totally Enclosed Fan Cooled	For outdoor applications (e.g. pumps, fans); not waterproof
TENV	Totally Enclosed Non-Ventilated	For damp, dirty indoor and outdoor locations

3 Studying motor nameplates

Now you study the nameplates of the motors that are used at the factory.

A **Work with a partner and write down as much information as you can about the motors below.**

A

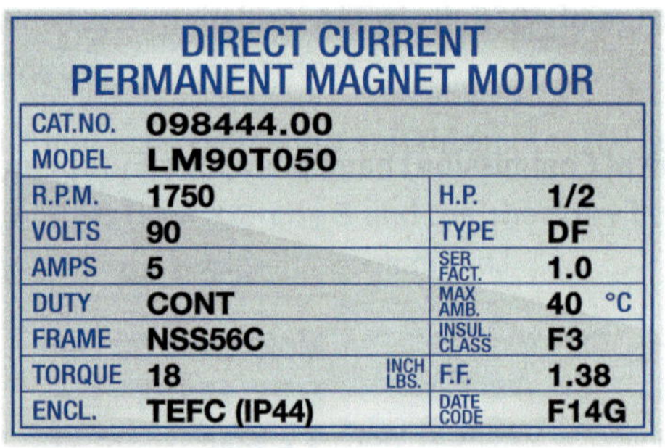

B

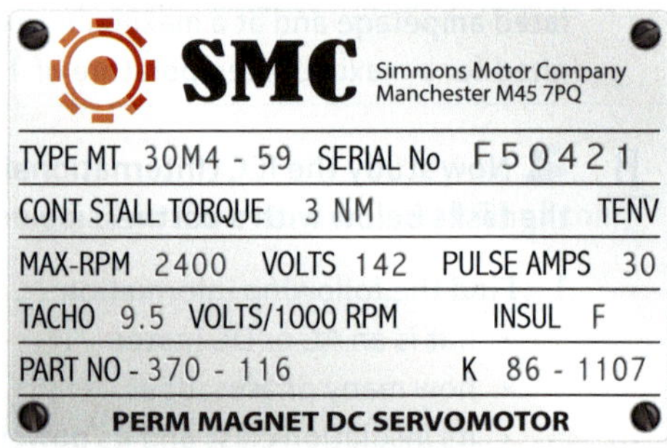

C

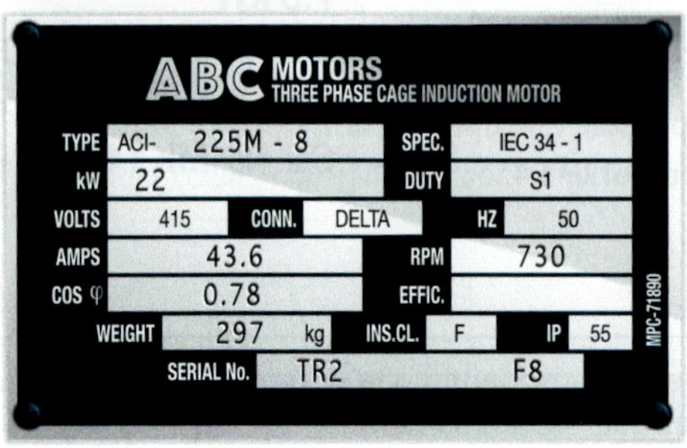

D

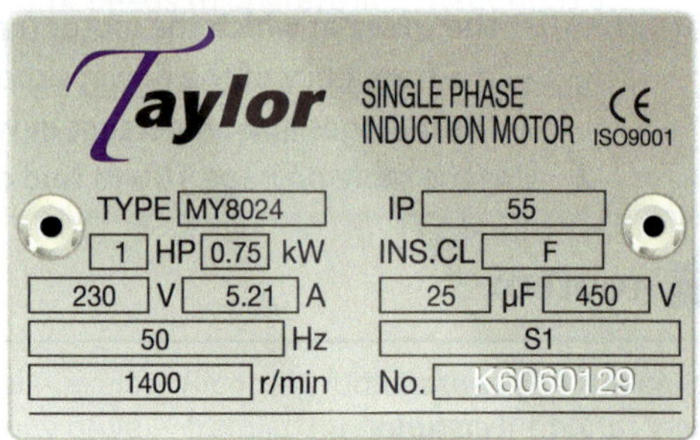

B **Work with a partner. Look back at page 103 and suggest a suitable application for each motor. What working environment (e.g. indoors, outdoors, etc.) is each one suitable for?**

4 Ordering an electric motor

One of the hoists in the factory is broken. It isn't capable of lifting heavy loads any more. Your supervisor talks to Braden O'Farrell, a salesman from Galway Electrics, about a retrofit.

34))) Copy the specification list and then listen to the conversation between Braden O'Farrell and your supervisor.
Complete the missing information.

Talking about necessity

The brushes **need replacing** = The brushes need to be replaced.
Does it **need repairing**? What **needs doing**?

› *Grammar: Gerunds, page 162*

<table>
<tr><td colspan="12">Motor specifications</td></tr>
<tr><td>Application</td><td colspan="2">AC single-phase</td><td colspan="3">AC 3-phase</td><td colspan="3">DC brushed</td><td colspan="3">DC brushless</td></tr>
<tr><td></td><td colspan="2"></td><td colspan="3"></td><td colspan="3"></td><td colspan="3"></td></tr>
<tr><td colspan="4">Retrofit</td><td colspan="4">Brushwear detection</td><td colspan="4">Drive</td></tr>
<tr><td>Yes</td><td></td><td>No</td><td></td><td>Yes</td><td></td><td>No</td><td></td><td>With</td><td></td><td>Without</td><td></td></tr>
<tr><td colspan="2">Continuous use</td><td colspan="2">Intermittent use</td><td colspan="3">Indoors / clean</td><td colspan="3">Indoors / dusty</td><td colspan="2">Outdoors</td></tr>
<tr><td colspan="2"></td><td colspan="2"></td><td colspan="3"></td><td colspan="3"></td><td colspan="2"></td></tr>
<tr><td colspan="3">Enclosure</td><td>ODP</td><td></td><td colspan="2">TEFC</td><td></td><td colspan="2">TENV</td><td colspan="2"></td></tr>
<tr><td colspan="3">Motor HP / kW</td><td colspan="3">Motor rpm</td><td colspan="3">Motor voltage</td><td colspan="3">Full load amps</td></tr>
<tr><td colspan="3"></td><td colspan="3"></td><td colspan="3"></td><td colspan="3"></td></tr>
<tr><td>Motor price</td><td colspan="2"></td><td>Drive price</td><td colspan="2"></td><td colspan="3">Delivery</td><td colspan="3"></td></tr>
</table>

5 Role-play: Placing an order

Now it is time to role-play a telephone conversation about an order for a new electric motor.

Work with a partner. Partner A: Look here. Partner B: Look at File 16 on page 141.

You are a salesperson at Galway Electrics in Ireland. Partner B rings your company and wants to order an electric motor.

Use the form in exercise 4 above to ask Partner B questions about the motor he/she needs.

› *Useful phrases: Telephoning, page 150; Taking telephone calls, page 151*

PARTNER A: Salesperson at Galway Electrics

- Answer the phone (company name, your full name; "How can I help?").
- Ask what the motor is to be used for.
- Use the motor specifications form to ask more questions.
- Invent a price.
- Say when delivery will be (e.g. immediate / in a week).
- End the call politely (e.g. "Thanks for ordering with Galway Electrics.")

TOOLBOX

hoist – *Hebezeug*

retrofit – *Nachrüstung*

COMMUNICATION: Enquiries, offers and orders

Situation: You are helping out in the office at World Medical, a company that manufactures and repairs medical equipment.
→ **You write an enquiry and an order to a supplier; then you write an offer to a customer.**

1 Checking language for enquiries

You check that you know suitable English phrases for writing a letter of enquiry.

Match the phrases and sentences from a German letter of enquiry (a–i) to the English equivalents (1–9).

TIP

You will find similar phrases in the model letter on page 99.

a Wir haben Ihre Anzeige … gesehen.
b Wir sind einen/eine … in Deutschland.
c Wir haben vor, …
d Wir interessieren uns …
e Wir möchten eine Probebestellung … aufgeben.
f Wenn die Dienstleistungen Ihrer Firma unsere Voraussetzungen erfüllen, …
g Bitte nennen Sie uns Einzelheiten …
h Die … Bank wird Ihnen gerne Referenzen zukommen lassen.
i Wir freuen uns, bald von Ihnen zu hören.

1 If the product is suitable …
2 … *(name of bank)* will be happy to supply references.
3 Please let us have details …
4 We are a … *(type of firm)* in Germany.
5 We are interested in …
6 We are planning …
7 We have seen your advertisement …
8 We look forward to hearing from you soon.
9 We would like to place a trial order …

2 Writing an enquiry for calibration equipment

World Medical is looking for a supplier of calibration equipment. Jan Dube, the Quality Control Manager, asks you to write a letter of enquiry to a manufacturer. He gives you the following details.

Work with a partner. Write a letter of enquiry to MCE using the notes on the right. Add today's date and your own reference numbers. Remember to use the correct salutation and complimentary close.

› *Useful phrases: Writing enquiries, page 154*

TIP

The letter on page 99 will help you with the layout.

Enquiry to MCE – Medical Calibration Equipment, Silverbank Industrial Estate, B5, Ferry Road, Edinburgh EH4 2EF
I found their details online.

- *Tell them who we are and what we do.*
- *Say that we're extending the Quality Control Department and we need more calibration equipment.*
- *Ask about a trial order for one calibration machine.*
- *Say that if the trial order is OK, we'll place another order.*
- *Ask for terms of delivery / payment.*
- *Give the Triodod Bank, Berlin as a reference.*
- *Sign it with your name and let me have a copy.*

Thanks, Jan

TOOLBOX

calibration equipment – *Kalibriergerät*

3 Writing an order for calibration equipment

Neil McCain, the sales manager from Medical Calibration in Edinburgh, has replied to your enquiry. Jan Dube, your Quality Control Manager, is happy with the offer and asks you to write the order.

Write the complete order using Jan Dube's notes.

- *Thank Mr McCain for his reply to our letter of enquiry.*
- *Confirm the trial order for one calibration machine.*
- *The price we agreed is 352 euros including VAT.*
- *Agree to the Terms of Delivery (Documentary Letter of Credit).*
- *Thank Mr McCain for his attention to our order.*
- *Say that if the product is suitable, we will place a second order.*

Start like this and end with a suitable complimentary close.

Dear Mr McCain
Thank you for your reply to our letter of enquiry.
My supervisor, Jan Dube, has asked me to confirm our trial order for ...

› *Useful phrases: Writing orders, page 155*

4 Writing an offer for wheelchairs

Your supervisor took a call from a customer earlier today. She gives you her notes and asks you to write an offer.

Read your supervisor's notes then write the offer following the scheme below.

Call from: Ms Smith, Administrator, Toll Road Hospital, Manchester M30

Re. our product no. BP Chair 07
Amount: 25 battery-powered wheelchairs
Terms of delivery: EXW
Delivery within one week of order
Price: 232 euros per item. Discount for bulk order 0.5%
Would like a price list

- Thank customer for the enquiry (give today's date).
- Thank for the interest in your company's products.
- Give details of terms of delivery and payment.
- Say that you are enclosing a price list as requested.
- Express hope that you will hear from Ms Smith soon.

› *Useful phrases: Writing offers, page 154*

DAS KANN ICH (Unit 10)

- Eine Bestellung per E-Mail bestätigen. (Foundation)
- Einem/Einer englischsprachigen Kunden/Kundin den passenden elektrischen Motor empfehlen. (Part A)
- Englischen Motoren-Typenschildern wichtige Daten für eine Bestellung entnehmen. (Part B)
- Eine Anfrage und ein Angebot auf Englisch verfassen. (Communication)

KMK Exam practice 5

1 Leseverstehen

Sie arbeiten im Ausland für einen Stromkonzern, wo in Sitzungen häufig von ‚HVDC' bzw. von ‚DC' und ‚AC' gesprochen wird. Um mitreden zu können, beschließen Sie, sich über dieses Thema zu informieren und stoßen auf folgenden Artikel im Internet.

Beantworten Sie die Fragen zu dem Artikel auf Deutsch.

New generation DC may win next round in 'war of currents'

The story is well-enough-known. The contest over a century ago between AC or DC about which type of current would become the standard for delivering power to homes and businesses was won by AC. The basic reason for this was that AC was more suited to transporting electricity over long distances on large-scale grids than DC was.

Now, however, a high-voltage version of DC, known as HVDC, looks set to challenge AC's position as the standard for electricity grids. AC grids suffer quite dramatic losses in electricity over long distances. Over a distance of 1,000 miles, an AC grid will lose between 12% and 25% of the power it is transporting. But with an HVDC grid the losses are of a lower order: over the same distance they only amount to between 6% and 8%. The results of this greater efficiency in both cash and environmental terms should be immediately clear.

All this is being brought one step closer by the development of new technology which looks set to solve a major problem of HVDC systems. In the past, power surges on HVDC systems resulted in entire grids going down and far-reaching power outages. However, new HVDC breaker technology means that the section of a grid experiencing a surge can be quickly isolated, and the problem dealt with while the rest of the grid continues to operate normally.

Some experts believe that these developments clear the way for the harnessing of renewable sources of energy on a truly grand scale. According to Alan Peekson, energy technology analyst at the consultancy SynroCross, 'The new efficiencies over very long distances offered by HVDC could make the development of enormous wind farms in isolated, far-flung regions practicable for the first time. Basically, we could turn the Canadian tundra regions into wind farms which could power Canada and the United States.'

Energy technologists could start to consider power-generating schemes which have up until now seemed rather more like science fiction than potential reality.

'The idea of the wastes of the Sahara desert becoming a gigantic source of solar power for Africa, Europe and parts of Asia could now be realizable,' says Peekson.

In any case, thanks to HVDC we can now see a future for power beyond fossil fuels which we can look forward to with optimism.

1 Warum wird bei Energieübertragungen über weite Entfernungen Wechselstrom gegenüber Gleichstrom bevorzugt?
2 Welche statistischen Angaben werden im Artikel zur jeweiligen Effizienz von Wechselstrom und HGÜ gemacht?
3 Welches Hauptproblem hatten HGÜ-Netze in der Vergangenheit?
4 Welche Entwicklung könnte dieses Problem jetzt lösen? Wie?
5 Inwiefern vereinfacht die HGÜ das Nutzen von erneuerbaren Energiequellen?

2 Interaktion

Verwenden Sie die Rollenkarten, um ein Telefongespräch zwischen einem Kunden / einer Kundin und einem Mechatroniker / einer Mechatronikerin als Rollenspiel durchzuführen.

Prüfling A

Sie sind Techniker/in in der Produktion bei einer kleinen Leichtmaschinenbaufirma. Der Motor einer Ihrer Produktionsmaschinen ist leistungsschwächer geworden. Rufen Sie die Kundenbetreuung an und fragen Sie um Rat. Bereiten Sie sich auf das Gespräch mit folgenden Punkten vor:

- Der Motor läuft nicht so schnell wie vorher. Das verringert die Leistung der Maschine, die er antreibt.
- Der besagte Motor ist ein Gleichstrommodell, das 1996 hergestellt wurde.
- Der Motor summt und startet manchmal nicht. Er vibriert leicht und fühlt sich ziemlich warm an.
- Ihre Firma würde das Ersetzen des Motors in Erwägung ziehen, wenn das Ersatzteil eine langfristige Geldersparnis darstellt.
- Geben Sie Ihre E-Mail-Adresse an, wenn Sie danach gefragt werden: bothingwood@lexitec.com.

Prüfling B

Sie sind Techniker/in bei der Kundenbetreuung einer Elektrofirma für industrielle Komponenten. Sie erhalten den Anruf eines Kunden / einer Kundin, der/die Probleme mit einem Motor hat. Bereiten Sie sich auf das Gespräch mit folgenden Punkten vor:

- Finden Sie heraus, um welche Art Motor es sich handelt und wann dieser produziert wurde.
- Fragen Sie, welche Probleme der Kunde / die Kundin mit dem Motor hat.
- Empfehlen Sie, dass der Kunde / die Kundin es in Erwägung ziehen sollte, den Motor gegen einen neuen Drehstrommotor auszutauschen. Sagen Sie, dass Sie ihm/ihr gerne eine E-Mail schicken, in der Sie ihm/ihr genau auflisten, was die Vorteile eines solchen Modells wären.
- Fragen Sie den Kunden / die Kundin nach seiner/ihrer E-Mail-Adresse und bedanken Sie sich für den Anruf.

3 Produktion

Herr Rowe ist ein Kunde, den Sie betreuen. Er besitzt momentan einen Gleichstrommotor. Sie haben ihm angeboten, einen Drehstrommotor zu installieren. Daraufhin hat er Sie in einer E-Mail nach den Vorteilen dieses Motors gefragt.

Schreiben Sie Herrn Rowe eine Antwort und verwenden Sie folgende Punkte.

Drehstrommotoren ...
- sind leiser als Gleichstrommotoren.
- benötigen weniger Wartung.
- sind in Hinblick auf den Stromverbrauch effizienter.
- werden auf lange Sicht zu Stromersparnissen führen.

11 Problems and complaints

FOUNDATION: Recycling

Situation: You work in the production department of an international smartphone manufacturer.
→ **You reply to a comment on a web forum.**

1 Reading about environmental issues

As smartphones contain many different chemical elements and compounds, you are attending a workshop on environmental issues. During the workshop, the trainer asks you to read the following text.

Reversing the damage done by mining

As studies show, mining can have a huge impact on the environment.

The most common environmental effects of mining are soil erosion, the formation of sinkholes and loss of biodiversity. Apart from these problems, chemicals from mining processes can contaminate soil, groundwater and surface water. In some cases, trees around mines are cut down to clear space for storage of soil and rocks from the mine.

Studies have discovered that these environmental problems are not only limited to the area directly beside the mine. The erosion of hillsides, water pollution and waste dumps can also have a negative effect on the surrounding areas.

In areas of wilderness, mining may cause the destruction of ecosystems and habitats. In farming areas, it may disturb or destroy grazing and croplands. In urban environments, mining may produce noise and dust, two elements which can affect people's health. Contamination resulting from leakage of chemicals used in some types of mining may also affect the health of the local population and of animals.

As a result of these studies, many governments around the world insist that mining companies follow environmental rules. Some governments also insist that, when mining is over, the companies clean up the mine and its surroundings and restore the environment for future use.

In many countries, before they are allowed to start mining, the mining companies have to pay a fixed amount of money into an account which is held by a third party until the land has been successfully cleaned up. Since 1978, the mining industry in the USA has reclaimed more than 2 million acres (8,000 km^2) of land. Vegetation is growing on this reclaimed land and wildlife has returned to live and breed there. Some of the land is being used for farming and ranching.

Do the following tasks using your own words as often as possible.

1 Explain why some governments have developed rules for mining companies.
2 Describe the rules and say what mining companies have to do.
3 Give examples from the text to show that the rules are working.

2 Understanding a presentation

The trainer talks about a study into environmental issues related to the production of smartphones.

A Before you listen, match the German words (1–8) to the English words in the list.

built-in battery · carbon footprint · dissolve · environment · glued · greenhouse gas · incinerator · toxic

1	Umwelt	3	CO_2-Fußabdruck	5	Müllverbrennungsanlage	7	eingebauter Akku
2	Treibhausgas	4	giftig	6	auflösen	8	verklebt

B 35 Read the statements below. Then listen and complete the notes.

1 The organization that conducted the survey hoped that manufacturers would …
 a) clean up their products by eliminating hazardous ___. **b)** take back and ___ old phones.
2 The study looked at three environmental areas:
 a) energy and ___. **b)** greener ___. **c)** the use of natural products and ___.
3 Manufacturing a smartphone is estimated to cause ___ kilogrammes of CO_2-equivalent emissions.
4 A smartphone contains heavy metals, including lead, mercury,
 a) ___, **b)** ___ and **c)** ___.
5 One million phones contain …
 a) ___ pounds of copper, **b)** ___ pounds of silver and **c)** ___ pounds of gold.
6 You can pay the phone company about ___ euros for a new battery.

3 Suggesting improvements

The trainer asks you to discuss what smartphone manufacturers could do to improve their record on environmental issues. She writes some points on the board.

Talk in groups. Expand on the suggestions for dealing with environmental issues related to the manufacture of smartphones above. Add your own ideas.

recycle / extract and reuse components and metals
change contract length / offer customers longer contracts
greener / fewer materials / organic radical batteries (ORB)
cut down on packaging / accessories

4 Replying to a comment on a forum

At the end of the workshop, the trainer points out the following comment on a forum. She asks you to write a reply.

"So many people complain about the effects of technology on our surroundings. Why don't people understand that we can't produce technological equipment without damaging the environment?"

Give your opinion on the topic. Mention the pros and cons you have discovered and discussed on these pages to give examples to illustrate your opinion.

TOOLBOX

biodiversity – *Artenvielfalt*
cadmium – *Cadmium*
chromium – *Chrom*
circuit boards – *Leiterplatten (PCBs)*
ecosystem – *Ökosystem*
habitat – *Lebensraum*
leakage – *Versickern; Leck*
mercury – *Quecksilber*
tin – *Zinn*
water pollution – *(Trink-)Wasserverschmutzung*

PART A: A delivery of an assembly robot

Situation: You are doing work experience at KS Engineering, a British company that produces components for the automotive industry.
→ **You write an email of complaint to the supplier about a delivery.**

1 Discussing robots in industry

During your work, you often think about how widespread robots are in modern industrial applications.

A **Work with a partner. Make a list of some of the tasks which robots perform in the automotive industry.**

arc welding, assembly systems, cutting, heavy material handling, milling, ...

B **Compare your list with another pair.**

C **In your group, think of areas where humans and robots collaborate, and where there is robot-robot collaboration. Give examples, if possible, from your own training companies.**

D **Discuss in class: Do you think robots will replace humans in the workplace in the near future?**

2 Reading a data sheet and a delivery note

Before you and your colleagues take delivery of a robot for mounting purposes, you read the data sheet and the delivery note.

A **Match these definitions to words in the data sheet on this page and the delivery note on page 115.**

1 amount a robot can carry
2 extent or distance
3 amount or quantity of heaviness or mass
4 overhead interior surface of a room
5 safety code against contact of water and dirt
6 number assigned for identification
7 insulated electrical conductor to provide electricity to a machine
8 hardware designed to communicate information between hardware and software devices

RobAG R500 SXJ	Data sheet
Payload	6 kg
Working envelope / max. reach	706.7 mm
Number of axes	6
Weight	52.5 kg
Mounting positions	Floor, ceiling, wall
Controller	CU555 compact
Protection class	IP 54

TOOLBOX

assembly system – *Montageanlage*
collaboration – *Zusammenarbeit*
complaint – *Beschwerde*
supplier – *Lieferant*

RobAG, Dortmund

Delivery note: Order no. 079819908

Material no.	Name	Price per unit in €	Quantity in pcs	Total price in €
0021631003	**RobAG Robot R500 SXJ** Serial no. 282842	**27,486.00**	**1**	**27,486.00**
			1	
0003811085	**CU555 compact S55/X55/J55 Controller** Serial no. 506058		**1**	
0000302268	Power supply cable EU 3 m CEE 7 / VII		1	
0000205668	Set of labelling plates English – German		1	
0000591430	CONFIGURATION PROFITECH		1	
0000228319	PROFIBUS M/S		1	
0000739211	INTERFACE 24V PWR IN X55		1	
0000191987	CU555 Docs & parts standard		1	
0000174213	LMN 8.3 Software package		1	
0000842449	RobAG NetPro controller/device 3.2		1	
0000672135	RobAG Programming tools: TechExpert 3.2, GripExpert 3.2, VisualExpert 3.2		1	
			1	
0044167005	**Mobile teaching unit Activate V2** Serial no. 175348		**1**	
0000204433	Labelling plate Activate V2		1	
0000749382	**RobAG smartPAD cable 10 m** Serial no. 5137845		**1**	

B **Find the following information in the data sheet and the delivery note:**

1 the weight of the robot
2 the serial number of the robot controller
3 the length of the power supply cable
4 the voltage of the interface
5 the type number of the software package
6 the names of the tools for easy programming

3 Checking the delivery note

While your colleagues Andy and Ray are unpacking the robot, they check the contents against the delivery note.

36 **Listen to their conversation and write down the problems with the delivery.**

Details on delivery note	Problems with delivery
RobAG Robot R500 SXJ Serial no. 282842	1
Power supply cable EU 3m CEE 7 / VII	2
RobAG NetPro controller/device 3.2	3
Mobile teaching unit Activate V2 Serial no. 175348	4
RobAG smartPAD cable 10 m Serial no. 5137845	5

TOOLBOX

data sheet – *Datenblatt*
delivery – *Lieferung*
delivery note – *Lieferschein*
payload – *Nutzlast*
protection class – *Schutzklasse*
type plate – *Typenschild*

4 Writing an email of complaint

Andy asks you to write an email of complaint to RobAG's UK sales department about the delivery.

Use your notes from exercise 3 to inform RobAG about the problems with the delivery and ask about the missing or wrong items.

› *Useful phrases: Making complaints, page 155*

To: sales@robag.co.uk
From: production@ks-engineering.co.uk
Subject: Order no. 019908798

Dear Sir or Madam
We received our R500 SXJ today but when we unpacked the delivery, we found the following problems:
...

5 Role-play: A conversation with the sales representative

The day after you write the email, a RobAG sales representative calls your department.

Role-play the telephone conversation, using the German prompts below.

RobAG sales representative

Sagen Sie, dass Sie die E-Mail an RobAG weitergeleitet bekommen haben und dass Ihnen die Probleme sehr leid tun.

You

Fragen Sie, wie die Probleme gelöst werden könnten.

RobAG sales representative

Antworten Sie, dass die Seriennummern im Lieferschein falsch sind und KS Engineering einen neuen Lieferschein erhalten wird.

You

Fragen Sie, warum für die Steuerung eine falsche Software geliefert wurde.

RobAG sales representative

Antworten Sie, dass dies ebenfalls ein Fehler von RobAG ist.

You

Fragen Sie nach dem zu kurzen Kabel für das smartPAD.

RobAG sales representative

Antworten Sie, dass das Kabel für das neue smartPAD nur noch 5 m lang ist.

You

Fragen Sie nach dem fehlenden Anschlusskabel.

RobAG sales representative

Antworten Sie, dass Sie so schnell wie möglich bei KS Engineering mit dem fehlenden Kabel vorbeikommen und dabei auch die neue Software für die Steuerung installieren wollen.

You

Antworten Sie, dass Sie morgen nicht in der Firma sein werden, aber übermorgen um 9 Uhr ein guter Zeitpunkt wäre.

RobAG sales representative

Antworten Sie, dass Sie kommen werden und entschuldigen Sie sich noch einmal für die Probleme.

You

Antworten Sie, dass dies kein Problem sei und dass Sie übermorgen wieder in der Firma seien.

RobAG sales representative

Verabschieden Sie sich.

You

Verabschieden Sie sich.

PART B: Problems with a 3D printer

Situation: You work in the Customer Services department of PrinTec, a manufacturer of 3D printers based in Leeds.
→ **You write a reply to an email of complaint from a customer.**

1 Identifying printer problems

To improve your English vocabulary, you check the names for printer problems by looking at the website below.

SIMPLIFY3D® www.simplify3d.com/support/print-quality-troubleshooting/

Gaps in Top Layers
Holes or gaps in the top layers of the print

Stringing or Oozing
Lots of strings and hairs are left behind when moving between different sections of the print

Overheating
Small features become over-heated and deformed

Layer Shifting
Layers are misaligned and shift relative to one another

Layer Separation and Splitting
Layers separate and split apart while printing

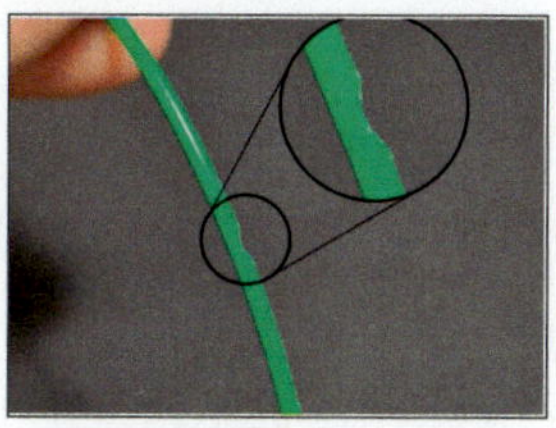

Grinding Filament
Plastic is ground away until the filament no longer moves, otherwise known as „stripped" filament

Clogged Extruder
Extruder is clogged or jammed and no longer extrudes plastic from the nozzle tip

Stops Extruding Mid Print
Printer stops extruding plastic randomly in the middle of a print

Which English words from the website match these German words?

1 drahtförmige thermoplastische Kunststoffe (ABS und PLA)
2 Düse
3 etw. herauspressen, drücken
4 Fadenzug
5 falsch ausgerichtet
6 Schicht
7 Trennung
8 Überhitzung
9 verformt
10 verstopft

2 Reading about printer problems

You also read the following text about 3D printer problems.

Printer problems: Troubleshooting

Most 3D printers come equipped with a nozzle with a 0.4 mm diameter hole in the tip that allows accurate reproduction of very small features. The standard size nozzle works well for most parts, but may cause problems when trying to print extremely thin features that are smaller than the nozzle diameter. For example, the printer cannot accurately produce a 0.2 mm extrusion from a 0.4 mm nozzle. The extrusion width should always be equal to or greater than the nozzle diameter. Nozzles with a smaller diameter are usually available from the manufacturer.

The 3D printer and software interact constantly to make sure that the nozzle extrudes the correct amount of printer resin. If the extrusion settings are not configured properly, the printer may extrude more resin than programmed. This will result in excess resin that can distort the outer contours of your print. To resolve this issue, the settings need to be adjusted in the software. For example, the extrusion multiplier needs to be increased in cases of under-extrusion, or decreased for over-extrusion issues.

Oozing, or stringing, occurs when small strings of resin are deposited on a 3D printed model. This is typically due to resin oozing out of the nozzle while the extruder is moving to a new position. Before printing begins in a new location, the filament is pushed back into the nozzle so that resin can extrude from the tip. Ensure that the retraction option is enabled for each of your extruders (click on "Edit Process Settings" and select the Extruder tab). You can also increase the speed of your printer head, which reduces the amount of time that the extruder can ooze when moving between parts.

3D printers melt and extrude many kilograms of filament over the course of their working life. If the extruder is no longer able to push filament through the nozzle, a jam or clog occurs. This is usually due to something inside the nozzle that is blocking the resin from freely extruding. Heat the extruder to 100 °C and then manually pull the filament out, removing any foreign material jamming the nozzle. TIP: Use a thin wire to push the material back through the nozzle tip.

Ringing is a wavy pattern that may appear on the surface of a print due to printer vibrations or wobbles. This pattern may occur when the extruder makes a sudden change of direction, for example near a sharp corner. The inertia of the extruder can create vibrations when these sudden direction changes occur, which will be visible on the print itself. One reason might be that the printer is moving too fast, so reduce the print speed setting (click on "Edit Process Settings" and select the Print speed tab). A loose screw or a broken bracket might also cause excessive vibrations.

A Answer the questions on the different printer problems.

1 What is the diameter of the standard nozzle hole in most 3D printers?
2 What do you need to produce smaller features?
3 Why do the nozzles sometimes extrude too much resin?
4 How can you solve the problem of over-extrusion?
5 What should you do if your prints suffer from stringing?
6 How can you clean the nozzle if it is clogged?
7 Why may ringing appear on the surface of your workpiece?
8 How can you avoid the problem of ringing?

B Which two troubleshooting problems from the website on page 117 are also mentioned in the text above?

TOOLBOX

bracket – *Halterung*
to configure – *einrichten*
printer resin – *geschmolzener Filamentkunststoff*
string – *Faden*

3 Discussing a customer's problem

One day the Customer Services department receives the following email of complaint from a customer.

From: dave.holdenby@prime-engineering.co.uk
To: customerservice@printec.com
Subject: **Printer fails on our PT2002 printer**

Dear Sir or Madam

About six months ago we bought the PT2002 to produce special parts for our machine prototypes. At the beginning we were very satisfied with the printer but now, as you can see in the attached photo, the results are no longer satisfactory.

We would like to know what the cause of the problem is. The printer is still under warranty, so please inform us whether we should return it to you for inspection or if you can send a technician to carry out repairs on site.

Yours faithfully
Dave Holdenby
Head of Construction

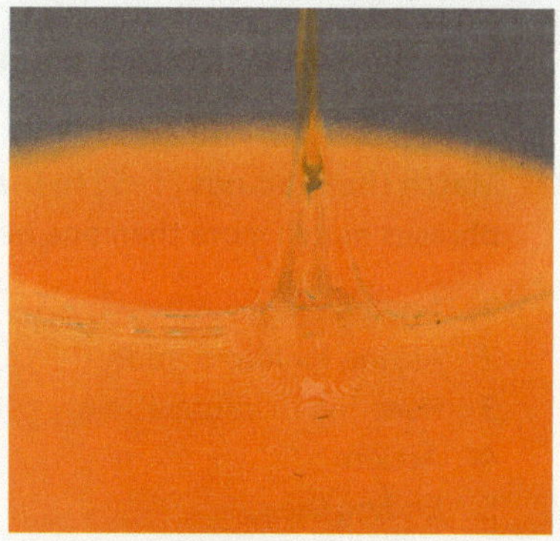

A **Work with a partner. Read the email and explain the situation: Who is the customer, what is the problem, what does he want PrinTec to do?**

B 37 **Wayne and Louise, two colleagues in the Production department, are discussing the problem. Listen to their conversation and answer the following questions.**

1 Which two features of the print results are unsatisfactory?
2 Which feature of the printer hardly ever breaks?
3 Why does Louise think Prime Engineering might not be using the original filament?
4 What other problem might be a result of that?
5 What is the maximum workpiece height for this type of printer?
6 What is the temperature of the resin when it exits the extruder nozzle?
7 What do they think the main cause of Prime Engineering's problem might be?

4 Answering the email of complaint

Your supervisor in the Customer Services department asks you to write an email to Prime Engineering Ltd.

Answer Dave Holdenby's email from exercise 3. Use your answers to exercise 3 and mention these points:

- not the resin heating system because ...
- original filament coils? cheap copies can cause ...
- working height? maximum working height for PT2002 is ...
- please check; otherwise 2-year on-site warranty

› *Useful phrases: Writing emails, page 151; Dealing with complaints, page 156*

Talking about consequences

If the filament **doesn't cool** quickly, it **loses** its shape.
If you **use** the correct filament coil, you **won't have** any problems.

› *Grammar: Conditional sentences, page 160*

TOOLBOX

to contaminate – *verschmutzen*
filament coil – *Filamentspule*
to harden – *aushärten*
to solidify – *fest werden*

COMMUNICATION: A telephone complaint

Situation: You work at World Medical, a company that manufactures medical equipment.
→ **You deal with a telephone complaint.**

1 Dealing with complaints on the telephone

Your supervisor gives you a list of phrases for dealing with complaints and tells you to keep it by the phone.

Match the headings (1–5) to the phrases (a–j). There are at least two phrases for every heading. Some phrases match more than one heading.

1 Apologizing
2 Asking for information
3 Reacting to information
4 Action
5 Ending the call

› *Useful phrases: Dealing with complaints, page 156*

a Can I just check with you that I've understood everything?
b Could you tell me what it's about, please?
c Could you give me the order number, please?
d I'll have a replacement sent out as soon as possible.
e I'm sorry to hear that.
f Is there anything else I can do for you today?
g Just a moment while I write that down.
h Oh, no. That doesn't sound at all good.
i Thank you for your call. Once again, I'm sorry that there was a problem.
j We're prepared to replace the goods at our expense.

2 Dealing politely with customers

A new customer, Jerzy Adamczyk, calls to complain about a trial order of X-ray machines. Your colleague, Melissa Wolf, takes the call. She is not very polite.

A 38 **With a partner, listen to the phone call and decide together how you would improve it. Make a list.**

B 39 **Now listen to how Melissa should have dealt with the phone call with Jerzy Adamczyk. Which (if any) of your improvements does she make?**

TIP

Making / Dealing with complaints on the phone
Give your name clearly at the start of the call and write down the name of the person you are speaking to immediately. If necessary, check the spelling of the name.

3 Complaining to a supplier

World Medical ships their orders in special containers made by Sheffield Metal, a company in England. The latest consignment has not arrived, so your supervisor phones to complain about the delay in delivery. Jeanette Hogg answers the phone.

A **Work with a partner. Look at the phrases (a–h) below and decide who says what – the caller or the person taking the call. (There are four phrases for each speaker.)**

a delivery was promised
b How can I help you?
c I will do my best
d it's an order for
e the exact details
f the order number?
g to enquire about my order
h We can't fulfil our orders

B **When you have finished, match the phrases (a–h) with the gaps (1–8) in the text to complete the transcript of the phone call.**

Jeanette Good morning. Sheffield Metal, Sales Department. Jeannette Hogg speaking.
Supervisor Good morning. This is Max Jahn from World Medical in Germany.
Jeanette Good morning, Mr Jahn. ___[1]
Supervisor I'm calling ___[2] for containers for medical equipment. The order was sent almost one month ago, on 18 April, and ___[3] by 3 May but, so far, nothing has arrived.
Jeanette Oh. I'm sorry to hear that. Could you give me ___[4]
Supervisor Yes. It's DF54736.
Jeanette DF54736. Just a moment, please. I'll check. I'm sorry, Mr Jahn. I don't seem to have any record of your order. Can I just check that I've understood everything? The order number is DF54736 and you ordered the containers on the 18th of April. Could you give me ___[5] of the order, please?
Supervisor Yes, ___[6] your aluminium containers for medical equipment.
Jeanette Aluminium containers for medical equipment. Mr Jahn, I'll have to speak to my colleague to find out what the problem is. Can I get back to you later?
Supervisor Well, yes. But I hope it won't take long. ___[7] until we have your containers.
Jeanette Yes. I realize that, Mr Jahn. I'm very sorry about this and ___[8] to get back to you as soon as possible.
Supervisor Many thanks for your help, Ms Hogg.

C 40 **Now listen and check your answers.**

4 Role-play: Making a complaint by telephone

Now it is time to practise dealing with telephone complaints.

A **Work with a partner and role-play a telephone complaint using the prompts below.**

PARTNER A

You work for the supplier. You take a call from a customer who makes a complaint. Before you begin, refresh your knowledge of phrases for dealing with complaints (exercise 1).

› *Useful phrases: Telephoning, page 150; Making complaints, page 155; Dealing with complaints, page 156*

PARTNER B

You are the customer. Before you begin, make some notes as follows:

- the name of your firm
- the order number
- the date of delivery
- the problem (e.g. damaged/wrong goods, delay in delivery)
- what you hope from Partner A

B **When you have finished the phone call, change roles and do it again using different details.**

DAS KANN ICH (Unit 11)

- Einen Kommentar zu einem Beitrag in einem Webforum auf Englisch schreiben. (Foundation)
- Eine Beschwerde per E-Mail auf Englisch verfassen. (Part A)
- Eine Antwort auf eine Beschwerde per E-Mail auf Englisch verfassen. (Part B)
- Mit telefonischen Beschwerden auf Englisch richtig umgehen. (Communication)

12 A job application

FOUNDATION: Where do I go from here?

Situation: You are thinking about applying for a work placement abroad. You start to think about what you have learned in your apprenticeship and where you might work when you have qualified.
→ **You write a description of your apprenticeship for a European job agency.**

1 Listening to newly-qualified technicians

You listen to an interview with three newly-qualified technicians. They are talking about the jobs they do and where they would like to find a permanent position.

Panel Building Electrician

CAD Technician

Mechatronics Technician

A 41 **Listen and say what the speakers liked best about their apprenticeship.**

1 Who enjoyed learning from experienced people?
2 Who liked the mixture of going to vocational college and doing practical work?
3 Who enjoyed making things in the workshop?

B 41 **Listen again and complete the table with the missing information.**

Name	What I do at work	Sector?
Maren	*designing ___[1] and producing ___[2]*	___[3]
Garry	*fix ___[4] so that the ___[5] can go on with their work*	___[6]
Delon	*install ___[7] equipment* *do ___[8] tasks such as checking or cleaning* *___[9] the machine if there is a problem*	___[10]

2 Thinking about your skills

You think about the skills you have learned during your apprenticeship.

A What do you enjoy most about your apprenticeship? What skills are you learning? How do you learn and develop these skills. First make notes on your own.

B Now talk to a partner about the skills you are learning.

C Now compare your ideas with another pair and make a list of the skills you are all learning, for example, soldering, welding, machine maintenance, etc. (Keep this list; you will need it for Part A, exercise 2, page 125.)

D Report your ideas to the class. In class, make a list in English of the different job titles in your field, e.g. installation technician. How can you use the skills you are learning in your preferred area of work?

Talking about skills; thinking about possibilities

I **can** solder cables.
We**'re able to** fix the machines without any help.
They **might be able to** get a job in the UK.
You **could** look for work in the automotive sector.

› *Grammar: Modals and their substitutes, page 163*

3 Doing internet research

You search the internet for job opportunities in Europe.

A Work with a partner. Do internet research to find suitable career prospects in Europe. Make a poster showing job offers and companies in your sector. Present your ideas to the class.

B When you have finished, pin your poster to the wall and do a gallery walk. Rank the posters using the categories below. Give points from 1–5 for each category.

headline · design · photos/pictures · content · overall effect

4 Reading about the Europass

While you are doing your research online, you come across the European Skills Passport (Europass). You decide to use it to collect your own personal details for applications and your CV.

Download the Europass and start to complete it with your details. (Your teacher has the correct URL.)

INFO

The European Skills Passport (Europass)
This is a standardized CV and language document that can be created online or on your own computer. Potential employers throughout Europe can clearly see your skills and qualifications.

The following sections might be of particular interest to you:
- **Language Passport** – a self-assessment tool for language skills and qualifications;
- **Europass Mobility** – a record of skills acquired during a learning experience in a European country;
- **Certificate Supplement** – a description of skills acquired by holders of vocational training certificates.

5 Describing your apprenticeship

You have contacted an EU job agency asking for help in looking for work experience in Europe. The agent for Germany asks you to write a short description of your apprenticeship in English for the agency file.

Write a short description of your apprenticeship. Before you begin, think about the aspects you should include, e.g. type of training, skills you learned, qualifications you gained, and make notes.

PART B: Job interviews

Situation: You have been shortlisted for a job in the UK.
→ **You prepare for and practise a telephone interview and a face-to-face interview.**

1 Handling telephone interviews

You and a colleague have decided to practise telephone interviews together.

A **With your partner, read the text below and decide which sentences (1–8) fit the gaps (A–F) in the text. There are two more sentences than you need.**

YOUR TELEPHONE INTERVIEW

One short phone call is all it takes to get you to the next level in your job application process – or not. Here are some tips to help you get that job.

Be prepared!
Gather the following documents and lists the day before the interview:
- a copy of the job description;
- a copy of your letter of application, your CV and your references;
- a list of questions you want to ask the interviewer;
- a list of your strengths and weaknesses.

So that the interviewer doesn't get irritated by the sound of you flicking through papers, **A** .

On the day of the call
- Place a notebook and a couple of pens beside the phone **B** .
- Make sure the room you are in is quiet.
- Switch off your computer and disconnect all social media.
- If possible, use a landline. If you use your mobile phone, make sure it is fully charged **C** .
- Get the interviewer's phone number in case you get disconnected.

Dress for the job
You should dress as you would for a face-to-face interview. Strange as it sounds, **D** .
Remember to smile: You can't sound bored or uninterested if you have a smile on your face.
To keep your voice sounding good, **E** .

During the call
Concentrate and stay focused. Listen carefully and reply to the interviewer appropriately.
Be professional and polite. At the end of the call, you can ask, "Do my qualifications meet the company's needs?" However the interview goes, always end with "Thank you for your call." The last few words of a conversation are often the ones that people remember **F** .

1 and that you take the call in a place where reception is good
2 ask the interviewer how many candidates he/she has spoken to today
3 pin these documents and lists to the wall so that you can check them during the call
4 please hang on while I think of the answer
5 so always leave a good impression at the end
6 so that you can take notes during the interview
7 swallow a teaspoon of honey just before the call
8 you're more likely to feel and sound professional if you look the part

2 Practising a telephone interview

You and your colleague decide to practise a telephone interview together.

A **Work with a partner. Study the list of common questions for interviews and how to answer them in File 18 on page 143.**

B **With your partner, prepare a dialogue and role-play a telephone interview.**

Asking for clarification

I'm sorry, could you say that again?
So, if I understand you correctly ...
I don't quite understand what you mean by ...

› *Useful phrases: Telephoning, page 150*

3 Preparing for a face-to-face interview

You listen to a podcast in which an expert gives tips about how to handle face-to-face job interviews.

A **What is the expert likely to say? With a partner, brainstorm a list of expressions you might hear and make notes under the headings below.**

Here are a few expressions from the podcast to start you off.

Stage 1: Greetings and introductions
arrive at the interview on time

Stage 2: Small talk
talk about the weather

Stage 3: The main part of the interview
talk about yourself

Stage 4: Questions from the candidate
do background research into the company before the interview

Stage 5: Further arrangements and the end of the interview
ask when you can expect to hear from the company again

B 42 **Now listen and check. How many of your expressions did you hear?**

4 Practising for an interview

You and your colleague decide to practise the main part of an interview together.

A **First of all, study the list of common interview questions (File 18 on page 143) and how to answer them.**

B **Work with a partner.**

Partner A: **Choose one of the job advertisements you read in Part A (page 124, File 7 or File 17) and tell your partner which one you have chosen. Think about the questions the interviewer might ask and how you might answer. Make notes.**

Partner B: **Study the job advertisement your partner has chosen. Make a list of questions you might ask.**

C **When you are both ready, role-play the job interview. When you have finished, change roles if you wish.**

COMMUNICATION: A CV and a covering letter

Situation: You find out online about the documents which you will need for job applications.
→ **You study an English CV and covering letter and tips on how to prepare them.**

1 Reading a website about CVs

You find an interesting website with tips, but the headings have got mixed up.

Work with a partner. Read the tips (1–9) and match them to the headings (a–i).

a Education and training
b Hobbies and interests
c Personal statement
d Personal details
e References
f Key skills
g Work experience
h Contact details
i Further skills

www.internationalCVs_Technical

TIPS for writing your CV

International CVs

Your CV is a summary of your abilities, work experience, education and qualifications. There is no set format for a British CV but you should keep it short, using clear headings to guide the reader.

1 Give your name and address, telephone number(s) (home/mobile) and email address.

2 This should be a short message that grabs the attention of the reader. Use note form. This helps to keep your CV focused and direct, for example: *Motivated electronic technician with experience in German engineering industry.*

3 Here you can summarize your skills and experience which are relevant to the job for which you are applying.

4 As a general rule, CVs should be in reverse chronological order, listing the most recent position first. For each position held you should provide the dates of the start and end of employment, the employer's name and address, the job title, the main duties and responsibilities and achievements.

5 Give a brief description of qualifications (school, academic and/or professional). Give the names of schools or colleges in reverse chronological order.

6 Here you should write about common skills gained throughout your education and work experience, such as languages, IT skills, good maths skills or a full, clean driving licence. These skills are of interest for any employer.

7 This feature is optional, but could provide something more personal to discuss at an interview. Be careful about what you write; a dangerous sport or *socializing with friends* may not be what an employer wants to hear!

8 Write your date of birth and nationality under this heading.

9 Due to data protection laws, candidates should not provide referees' names, addresses or any other contact details on CVs, but should state that details are available on request. Always ask your referees' permission before you give someone their contact details.

2 Analysing a CV

You also find an example of a British-style CV online.

Study the CV below. What differences can you find between this CV and a German CV?

MARTIN BIENEK
Am Kattenkamp 236, 33611 Bielefeld, Germany
Landline: (+49) 521 394677
Mobile: (+49) 176 3628419
Email: martin.bienek43@gmx.com

PERSONAL STATEMENT
Mobile and flexible apprentice mechatronics technician, in final year of 3-year course, seeking position abroad.

KEY SKILLS
Industrial electrical installation work
Experience in industrial test, measurement and automation systems
AC and DC motor maintenance and repair
Excellent spoken and written English
Good spoken and written Polish

WORK EXPERIENCE

Since 20..	Experience during apprenticeship of installation and electric motor repair work in industrial and commercial locations, installation and programming of industrial automation systems
20..	5-day placement at Elektro Friedrich (local electrical contractor) doing maintenance and repairs of household wiring

EDUCATION AND TRAINING

Since 20..	3-year apprenticeship at Schmidt Installations- und Antriebstechnik GmbH and Vocational Training College for Metalwork and Electrical Engineering in Bielefeld, Germany
June 20..	Abitur (Final examination similar to A-Levels) Main subjects: Physics, Computer Studies
20..–20..	Primary and secondary education in Bielefeld

FURTHER SKILLS
MS Office and database management
Full driving licence
First aid certificate

HOBBIES AND INTERESTS
Athletics, football
Training local junior football team

PERSONAL DETAILS
Date of birth: 06 April 20..
Nationality: German

REFERENCES
Available on request.

3 Analysing a covering letter

Martin has applied for a job as a mechatronics technician at an electrical engineering company in Ireland.

Read Martin's covering letter on the opposite page and match the parts (1–5) with explanations from the list.

a asking the employer to invite you for an interview
b reference to details on your CV
c reference to the position
d saying why the applicant is applying for the position
e stating why the applicant is the best person for the job

4 Mediation: Writing a covering letter

Your supervisor gives you the following text and asks you to make notes on the contents in German for the apprentice file.

Read the text and make notes in German for the file.

Writing your covering letter

A covering letter is a formal letter with a standard structure. Do not use the same letter for all companies and all jobs but include a different covering letter with your CV for each job you are applying for. Your covering letter should be one page long. Try to avoid having too many sentences beginning with "I".
In the letter you should ...

1 refer to the position for which you are applying; give the source of the employer's address;

2 give details of your education and training; explain what you are doing at the moment;

3 explain why you are applying for the position;

4 explain what you can offer the employer;

5 close politely, referring to enclosures (attachments in the case of online applications) and asking the employer to invite you for an interview.

Here are some things to remember:

» After "Dear ..." all letters and emails then start with a capital letter.
» If you start a letter / an email with a personal name (*Dear Anne, Dear Ms Green*), you finish it with "Yours sincerely".
» If you begin a letter / an email with no personal name (*Dear Sir/Madam*), you always finish it with "Yours faithfully".

› *Useful phrases: Writing a covering letter, page 157*

Am Kattenkamp 236, 33611 Bielefeld, Germany
Phone: (+49) 521 394677, Mobile: (+49) 176 3628419
Email: martin.bienek43@gmx.com

20 April 20..

Scott Electrics Ltd
Silverbank Industrial Estate
DUBLIN
D11 D4E2
IRELAND

Attn. Mr Haig, Human Resources Director

Dear Mr Haig

Mechatronics technician

1 With reference to your advertisement Ref. No. 17673 on the internet, I would like to apply for the post described.

2 I am very interested in the job you are offering as I feel sure it will give me the opportunity to develop both personally and professionally. I am particularly keen to work where I can apply my skills on a daily basis.

3 As you can see from the enclosed CV, by June of this year I will have completed the final year of a three-year apprenticeship at Schmidt Installations- und Antriebstechnik GmbH with theoretical instruction at the Vocational Training College for Metalwork and Electrical Engineering in Bielefeld, Germany. I will then be a fully qualified mechatronics technician.

4 As I have practical skills and experience, am flexible and mobile and speak fluent English, German and Polish, I believe I will be a strong member of any team I join and will benefit your company.

5 My CV is enclosed and I am available for an interview at short notice.

I would very much appreciate it if you would consider my application and hope that you will grant me an interview.

I look forward to hearing from you soon.

Yours sincerely

M. Bienek

Martin Bienek

Encl.

DAS KANN ICH (Unit 12)

- Eine Beschreibung meiner Ausbildung auf Englisch verfassen. (Foundation)
- Englische Stellenanzeigen analysieren und mich darauf bewerben. (Part A)
- Mich auf ein Bewerbungsgespräch auf Englisch gut vorbereiten. (Part B)
- Bewerbungsunterlagen auf Englisch richtig verfassen und gestalten. (Communication)

P Partner files

FILE 1: Unit 1, Part A, exercise 3

Partner A

A **Answer Martin Foster's (= Partner B's) questions about the organization chart below. Spell all the names that are not familiar to you.**

B **Some of the information in the chart is missing, so ask Partner B questions to complete the chart.**

What does Lukas Hanitzsch do?
Who works in the Construction department?
What's the name of the supervisor in ... ?

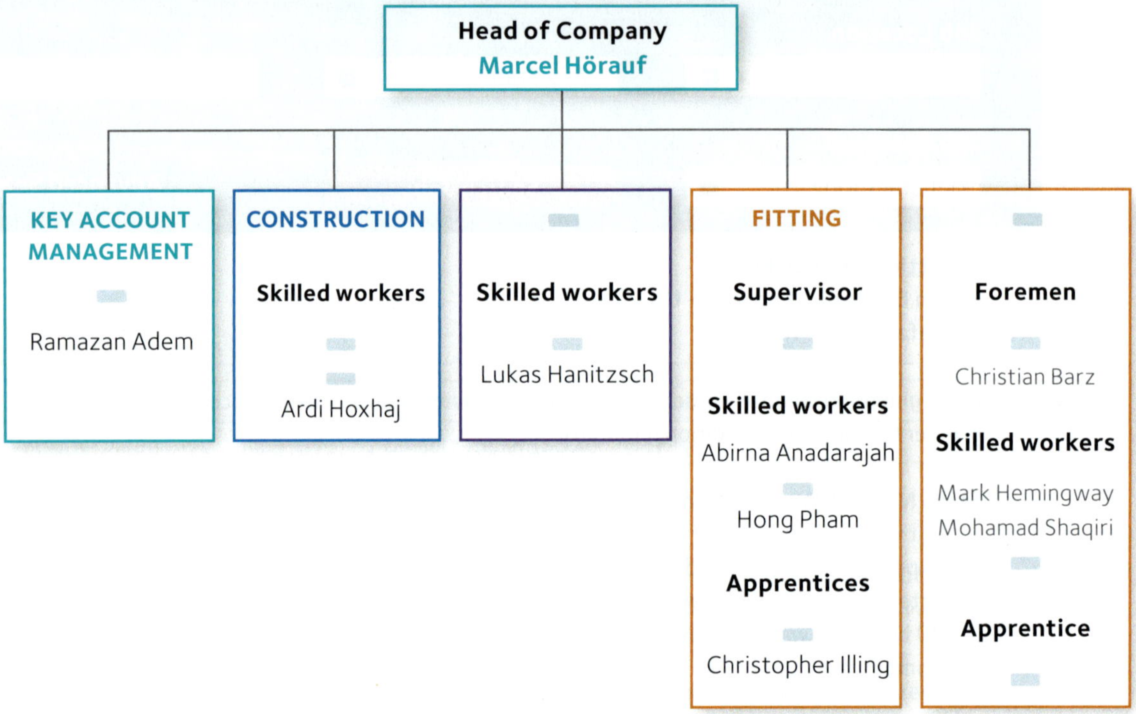

C **Compare your charts when you have finished.**

FILE 2: Unit 3, Communication, exercise 1C

Partner A

Dictate these email addresses to Partner B. Check B's answers.

1 DavidMcCarthy+list@net.us
2 sergei-nikitin@com.ru
3 your own email address
4 the email address of your firm or another email address you often write to

FILE 3: Unit 2, Communication, exercise 5

Partner A and Partner B

Partner A: You work for your training company. (Use your own name and the name of your company.)
Partner B: You work for Trent Electrical Equipment Ltd in Stoke. (Make up an English name for yourself.)

Role-play a telephone call and taking a message. Partner A starts:
Good morning, (name of company). (Your name) speaking. ...

Partner A

Answer the phone. Introduce yourself and ask how you can help.

Partner B

Introduce yourself and ask to speak to Mr Schmidt in the Production department.

Partner A

Say that Mr Schmidt is out of the office at the moment.

Partner B

Ask to speak to Frau Wendlinger.

Partner A

Say that Frau Wendlinger is in a meeting. Ask if the caller would like to leave a message.

Partner B

Say that the electric drills the company ordered are not available. Ask for somebody to call you back to discuss an alternative.

Partner A

Ask the caller for his/her contact details.

Partner B

Give your contact details.

Partner A

Say that you will pass on the message.

Partner B

Thank Partner A and end the call politely.

Partner A

Thank Partner B for calling.

FILE 4: Unit 5, Foundation, exercise 1B

Partner B

Read out these mathematical equations. Partner A will write them down. When you have finished, check that Partner A has written them correctly.

1 $13^2 = 169$
2 $579 \div 26 = 22.26923$
3 $1.234 + 56,789 = 58,023$
4 $70° < 180°$
5 $a2 \approx b2$
6 $48,571,053 - 27,640,598 = 20,930,455$

FILE 5: Unit 5, Communication, exercise 1C

Partner B

Describe this line graph to Partner A. Partner A will draw it. Check Partner A's graph when you have finished.

> **Describing graphs**
>
> The graph/chart shows …
> The horizontal/vertical axis is divided into … units/sections each representing …
> The x axis / The y axis has a scale from … to …

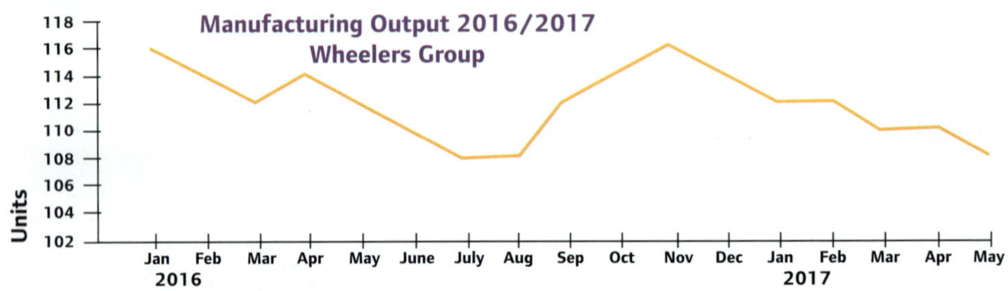

FILE 6: Unit 4, Part B, exercise 4B

Partner A

Describe the two workpieces from the turning machine to Partner B. Answer any questions your partner has.

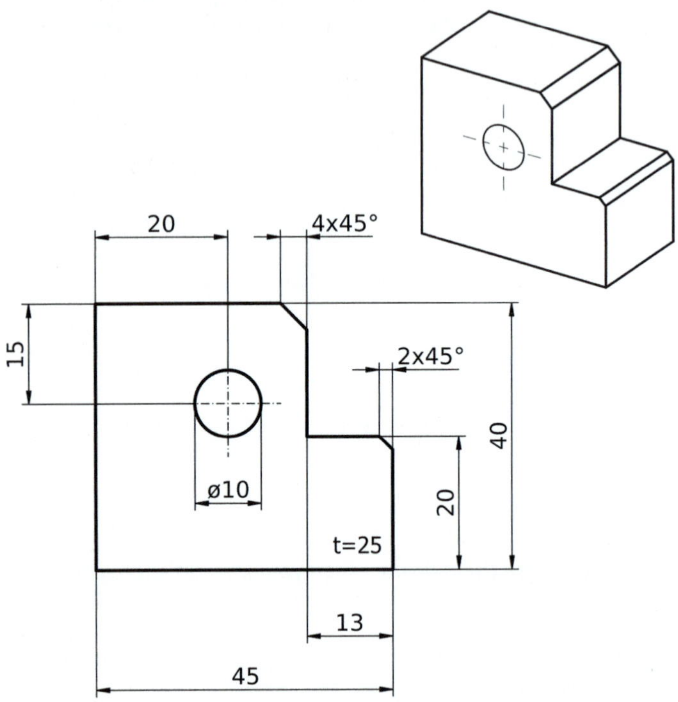

headstock

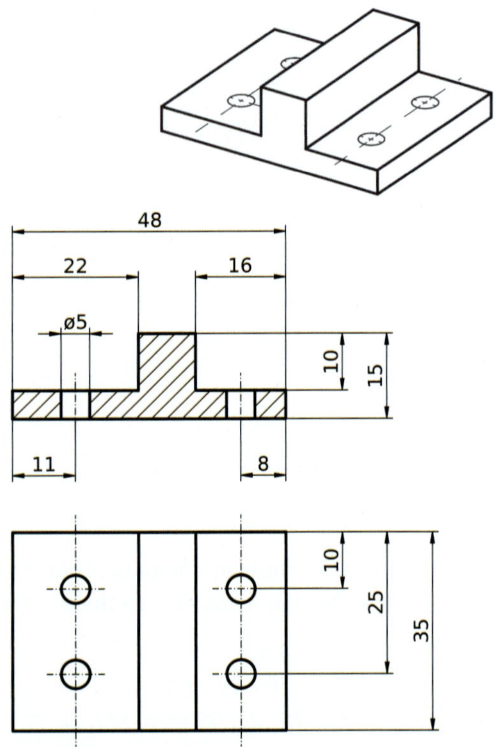

saddle

Which parts (1–5) of the turning machine on page 41 do the drawings match?

FILE 7: Unit 12, Part A, exercise 2A

Partner B

Read the job advertisement below and be ready to answer your partners' questions about it. Ask your partners questions about their job adverts. Find out about ...

1 the type of employer.
2 what the job is.
3 what the requirements are.
4 the salary and benefits.
5 how to apply.
6 what happens if the application is shortlisted.

Sheet Metal Worker/Fabricator

Oxford Fabrications Ltd – Oxford, England

We are a large sheet metal company, established in 1986. We are looking for workers for all types of sheet metal fabrication to work with stainless steel, aluminium and mild steel.
Ability to weld would be an advantage but not essential.

Hours of work are Monday–Thursday 8.00–4.30 and Friday 8.00–1.15.
Salary is dependent on experience.
The ideal candidate needs to be reliable, show they have a good initiative, able to work as part of a team or on their own.
Good working conditions.
Use of company van.

If you feel you are suitable for this role, please apply with your CV and a covering letter to Oxford Fabrications Ltd. Unit 7, Oxford Industrial Estate, OX22 7JY, UK.
Successful candiates will be invited to a preliminary interview at a local assessment centre.

Job type: Full-time
Pay: starts at £10.44 per hour; 25 days paid holiday
Job location: Oxford, UK
Required education: Vocational Technical School qualification

FILE 8: Unit 9, Part B, exercise 5B

In the table below you can find the different prices (excl. VAT = value added tax) for Stepcraft CNC milling machines.

Type	Clamping Surface (X Y)	Working Space (X Y Z)	Overall Size (L x W x H)	Weight (kg)	Price Construct-ion Kit (€)	Price Ready to Run System (€)
1-210	210 x 290	210 x 210 x 40	320 x 342 x 350	11	729	1078
2-300	232 x 380	210 x 300 x 105	430 x 345 x 410	13	829	1178
2-420	312 x 500	300 x 420 x 140	552 x 440 x 510	15	979	1328
2-600	432 x 680	420 x 600 x 140	737 x 558 x 510	19	1279	1728
2-840	615 x 920	600 x 840 x 140	968 x 745 x 510	31	1499	1948

FILE 9: Unit 1, Part A, exercise 3

Partner B

A **You are Martin Foster. You want to know about the structure of the head office in Nuremberg. Ask Partner A questions about the organization chart:**

What does Julia Schreiber do?
Who works in the Production department?
What are the names of the skilled workers in … ?

B **Some of the information in Partner A's chart is missing, so answer Partner A's questions. Spell all the names that are not familiar to you.**

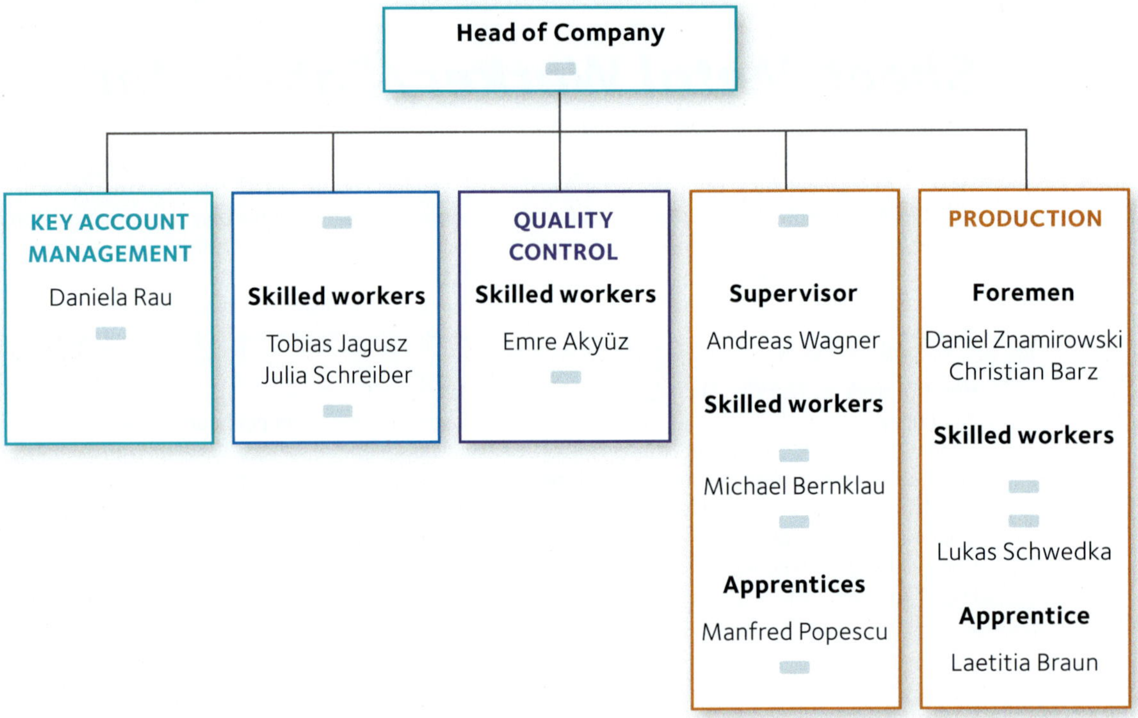

C **Compare your charts when you have finished.**

FILE 10: Unit 3, Communication, exercise 1C

Partner B

Dictate these email addresses to Partner A. Check A's answers.

1 beatrice-kuhn@berlin_tools.de
2 Hamish.MacPherson@net.uk
3 your own email address
4 the email address of your firm or another email address you often write to

FILE 11: Unit 5, Foundation, exercise 3

Partner B

You work for Walker Aluminium (UK) Ltd. Your supervisor has sent Partner A an email with information about a platform trolley his/her company is interested in. Unfortunately, some of the information is incorrect.

Call Partner A to correct the information.

> **Clarifying details**
>
> **Asking about and giving dimensions**
> What does is say about … ?
>
> **Confirming information**
> I'm afraid the dimensions of the … are wrong/incorrect. They should be …
>
> The trolley is made of …
> The castors are made of …

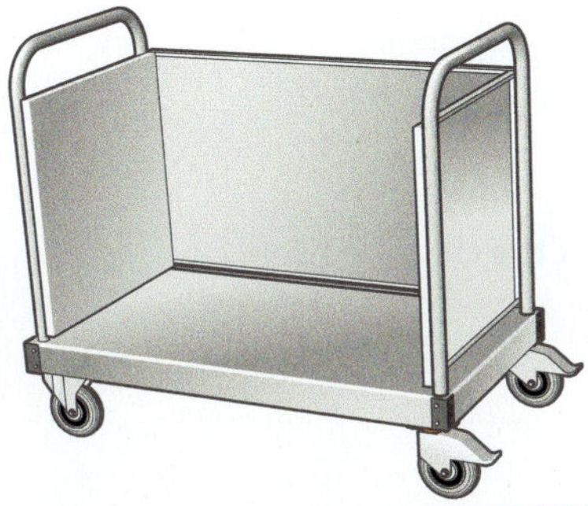

PLATFORM TROLLEY
Platform trolley / aluminum
1000 x 655 x 620 mm

Other information: Four castors on the bottom made of rubber.
They measure approximately 160 mm in diameter and 40 mm in width.
Both back wheels are fitted with wheel brakes.

When you have finished, check the information with Partner A. Does he/she now have the correct information?

FILE 12: Unit 10, Foundation, exercise 2

Partner B

You are Tom Young. You organize festivals in Scotland. An employee at AluBox (Partner A) is going to phone you to give you information about aluminium containers. You are not sure about what you want so you may need to ask the caller to repeat information.

Before you start, read the prompts below carefully. You start the conversation by answering the phone:

Hello, Tom Young speaking. …

- Explain that you would like some information about aluminium containers for transporting electronic equipment, such as lights, microphones, cables, speakers, etc.
- You would like the following information:
  - How big is the medium-sized container?
  - Can the storage containers also be used for transport?
  - Can the containers be locked in any way?
  - Are the containers suitable for transporting goods that might break?
- Say that you would like to place a trial order for 2 containers.
- Ask for a copy of the latest catalogue and price list.
- Thank the caller for his/her help and say you look forward to receiving confirmation of the order.
- End the phone call politely.

FILE 13: Unit 6, Foundation, exercise 2

Partner B

You are a GP (general practitioner = *Hausarzt*) visiting the trade fair. You go to the World Medical stand to enquire about portable X-ray equipment.

Before you start, read the instructions below and prepare to take notes.

Explain that you often deal with accidents on construction sites and need portable X-ray equipment. Ask Partner A …

… for general information about the equipment
… if the equipment can be used outdoors
… about specifications
… the price
… the delivery details
… the packaging details

Make notes as Partner A answers your questions.

Change roles if you want. Prepare to perform your role-play for the class.

FILE 14: Unit 4, Part B, exercise 4B

Partner B

Describe the two workpieces from the turning machine to Partner A. Answer any questions your partner has.

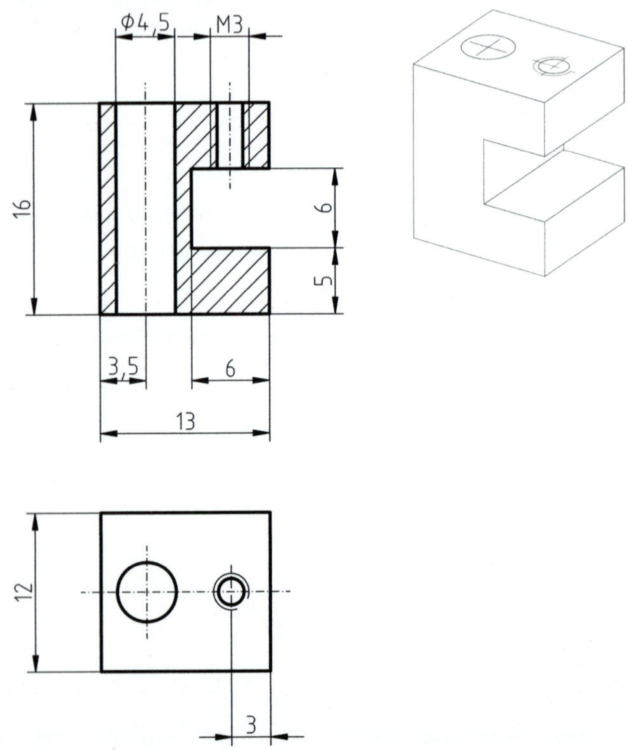

toolholder

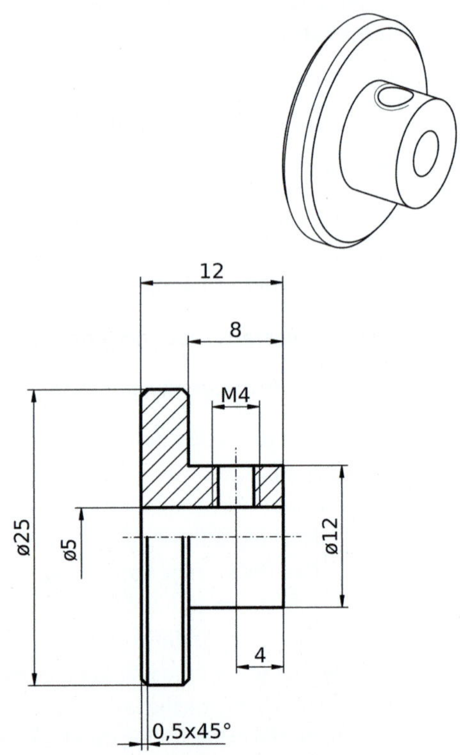

handwheel

Which parts (1–5) of the turning machine on page 41 do the drawings match?

FILE 15: Unit 7, Part A, exercise 1C

Partner A

You and your partner have the same schematic on which five different components have been ringed. Take it in turns to ask each other questions, using the useful phrases.

> **Asking about schematics**
>
> What's the component in square E5/H6/... ?
> What is it attached to?
> Where is the ... ?
> How many ... are there in the circuit?
> Where is it / are they?
> What is there between square ... and square ... ?

Amplifier

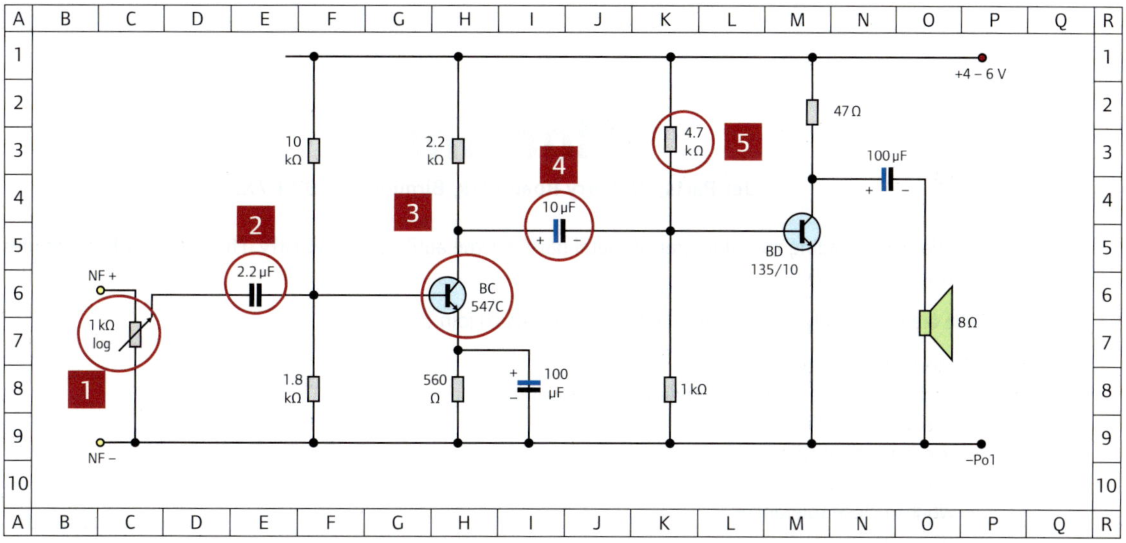

FILE 16: Unit 10, Part B, exercise 5

Partner B

You are a mechatronics technician at your own training company. (Use your own name.) You call Galway Electrics in Ireland to order a new electric motor.

Use the prompts below to role-play a telephone conversation with the salesperson at Galway Electrics (Partner A).

PARTNER B

(Partner A answers the phone.)
- Introduce yourself (full name, company).
- Explain that you need to order an electric motor. A motor is losing power quickly.
- Invent an application for the motor, e.g. a crane/pump, etc.
- Improvise answers to Partner A's questions using a nameplate from page 106 or your own training company.
- Ask about the price and delivery date.
- End the call politely.

The Hybrid Power Solution

Firefly solves the problem of temporary power. Combining existing diesel generators with battery storage systems has a number of benefits including:

Reduced operating costs

Hybrid power can reduce fuel consumption by up to 30% and reduce maintenance of the diesel generator by 50%.

Lower environmental impact

A hybrid system can reduce carbon emissions by up to 30% compared to using a diesel generator. Local residents and staff can also benefit from silent operation and no exhaust fumes.

Cygnus Hybrid Power Generator (HPG) 12–24 kVA

Product Overview

Firefly is proud to announce the latest member of the family. Cygnus HPG is an extremely versatile power solution for a wide range of temporary applications including live events, broadcast, construction and disaster response. The HPG can deliver single or 3-phase 415 V, with integral transfer switching that moves between external and inverter power – avoiding the need to run twin diesel sets for UPS.

With significant storage, the intermittent nature of renewable energy sources is no longer a concern. Auxiliary control function is determined by flexible user-defined parameters, such as maximum battery discharge and load.

Product Features

- Up to 24 kVA 240 V 50 Hz continuous output
- 72 kVA peak output (5 seconds)
- 48 kWh usable stored energy
- IP 44 rated
- Rental specification
- Backup or stand-alone operation
- Remote generator start
- Lifting ring & forklift pockets
- Compact design
- Pure sine wave output
- One-piece lift canopy
- Easy access for maintenance
- Buzz bar for hard wiring
- RCD/MCB protection

Options

- Power storage extender pack (12 kWh)
- Solar prep
- Remote monitoring kit
- Road tow
- Harsh environment kit (hot)
- Harsh environment kit (cold)
- 110 V/60 Hz inverter

Benefits

- Reduces carbon emissions by up to 30%
- Reduces fuel consumption by up to 30%
- Reduces maintenance costs by 50%
- Truly silent – zero noise
- Zero emissions in stand-alone mode
- 2-year standard warranty

1 Wann ist es sinnvoll, den hier beschriebenen Generator einzusetzen?
2 Warum wird der Generator als Hybrid bezeichnet?
3 Um wie viel ist der hier beschriebene Generator sparsamer als ein herkömmlicher?
4 Warum wird der Einsatz eines solchen Generators von Bevölkerung und Personal begrüßt?
5 Welche Leistungen hat ein Cygnus HPG?
6 Warum ist es beim Cygnus HPG nicht notwendig, zwei Dieselmotoren zu haben, um unterbrechungsfreie Stromversorgung (UPS) zu gewährleisten?
7 Welche Parameter kann der Benutzer dieses Geräts selber einstellen?
8 Welche Sicherheitsvorkehrungen hat das Gerät?
9 Erläutern Sie drei der aufgeführten Produkteigenschaften unter der Überschrift ‚Product Features'.
10 Woher weiß man, dass das Gerät auch unter extremen Witterungsverhältnissen eingesetzt werden kann?

Mediation

Sie arbeiten für eine Bühnentechnikfirma, die ihren Kunden umweltfreundliche Lösungen anbietet. Ihr Geschäftsführer bittet Sie, über die britische Firma Firefly Solar Generators Limited Auskünfte einzuholen und insbesondere herauszufinden, ob deren Aggregate für größere Events geeignet sind. Sie finden auf der Webseite von Firefly untenstehenden Bericht über ein Festival, das die Firma mit Strom versorgt hat.

Übertragen Sie die wichtigsten Inhalte des Berichts ins Deutsche.

Lowlands Festival – solar powered eco-houses

PROJECT SUMMARY

Essent Energy, the largest producer of renewable power in the Benelux countries, needed an environmentally friendly and sustainable means of powering the Lowlands interactive experience festival – the largest in the Netherlands. Firefly Solar Generators Limited, UK installed a 15 kVA solar unit which provided enough power for the whole event.

BACKGROUND

Lowlands is an annual music festival located in the Netherlands. The festival is one of the biggest in the country with over 60,000 visitors, 200 acts and more than ten stages every year. Lowlands festival started in 1967 and has since hosted some of the world's most famous alternative acts and musicians. Lowlands not only provides music but also a wide variety of acts, including stand-up comedy, film, visual arts, literature and theatre.

Essent Energy is the leading producer of sustainable energy in the Netherlands and always uses the most affordable, reliable and sustainable means possible. It looks for solutions that are better for people, the environment and society as a whole.

TASK & SOLUTION

Essent Energy were unable to locate a suitable supplier in the Netherlands or elsewhere in mainland Europe, so they contacted Firefly, UK to enquire about a renewable energy solution to power a large, interactive exhibition.

Firefly quickly decided that its 'Fold Array' was ideal for this project, and designed a sustainable power distribution system combining three of its Orion generators and a number of Fold Arrays. The Fold Arrays were adapted to be mounted on the roofs of the flat-pack houses built by Essent for their interactive experience.

RESULTS

Lowland's 60,000 festival attendees saved a total of 37,821 kg of CO_2 demonstrating how the green festival movement is now spreading across international borders and how willing and enthusiastic the public are to take responsibility and make a difference.

Produktion

Ihre Firma, Bühnentechnik Funlight GmbH in Freiburg, interessiert sich für den Stromgenerator der britischen Firma Firefly Solar Generators Limited.

Schreiben Sie im eigenen Namen als Projektleiter/in eine E-Mail-Anfrage an info@fireflysolar.co.uk unter Berücksichtigung folgender Punkte:

- Sie haben die Webseite der britischen Firma im Internet gesehen.
- Kurzbeschreibung Ihrer Firma: mittelständisches Unternehmen; Versorgung von Festivals mit Bühnentechnik; überall in Europa tätig
- Interesse an Cygnus HPG Generator
- Bitte um nähere Beschreibung des Geräts
- Bitte um Preisangabe bei Vermietung und Kauf
- Lieferzeit? Lieferbedingungen?
- Bei einem günstigen Mietangebot wird Ihr Unternehmen ein Gerät für eine Woche mieten und evtl. bei Entsprechung Ihrer Erwartungen anschließend kaufen.
- Höfliche Schlussformel

Mündliche Prüfung

Die Prüfung ist eine Gruppenprüfung, bei der Sie Gespräche persönlichen und fachlichen Inhalts in der Fremdsprache führen sollen. Es wird von Ihnen erwartet, dass Sie der vorgegebenen Situation entsprechend sprachlich agieren und reagieren. Es kommt dabei vor allem darauf an, dass Sie sich spontan äußern, dass Sie versuchen, sich verständlich zu machen, und dass Sie gut zuhören.

Die Prüfung besteht aus zwei Teilen und dauert insgesamt ca. 20 Minuten. Sie erhalten eine angemessene Vorbereitungszeit, wenn die Aufgabe dies verlangt.

Im **ersten Teil** der mündlichen Prüfung werden Sie gebeten, sich zu persönlichen oder beruflichen Themen zu äußern.

Im **zweiten Teil** sollen Sie zusammen mit einem/einer anderen Kandidaten/Kandidatin ein Rollenspiel durchführen. Dazu erhalten Sie vom Prüfer / von der Prüferin Rollenkarten, auf denen eine Situation beschrieben ist, die Sie vorspielen sollen.

Hilfsmittel: allgemeines zweisprachiges Wörterbuch

Mündliche Prüfung Teil I

Erzählen Sie uns etwas über ...

- sich selbst und Ihre Familie.
- die Firma, in der Sie Ihre Ausbildung machen.
- Ihre Berufsschule.
- Ihre Hobbys.
- Ihre Pläne für die Zukunft.
- wo sie beruflich gerne in fünf Jahren wären.

Mündliche Prüfung Teil II

Es ist Winter. Ihre Chefin teilt Ihnen und Ihrem Partner / Ihrer Partnerin mit, dass Sie morgen früh nach Schottland fliegen müssen, um dort dringende Reparaturen am Stromgenerator eines entlegenen Hotels im schottischen Hochland bei Inverness vorzunehmen. Ihre Firma hatte vor einigen Jahren dort einen Generator installiert, der nun jedoch unter extremen Witterungsverhältnissen gelegentlich aussetzt. Ein Mietwagen wird morgen für Sie am Flughafen Edinburgh bereitstehen.

Besprechen Sie mit Ihrem Partner / Ihrer Partnerin ...

- welche Dokumente Sie für Ihre Reise nach Schottland benötigen.
- welche Werkzeuge Sie auf jeden Fall mitnehmen werden.
- welche Werkzeuge Sie evtl. nachschicken lassen werden.
- was Sie sonst noch alles an Kleidung und Toilettenartikeln mitnehmen werden.
- weitere Angaben nach Wahl.

Scottish Highlands

Useful phrases

Describing your company	Unit 1
– We are a small family business / medium-sized company in the automotive sector.	– *Wir sind ein kleiner Familienbetrieb / ein mittelständisches Unternehmen in der Automobilbranche.*
– The company is based in …	– *Das Unternehmen hat seinen Sitz in …*
– We manufacture components for the … industry.	– *Wir fertigen Bauteile für die …-Industrie.*
– We supply/produce machines for customers in the … sector.	– *Wir liefern/produzieren Maschinen für Kunden in der …-Branche.*
– Our products are used in …	– *Unsere Produkte werden in … eingesetzt.*
– We install/manufacture/export …	– *Wir installieren/fertigen/exportieren …*
– The company maintains / carries out …	– *Das Unternehmen hält … instand / führt … aus.*

Making introductions	Unit 1
Greeting people you do not know	
– Good morning/afternoon/evening. I'm …	– *Guten Morgen/Tag/Abend. Ich bin …*
– How do you do? My name is …	– *Freut mich. Mein Name ist …*
– Nice/Pleased to meet you.	– *Es freut mich, Sie kennenzulernen.*
– Nice to meet you, too.	– *Ganz meinerseits.*
– Excuse me. Are you … ?	– *Entschuldigung. Sind Sie … ?*
– Yes, I am. / No, I'm not. I'm …	– *Ja, das bin ich. / Nein, das bin ich nicht. Ich heiße …*
– Welcome to …	– *Herzlich willkommen in/bei …*
– Thank you. It's nice to be here.	– *Dankeschön. Es ist schön, hier zu sein.*
Introducing people	
– This is … . / These are my colleagues, John and Mary.	– *Das ist … / Das sind meine Kollegen, John und Mary.*
– I'd like to introduce … from the … department.	– *Darf ich Ihnen … aus der …-Abteilung vorstellen?*

Showing visitors around the company	Unit 1
Giving a tour of the company	
– Let's start by visiting …	– *Lassen Sie uns mit dem Besuch der/des … beginnen.*
– Here we have the … department.	– *Hier haben wir die Abteilung …*
– On the left/right, you can see …	– *Zu Ihrer Linken/Rechten sehen Sie …*
– This is where we make/assemble …	– *Hier stellen wir … her / bauen wir … zusammen.*
Asking for and giving directions	
– Could you tell me the way to …, please?	– *Könnten Sie mir bitte sagen, wie ich nach / zu/r/m … komme?*
– Yes, certainly.	– *Ja, selbstverständlich.*
– Go down the corridor until you get to …	– *Gehen Sie den Flur entlang, bis Sie zu/r/m … kommen.*
– Turn left at the first/second/last door on your right.	– *Nehmen Sie die erste/zweite/letzte Tür rechts.*
– Turn right at the end of the corridor.	– *Biegen Sie am Ende des Flures rechts ab.*
Offering help/refreshments	
– Can I take your coat?	– *Möchten Sie Ihren Mantel ablegen?*
– Would you like something to drink?	– *Darf ich Ihnen etwas zu trinken anbieten?*
– Would you like some tea/coffee/water?	– *Möchten Sie Tee/Kaffee/Wasser?*

Describing your job	Unit 2
– I work in a workshop/factory.	– *Ich arbeite in einer Werkstatt/Fabrik.*
– I install/test/replace/inspect …	– *Ich installiere/teste/ersetze/kontrolliere …*
– I maintain/repair machines.	– *Ich warte/repariere Maschinen.*
– I diagnose problems/faults.	– *Ich stelle Probleme/Fehler fest.*
– I advise customers.	– *Ich berate Kunden/Kundinnen.*

Writing business letters	Unit 9
Salutation	
– Dear Sir or Madam (*to a firm*)	– *Sehr geehrte Damen und Herren,*
– Dear Mr Brown	– *Sehr geehrter Herr Brown,*
– Dear Sharon	– *Liebe Sharon,*
Complimentary close	
– Yours faithfully (*BE: to a firm*)	– *Mit freundlichen Grüßen*
– Yours very truly / Cordially yours (*AE: to a firm*)	– *Mit freundlichen Grüßen*
– Yours sincerely (*BE*)	– *Mit freundlichen Grüßen*
– Sincerely yours / Best personal regards (*AE*)	– *Mit freundlichen Grüßen / Beste Grüße*

Writing enquiries	Unit 9
Source of address	
– We saw your advertisement/brochure/catalogue in …	– *Wir haben Ihre/n Anzeige/Prospekt/Katalog in … gesehen.*
– We visited your stand/presentation at the trade fair in …	– *Wir haben Ihren Stand / Ihre Präsentation auf der Messe in … besucht.*
About your firm	
– We are a small/medium-sized company in the … sector.	– *Wir sind ein kleiner/mittelständischer Betrieb in der …-Branche.*
– We are interested in your … (products).	– *Wir interessieren uns für Ihre … (Produkte).*
What you require	
– Please send us samples of your … / your latest catalogue.	– *Bitte schicken Sie uns Muster/Proben Ihrer … / aus Ihrem aktuellen Katalog.*
– Please give us / let us have a quotation for … / details of all discounts.	– *Bitte schicken Sie uns / machen Sie uns ein Angebot für … / informieren Sie uns zu allen Einzelheiten Ihrer Rabatte.*
– Full details of your terms of delivery and payment would be appreciated.	– *Wir würden uns freuen, genaue Informationen zu Ihren Versand- und Zahlungsbedingungen zu erhalten.*
References	
– References can be obtained from … (name of bank/company).	– *Referenzen können von … (Name der Bank/Firma) angefordert werden.*
Polite ending	
– If your products find our customers' approval, …	– *Wenn Ihre Produkte unseren Kunden zusagen, …*
– … we will be able to place a sizeable order very soon.	– *… werden wir in naher Zukunft eine größere Bestellung in Auftrag geben.*
– We look forward to hearing from you soon / receiving your offer within the next few days.	– *Wir würden uns freuen, bald von Ihnen zu hören / Ihr Angebot in den nächsten Tagen zu erhalten.*

Writing offers	Unit 9, Unit 10
Reference to enquiry	
– Many thanks for your letter of … (date) enquiring about … (*general enquiry*)	– *Vielen Dank für Ihren Brief vom … (Datum) mit Ihrer Anfrage bzgl. …*
– We refer to your enquiry of … (date) for … (*specific enquiry*)	– *Wir beziehen uns auf Ihre Anfrage vom … (Datum) bzgl. …*
Reference to information, samples, etc.	
– Enclosed (please find) our latest brochure / catalogue / price list.	– *Anbei finden Sie unsere(n) aktuelle(n) Prospekt/Katalog/Preisliste.*
– We are sending you a selection of samples.	– *Wir übersenden Ihnen eine Auswahl an Mustern/Proben.*

Terms	
– We would like to point out that our prices are quoted DAP / EXW / …	– *Wir möchten darauf hinweisen, dass sich unsere Preise DAP / EXW / … verstehen.*
– We draw your attention to the fact that our guarantee/warranty period extends over … / is valid for …	– *Wir möchten Sie darauf hinweisen, dass unser Garantie-/Haftungszeitraum … beträgt.*
– Terms of payment: we offer a …% cash discount for payment within … days.	– *Zahlungsbedingungen: Bei Zahlung innerhalb von … Tagen gewähren wir … % Skonto.*
– For orders over … we offer a discount of …%.	– *Für Bestellungen über … räumen wir einen (Mengen-) Rabatt von … % ein.*
Further information	
– Our delivery date is approximately … days/weeks after receipt of your order.	– *Die Lieferung erfolgt etwa … Tage/Wochen nach Eingang Ihrer Bestellung.*
– Delivery time is about … weeks/months.	– *Der Lieferzeitraum beträgt etwa … Wochen/Monate.*
– We can guarantee immediate delivery.	– *Wir können Ihnen eine sofortige Lieferung garantieren.*
Polite ending	
– We look forward to receiving your order and assure you that we will give it our prompt and careful attention.	– *Wir freuen uns auf Ihre Bestellung und sichern Ihnen eine zügige und gewissenhafte Abwicklung zu.*

Writing orders	Unit 10
– Thank you for your quotation of …	– *Vielen Dank für Ihr Angebot für …*
– Many thanks for your quotation.	– *Vielen Dank für Ihr Angebot.*
– We agree to your terms and are pleased to give you an order for …	– *Wir stimmen Ihren Bedingungen zu und freuen uns, Sie mit einer Bestellung über … zu beauftragen.*
– We enclose / are enclosing order no. …	– *Wir fügen Bestellnr. … bei.*
– We understand that all prices are DAP / EXW / … / include VAT.	– *Wir sind uns bewusst, dass sich alle Preise DAP / EXW / … / inklusive Mehrwertsteuer verstehen.*
– Payment will be made by … (method of payment) on delivery of the goods.	– *Die Zahlung erfolgt durch … (Zahlungsmethode) bei Lieferung der Ware(n).*
– Payment will be made within … days of receipt of the goods.	– *Die Zahlung erfolgt innerhalb von … Tagen nach Eingang der Ware(n).*
– Please acknowledge this order by return of post.	– *Bitte bestätigen Sie diese Bestellung postwendend.*
– We look forward to receiving the goods as soon as possible.	– *Wir würden uns freuen, die Ware(n) sobald wie möglich zu erhalten.*
– We trust you will give this order your prompt/careful attention.	– *Wir erwarten eine zügige/gewissenhafte Abwicklung dieser Bestellung.*

Making complaints	Unit 11
Situation	
– With reference to our order number … which arrived / was due on … (date), …	– *Mit Bezug auf unsere Bestellnummer …, die am … (Datum) eingetroffen ist / fällig war, …*
– I'm sorry to have to inform you that …	– *Leider müssen wir Ihnen mitteilen, dass …*
– When we opened the containers/boxes, we discovered/saw that …	– *Beim Öffnen der Behälter/Container bemerkten/sahen wir, dass …*
– … some/all of the items/parts were broken/damaged/missing.	– *… einige der / alle Artikel/Teile kaputt/beschädigt waren / fehlten.*
– While testing the equipment, we saw that it was not working properly / it became apparent that it was not up to standard.	– *Beim Testen des Geräts / der Geräte stellten wir fest / stellte sich heraus, dass es/sie nicht funktionierte(n) / es/sie den Anforderungen nicht entsprach(en).*

Request

- Please investigate the matter as soon as possible. – *Bitte untersuchen Sie diese Angelegenheit so schnell wie möglich.*
- Please let us know what can be done to solve this problem. – *Bitte teilen Sie uns mit, welche Maßnahmen getroffen werden können, um dieses Problem zu beheben.*
- Could you please explain (why) ... ? – *Könnten Sie bitte erklären (warum) ... ?*

Reason

- We have a large order from a regular customer, which we have to fill quickly. – *Wir haben eine große Bestellung eines Stammkunden, die wir schnell ausführen müssen.*
- We are unable to continue production until we have the equipment. – *Wir können mit der Produktion nicht fortfahren, solange die Geräte nicht da sind.*
- If we do not receive the goods within the next ... days, we will have to stop production. – *Wenn wir die Ware nicht innerhalb der nächsten ... Tage erhalten, müssen wir die Produktion einstellen.*

Polite ending

- We hope to receive your answer / an explanation immediately / without delay / by ... (date). – *Wir hoffen auf Ihre sofortige Antwort/Erklärung / bis zum ... (Datum).*
- We must point out that our further business relationship will depend on a satisfactory solution to the problem. – *Wir müssen darauf hinweisen, dass unsere weitere Zusammenarbeit von einer zufriedenstellenden Lösung des Problems abhängt.*

Dealing with complaints — Unit 11

Polite opening

- We are very sorry (to hear) that the goods arrived damaged/broken/late. – *Wir bedauern sehr, dass die Ware bei Ihnen beschädigt/kaputt/verspätet eingetroffen ist.*
- We are very sorry (to learn) that you have received faulty/damaged / the wrong goods. – *Es tut uns sehr leid, dass Sie mangelhafte/ schadhafte / die falsche Ware erhalten haben.*
- Please accept our sincere apologies. – *Wir bitten vielmals um Entschuldigung.*
- We apologize for the inconvenience caused. – *Wir entschuldigen uns vielmals für die entstandenen Unannehmlichkeiten.*

Reason

- Unfortunately, there was a mix-up in our sales department. – *Leider ist es in unserer Vertriebsabteilung zu einer Verwechslung gekommen.*
- We are sorry to say that one of our staff was ill and could not complete the order. – *Leider war einer unserer Mitarbeiter krank und konnte daher die Bestellung nicht bearbeiten.*
- The damage was caused by bad handling in transit / a problem with the packing. – *Der Schaden ist durch mangelhafte Abfertigung während des Transports / ein Problem bei der Verpackung entstanden.*
- We have had some problems with new software but these have now been solved. – *Wir hatten einige Probleme mit der neuen Software, aber diese konnten behoben werden.*

Action taken

- We have sent a replacement consignment by courier / by express delivery which you will receive by ... at the latest. – *Wir haben Ihnen per Kurierdienst/Expressversand eine Ersatzlieferung geschickt, die Sie spätestens bis ... erhalten werden.*

Polite ending

- We hope that we can continue our successful business relationship, despite this problem. – *Wir hoffen sehr, dass wir trotz dieses Problems unsere erfolgreiche Zusammenarbeit fortsetzen können.*
- We assure you that we will make every effort to ensure there are no problems in the future. – *Wir versichern Ihnen, dass wir alles tun werden, um derartige Probleme in Zukunft zu vermeiden.*
- We hope that this solution solves the problem to your satisfaction. – *Wir hoffen, dass diese Lösung das Problem zu Ihrer Zufriedenheit behebt.*
- Don't hesitate to contact us again if you have any further difficulties. – *Bitte kontaktieren Sie uns, sollten Sie weitere Schwierigkeiten haben.*

Writing a covering letter — Unit 12

Opening phrases	
– With reference to your advertisement in … (newspaper) of … (date), …	– *Bezugnehmend auf Ihre Ausschreibung in … (Zeitung) vom … (Datum), …*
– I would like / wish to apply for the above-mentioned position/post of … (job).	– *Hiermit möchte ich mich für die oben genannte Stelle als … (Berufsbezeichnung) bewerben.*
Education/Training / Present employment	
– I attended … (school/college) for … (length of time).	– *Von … bis … (Jahr) besuchte ich (Schule/ Hochschule).*
– I studied … (subjects) at vocational school in … (town/city) from … (date) to … (date).	– *An der Berufs(fach)schule in … (Ort) lernte/belegte ich … (Fächer) von … (Datum) bis … (Datum).*
– At present I am working for a(n)… (type of company) as a(n)… (job).	– *Zurzeit arbeite ich für eine / bei einer … (Firmenbezeichnung) als … (Berufsbezeichnung).*
– I will complete my period of training on … (date).	– *Am … (Datum) werde ich meine Ausbildung abschließen.*
Closing paragraph	
– I enclose / Enclosed is my CV/résumé / a list of my qualifications and experience.	– *Anbei finden Sie meinen Lebenslauf / eine Übersicht meiner Qualifikationen und Erfahrungen.*
– I am available for interview at your earliest convenience.	– *Für ein Vorstellungsgespräch stehe ich Ihnen jederzeit gern zur Verfügung.*
– I hope you will consider my application favourably and …	– *Über eine positive Antwort freue ich mich sehr und …*
– … (I) look forward to hearing from you in the near future.	– *… (ich) freue mich darauf, von Ihnen bald zu hören.*

G Grammar

Simple present

1 I **work** for a mechanical engineering company. I **maintain** and **repair** machines.
2 The company **produces** components for the automobile industry.
3 The new milling machine **doesn't work** when you switch on the power.

- Das *simple present* wird für wiederholte, oft regelmäßige Handlungen in der Gegenwart verwendet.
- Signalwörter: *regularly, sometimes, often, always, normally* usw.
- Manche Verben, die keine Handlung, sondern einen Zustand ausdrücken (*need, like, want, hate, love, know, believe*), stehen (fast) ausschließlich im *simple present*.
- In der 3. Person (*he, she, it, Peter, the firm* usw.) wird ein *-s* angefügt (2).
- Verneinungen werden mit *doesn't/don't* gebildet (3).

Present progressive

1 One of our customers **is** currently **having** a problem with the power supply.
2 The mechatronics technicians **are looking** at the plans on their laptop.

- Das *present progressive* wird gebraucht, wenn man gerade ablaufende oder noch nicht abgeschlossene Handlungen beschreibt.
- Signalwörter: *at the moment, (right) now, just, currently* usw.

Questions and short answers

1 **Do** you **use** a digital multimeter often? – Yes, I **do**. / No, I **don't**.
2 **Did** you **make** the voltage meter yourself? – Yes, I **did**. / No, I **didn't**.
3 **Can** you **carry** it in your pocket? – Yes, you **can**. / No, you **can't**.
4 **Is** it small? – Yes, it **is**. / No, it **isn't**.
5 **When/Why/How did** you **change** the fuse?

- Fragen im *simple present* werden mit *do/does* gebildet (1).
- Fragen im *simple past* werden mit *did* gebildet (2, 5).
- In Sätzen mit Hilfsverben (*is/have/can/will/should/...*) bildet man Fragen, indem man das Hilfsverb des Aussagesatzes vor das Subjekt stellt (3, 4).
- Kurzantworten bestehen aus *yes/no* + Personalpronomen + Hilfsverb (+ *n't*) (1–4).
- Fragewörter stehen immer am Anfang des Fragesatzes (5).

Imperatives

1 **Do not / Don't block** emergency exits.
2 **Keep** emergency stop buttons free.
3 **Switch off** machinery before you remove the safety cover.
4 **Never touch** a live power cable.

- Man verwendet den Imperativ für Hinweise, Befehle, Warnungen und Erklärungen.
- Der Imperativ ist die Grundform (= Infinitiv) des Verbs. Man verwendet die gleiche Form, wenn man zu einer oder mehreren Personen spricht (2, 3).
- Negativformen werden mit *do not* bzw. *don't* gebildet (1).
- Bei Negativformen mit *never* entfällt *don't* (4).

Simple past

1 I **talked** to my supervisor about the job last week.
2 Yesterday I **made** a workpiece on a CNC milling machine.
3 I **didn't finish** it until late in the afternoon.
4 What time **did** you **start** work?
5 My first day at work **was** a disaster.

- Das *simple past* verwendet man, um zu sagen, wann etwas geschehen ist (1, 2, 3), oder um über Vergangenes zu berichten.
- Signalwörter: *yesterday, last week, two days ago, in 1998, When ...?* usw.
- Bei den regelmäßigen Verben wird im *simple past* in allen Personen *-(e)d* angehängt.
- Verneinungen und Fragen werden in allen Personen mit *did/didn't* gebildet.
- Eine Liste der unregelmäßigen Verben befindet sich auf S. 230.

Past progressive

1 I **was working** in a factory last week.
2 I **was standing** on a ladder when a colleague **bumped** into it and I **fell** off.

- Mit dem *past progressive* drückt man aus, dass eine Handlung oder ein Vorgang zu einer bestimmten Zeit in der Vergangenheit gerade im Verlauf war (1).
- Es beschreibt oft eine Handlung, die gerade im Verlauf war, als eine zweite Handlung einsetzte. Die zweite Handlung steht im *simple past* (2).

Present perfect

1 He **has worked** here for six months.
2 They **haven't found** the cause of the problem yet.
3 I**'ve talked** to her twice today.
4 **Have** you **been able to** repair the motor?

- Mit dem *present perfect* sagt man, dass (nicht: wann!) etwas geschehen ist. Man drückt damit auch aus, seit wann oder wie lange ein Zustand schon andauert.
- Signalwörter (Zeitadverbien): *for two years, this week, since 2017, already, yet* usw. Sie benennen einen Zeitraum, auf den sich der Satz bezieht und der bis in die Gegenwart reicht.

Future with *will* and *going to*

1 I think the installation **will take** about two days.
2 **I'll (will) order** the spare parts this afternoon.
3 We **won't (will not) need** the spare parts until next week.
4 We**'re going to replace** the electric motor tomorrow.
5 This old motor **is going to break down** soon.

- *Will* wird verwendet, um Vorhersagen zu machen oder Vermutungen über die Zukunft auszudrücken (1).
- *Will* wird für spontane Entscheidungen, Angebote und Versprechen verwendet (2).
- Im gesprochenen Englisch lautet die Verneinung *won't*, ansonsten *will not* (3).
- *Be going to* (+ Infinitiv des Verbs) wird verwendet, um über Pläne oder Absichten zu sprechen (4), oder wenn die Gewissheit (oder ein Anzeichen dafür) besteht, dass etwas geschehen wird (5).

Passive forms

1 The machine **is bolted** to the floor.
2 The new power unit **was installed** on Tuesday morning.
3 The cables **have** already **been laid** under the floor.
4 The desktop CNC milling machine **could be bought** on the internet.
5 The control unit **will be installed by** us as part of our service.

- Das Passiv wird oft verwendet, wenn man auf eher unpersönliche Art und Weise über Fakten, Vorgänge und Zahlen berichtet.
- Das Passiv wird mit der entsprechenden Form von *be* + Partizip Perfekt (3. Verbform) gebildet. Es können alle Zeiten gebildet werden.
- Passivsätze mit modalen Hilfsverben werden mit einem modalen Hilfsverb + *be* + Partizip Perfekt (3. Verbform) gebildet (4).
- „Von" und „durch" werden in Passivsätzen durch *by* ausgedrückt (5).

Conditional sentences

1 Type 0: If it **trips** the switch, it **turns on** the alarm.
2 Type 1: If you **touch** the overhead power cable, you **will get** an electric shock.
3 Type 2: If there **was** a short circuit, the circuit breaker **would trip**.
4 Type 2: **I wouldn't do** that **if** I **was/were** you.

- Bedingungen, die allgemeingültig sind bzw. die immer eintreffen, werden mit einem *if*-Satz des Typs 0 ausgedrückt. Hier sind beide Satzteile im *simple present*.
- Ein *if*-Satz des Typs 1 drückt eine Bedingung aus, die der Sprecher für durchaus möglich oder wahrscheinlich hält. Der damit verbundene Hauptsatz drückt eine Vorhersage aus, die je nach Situation als Warnung, Versprechen o. ä. zu verstehen ist (2).
- Durch einen *if*-Satz des Typs 2 gibt der Sprecher seinem Gesprächspartner einen Ratschlag oder teilt ihm mit, dass er die Erfüllung der Bedingung für unmöglich, unwahrscheinlich (3) oder nicht wünschenswert (4) hält.
- Steht der *if*-Nebensatz an erster Stelle, wird er durch ein Komma vom Hauptsatz abgetrennt (1, 2, 3).

Verb + *to*-infinitive or *-ing* form

1 I enjoy **working** in a team.
2 I expect **to qualify** as a mechatronics technician in June.
3 I love **repairing / to repair** old cars.
4 I'd love **to have** the chance to work on a big production line.
5 I'm interested in **getting** some work experience abroad.

- Auf eine Gruppe von Verben folgt immer die *-ing*-Form (1). Zu diesen Verben gehören *dislike, enjoy, finish, give up, imagine, involve, keep, mind, miss, practise, risk, stop, suggest*.
- Auf eine zweite Gruppe von Verben folgt immer ein *to*-Infinitiv (2). Zu diesen Verben gehören *agree, arrange, choose, decide, expect, hope, learn, offer, plan, promise, want*.
- Auf eine dritte Gruppe von Verben kann sowohl die *-ing*-Form als auch ein *to*-Infinitiv folgen (3). Zu diesen Verben gehören *begin, continue, hate, like, love, prefer, start*.
- Nach *would hate, would like, would love* and *would prefer* (Kurzform *'d like* usw.) steht nur der *to*-Infinitiv. (4)
- Nach einer Präposition kommt immer die *-ing*-Form (5).

Gerunds

1 [illegible] e is a lot of variety in my job.
2 [illegible] ends?
3 [illegible] gear.
4 [illegible] the circuit.

- [illegible] s) kann die Rolle eines Nomens übernehmen.
- [illegible] bjekt (2) oder nach Präpositionen (3, 4) verwendet werden.

Relative clauses

1 [illegible] hat enable goods to enter other countries.
2 [illegible] international standards.
3 [illegible] was defect.
4 [illegible] follow these regulations.
5 [illegible] s harmonized the rules worldwide.

- [illegible] in.
- [illegible] t notwendigen Relativsatz. Notwendige Relativsätze sind für das Verständnis des Satzes unbedingt erforderlich (1, 2, 3, 4) und stehen ohne Komma. Nicht notwendige Relativsätze geben lediglich Zusatzinformationen und werden durch Kommata getrennt (5).
- In notwendigen Relativsätzen kann das Relativpronomen wegfallen, wenn es Objekt ist, d. h. wenn im Relativsatz ein Subjekt steht (3).

Adjectives and adverbs

1 Repairing the assembly robot is an **easy** job.
2 We need it to be fixed **quickly**.
3 It's **really** hard to get the settings right.
4 Can it be fixed **easily**?
5 I don't speak German very **well**.

- Man verwendet Adjektive, um Personen oder Sachen näher zu beschreiben (1).
- Adverbien beziehen sich auf Verben (2, 4, 5) oder Adjektive (3).
- Adverbien haben in der Regel eine andere Form als Adjektive. Man fügt normalerweise die Endung *-ly* an das Adjektiv an (2, 3). Endet das Adjektiv auf *-y*, wird die Endung zu *-ily* (4).
- Das Adverb von *good* lautet *well* (5).

Much, many, a lot (of)

1 How **much** time do you spend answering emails?
2 How **many** text messages do you get at work every day?
3 I get **a lot of** text messages. **Lots of** them are instructions from my supervisor.
4 We have **too many** meetings at work. We waste **too much** time on them.

- *Much* verwendet man nur bei nicht-zählbaren Nomen, z.B. *time*. (1)
- *Many* verwendet man nur bei Nomen im Plural. (2)
- *Much* und *many* werden meist in verneinten Aussagesätzen und in Fragen verwendet. In bejahten Aussagesätzen ist *a lot of* bzw. *lots of* gebräuchlicher. (3)
- Nach *too, so, as, very* und *how* werden immer *much* und *many* verwendet. (4)

Thomas	Yes, we do. We make them in the next workshop, which is the metal workshop. It's next door to the copper workshop just over here. Here in the metal workshop we have another special machine to cut the metal, and you can also see three welding bays over there by the wall, which is where we join the panels
Stig	Very impressive! I thought you would buy these parts from an external supplier.
Thomas	No, we make them ourselves, so we can guarantee the quality of the product. OK, let's now walk back the way we came to the last workshop I want to show you. We first have to walk by the testing section. Over there on our left you can see the lathes and some more welding equipment, and now we're in the assembly, wiring and training workshop.
Stig	Assembly, wiring and *training*. Does that mean you train your apprentices here?
Thomas	Yes, we have a master electrician who shows them how to do basic installation work. Over there, for example, you can see two practice installation boards on the wall. The apprentices use them to practise wiring. Our last stop is the break room, where we can sit down and talk to some of the apprentices.
Stig	Great idea! By the way, do you have a design department?
Thomas	Yes, the design department is in a separate building outside the factory. I can show it to you later. Now what would you like, tea or coffee?

Track 6: Unit 1, Communication, exercise 1A

Martyna	Hello. I'm Martyna Nowak. I'm 42. I was born in Poland. I'm a line manager.
Halil	Good morning. My name is Halil Özdemir. I'm 29 years old. I was born in Germany. I'm a training supervisor.
Deema	Good afternoon. My name is Deema Mansour. I'm 19. I was born in Syria. I'm an apprentice.
Robert	Hallo. I'm Robert Klein. I'm 21. I was born in Austria. I'm a skilled worker.
Canan	Hallo. I'm Canan Tolon. I'm 25 years old. I was born in Turkey. I'm a CAD engineer.
Alexei	Good morning. My name is Alexei Melnyk. I'm 39 years old. I was born in Ukraine. I'm an electrical engineer.

Track 7: Unit 2, Foundation, exercise 1A

Soldering, testing, routine maintenance checks – these are just three of the jobs you might be doing in workshop. We all enjoy what we're doing there, but there could be some dangers attached to the work. Take soldering for example. The tip of a soldering iron is at a temperature around 300 to 350 degrees and can burn your skin. Apart from that, the soldering process gives off fumes and these fumes can be harmful if you're soldering for a long time.
Safety in the workshop is very important. ...
Now, the first thing I want to talk about is what you wear in the workshop. I'm talking about protective clothing – hard hats or overalls, for example. Now, I know that safety shoes might not look very cool, but you're given them for a reason – to keep you safe. Wear them!
Now, here are a few problems that might lead to accidents in your workshop. Sometimes, messiness can lead to minor accidents. I don't know how many times I've walked into a workshop and seen dirt and rubbish on the floor. Have a good look around your workshop and clean it up. Make sure everything is in the right place.
Another thing which is very dangerous – and I've seen this a few times, too – is when emergency cut out switches are covered or hidden by piles of boxes. If there's an emergency in the workshop, you need to be able to switch everything off quickly, so, the safety rule for emergency switches is: Keep them free!
Top-heavy shelving, now that's another dangerous thing. When you fill a shelf, put the heavy stuff at the bottom and light stuff at the top. It's a matter of common sense, really.
One of the biggest dangers I see is poor ventilation. Don't block the ventilators and open the windows, even in winter.
Now, as far as machinery or equipment is concerned, not using guards or screens or using damaged guards or screens or the wrong guards or screens can also cause trouble. And please, please, please, use the right tool for the job. Do not use a wrench as a hammer.
As I say, these are just a few of the problems. I'd like you now to work in groups and brainstorm a list of other things that might make your workshop a dangerous place.

Track 8: Unit 2, Part A, exercise 2C

Hi, I'm Jarek Król and I live and work for Everlight in Krakow in Poland. It's a beautiful city! I'm a machine maintenance technician, so I spend my time installing, checking, maintaining and repairing hi-tech machinery in our big factory here. There's always something to do in my job and even brand new machines sometimes break down and have to be repaired. It's also very important to maintain all machines regularly to minimize downtime.
The factory employs hundreds of workers and the plant operates 24 hours a day, seven days a week. An electrician always has to be on duty to deal with problems, so the other electricians and I work in three 8-hour shifts. Last month, I worked nights but I prefer the early and late shifts. I like my job because I enjoy troubleshooting and I have good promotion chances.

Track 9: Unit 2, Communication, exercise 4

Julie	Hamm Machines Ltd. Julie Matthews speaking.
Liam	Can I speak to Martin Brown in the workshop, please?
Julie	Who's calling please?
Liam	This is Liam Donnelly.
Julie	I'm sorry, could you spell your name, please?
Liam	It's L I A M D O double-N E double-L Y. I'm calling from Machine Tools in Manchester. It's about the drills Mr Brown ordered.
Julie	Thank you, Mr Donnelly. I'll try Mr Brown for you. Please hold the line.
Liam	Thank you.
Julie	Mr Donnelly. I'm sorry, Mr Brown is unavailable at the moment. Would you like to speak to someone else?
Liam	Yes. All right. Anyone in the workshop will do.
Julie	Thank you. I'll put you through.
Julie	I'm sorry, Mr Donnelly. I'm afraid the line is engaged. Would you like to leave a message for Mr Brown?
Liam	Yes, please. Would you tell Mr Brown that the drills he ordered aren't available and ask him to call me to discuss an alternative. My telephone number is 161 839 5005 and the extension is 822.
Julie	I'm sorry. I didn't understand. Could you repeat that, please?
Liam	Sure. It's 161 839 5005, extension 822.
Julie	Thank you, Mr Donnelly. I'll make sure that Mr Brown gets the message.

Track 10: KMK Exam practice 1, exercise 1, Hörverstehen

Good morning, everybody, and thank you for taking the time to come to this presentation. My name's Chuck Henderson. I work for Eaton Industries in Cleveland, Ohio and I'm here to tell you all about our corporation's activities in Germany.

Many of you will remember the famous German Moeller Group which was founded in Cologne in 1899. In the 1920s Hein Moeller introduced assembly line production. Today, the Moeller Group has its headquarters in Bonn and is fully owned by Eaton Industries. It's a great example of a successful German-American partnership.

The Moeller Group first became famous for its contactors. For those of you who are not experts, a contactor is an electrically controlled switch. Way back in the 1910s, Moeller was the first ever European manufacturer to make a three-phase *oil* contactor. It was a breakthrough discovery, and there were many more to come. Today we still sell a lot more than just contactors. Our range includes switchgear devices, foot and palm switches – you know those big red emergency on-off switches you see everywhere? – and programmable logic controllers. In addition to this, we have a wide range of relays and ground fault circuit interrupters – I believe you call them RCDs over here in Europe. In 2008 the Moeller Group, which by then was 100% owned by Eaton, brought out the first digital RCD and also introduced its SmartWire-DT system, which is an 8-pole flat cable which makes interconnecting all the electronic devices in a system a piece of cake. A piece of cake? Sorry, I should have said that the system makes interconnecting devices child's play. Anyone can do it.

Our turnover in Germany is now over a billion euros a year and we have a workforce of 8,600. Oh, and one more thing. We also sponsor a handball club called VfL Gummersbach. They're a great team!

Thanks for coming to the presentation. If you have any questions, please don't hesitate to ask them, and remember to visit our website.

Track 11: Unit 3, Foundation, exercise 1A

a I enjoy working with my vernier callipers. They're used for measuring thicknesses, inside diameters, outside diameters and depth. It's the best measuring tool ever. It's much more accurate than a normal ruler. That can only measure down to 1 millimetre, or maybe 0.5 millimetres if you have a good one. Good vernier callipers can measure within 0.1 millimetres. The second tool I like is my inspection mirror. I use it when I'm working on machines to check for screws and things that might have become loose during vibration testing. This is the most useful tool a mechatronics technician like me can have.

b I spend a lot of time on the factory floor, checking and repairing machinery and devices. If something's not working properly, I have to diagnose the problem – find out what's wrong – then I have to fix it. In this case, I use a multimeter that measures voltage, current and resistance or one that can measure the capacitance, inductance and current gain of transistors. That one's a very advanced, high-tech tool. At the other end of the scale, I often have to use a soldering iron which is a very simple tool. My father taught me how to use a soldering iron when I was a kid. He was a machine builder, too.

c I like working with the centre punch I made myself. Basically, you use a centre punch to mark the centre of a hole when drilling holes. A drill can wander if it doesn't start in a hole, so you use the punch to form a dent to guide the tip of the drill. You place the tip on the point where you want the hole, then hit it hard with a hammer. An automatic centre punch operates without the need for a hammer, but I really prefer the one I made. It's just a metal rod with a shaped tip on the end that has been hardened. I always use it when I need to drill holes in metal sheets.

Track 12: Unit 3, Part A, exercise 2

Peter Right, Aleksi. This is where we're going to be working today.

Aleksi OK. And what are we going to do?

Peter We're going to lay a cable in a concrete floor but first we need to cut a channel for it about four metres long. How do you think we're going to do that?

Aleksi Start by making a hole in the concrete with an electric drill and then use a mallet and chisel to cut the channel?

Peter We could do that ... but I think it would take all day! How about a power tool?

Aleksi Ah yes, of course! What about an angle grinder? We could cut two slits in the concrete with that.

Peter That's true, but the problem with using an angle grinder is that the two slits wouldn't be parallel. Have you ever seen this tool? It's a special power tool for cutting parallel slits in brick and concrete. It has two parallel cutting blades and you can adjust the distance between the blades and the depth of the cut and it's really fast. Do you know what it's called in English?

Aleksi I'm sorry, I don't know.

Peter It's called a wall chaser. There's nothing better than a wall chaser for cutting channels.

Aleksi A wall chaser. OK, and then we can use the mallet and chisel to knock out the concrete between the slits.

Peter Exactly. Now let's go over to the other side of the room and I'll show you where we're going to cut the channel. You bring the mallet and the chisel, oh and that extension reel, too. I'll bring the wall chaser and the cable.
OK, here we are. I talked to the boss yesterday and he said that the cable has to run from under this junction box to the other side of the room. I've already marked the floor to show exactly where we have to cut the channel, so let's get started.

Aleksi Great. Can I do it?

Peter Yes, OK ... but I'll cut the first 50 centimetres, so you see what to do. OK, plug the wall chaser into the extension reel first ... and then line it up with the markings on the floor ... and then switch on and ... . Wait a minute. That doesn't sound too good. It sounds like there's something wrong with the motor and the blades are hardly moving.

Aleksi Yes, and there's a smell of burning.

Peter OK, this chaser's broken, which is really annoying. We need to go back to the office and pick up another one.

Aleksi OK, but what about this one? Can we repair it?

Peter We'll first have to find out if it's still under warranty. If it is, we shouldn't try to repair it ourselves or else the warranty will be void. If it's not in warranty anymore, it's not worth repairing it. It's easier to buy a new one and throw this one away.

Aleksi Oh, I see ...

Track 14: Unit 3, Communication, exercise 1B

Supervisor I'll just give you my email address. It's t m dot martin at technical underscore tools dot de.

Mary-Anne Sorry, could you repeat that, please?

Supervisor No problem. t m dot martin at technical underscore tools dot de. You can reach me directly with that address.

Mary-Anne Thank you. Well, my email address is mary hyphen anne hyphen brown at five plus five services dot net. The fives are written as numbers. Oh, and my first name, Mary-Anne – Anne is written with an e.

Supervisor OK. I'll just read that back to you. Mary hyphen anne hyphen brown at five plus five services dot net. Mary-Anne with a hyphen, the fives written as numbers and Mary-Anne written with an e at the end of Anne.

Mary-Anne Yes. That's correct.

Track 15: Unit 4, Part A, exercise 4

Interviewer Welcome, Professor Bassford. We're really glad to have you here for our in-company training this morning!

Bassford My pleasure. It's nice to be here.

Interviewer Professor Bassford, you've done a lot of research on materials used in electronics. What are electronic materials? Could you give us a short overview of the different kinds of materials that can be found in electronic devices?

Bassford Well, first of all, electronic materials are materials that are typically used as core elements in device applications. Electronic devices consist of a great variety of materials. We find them, of course, in the PCBs, which are populated by all kinds of electronic components, but also for example in the casings of the devices.
Generally speaking, we have to deal with three types of materials: conductors, insulators and semi-conductors.

Interviewer I see. Well, electrical conductors are those metals that allow electricity to flow through them easily; and electrical insulators, like most plastics for example, prevent electrical flow ... but perhaps you could tell us a bit more about the properties and applications of semi-conductors in electronics?

Bassford Of course. Well, semi-conducting materials can exhibit both conducting and insulating properties. The most common semi-conducting material is silicon. Silicon needs to have very small amounts of other elements such as boron and phosphorous added to it in order to become a semi-conductor. This is called doping. Doped silicon is used to make components such as diodes, transistors, or integrated circuits.

Interviewer And these components are typically found soldered to PCBs.

Bassford That's right.

Interviewer Are there any precious materials used in PCBs?

Bassford PCBs are typically manufactured using thin copper foils on glass-fibre-reinforced laminate materials. The outer copper layers can, for instance, be gold-or-tin-plated and the board can have a solder mask and sometimes even a conformal polymer coating. So, PCBs and electronic components contain a wide variety of precious metals including gold, silver, platinum, rhodium and palladium ... and this makes recycling of these materials very interesting. Also, you mustn't forget the solder itself, which has become a significant factor in the production costs.

Interviewer Oh, I see, you're talking about the recent transition to lead-free assembly in PCB production ...

Bassford That's right! You see, when the RoHS directive came into effect ...

Interviewer Excuse me – could you explain for the audience what "RoHS", spelled R-O-H-S, stands for?

Bassford RoHS stands for "Restriction of certain Hazardous Substances", and it is an EU directive on the use of hazardous substances in electrical and electronic equipment. According to this directive, leaded solders are prohibited and have to be replaced in production. Unfortunately, all the available replacement alloys also have significant disadvantages ...

Interviewer I see. Which problems do the lead-free solders cause?

Bassford Well, there are several potential problems: different temperatures, higher costs, altered soldering processes, corrosion and so on. Let's look at the higher soldering temperatures as an example: All affordable replacement alloys have a much higher melting point than traditional tin-lead solders. But higher temperatures can destroy the electronic components – so the whole soldering processes has to be changed ...

Interviewer But there are some lead-free solders with even lower melting points than leaded solders ...

Bassford Yes, of course, but these alloys contain bismuth and indium, which not only makes them much more expensive, but causes even more unwanted effects in soldering.

Interviewer That's very interesting. Maybe we should take a break for questions here ...

Track 16: Unit 4, Part B, exercise 1

Börne Wilsberg Metall. Börne am Apparat. Wie kann ich Ihnen helfen?

Supervisor Good morning, Mr Börne. Julia Saunders here.

Börne Good morning, Ms Saunders.

Supervisor I got your message about the workpiece. I'm sorry, I don't understand why some information is missing, but maybe we can sort it out now on the phone.

Börne Thanks. That would be great. Maybe you could just talk me through the whole thing.

Supervisor Fine. OK ... It's an almost square plate with a side length of 120 mm.

Börne OK, square, 120 mm. I've got that.

Supervisor On the left side on the top there's a chamfer of 10 by 10 mm.

Börne Yes, got it. OK.

Supervisor On the top at the right there's a convex semicircle with a radius of 20 mm ...

Börne Aha ...

Supervisor ... followed by a concave semicircle of another 20 mm.

Börne OK. Top right, a convex semicircle with a radius of 20 mm, followed by a concave semicircle of another 20 mm.

Supervisor That's right. So, now, on the base line, there's a groove that's 15 mm deep topped by a semicircle with a radius of 15 mm.
Börne Where is that on the base line?
Supervisor Sorry. It's exactly in the middle.
Börne Ah, OK.
Supervisor Now, there are 4 boreholes with a diameter of 6 mm. Number 1 is 30 mm from the bottom line and 25 mm from the left side.
Börne Does it have a thread?
Supervisor No, just a bore. The next one is 85 mm from the bottom and 15 mm from the left.
Börne OK.
Supervisor Then 60 mm from the bottom and 60 mm from the left and 85 mm from the bottom and 60 mm from the left.
Börne Got it. Anything else?
Supervisor The last feature is a 24 mm hole at 60 mm from the bottom and 25 mm from the left. And that's all.
Börne OK. That's clear now. What material do you want it in?

Track 17: Unit 5, Foundation, exercise 1A

1	is approximately equal to	7	minus
2	degree	8	multiplied by / times
3	divided by	9	per cent
4	is equal to / equals	10	squared
5	is greater than	11	plus or minus
6	is less than	12	is not equal to

Track 18: Unit 5, Part A, exercise 2

Märta Wow, it's a big warehouse!
Supervisor Yes, it must be 40 or 50 metres long.
Märta And look at that high ceiling!
Supervisor It's about 12 metres high. Just check on the floor plan will you, Märta?
Märta Yes, I have it here. The warehouse is 50 metres long, 20 metres wide and 10 metres high. It's a big area.
Supervisor So we'll need to install a number of motion detectors to cover the main areas.
Märta OK, so first we must calculate how many we need.
Supervisor That's right. Let's have a walk round and see where they need to go …
Märta I think we'll need two here over the vehicle entrance.
Supervisor Why two?
Märta Because it's a very high ceiling.
Supervisor According to the booklet the High Bay motion detector will detect a person at a height of 10 metres and a vehicle at 13. The vehicle entrance is only 5 metres wide, so one will be enough.
Märta Ah yes, good point.
Supervisor OK, so let's take a look at the rest of the building. Ah look, there's a skylight in the ceiling.
Märta So we'll need one next to it in case someone breaks in through the roof.
Supervisor I think we will need two.
Märta Are you sure? According to this booklet the detection zone is 18 metres wide. Isn't that enough?
Supervisor But the building is 20 metres wide and also if the skylight is opened to let in fresh air, the movement of the air will trip the motion detector if it is too close. We should put one on either side of the skylight, each about two metres away from it.
Märta Ah, I understand …
Supervisor Now let's walk to the far end of the warehouse … OK, there are two back entrances on the left and right …
Märta … so we'll need one over each of those. So, that's it then. Five detectors in all.
Supervisor We'll need more than that.
Märta Why's that?
Supervisor You've forgotten the office. The office is inside the warehouse.
Märta Ah yes, of course. One for the office, so that's six.
Supervisor We'll need two.
Märta Two?
Supervisor The office has two rooms. Each room also has a window. We'll need one for each room.
Märta Right again …
Supervisor So how many do we need, Märta?
Märta Seven.
Supervisor OK, seven it is. Let's get started, shall we?

Track 19: Unit 5, Part B, exercise 3A

Supervisor So … this is an assembly line for the production of tumble dryers. At this stage, the tumble dryers have already been tested and they are ready for packaging. Can you see the packaging lines over there? When the tumble dryers reach this point, the transport system is programmed to guide the approaching device to one of the packaging lines. If there is no empty packaging station, the line is supposed to stop automatically and wait.
Vasil Ah, OK. So what's the problem?
Supervisor Well, sporadically … meaning every now and then … the transport system doesn't stop the line and this causes the approaching tumble dryer to bump into one of the packaging stations.
Vasil Hmmm, … I have the schematic here – it's probably one of the proximity sensors that's causing the sporadic fault. We should check the sensors first!
Supervisor Well, I'm not so sure about that. It's very uncommon for a proximity sensor to fail sporadically and if we want to check the sensors properly, we'll have to bring the entire production line to a halt. So I think we should check the operating voltage of the sensors first.
Vasil OK, the control system and the sensors operate at 24 volts. So it's safe to open the cover and measure the supply voltage with a multimeter … Ahhmm, it's around 18 volts!
Supervisor That's definitely too low. So we need to check the 24 volt rail with the portable digital oscilloscope.
Vasil Ah, that doesn't look good either! There are spikes and noise on the 24 volt rail.
Supervisor OK … I'm afraid we'll have to stop the production line anyway and replace the power supply unit! So, Vasil, switch off the circuit while I call the production supervisor and ask her to stop the line. Don't forget to tag the circuit breaker!
Vasil Sorry, what does that mean – tag the circuit breaker?
Supervisor Put a sign on the circuit breaker, so that nobody switches it back on again. Use this one. I've signed it.
…

Marta You can share selected information with clients on the cloud, too, can't you? Maybe we should mention that to the supervisor?

Janek Hey. That's a good idea. Let's tell the supervisor that we use emails and the intranet, but we feel that using the cloud might be more useful. Yes? And, of course, the advantage of using the cloud is that the company can share information with clients. He can bring that up at the meeting.

3: Discussing a project

Janek He can bring that up at the meeting.

David Oh, yes. The meeting. That's another type of internal communication, isn't it? In this case, they're discussing the project. I'm glad I don't have to go to a lot of meetings. Meetings take up too much time. I'd rather be out doing my job.

Marta Me, too. I hate meetings. Especially when somebody stands up and reads things from slides.

Janek I can only agree with you there. When they're full of writing, slides are a real waste of time. When it's written information, a hand-out is always better.

David Right, well, I think we have enough now. Face-to-face meeting, phone calls and text messages for making quick decisions; emails and intranet for sharing information, and a suggestion that the company might consider cloud storage.

Marta And, don't forget to mention that, at meetings, slides should only be used for graphic images and not for a lot of text. If it's written information, we'd rather have a hand-out.

Track 24: Unit 7, Part A, exercise 2

Randy Our next question tonight is from Armin in Germany. How are you doing, Armin?

Armin Good!

Randy And It's good to have you at this webinar, Armin. What are you working on right now?

Armin Hi everyone. I'm working on this guitar amp here in my workshop. Let me just get the camera on it ... Can you all see it clearly?

Randy Yes, we can all see the amplifier.

Armin Well, yesterday it suddenly just cut out. Since then I've replaced one of the glass fuses, which was blown, and checked the mains lead, which was fine. I've now just switched the amp back on again and, as you can see, the mains and standby control lights have come on but the amp is still dead. Any ideas?

Randy I hope your workshop has a GFCI, Armin. If not, you could electrocute yourself!

Armin A GFCI ... ?

Randy ... a ground fault circuit interrupter ...

Armin Ah yes, we call a ground fault circuit interrupter an RCD over here. Yes, I have an RCD in the circuit. No worries.

Randy That's good to hear. So now show us the back of the amp, so we can see if the tubes have come on. They should be illuminated.

Armin OK, I'll just get the camera on the tubes ... Yes, the tubes have come on.

Randy Well, that's good because that shows they haven't blown, so please disconnect the AC mains lead and remove the back panel of the amplifier.

Armin OK ... I've done that and now we can see inside the amp.

Randy And the next thing is the sensory check. Is there a smell of burning?

Armin No, it smells fine.

Randy Can you see charred wires anywhere?

Armin No, nothing at all.

Randy What's that piece of paper in the corner of the amp on the right?

Armin Just a moment ... Here we are. It's the schematic of the amp!

Randy Well, I think we're in luck now, Armin because we can trace the fault much more easily. Will you get the camera on the schematic, so we can all take a look at it?

Armin Just a moment ... Here we are. Can you see it?

Randy We can all see it just fine. First find the part of the schematic with the transformer put the camera on that.

Armin Just a moment ... Got it.

Randy Now we need to look at the output voltages from the transformer. What can you see, Armin?

Armin I can see that the transformer has five output voltages. Three rectified low voltage outputs for the semi-conductors, one to heat the tubes and one high-voltage output to a bridge rectifier.

Randy Well, I guess the high voltage rectifier provides the DC output to power the tubes, so the DC output is what we need to check first. Do you have a multimeter there, Armin?

Armin Yes, I do.

Randy So measure the output voltage of the rectifier. I think I know what it's going to be ...

Armin OK, the camera's now on the multimeter, which I've attached to the output voltage of the rectifier and the reading is zero!

Randy Just as I thought. So now we know where the fault is, but we still need to know if the transformer's not supplying the voltage to the rectifier or if the rectifier's not changing AC into DC.

Armin Exactly. So I'll either need a new transformer or some diodes for a new rectifier. I'll get started on that now. Thanks for your help, Randy!

Randy You're welcome, Armin. Now let's go over to Bill in Buffalo, New York. Hi Bill ...

Track 24: Unit 7, Part A, exercise 2

Kate Good morning, Mr Meesang. How are you today?

Surat Fine, thank you. I hope you're well, too, Ms O'Brien.

Kate Yes, I'm fine, thanks. But, please, call me Kate.

Surat Thank you. My first name is Surat.

Kate Surat. OK ... Listen, my colleague and I will arrive in Bangkok on the 30th of November so I'd just like to check a few things with you before we arrive. Has the resin-sealing unit arrived at the factory yet?

Surat Not yet, but I've been told that it's already in Bangkok port and should be delivered to our factory on the 29th November. It will be waiting for you when you arrive in Bangkok the next day.

Kate OK. That's excellent. One important thing, though, Surat. Please, don't unpack the machine before my colleague and I arrive. Please leave it in the crate. The resin-sealer must be handled very carefully.

Surat Don't worry. I understand. I'll tell my colleagues to leave the machine in the crate until you are here. I expect it's very heavy.
Kate Yes, it weighs 4 tons. Do you have a forklift truck that can carry that weight?
Surat Well, we have a DFG 435. I think that is strong enough for transportation within the factory building.
Kate Sorry, Surat, but I don't think it is. We really need a more powerful one, like a TFG 540. Can you get a TFG 540?
Surat Er ... yes, I think so. I don't think that will be a problem. There's a factory nearby that has a TFG 540. My cousin works there. He'll help us with that. ... What do you need to fix the machine on the floor? Nuts and bolts?
Kate Yes. Sixteen bolts – M18x150 – and the nuts as well.
Surat Right, no problem.
Kate And we'll need a drill and some 18 millimetre drill bits. We'll also need glue to fix the bolts to the floor.
Surat Drills, drill bits, glue. You don't have to worry, Kate, our electricians have all of these things.
Kate Yes. I know, but I just want to be sure. Now, how about the electricity supply? We need to lay data cables and power cables. Do we have to lay cable trunks?
Surat No, that's not necessary. There's enough space for cables under the flooring.
Kate And the pneumatics? Can the cables and the pneumatic hose be laid under the floor, too?
Surat No problem, we can lay a pneumatic hose under the flooring, too.
Kate Fine. I think that's it. Or, do you have any questions about the installation?
Surat No, no. Everything will be fine.
Kate I'm sure it will. If possible, I'd like to have everything up and running by the 3rd of December so that you can start production the following week.
Surat No problem at all, Kate. My men and I will work hard to get the job done on time.
Kate Thank you, Surat. I'm looking forward to meeting you soon.
Surat You, too, Kate. Have a good flight.

Track 26: Unit 8, Part A, exercise 2A

Liu ... one of our contracts is cutting rubber mats for an important customer.
Derek So what exactly is the problem?
Liu The thing is, we cut these rubber mats with our water-jet cutter, of course, but there is also abrasive sand mixed in with the water.
Derek OK ...
Liu This sand helps to cut the rubber, but some sand remains on the rubber mats and we have to wash it off after cutting. So ... we have to wash down the mats manually, and we can't do that within the air-conditioned plant, so we have to do it outside in the heat.
Derek And that also takes a lot of time probably.
Liu That's true. It's actually about four minutes per mat.
Derek Oh, that's a lot. OK, how can we help?
Liu What we need is a kind of washing machine for these mats.
Derek All right, do you have an idea of how that could work?
Liu Yes, well, we thought about a kind of conveyor that cleans the mats on both sides, dries them and palletizes them.
Derek OK. I think we can come up with something like that ... let me just write this down: cleans mats on both sides ... dries and palletizes them ...
Liu That's right.
Derek First of all, what are the dimensions of the mats?
Liu Length 1000 mm, width 500 mm and 20 mm thick.
Derek OK. 1000 mm, width 500 mm and 20 mm thick. And how about the water? It's polluted with sand after the cleaning process ...
Liu That's another problem. Could we filter the sand out, so that we can reuse both the sand and the water? You know, the environmental legislation in Shenzhen is rather strict.
Derek We'll try our best. filter sand out of water ... and then you want the system to dry the mats before palletizing them?
Liu That's right. That will save us lots of time and money.
Derek Well, OK. I have all the information I need now. Give me two weeks and then I think I can send you some ideas about what we could do.
Liu Fine, thank you. I look forward to ...

Track 27: Unit 8, Communication, exercise 1A

1

Receptionist Good morning. Welcome to the International Hotel.
Giovanni Good morning. My name is Rossi – Giovanni Rossi. I have a reservation.
Receptionist Here we are. Giovanni Rossi.
Giovanni Yes. From Rossi Technology, Rome.
Receptionist Thank you. You're in room 303, on the third floor.
Giovanni What time is breakfast served?
Receptionist We serve a buffet breakfast in the dining room between 8 and 10 a.m.
Giovanni Eight till 10? Can I have a swim before breakfast?
Receptionist Yes, of course. The swimming pool is open from 6 a.m. till 10 p.m.
Giovanni That's great. Thank you.
Receptionist You're welcome. Enjoy your stay, Mr Rossi.

2

Receptionist Good morning. Welcome to the International Hotel.
Mary Good morning. I have a reservation under McGregor, McGregor Robotics.
Receptionist Mary McGregor, from Glasgow.
Mary Yes. That's right. I booked a room on the ground floor, with wheelchair access.
Receptionist Yes, that's correct. You're in room 15, on this floor.
Mary Does the dining room have wheelchair access?
Receptionist Yes, it does. All of our rooms and facilities have wheelchair access.
Mary Good. Thank you.
Receptionist Let me know if you need any extra towels or pillows.
Mary That's very kind of you.
Receptionist My pleasure. Have a good stay, Ms McGregor.

3

Receptionist Good morning. Welcome to the International Hotel.
Yusuf Thank you. I would like to check in.
Receptionist Of course. What name is the reservation under?
Yusuf My name is Yusuf Zuabi.
Receptionist Could you spell your surname, please?
Yusuf Yes. It's Z U A B I, "Zuabi", with a Z. The reservation may be under the name of my company, Tech Solutions.

Receptionist	Thank you. Ah, yes, here it is, Tech Solutions, Berlin, Mr Yusuf Zuabi. You're in room 201, on the second floor. Here's your key. The buffet breakfast is served in the dining room between 8 and 10 a.m.
Yusuf	Thank you. I have a question. Where can I park my car?
Receptionist	There's a secure car park at the back of the hotel. The man at the gate will let you in.
Yusuf	Good. Thank you.
Receptionist	No problem. Enjoy your stay.

Track 28: Unit 8, Communication, exercise 1C

Receptionist	Good morning, Ms Banerjee. How are you this morning?
Akira	Good morning. I'm very well, thank you.
Receptionist	Howcanlhelpyou?
Akira	I'm going home today so I would like to check out.
Receptionist	Of course. What room were you in?
Akira	I was in room 207.
Receptionist	Did you have a nice time in Amsterdam?
Akira	It's been great. I love Amsterdam.
Receptionist	Was everything OK for you in the hotel?
Akira	Yes, thank you. Everything was fine. I'll definitely be back.
Receptionist	I'm pleased to hear that. Have a good trip home.
Akira	Thank you. I'm flying KLM. They're very good.

Track 29: KMK Exam practice 4, exercise 2, Hörverstehen

Lecturer	Good morning everybody. Today we're going to be looking at some simple breadboard circuits built by members of this class and I'd like you to take notes while you listen. I'll put the schematic on the screen and then each student will describe the components on the breadboard. Would you like to begin, Fabiola? Tell us about your circuit, please.
Fabiola	Hi everyone. My breadboard circuit is a touch switch that turns on another device. Here it's an LED and ... as you can see ...it actually works!
Lecturer	Well done, Fabiola! We can all see that the LED is on but would you tell us how you built it?
Fabiola	Yes, certainly. The components needed are two npn transistors, two resistors, an LED, a 6-volt battery, two connecting wires and two bare metal conductors. First I connected the battery to the breadboard and then I put on the two transistors and connected them to each other with one of the connecting wires. I used the other connecting wire to attach the second transistor to the negative terminal of the battery.
Lecturer	What sort of transistors are you using here, Fabiola?
Fabiola	They're both BC 547 transistors.
Lecturer	And then what did you do?
Fabiola	Then I added a two-hundred-and-seventy-ohm resistor to the circuit. I placed it between the LED and the second transistor. Then I connected the second resistor to the first transistor and the positive terminal of the battery.
Lecturer	And what rating is the second resistor?
Fabiola	Oh, sorry! I forgot to say that the second one is a hundred kiloohms.
Lecturer	Yes, that's important. What did you do next?
Fabiola	Then I connected the two bare metal conductors to the two free terminals of the first transistor, making it all into a simple touch switch. Now if you put your finger across the two bare conductors, it switches on the LED – like this.
Lecturer	Excellent! Now could you tell us what's happening in this circuit?
Fabiola	Yes, when you put your finger across the two bare wires, a very small current flows between the conductors and this isn't enough to light up the LED. This circuit therefore uses the two transistors to amplify the current twice. Each time the current passes through a transistor it's amplified two hundred times, so in fact the tiny current between the two bare conductors is magnified forty thousand times, which is enough to power the LED.
Lecturer	Thanks for that, Fabiola. Our next circuit is ...

Track 30: Unit 9, Foundation, exercise 1B

Claudia	Good morning, Mr Camilleri. It's Claudia here. You wanted to talk about the video conferencing system?
James	Ah. Hallo there, Claudia. Thanks for calling. How's the weather there in Berlin? It's a beautiful day here in Valletta.
Claudia	You're lucky. It's raining here.
James	Oh, dear. Well, never mind. Perhaps it will be nice tomorrow. Do you have my email there?
Claudia	Yes, I do.
James	Good. Let's start. First of all, I'd like to be able to store data that everyone can access wherever they are. What do you think of that idea?
Claudia	It's a good idea. We'll need cloud storage.
James	Cloud storage? Oh, yes. I've heard of that. Fine. And I'd like the system to let us re-play the sessions later.
Claudia	So, we'll need a video recording function.
James	Right. That makes sense. It's a video conferencing system, so it should be able to make video recordings.
Claudia	Yes. That's right.
James	Of course. Right, well, only two more things. Will the makers supply a guide that helps us to use the system?
Claudia	A user manual? Yes. Probably. If not, there will be some other kind of help available.
James	Oh. All right. Then, the last thing is, will they let us try out the system for nothing so that we know if it is the right one for us?
Claudia	Sure. Most of them offer a free trial.
James	Good. Well, I think that's it. I'd like you to get started on that today.
Claudia	I'll do that, Mr Camilleri, but I wanted to suggest two other functions.
James	Oh. All right. You're the expert. What else do you suggest?
Claudia	Hmm. I wondered about multi-language support.
James	Why would we need that?
Claudia	Hmm. Just in case someone doesn't speak good English?
James	Oh, no. I don't think we need that. What was the other thing?
Claudia	Well, some video conferencing systems have calendar integration so that you can schedule more meetings. I think you'll want to arrange more meetings.
James	Well, yes, but my secretary, Maria, does that for me.
Claudia	Oh, of course. I just thought it might be useful.
James	All right. I'll probably never use it but you can add the calendar thing to the other items we discussed.
Claudia	Very well, Mr Camilleri. I'll get on with it right away.
James	Thanks, Claudia. Goodbye.

Track 31: Unit 9, Part B, exercise 2

Harry Hi, Sina. How are things going?
Sina Hi, Harry. Not so good at the moment. We have a problem with one of our aggregates again.
Harry Oh, what is it?
Sina You can't read the numbers we engraved on the labelling plates any more. The colour came off.
Harry Oh, no. Not again.
Sina Maybe we should order our labelling plates from Bensons again. They're more expensive, but the plates at least keep their colour.
Harry You're right. But we had a few problems with Bensons as well in the past. That's why we stopped using them.
Sina I know. Some plates were delivered late for one of our orders and two were missing.
Harry ... so we couldn't dispatch that aggregate to Norway on time. ... But what can we do now?
Sina Maybe we could produce our labelling plates ourselves?
Harry Hmm. That's a good idea. That would make us a lot more independent. But you know what a CNC machine for that kind of job costs, don't you?
Sina I do ... but maybe we could find a smaller machine, you know, the type that model-makers use? We only need a relatively small machine.
Harry Yeah ... one we could use to produce our labelling plates from metal and plastics.
Sina Right. Let me look on the internet. Maybe we can find something suitable.
Harry Yeah, go ahead. ... Ah, what's that?
Sina OK ... This looks interesting. A kind of desktop CNC machine ...
Harry ... desktop gantry CNC machine ... with linear drives ...
Sina Could be just what we need ...

Track 32: Unit 9, Part B, exercise 4

Sina ... then we can decide whether we want to buy it.
Harry We need to find out first whether there are any optional extras for the 2-240 model that we need.
Sina I don't think there are. It says here: "Complete DIY kit including all mechanical and electronic components". It also says that there are easy-to-follow assembly instructions with pictures, so the assembly only takes a couple of hours.
Harry OK, that sounds good.
Sina Now there's one thing in the list of features which I think is really important. It's the 6-point ball bearing cage in all the linear profiles ... and the play-free movement of the carriages
Harry Well that's absolutely necessary, of course. We need maximum precision ... especially for the smaller plates.
Sina And look what it says here: "The carriages can be continuously adjusted and are freely accessible externally without disassembly."
Harry That's a real advantage if you don't have to dismantle the whole system for cleaning or any other purposes. What's the minimum feed rate?
Sina Er ... let me see ... It says the feed rate is at least 3000 mm/min ... divided by 60 seconds ...
Harry So 50 mm/sec?
Sina Yes, 50 mm/sec.
Harry Have you found anything on the thickness of the materials we can machine on it?
Sina Yes, it's 15 mm.
Harry Great. That's perfect for our purposes. By the way, is there an additional box for the electronic controller?
Sina No, there isn't. The control electronics are integrated in the machine housing and there is only one connecting cable from the machine to the computer.
Harry Do we need 3-phase current to operate it?
Sina No, it works between 100 and 240 V.
Harry That sounds good. Now, one final question: Does it come with a warranty?
Sina Yes, there's a 2-year warranty. But surely the most important question is: How much does it cost?
Harry Yes, go on then. How much does it cost?
Sina It says here the 2-240 costs ...

Track 33: Unit 10, Part A, exercise 3

Colleen Good morning, Galway Electrics. You're through to Colleen. How can I help?
Marco Good morning. It's Marco Meier from Elektro Merkel in Dortmund, Germany. I'm phoning to enquire about an electric motor for an industrial site in Dunmore.
Colleen For Dunmore! That's just down the road from us here.
Marco Excellent!
Colleen We have a lot of very different motors, sir, so could I just take down the details? *Marco* Yes, of course.
Colleen What is the motor to be used for?
Marco It's for a conveyor belt in a food-processing factory.
Colleen What power output do you need?
Marco Between 4 and 5 kilowatts.
Colleen Between 4 and 5 kilowatts. And what voltage is the electricity supply?
Marco 3-phase AC.
Colleen So it's 400 volts ... OK, I've got that. And is it for a monodirectional or reversible conveyor?
Marco Just let me think ... Well, at the moment the old motor is very slow and only works in one direction and that's a problem, so the customer wants a reversible motor.
Colleen ... So it's a reversible motor. Now what about the speed? Do you want it to operate at a fixed or variable speed?
Marco Well, as I said the old motor is very slow, so we need a variable speed motor.
Colleen Right, I've got that. So we're talking about a 4 to 5 kilowatt reversible, variable speed motor with a 3-phase power supply.
Marco Yes, that's right.
Colleen Now I have just one more question and that is if it's for indoor or outdoor use.
Marco It's for indoor use.
Colleen In that case, we can install an ODP motor.
Marco Sorry, I didn't understand that.
Colleen ODP refers to the enclosure of the motor, the housing it's in. An ODP motor is an open drip-proof motor. If some water splashes on it, it's fine but you can't use it outdoors in the wind and rain. We supply TEBC motors for outdoor use. TEBC motors are totally enclosed blower cooled motors.
Marco I see. Do you have an ODP motor with these specifications?

Colleen We certainly do, sir. I would suggest an ODP three-phase squirrel-cage induction motor with an output of 5 kW, together with a VFD so you can reverse it and vary the speed.
Marco VFD?
Colleen A variable frequency drive. That will give you all the flexibility you need. Now can I just take down your details, so we can send you an offer with a data sheet?

Track 34: Unit 10, Part B, exercise 4

Braden ... So let's just take a look at the motor that needs replacing, shall we?
Marco Yes, please come this way. It's in a hoist. It's pretty old but we use the hoist a lot.
Braden A hoist. I see. If it's old I think it'll be a DC motor ...
Marco Here it is.
Braden Yes, it's a brushed DC motor ... made 20 years ago! I'm sure the brushes have worn out but I would say you need a new hoist. We have some very good ones in stock at the moment.
Marco Well, the mechanism of the hoist is still good. It's just the motor that's worn out. We really only need to replace the motor.
Braden All right. Perhaps we can do a retrofit for you, which means you have a new motor in an old enclosure. Just let me look at it ... Yes, I think we can do a retrofit, but this time with brushwear detection.
Marco Brushwear detection? How does that work?
Braden The new models have sensors that warn you when the brushes are nearing the end of their working life, so you can replace them in good time before they wear out.
Marco That sounds like a good idea.
Braden Yes, it's a very popular feature. Now let me take down some more details. Do you always lift the same loads with it or do they vary?
Marco They vary a lot. We have a wide range of loads.
Braden Well, in that case you need a drive – a DC speed control. It will make you very flexible.
Marco All right.
Braden And as it's for a hoist, it isn't for continuous use.
Marco But we use it all day, really. Perhaps a hundred times a day.
Braden Yes, but it doesn't run around the clock like a pump or a fan. A brushed DC motor is fine for intermittent use, which means you use it for two or three minutes and then you turn it off again.
Marco Yes, I see what you mean.
Braden And the motor enclosure is ODP, which is fine in a clean, indoor environment like this.
Marco Good.
Braden I'll just make a note of the other ratings on the nameplate. One horse power; one thousand seven hundred and fifty rpm; ninety volts DC and 10 amps at full load.
Marco And can you supply exactly the right drive for these specifications?
Braden Yes, we have a drive for 90 volts DC, one horsepower, maximum 10 amps. No problem at all.
Marco So how much will it all cost?
Braden A retrofit DC motor like this, with brushwear detection will cost about €800 and the drive will cost about €400.
Marco So we're talking about !1,200. And when can you install it?
Braden Immediate delivery. We have the parts and the drive in stock.
Marco Fine. I'll talk to the customer and then get back to you ...

Track 35: Unit 11, Foundation, exercise 2B

Good morning, everyone. Thank you. I'd like to talk this morning about some of the environmental issues related to the production of smartphones.
Right. There was a study recently, which aimed to find out the answer to the question: How well do manufacturers of smartphones protect the environment?
The aim of the study was to gather information that would help persuade phone manufacturers to reduce emissions of greenhouse gases. The organization that conducted the survey also hoped that they would clean up their products by eliminating hazardous substances and that they would take back and recycle old phones.
The organizers of the study looked at three environmental areas: one, energy and climate, two, greener products and, three, the use of natural products and energy in a way that does not harm the environment.
The study looked at the carbon footprint of a mobile phone and saw that the main problem lies in the manufacturing processes. Basically, more carbon is used to make and put together smartphones than consumers ever use after buying them. According to the study, manufacturing a smartphone is estimated to cause 16 kg of CO_2-equivalent emissions.
Now, apart from using huge amounts of energy and materials, manufacturing smartphones requires using toxic chemicals. Toxic, hazardous, poisonous materials – call them what you will – it's easy to forget that your sexy new smartphone contains heavy metals, including lead, mercury, tin, cadmium and chromium. All of these are very dangerous for the environment.
Some of you are probably thinking, "Why does it matter? We don't come into direct contact with these toxic materials." The thing is, these hazardous substances don't just disappear when you throw your phone away. When they aren't recycled, phones often end up in landfills or incinerators and they can release heavy metals into groundwater and air. Contaminated groundwater is linked to several diseases.
Of course, there are also precious metals in electronics. One million phones contain 35,000 pounds of copper, 772 pounds of silver, and 75 pounds of gold, so the phones are worth recycling. In a lot of African countries where old phones are sent to be dumped, workers dissolve or burn circuit boards to get at the precious metals. This may be profitable, but it can cause serious health problems.
Batteries are another problem. Some phones contain built-in batteries that you can't change so, once the batteries are dead, the phone is useless and it gets thrown away. Sure, you can pay the company about 70 euros for a new battery but ...
Yes, I know there are guides on the internet showing you how to do it yourself, but it's not easy. A lot of phones are glued so they can't be opened or they have special screws ...
OK. OK. Let's take a break there. When we come back, we'll have a look at some improvements that the manufacturers of smartphones and other electronic equipment might make.

Track 36: Unit 11, Part A, exercise 3

Ray Oof! It's pretty heavy, isn't it?
Andy Yes, it weighs over 50 kilos according to the data sheet. I think we'll need a gantry crane to install it. But let's check the contents of the package with the delivery note first.
Ray OK, ... Well here on the type plate it says R500 SXJ.
Andy Yes, that's correct.
Ray ... and the serial number is 282824.
Andy Hold on. Say that again.
Ray 282824.
Andy There's something wrong here. It should be 282842 according to the delivery note. I think we need to check that with the supplier. I'll make a note of that.
Ray So, what's next on the list?
Andy OK. The next item is the robot controller, the CU555 compact.
Ray Yes, that must be this grey box here.
Andy Then it says here: power supply cable EU 3m CEE 7 / VII.
Ray Hmmm. Can't find that anywhere.
Andy OK, so we'll have to add that to the email, too.
Ray Yeah, but let's check the other things first.
Andy Right. What about the interface 24V PWR IN X55?
Ray Yes, that's OK. It's here on the back of the controller.
Andy Is there a handbook with it, too?
Ray Yes, this looks like the handbook and documentation.
Andy OK. Then it says LMN 8.3 ... That's the software package which should be installed on the controller already.
Ray Well, we can't check that before the robot is up and running.
Andy No, OK. And what's that? Is it the controller device?
Ray Yes, it says: NetPro 3.1 on the package.
Andy Uh-o. Another error. It should be version 3.2 according to the delivery note. We'd better check that with the supplier as well. Now, what about TechExpert 3.2? That's a software tool for easy programming, as well as GripExpert 3.2 and VisualExpert 3.2.
Ray Yes, they seem to be here in among the handbook and documentation.
Andy OK, the next item is the mobile teaching unit.
Ray Yes, got that here. Let's just check the serial number ... here it is: 175384.
Andy Wrong again. It says here 175348. Let's just make a note of that ... 175348.
Ray Now, here's the smartPAD cable ...
Andy ... that should be 10 metres.
Ray No, it doesn't look like 10 metres to me. Let me check. 2, 4, ... it's only 5 metres.
Andy OK, we'll have to mention that in the email as well.
Ray I think that's everything. So, are you going to write the email to RobAG?
Andy No, I have a meeting right now, but I know somebody who can do it for me ...

Track 37: Unit 11, Part B, exercise 3B

Louise Have you seen this email from Prime Engineering that Customer Services forwarded to us?
Wayne Yes, that print looks really terrible. Look at it: the top looks like a piece of chewing gum.
Louise Yeah, very funny. But it's not just the form, the surface also looks so rough. The surface is not as smooth as our printer resin usually is after it hardens.
Wayne Do you think the resin might be overheating?
Louise It looks a bit like that, doesn't it. But so far we've only ever had one broken heating element ... and that one was completely broken. I've never heard of a case of overheating, unless they are printing with the heat settings too high.
Wayne But what surprises me most is the strange colour. I'm not sure whether they're using our original filament coils. They might have bought cheap copies which work at first, but now they might be contaminating or even clogging the nozzle.
Louise Yes, it looks a bit like that, doesn't it? That could be the problem. By the way which printer model are they using?
Wayne The PT2002.
Louise OK. The PT2002 has a maximum working height of 200 mm. What is the height of this workpiece do you think?
Wayne I can't tell from the photo, but to me it looks more than that ... Do you think that could be the problem?
Louise I'm pretty certain it is. They must have ignored the software warning and started printing anyway. When the height of the printed workpiece reached the maximum working height, the machine stopped printing and the hot nozzle prevented the filament from cooling and solidifying quickly.
Wayne That makes sense.
Louise The filament may be anywhere between 190 to 240 degrees Celsius when it exits the extruder nozzle. When filament cools, it quickly hardens so that it retains the correct shape. You need to achieve the correct distance between the nozzle and the top of the workpiece, so that the filament can quickly solidify to produce the exact dimensions of your 3D printed part. In this photo, it looks like the filament extruded at the top of the workpiece was not able to cool quickly enough to retain its shape.
Wayne I think you're right. OK, so what do we do now?
Louise Can you ask Customer Services to write them a reply? They should tell them that we believe that they have either used different filament coils ... ones which are not our originals ... or the maximum working height has been exceeded.
Wayne OK, I'll get on to it now ...

Track 38: Unit 11, Communication, exercise 2A

Melissa Wolf.
Jerzy Oh. Hello. Erm. Do you speak English?
Melissa Yes.
Jerzy Oh. Good. This is Jerzy Adamczyk calling from the Denta Dental Clinic in Warsaw. Is that the sales department?
Melissa Yes.
Jerzy And, erm, who am I speaking to, please?
Melissa Wolf.
Jerzy Ah. Mrs Wolf. Erm. Is, erm, are you the correct person to take a complaint about a delivery?
Melissa What's the problem?
Jerzy It's about my order for X-ray machines. Both of the X-ray machines were damaged. One of them – the glass on one of the machines is scratched and the other machine is dented. I mean, the metal casing is dented. I think that ...
Melissa What's the order number?
Jerzy 942761.

Melissa OK. I can't do anything at the moment. I'll get it sorted after lunch.
Jerzy So, will you phone me back? My phone number is ...
Melissa It's here on the display.
Jerzy 0048 129 546 783?
Melissa Yes.
Jerzy And my name is Adamczyk. You will be sure to look into this? Well, thank you very much.

Track 39: Unit 11, Communication, exercise 2B

Melissa *Guten Morgen. Verkaufsabteilung. MelissaWolf am Apparat.*
Jerzy Oh. Hello. Erm. Do you speak English?
Melissa Yes, of course. How can I help you?
Jerzy Oh. Good. This is Jerzy Adamczyk calling from the Denta Dental Clinic in Warsaw. Is that the sales department?
Melissa Yes, this is the sales department. My name's Melissa Wolf.
Jerzy Ah. Mrs, erm, Ms Wolf. Hmm. Is, erm, are you the correct person to take a complaint about a delivery?
Melissa It depends on what it's about. Could you give me some details?
Jerzy It's about my order for X-ray machines. Both of the X-ray machines were damaged. One of them – the glass on one of the machines is scratched and the other machine is dented. I mean, the metal casing is dented. I think that there was a problem during transport.
Melissa Oh, I'm sorry to hear that. Could you give me the order number, please?
Jerzy It's 942761.
Melissa Just a moment, please. Right. 942761. I have it here. Two X-ray machines. And you say that both of them are damaged?
Jerzy That is correct. I am sorry, but I have to say that I am disappointed about this business. This is a trial order but I had to complain last week because the equipment did not arrive on the date we agreed. Now the machines are here and I can't use them.
Melissa Oh, dear. I'm extremely sorry to hear that you've had so much trouble. I'm sure my superior would like to discuss this with you. Can I ask her to phone you when she comes in to work tomorrow?
Jerzy Yes. All right. I'll be at home all day tomorrow so she should call me there. The number is 0048 129 546 993.
Melissa 0048 129 546 993. Yes. You'll get a call from my superior tomorrow, Mr Adamczyk.
Jerzy Could you tell me her name, please?
Melissa It's Mia Richter.
Jerzy Mia Richter. Good. Thank you very much, Ms Wolf.
Melissa You're welcome, Mr Adamczyk. Thank you for calling.
Jerzy Goodbye.

Track 40: Unit 11, Communication, exercise 3C

Jeanette Good morning. Sheffield Metal, Sales Department, Jeannette Hogg speaking.
Supervisor Good morning. This is Max Jahn from World Medical in Germany.
Jeanette Good morning, Mr Jahn. How can I help you?
Supervisor I'm calling to enquire about my order for containers for medical equipment. The order was sent almost one month ago, on the 18th of April, and delivery was promised by the 3rd of May but, so far, nothing has arrived.
Jeanette Oh. I'm sorry to hear that. Could you give me the order number?
Supervisor Yes. It's DF54736.
Jeanette DF54736. Just a moment, please. I'll check. I'm sorry, Mr Jahn. I don't seem to have any record of your order. Can I just check that I've understood everything? The order number is DF54736 and you ordered the containers on the 18th of April. Could you give me the exact details of the order, please?
Supervisor Yes, it's an order for your aluminium containers for medical equipment.
Jeanette Aluminium containers for medical equipment. Mr Jahn, I'll have to speak to my colleague to find out what the problem is. Can I get back to you later?
Supervisor Well, yes. But I hope it won't take long. We can't fulfil our orders until we have your containers.
Jeanette Yes. I realize that, Mr Jahn. I'm very sorry about this and I will do my best to get back to you as soon as possible.
Supervisor Many thanks for your help, Ms Hogg.

Track 41: Unit 12, Foundation, exercise 1

1 Maren
Presenter Hallo, and welcome to this week's podcast. This week, we're talking to a group of people who have recently gained their technical qualifications. Let's start with you, Maren. Would you like to introduce yourself?
Maren Sure. I'm Maren and I've just completed my apprenticeship as a Mechanical Engineering Technician.
Presenter What did you like best about your apprenticeship?
Maren I enjoy making things, so the best time for me was when we were in the workshop.
Presenter Apart from making things, what else do you do at work?
Maren Well, I install and service machinery.
Presenter Right. Hmm. A last question, Maren. Now that you're qualified, where would you like to work?
Maren Definitely in the automotive sector. A job at BMW would be great.

2 Garry
Presenter Hi. What's your name and what do you do?
Garry My name's Garry and I'm a CAD Technician.
Presenter Just in case any of our listeners don't know, what does CAD stand for?
Garry CAD stands for computer aided design.
Presenter OK. What did you enjoy most about your apprenticeship, Garry?
Garry I enjoyed learning from experienced people.
Presenter Nice. What do you do as a CAD Technician?
Garry Well, I work with computers, of course. I work with engineers who create drawings on computers. Sometimes there's a problem, then I have to fix the software so that the engineers can go on with their work.
Presenter That sounds interesting. What sector would you like to work in?
Garry I'd like to work in construction – Hochtief, for example. Everybody needs somewhere to live, and

every country needs offices, factories, hospitals, and so there will always be work for people like me.

3 Delon

Presenter Hello. Can you tell us your name and something about your apprenticeship?

Delon Yes. My name's Delon and I've just qualified as a Mechatronics Technician.

Presenter What did you like best during your apprenticeship?

Delon I liked the mixture of going to vocational college and doing practical work in the factory.

Presenter What do you do at work?

Delon Basically, I install electronic equipment; transmitters, antennas, that kind of thing. Then, I do regular maintenance tasks such as checking and cleaning so that we don't have any problems with the equipment. If we do have a problem, I repair the machine.

Presenter It sounds as if you have a lot of different things to do. What about the future? Where would you like to work?

Delon I'd like to work in the steel industry. I did my apprenticeship at Thyssenkrupp, so, ideally, I'd like to stay on there.

Track 42: Unit 12, Part B, exercise 3B

Presenter Thanks for coming along to talk to us today, Pat.

Pat My pleasure. It's nice to be here.

Presenter Good. Now, today you're going to give us advice about how to prepare for an interview.

Pat Correct. I'm going to go through each of the five stages of a job interview and talk about how candidates can prepare themselves. So, stage one, greetings and introductions. That's perhaps the easiest part of the interview but it still needs some preparation. First of all, you should find out where the interview location is and how to get there so that you arrive in good time. Try to give yourself enough time to relax and calm down. You should also make sure that you're wearing appropriate clothes.

Presenter First impressions count. Would you advise people to buy new clothes specially for the interview?

Pat No, not particularly. Your clothes need to be appropriate for the job, clean and smart, that's all. They don't have to be new.

Presenter Right. What about body language at the start of the interview?

Pat Body language is important. Walk into the room as confidently as possible, shake hands and make eye contact. Don't be shy. Look directly at the interviewer or interviewers. You'll be asked to take a seat, and there will be a bit of small talk.

Presenter Talking about the weather, your journey, that kind of thing?

Pat That's right. There might also be a question about where you live or your hobbies.

Presenter Some people find it difficult to make small talk, even in their own language. What advice can you give us there, Pat?

Pat I think the best thing to do is to simply get into the habit of making small talk in English with a colleague or a friend.

Presenter That's a good idea. Practise making small talk whenever you can.

Pat That's it. Now, let's move on to the main part of the interview. You'll be asked questions by one or more interviewers.

Presenter The interview might be conducted by more than one person?

Pat That's correct. Sometimes there's a panel of interviewers. Now, preparation for this part is extremely important. Think about the questions you might be asked and make a list. You'll definitely be asked to talk about yourself. Perhaps the interviewer will ask you about your strengths and weaknesses. Write down the questions – and think about how you're going to answer. And always remember to relate your answers to the job on offer.

Presenter Yes, that's important. Keep focused on the job. What should a candidate do if he or she doesn't understand a question?

Pat If you don't understand a question, ask the interviewer to clarify. You can say: "Could you explain what you mean by ... ?" – whatever it is. A good interviewer will ask the question again in a slightly different way.

Presenter Hmm. I hope so. Now, earlier you mentioned questions from the candidate. I remember my very first interview. I had no idea what to ask.

Pat Oh, dear. Some preparation would have helped. It's important to do some background research into the company before you go for the interview. Find out about the company's most recent developments and the future prospects of the company you hope to work for. Go to the firm's home page on the internet, read the business section of your newspaper, or look through business magazines. As you're doing your research, note down any questions that occur to you concerning the company. You should also, of course, prepare some questions about the job itself. Then, when you're asked if you have any questions, this is your chance to show your interest in the company and the job.

Presenter Right. Be prepared with questions about the company and the job! And that's the end of the interview and you can say goodbye.

Pat Well, not quite. Before the interview comes to an end, the interviewer usually says when the candidate can expect to hear from the company or if there's to be a further interview or a test – hmm – say, in the form of an assessment centre evaluation. So, only after these arrangements have been made, then your last task as a candidate is to say thank you and goodbye. Again, a good, firm handshake and a smile, and that's it.

Presenter Well, thank you, Pat, for these very helpful interviewing tips. I'm sure our listeners have learned a lot today and that they'll be able to put your tips to good use in their interviews. Now, next week's podcast is about ...

Track 43: KMK Exam practice 6, exercise 1, Hörverstehen

Call agent	Kelly Electrical Supplies, you're through to Ronan. How can I help?
Emily	Hello, it's Emily Winterstein from Ritter Installation in Dortmund, Germany. I'd like to order some tools, please.
Call agent	Certainly madam. Do you have an account with us?
Emily	No, we don't actually.
Call agent	Well, in that case I'll take down your details at the end of this phone call. What would you like to order, madam?
Emily	We need some tools but before we go on, how soon can you deliver?
Call agent	We can deliver the next day in Ireland, Northern Ireland and GB mainland, Monday to Saturday at no extra charge if you place your order before 1 p.m. the day before. Where do you want the tools sent?
Emily	To Limerick. Limerick Railway Station. Our customer is Irish Rail.
Call agent	No problem at all, madam. We can deliver the goods there tomorrow in the course of the day.
Emily	Not tomorrow morning?
Call agent	I'm afraid we can't guarantee that. If you want overnight delivery, that will cost you €50 more.
Emily	And then can you guarantee delivery tomorrow morning?
Call agent	Yes, madam. The tools will be there by 7 a.m.
Emily	In that case, I'd like to place an order now and pay the extra €50.
Call agent	No problem at all, madam. What would you like to order?
Emily	One pair of combination pliers and a hacksaw.
Call agent	Electrician's pliers?
Emily	Yes.
Call agent	So that's €35 plus VAT. Large or small hacksaw?
Emily	Large.
Call agent	€28.
Emily	Three Phillips screwdrivers, one each of sizes 2, 3 and 4.
Call agent	The three together will cost you €30.
Emily	OK, and I also need a set of open-ended and ring spanners.
Call agent	If you want both, I'll put you down for a set of 12 combination spanners for €26. Is that all right?
Emily	Yes, that's fine and we also need a multimeter.
Call agent	High-quality electrician's or handyman's pocket size?
Emily	High-quality, please.
Call agent	In that case you'll need a professional multimeter at €175. Anything else?
Emily	That's all, thanks. How much does that come to?
Call agent	The tools together come to two hundred and ninety-four euros, plus fifty euros for overnight delivery making the sub-total three hundred and forty-four euros. Add 23% VAT to that and ...
Emily	23% VAT?
Call agent	Yes, value added tax is 23% here, so that comes to another seventy-nine euros twelve, making the final price four hundred and twenty-three euros twelve.
Emily	Four hundred and twenty-three euros twelve ... Thanks. I've made a note of that.
Call agent	Now can I just have your details, please?

Track 44: KMK Mock exam, Rezeption 1, Hörverstehen

Apprentice	Schattauer Installationstechnik, Klopp. Was kann ich für Sie tun?
Caller	Good morning. I hope you speak English because I don't speak much German.
Apprentice	No problem, sir. How can I help you?
Caller	Well, my name's Jess Johnson and my company is Data Solutions Incorporated. We're building a data centre near Freiburg, Germany next year. We've been given your company's name by a German business partner who tells us that you do electrical installation work in high-security buildings.
Apprentice	That's exactly right, Mr Johnson. We're specialists in this field. Could you give me some more details of what your company needs?
Caller	Well, our data centre is going to be built next year, and we'll need a lot of security features. For example, we'll need an electronic alarm system that can be activated easily when the building is empty – at night or at weekends, for example.
Apprentice	We can do that for you, Mr Johnson. What other security features will you need?
Caller	Well, apart from a burglar alarm, we'll need access control, so we can log the movements of all employees and visitors entering the building and moving from place to place inside it. Our data is so sensitive and so attractive to data thieves that we must know who enters the building and where they go. Can you do that, too?
Apprentice	Oh yes, we can. We do a lot of work for banks over here and we install access control using the EIB system.
Caller	EIB? Never heard of it. How does it work?
Apprentice	Well, basically, every electrical device in the building has an actuator, which can be controlled digitally. In that way we can install and link all the actuators needed in the ceilings and walls and so on with a minimum of work. You then only need a laptop or a smartphone to program the system. And you can do that from anywhere in the world. Would you like us to send you some sales literature, Mr Johnson?
Caller	Sure, that would be great. And I'll be in Germany next week to talk to the architect, so let's set up a meeting.
Apprentice	I'll do that for you, Mr Johnson. May I have your email address and cell phone number, please?
Caller	Yes, my email's jess.johnson@dsi.org. I'll spell that for you. J–E–S–S dot J–O–H–N–S–O–N at D–S–I dot O–R–G. Have you got that?
Apprentice	Yes, and your cell phone number, please?
Caller	It's 001 707 499 3877.
Apprentice	001 707 499 3877. OK, I've got everything I need for the time being. We'll email you some brochures on EIB straight away. And I'll arrange that meeting.
Caller	Wonderful.
Apprentice	Thanks for calling, Mr Johnson.
Caller	Bye-bye.
Apprentice	Bye.

1–12 Unit word list

Dieses Wörterverzeichnis enthält alle neuen Wörter aus *Mechatronics Matters –2nd Edition* in der Reihenfolge ihres Erscheinens (Seitenzahlen sind angegeben). Nicht angeführt sind die Wörter aus dem Grundwortschatz (vgl. **Handreichungen für den Unterricht**). Wörter aus den Hörverständnisübungen sind mit einem T (Transkript) und Wörter aus den *Partner files* mit einem **P** gekennzeichnet. Die Zahl am linken Rand gibt die Seitenzahl an.

Abkürzungen			
	AE = amerikanisches Englisch	*jdm* = jemandem	*pl* = plural noun
	BE = britisches Englisch	*jdn* = jemanden	*sb* = somebody
	etw = etwas	*jds* = jemandes	*sth* = something

UNIT 1

6	**foundation** [faʊn'deɪʃn]	Grundlage
	profile ['prəʊfaɪl]	Porträt, Beschreibung, Profil
	apprentice [ə'prentɪs]	Auszubildende/r, Lehrling
	trainee [treɪ'niː]	Auszubildende/r, Praktikant/in
	global player [ˌgləʊbl 'pleɪə]	international agierendes Unternehmen
	producer [prə'djuːsə]	Hersteller, Produzent
	cable ['keɪbl]	Kabel
	connector [kə'nektə]	Verbinder, Stecker
	head office [ˌhed 'ɒfɪs]	Zentrale, Sitz
	to **found** [faʊnd]	gründen
	to **run** [rʌn]	(*Unternehmen usw.*) führen
	structure ['strʌktʃə]	Aufbau, Struktur
	chairman ['tʃeəmən]	Vorsitzende/r
	board [bɔːd]	Aufsichtsrat
	finance ['faɪnæns]	Finanz, Finanzen
	purchasing ['pɜːtʃəsɪŋ]	Einkauf
	partner ['pɑːtnə]	Gesellschafter/in
	sales [seɪlz]	Verkauf, Vertrieb
	to **employ sb** [ɪm'plɔɪ]	jdn beschäftigen
	including [ɪn'kluːdɪŋ]	einschließlich
	research [rɪ'sɜːtʃ]	Forschung
	scientist ['saɪəntɪst]	Wissenschaftler/in
	to **develop** [dɪ'veləp]	entwickeln
	to **manufacture** [ˌmænju'fæktʃə]	fertigen, herstellen
	mechanical engineering [mɪˌkænɪkl ˌendʒɪ'nɪərɪŋ]	Maschinenbau
	factory ['fæktəri]	Fabrik, Werk
	automation [ˌɔːtə'meɪʃn]	Automatisierung, Automation
	power generation ['paʊə dʒenəreɪʃn]	Stromerzeugung
	power distribution ['paʊə dɪstrɪbjuːʃn]	Stromverteilung
	industrial electronics [ɪnˌdʌstriəl ɪlek'trɒnɪks]	Industrieelektronik
	telecommunication [ˌtelikəˌmjuːnɪ'keɪʃn]	Fernmeldetechnik, Telekommunikation
	vocational training [vəʊˌkeɪʃənl 'treɪnɪŋ]	Berufsausbildung
	apprenticeship [ə'prentɪʃɪp]	Lehre, Ausbildung
	role [rəʊl]	Rolle
	headline ['hedlaɪn]	Überschrift
7	**according to** [ə'kɔːdɪŋ tə]	gemäß, entsprechend, zufolge
	multinational (company) [ˌmʌlti'næʃnəl]	internationaler Konzern
	well known [ˌwel'nəʊn]	bekannt
	works [wɜːks]	Fabrik, Werk
	production [prə'dʌkʃn]	Produktion, Fertigung, Herstellung
	sector ['sektə]	Bereich, Branche, Sektor
	grid [grɪd]	Raster
	size [saɪz]	Größe
	medium-sized ['miːdiəm saɪzd]	mittelgroß, mittelständisch
	solution [sə'luːʃn]	Lösung
	construction [kən'strʌkʃn]	Bau
	building ['bɪldɪŋ]	Bauwesen
	service ['sɜːvɪs]	Dienst, Dienstleistung
T	**equipment** [ɪ'kwɪpmənt]	Geräte, Ausstattung
	dealer ['diːlə]	Händler/in
	training ['treɪnɪŋ]	Ausbildung
	automative [ɔː'tɒmətɪv]	Automations-
	medical ['medɪkl]	medizinisch
	to **cover** ['kʌvə]	(Thema) behandeln
	employee [ɪm'plɔɪiː]	Angestellte/r, Beschäftigte/r
	target group ['tɑːgɪt gruːp]	Zielgruppe
	competitor [kəm'petɪtə]	Wettbewerber/in, Konkurrent/in
	on one's own [ɒn wʌnz 'əʊn]	alleine
	to **structure** ['strʌktʃə]	aufbauen, strukturieren
	prepared [prɪ'peəd]	bereit, vorbereitet
	audience ['ɔːdiəns]	Publikum
8	**branch** [brɑːntʃ]	Niederlassung

	chart [tʃɑːt]	Diagramm, Tabelle
	organization chart [ˌɔːgənaɪ'zeɪʃn tʃɑːt]	Organigramm
	first of all [ˌfɜːst əv 'ɔːl]	zunächst, zuallererst
	CAD engineer [ˌsiː eɪ 'diː endʒɪnɪə]	Technische/r Zeichner/in
	fitting ['fɪtɪŋ]	Montage
	fitter ['fɪtə]	Monteur/in
	turner ['tɜːnə]	Dreher/in
	foreman/-woman ['fɔːmən, 'fɔːwʊmən]	Vorarbeiter/in, Meister/in
	division [dɪ'vɪʒn]	Geschäftsbereich, Division, Sparte
	head of division [ˌhed əv dɪ'vɪʒn]	Bereichsleiter/in
	line manager [laɪn 'mænɪdʒə]	direkte/r Vorgesetzte/r
	quality control ['kwɒləti kəntrəʊl]	Qualitätskontrolle
	skilled worker [ˌskɪld 'wɜːkə]	Facharbeiter/in
	test technician ['test teknɪʃn]	Prüftechniker/in
T	**screen** [skriːn]	Leinwand, Bildschirm
	to **supervise** ['suːpəvaɪz]	überwachen, beaufsichtigen
	process ['prəʊses]	Ablauf, Prozess, Verfahren
	to **be in charge of sth** [bi ɪn 'tʃɑːdʒ əv]	für etw zuständig/verantwortlich sein
	to **list** [lɪst]	(in einer Liste) aufführen
	colleague ['kɒliːg]	Kollege/-in
	and so on [ənd 'səʊ ɒn]	und so weiter
	last but not least [ˌlɑːst bʌt nɒt 'liːst]	zu guter Letzt
	to **keep up sth** [ˌkiːp 'ʌp]	etw aufrecht erhalten
	reputation [ˌrepju'teɪʃn]	Ruf
9	**understanding** [ˌʌndə'stændɪŋ]	Verständnis
	excerpt ['eksɜːpt]	Auszug
	shaft [ʃɑːft]	Welle
	micrometre ['mʌɪkrəˌmiːtə]	Mikrometer
	diameter [daɪ'æmɪtə]	Durchmesser
	batch [bætʃ]	Charge, Los
	label ['leɪbl]	Etikett, Siegel
	tolerance ['tɒlərəns]	Toleranz
	out of tolerance [ˌaʊt əf 'tɒlərəns]	außerhalb der Toleranz
	flywheel ['flaɪwiːl]	Schwungrad
	to **drill** [drɪl]	bohren
	outer ring [ˌaʊtə 'rɪŋ]	Außenring
	to **reduce** [rɪ'djuːs]	senken, reduzieren, verringern
	weight [weɪt]	Gewicht
	to **make changes** [ˌmeɪk 'tʃeɪndʒɪz]	Änderungen vornehmen
	lifting system ['lɪftɪŋ sɪstəm]	Hubsystem
	hydraulic [haɪ'drɔːlɪk]	hydraulisch, Hydraulik-
	piston ['pɪstən]	Kolben
	to **fit** [fɪt]	passen
	properly ['prɒpəli]	richtig, genau
	to **mention** ['menʃn]	erwähnen, nennen
	lift cabin ['lɪft kæbɪn]	Aufzugskabine
	screw [skruː]	Schraube (zur Befestigung von Teilen mit Innengewinde)
	purpose ['pɜːpəs]	Zweck, Absicht
	to **tighten** ['taɪtn]	(Schraube) anziehen, festziehen
	lift shaft ['lɪft ʃɑːft]	Aufzugsschacht
	connecting pipe [kəˌnektɪŋ 'paɪp]	Verbindungsrohr, -leitung
	flange [flændʒ]	Flansch
	as far as [əz 'fɑːr əz]	soweit
	to **concern sth** [kən'sɜːn]	etw betreffen
	supplier [sə'plaɪə]	Zulieferer, Lieferant/in
	cooperation [kəʊˌɒpə'reɪʃn]	Zusammenarbeit
	to **go on** [ˌgəʊ 'ɒn]	währen, dauern
P	**key account management** [kiː əˌkaʊnt 'mænɪdʒmənt]	Großkundenbetreuung
	to **include** [ɪn'kluːd]	einbeziehen, aufnehmen
10	**slide** [slaɪd]	(Präsentation:) Folie
	to **switch** [swɪtʃ]	schalten
	switchgear ['swɪtʃgɪə]	Schaltgerät(e), Schaltanlage
	device [dɪ'vaɪs]	Gerät, Element
	switching device ['swɪtʃɪŋ dɪvaɪs]	Schaltgerät, Schaltelement
	industrial [ɪn'dʌstriəl]	Industrie-, industriell
	domestic [də'mestɪk]	häuslich, Haus-, Haushalts-
	wiring ['waɪərɪŋ]	Verkabelung, Verdrahtung
	rewiring [riː'waɪərɪŋ]	Neuverkabelung, Neuverdrahtung
	(cable) trunking ['trʌŋkɪŋ]	Leitungsführung
	tray work ['treɪ wɜːk]	Installation in Kabelpritschen
	(cable) sleeve [sliːv]	Kabeltülle, Kabelmuffe
	emergency service [ɪ'mɜːdʒənsi sɜːvɪs]	Notdienst
	(electrical) panel ['pænl]	Schaltanlage, Schalttafel
	customized ['kʌstəmaɪzd]	maßgeschneidert, individuell
	official [ə'fɪʃl]	amtlich, offiziell
	certification [ˌsɜːtɪfɪ'keɪʃn]	Zulassung, Abnahme, Zertifizierung
	control technology [kən'trəʊl teknɒlədʒi]	Leittechnik
	process visualization ['prəʊses vɪʒuəlaɪzeɪʃn]	Prozessvisualisierung
	remote system [rɪ'məʊt sɪstəm]	ferngesteuerte Anlage
	industrial communication [ɪnˌdʌstriəl kəˌmjuːnɪ'keɪʃn]	industrielle Kommunikation

	wireless ['waɪələs]	drahtlos, Funk-
	current ['kʌrənt]	Strom
	high-current [ˌhʌɪ 'kʌrənt]	Hochstrom-
	circuit breaker ['sɜːkɪt breɪkə]	Leitungsschutzschalter, Sicherungsautomat
	rail technology ['reɪl teknɒlədʒi]	Eisenbahntechnik
	compact construction [ˌkɒmpækt kən'strʌkʃn]	kompakte Bauweise
	maintenance ['meɪntənəns]	Wartung, Instandhaltung
	low maintenance [ˌləʊ 'meɪntənəns]	wartungsfreundlich
	available [ə'veɪləbl]	lieferbar, verfügbar
	overview ['əʊvəvjuː]	Überblick, Übersicht
	range [reɪndʒ]	Angebot(spalette), Sortiment
	to **specialize in sth** ['speʃəlaɪz ɪn]	sich auf etw spezialisieren
	sales director ['seɪlz dərektə]	Vertriebsleiter/in
	presentation [ˌprezn'teɪʃn]	Vortrag, Präsentation
	field [fiːld]	Bereich, Gebiet
	in detail [ɪn 'diːteɪl]	genau, detailliert
	household name ['haʊshəʊld neɪm]	(allgemein) bekannter Name
	to **operate** ['ɒpəreɪt]	geschäftlich tätig sein
	mobile ['məʊbaɪl]	mobil
	24/7 [twentiˌfɔː 'sevn]	rund um die Uhr
	operation [ˌɒpə'reɪʃn]	Betrieb
	heavy industry [ˌhevi 'ɪndəstri]	Schwerindustrie
	chemical ['kemɪkl]	chemisch, Chemie-
	power station ['paʊə steɪʃn]	Elektrizitätswerk
	data centre ['deɪtə sentə]	Rechenzentrum
	vital ['vaɪtl]	essenziell, lebenswichtig, entscheidend
	component [kəm'pəʊnənt]	Element, Bestandteil
	transportation [ˌtrænspɔː'teɪʃn]	Transport, Verkehr
	brief [briːf]	kurz, knapp
	to **be delighted to do sth** [bi dɪ'laɪtɪd]	etw sehr gerne tun
11	**guided tour** [ˌgaɪdɪd 'tʊə]	Führung, Rundgang
	assembly [ə'sembli]	Montage
	conference room ['kɒnfərəns ruːm]	Tagungsraum, Besprechungsraum
	copper ['kɒpə]	Kupfer
	workshop ['wɜːkʃɒp]	Werkstatt
	electrical design [ɪˌlektrɪkl dɪ'zaɪn]	Elektroplanung
	final assembly [ˌfaɪnl ə'sembli]	Endmontage
	pre-assembly [ˌpriː ə'sembli]	Vormontage
	showroom ['ʃəʊruːm]	Ausstellungsraum
	storeroom ['stɔːruːm]	Lagerraum
	entrance ['entrəns]	Eingang, Einfahrt
	goods *pl* [gʊdz]	Ware(n), Güter
	goods inwards examination [ˌgʊdz 'ɪnwədz ɪgzæmɪneɪʃn]	Wareneingangskontrolle
	lathe [leɪð]	Drehbank
	changing room ['tʃeɪndʒɪŋ ruːm]	Umkleide
	testing ['testɪŋ]	Prüfung, Prüf-
T	**this way** ['ðɪs weɪ]	hier entlang
	apartment block [ə'pɑːtmənt blɒk]	Mietshaus, Wohnblock
	control system [kən'trəʊl sɪstəm]	Steuerung, Steuer-/Regelsystem
	external [ɪk'stɜːnl]	extern, von außen
	corridor ['kɒrɪdɔː]	Flur, Gang
	past sth [pɑːst]	an etw vorbei
	competition [ˌkɒmpə'tɪʃn]	Konkurrenz, Wettbewerb
	tough [tʌf]	hart
	staff entrance [ˌstɑːf 'entrəns]	Personaleingang
	specifications *pl* [ˌspesɪfɪ'keɪʃnz]	Technische Daten, Spezifikationen
	component [kəm'pəʊnənt]	Bauteil
	to **assemble** [ə'sembl]	montieren, zusammenbauen
	unit ['juːnɪt]	Gerät, Einheit
	section ['sekʃn]	Abteilung, Abschnitt
	to **bend** [bend]	biegen
	panel ['pænl]	Blech, Tafel
	next door to [ˌnekst 'dɔː tə]	neben
	welding ['weldɪŋ]	Schweißen
	welding bay ['weldɪŋ beɪ]	Schweißplatz
	to **join** [dʒɔɪn]	(miteinander) verbinden
	impressive [ɪm'presɪv]	beeindruckend, eindrucksvoll
	installation board [ˌɪnstə'leɪʃn bɔːd]	Installationsplatte
	by the way [baɪ ðə 'weɪ]	übrigens, à propos
	separate ['seprət]	eigen, separat, getrennt
	training company ['treɪnɪŋ kʌmpəni]	Ausbildungsbetrieb
	to **consist of sth** [kən'sɪst əv]	aus etw bestehen
	member ['membə]	Mitglied
	layout ['leɪaʊt]	Raumaufteilung, Plan
	to **label** ['leɪbl]	bezeichnen, etikettieren
	to **take it in turns** [ˌteɪk ɪt ɪn 'tɜːnz]	sich abwechseln
12	**introductions** *pl* [ˌɪntrə'dʌkʃnz]	Bekanntmachen, Vorstellen

	supervisor ['su:pəvaɪzə]	Ausbildungsleiterer/in, Abteilungsleiter/in, Vorgesetzte/r
	computerized [kəm'pju:təraɪzd]	Computer-
	personnel [ˌpɜ:sə'nel]	Personal
	personnel file [ˌpɜ:sə'nel faɪl]	Personalakte
T	**electrical engineer** [ɪˌlektrɪkl ˌendʒɪ'nɪə]	Elektroingenieur/in, Elektrotechniker/in
	place of birth [ˌpleɪs əv 'bɜ:θ]	Geburtsort
	job description ['dʒɒb dɪskrɪpʃn]	Stellenbeschreibung
13	**formal** ['fɔ:ml]	formell, förmlich
	refreshment [rɪ'freʃmənt]	Erfrischung
	suitable ['su:təbl]	geeignet, passend
	to **avoid** [ə'vɔɪd]	vermeiden
	illness ['ɪlnəs]	Krankheit
	politics ['pɒlətɪks]	Politik
	journey ['dʒɜ:ni]	Fahrt, Anreise
	pay [peɪ]	Bezahlung, Gehalt
	response [rɪ'spɒns]	Antwort, Reaktion
	to **be based in ...** [bi 'beɪst ɪn]	seinen Sitz in ... haben, in ... sein
	view [vju:]	Aussicht
	in fact [ɪn 'fækt]	tatsächlich, eigentlich
	Excuse me. [ɪk'skju:z mi]	Verzeihung. Entschuldigung.
	to **hold up sb** [ˌhəʊld 'ʌp]	jdn aufhalten
	to **keep sb waiting** [ki:p 'weɪtɪŋ]	jdn warten lassen

UNIT 2

14	**health and safety** [ˌhelθ ənd 'seɪfti]	Arbeitssicherheit, Sicherheit am Arbeitsplatz
	training course ['treɪnɪŋ kɔ:s]	Lehrgang, Schulung
	hazard ['hæzəd]	Gefahr
	trainer ['treɪnə]	Ausbilder/in, Dozent/in
	talk [tɔ:k]	Vortrag
	to **discuss** [dɪ'skʌs]	diskutieren, besprechen, (über etw) sprechen
	panel building ['pænl bɪldɪŋ]	Schaltanlagenbau
	to **attach sth to sth** [ə'tætʃt]	etw mit etw verbinden, etw an etw anschließen
	electric shock [ɪˌlektrɪk 'ʃɒk]	Stromschlag
	faulty ['fɔ:lti]	defekt, fehlerhaft, schadhaft
	machinery [mə'ʃi:nəri]	Maschinen
	to **switch on/off** [ˌswɪtʃ 'ɒn, ɒf]	ein-/ausschalten
	tool [tu:l]	Werkzeug
	power tool ['paʊə tu:l]	Elektrowerkzeug
T	**protective clothing** [prəˌtektɪv 'kləʊðɪŋ]	Schutzkleidung
	hard hat [ˌhɑ:d 'hæt]	Schutzhelm
	overall [ˌəʊvər'ɔ:l]	Schutzanzug
	safety shoes *pl* ['seɪfti ʃu:z]	Sicherheitsschuhe
	to **keep sb safe** [ˌki:p 'seɪf]	jdn schützen
	messiness ['mesinəs]	Unordnung, Unsauberkeit
	minor ['maɪnə]	klein(er/e/s), geringfügig
	dirt [dɜ:t]	Schmutz, Dreck
	rubbish ['rʌbɪʃ]	Abfall, Müll
	emergency cut out switch [ɪˌmɜ:dʒənsi 'kʌt aʊt swɪtʃ]	Not-Aus-Schalter
	to **cover** ['kʌvə]	verdecken, abdecken
	pile [paɪl]	Stapel
	rule [ru:l]	Vorschrift, Regel
	top-heavy [ˌtɒp 'hevi]	kopflastig
	shelving ['ʃelvɪŋ]	Regale
	to **fill** [fɪl]	(*Regal*) befüllen
	shelf, shelves [ʃelf, ʃelfvz]	Regal, Regale
	stuff [stʌf]	Sachen, Zeug
	common sense [ˌkɒmən 'sens]	gesunder Menschenverstand
	ventilation [ˌventɪ'leɪʃn]	Belüftung
	to **block** [blɒk]	versperren, blockieren
	ventilator ['ventɪleɪtə]	Abzug, Ventilator
	guard [gɑ:d]	Schutzvorrichtung
	screen [skri:n]	Schutzschirm
	damaged ['dæmɪdʒd]	beschädigt, defekt
	wrench [rentʃ]	Schraubenschlüssel
	hammer ['hæmə]	Hammer
	to **brainstorm** ['breɪnstɔ:m]	Ideen sammeln
	related to sth [rɪ'leɪtɪd tə]	bezüglich etw
15	**guideline** ['gaɪdlaɪn]	Richtlinie
	to **shut down sth** [ˌʃʌt 'daʊn]	etw ausschalten
	to **distract** [dɪ'strækt]	ablenken
	jewellery ['dʒu:əlri]	Schmuck
	electrical appliance [ɪˌlektrɪkl ə'plaɪəns]	Elektrogerät
	to **plug in** [ˌplʌg 'ɪn]	einstecken, anschließen
	order ['ɔ:də]	Befehl
	emergency exit [i'mɜ:dʒənsi eksɪt]	Notausgang
	emergency stop button [ɪ'mɜ:dʒənsi stɒp bʌtn]	Not-Aus-Taster
	to **remove** [rɪ'mu:v]	entfernen, abheben
	safety cover ['seɪfti kʌvə]	Sicherheitsabdeckung
	due to ['dju: tə]	aufgrund von, wegen
	ladder ['lædə]	Leiter
	to **bump into sth** ['bʌmp ɪntə]	gegen etw stoßen
	to **fall off** [ˌfɔ:l 'ɒf]	herunterfallen
	to **recognize** ['rekəgnaɪz]	erkennen

	safety sign ['seɪfti saɪn]	Sicherheitsschild, Hinweisschild
	fire exit ['faɪər eksɪt]	Notausgang
	high voltage [ˌhaɪ 'vəʊltɪdʒ]	Hochspannung
	fire extinguisher ['faɪər ɪkstɪŋgwɪʃə]	Feuerlöscher
	gloves *pl* [glʌvz]	Handschuhe
	acid ['æsɪd]	Säure
	highly flammable [ˌhaɪli 'flæməbl]	leicht entzündlich
	no entry [nəʊ 'entri]	Einfahrt verboten
	naked lights *pl* [ˌneɪkɪd 'laɪts]	offene Flammen
	first aid [ˌfɜːst 'eɪd]	Erste Hilfe
	safety goggles *pl* ['seɪfti gɒglz]	Schutzbrille
	to **pin** [pɪn]	(mit einer Nadel) befestigen, anheften
	gallery walk ['gæləri wɔːk]	Galerierundgang
	to **rank** [ræŋk]	einstufen, (in einer Rangliste) bewerten
	category ['kætəgəri]	Kategorie
	overall effect [əʊvərˌɔːl ɪ'fekt]	Gesamteindruck, Gesamtwirkung
16	**corporation** [ˌkɔːpə'reɪʃn]	Unternehmen, Konzern
	to **recruit** [rɪ'kruːt]	(*Personal*) anwerben, einstellen
	panel builder ['pænl bɪldə]	Schaltanlagenbauer/in
	installation electrician [ˌɪnstə'leɪʃn ɪlektrɪʃn]	Elektroinstallateur/in
	machine maintenance technician [mə'ʃiːn meɪntənəns teknɪʃn]	Maschinenwartungstechniker/in
	powerline technician ['paʊəlaɪn teknɪʃn]	*Elektriker/in, der/die am öffentlichen Stromnetz arbeitet*
	to **pair** [peə]	koppeln, zuordnen
	speech bubble ['spiːtʃ bʌbl]	Sprechblase
	to **involve** [ɪn'vɒlv]	beinhalten, mit sich bringen, einbeziehen
	flat *BE* [flæt]	Wohnung
	commercial [kə'mɜːʃl]	gewerblich
	to **maintain** [meɪn'teɪn]	warten, instand halten
	(national) grid [grɪd]	Stromnetz
	to **transmit** [træns'mɪt]	übertragen
	voice-over ['vɔɪsəʊvə]	aus dem Off
	profession [prə'feʃn]	Beruf
	schematic [skɪ'mætɪk]	Schaltbild
	control panel [kən'trəʊl pænl]	Steuertafel, Schaltschrank
	to **solder** ['səʊldə]	löten
	circuit board ['sɜːkɪt bɔːd]	Leiterplatte, Platine

	working hours *pl* [ˌwɜːkɪŋ 'aʊəz]	Arbeitszeiten
	heating ['hiːtɪŋ]	Heizung
	air-conditioning system ['eə kəndɪʃnɪŋ sɪstəm]	Klimasteuerung, Klimaanlage
	well-equipped [ˌwel ɪ'kwɪpt]	gut ausgestattet
17	**conduit** ['kɒndjuɪt]	Kabelkanal
	to **attach** [ə'tætʃ]	anbringen, befestigen
	cooker ['kʊkə]	Herd
	water-heater ['wɔːtə hiːtə]	Warmwasserbereiter, Boiler
	variety [və'raɪəti]	Abwechslung, Vielfalt
T	**brand new** [ˌbrænd 'njuː]	brandneu
	to **break down** [ˌbreɪk 'daʊn]	kaputtgehen
	to **minimize** ['mɪnɪmaɪz]	gering halten, minimieren
	downtime ['daʊntaɪm]	Ausfallzeiten
	to **operate** ['ɒpəreɪt]	in Betrieb sein
	on duty [ɒn 'djuːti]	im Dienst
	to **deal with sth** ['diːl wɪð]	sich um etw kümmern, mit etw umgehen
	shift [ʃɪft]	Schicht
	troubleshooting ['trʌblʃuːtɪŋ]	Fehlersuche
	promotion [prə'məʊʃn]	Beförderung
	overhead power cable [ˌəʊvəhed 'paʊə keɪbl]	Freileitung, Überlandleitung
	to **lay** [leɪ]	legen
	underground cable [ˌʌndəgraʊnd 'keɪbl]	Erdleitung
	to **connect** [kə'nekt]	verbinden, anschließen
	substation ['sʌbsteɪʃn]	Umspannwerk, Transformatorenstation
	pylon ['paɪlən]	Strommast
	standby ['stændbaɪ]	Bereitschaft
	fresh [freʃ]	frisch
	to **be one's turn** [bi wʌnz 'tɜːn]	an der Reihe sein
	to **record** [rɪ'kɔːd]	aufzeichnen, aufnehmen
	to **accompany** [ə'kʌmpəni]	begleiten
18	**dual system** [ˌdjuːəl 'sɪstəm]	duales System
	in-company ['ɪn kʌmpəni]	innerbetrieblich
	to **enter sth** ['entə]	etw (Ausbildung usw.) beginnen, mit etw anfangen
	scheme [skiːm]	Programm, Plan
	vocational college [vəʊˌkeɪʃənl 'kɒlɪdʒ]	Berufsschule
	to **combine** [kəm'baɪn]	verknüpfen, kombinieren
	hands-on [ˌhændz 'ɒn]	praktisch
	job experience [ˌdʒɒb ɪk'spɪəriəns]	Berufserfahrung
	deep [diːp]	tief, vertieft
	trade [treɪd]	Gewerbe, Branche

	to **act out** [ˌækt 'aʊt]	spielen
29	**machine tool** [mə'ʃiːn tuːl]	Werkzeugmaschine
	bandsaw ['bændsɔː]	Bandsäge
	milling machine ['mɪlɪŋ məʃiːn]	Fräsmaschine
	off-hand grinder [ˌɒfhænd 'graɪndə]	Handschleifmaschine
	power hacksaw ['paʊə hæksɔː]	Maschinenbügelsäge
	column ['kɒləm]	Säule
	chuck [tʃʌk]	Spannfutter, Bohrfutter
	dial ['daɪəl]	Anzeige, Regler
	motor ['məʊtə]	Motor
	to **swivel** ['swɪvl]	schwenken
	to **be composed of sth** [bi kəm'pəʊzd əv]	aus etw bestehen
	base [beɪs]	Basis, Sockel
	to **support** [sə'pɔːt]	tragen, halten, stützen
	in turn [ɪn 'tɜːn]	wiederum, seiner-/ihrerseits
	hold down clamp [ˌhəʊld daʊn 'klæmp]	Niederhalter
	to **contain** [kən'teɪn]	enthalten
	to **turn** [tɜːn]	drehen
	spindle ['spɪndl]	Spindel
	control dial [kən'trəʊl daɪəl]	Drehregler
	to **hold** [həʊld]	halten
	cutting tool ['kʌtɪŋ tuːl]	Schneidwerkzeug
30	to **machine** [mə'ʃiːn]	(maschinell) bearbeiten
	flat [flæt]	eben
	surface ['sɜːfɪs]	Oberfläche, Fläche
	irregular [ɪ'regjələ]	uneben
	to **bore** [bɔː]	innendrehen
	swivelling head ['swɪvlɪŋ hed]	Schwenkkopf
	to **remove** [rɪ'muːv]	entfernen, abtragen
	to **rotate** [rəʊ'teɪt]	rotieren, sich drehen
	multi-toothed cutter [ˌmʌlti tuːθt 'kʌtə]	mehrzahniges Fräswerkzeug
	equipped with sth [ɪ'kwɪpt wɪð]	mit etw ausgestattet
	power feed ['paʊə fiːd]	automatischer Vorschub
	smooth [smuːð]	glatt, ruhig
	manual feed [ˌmænjuəl 'fiːd]	manueller Vorschub
	surface finish [ˌsɜːfɪs 'fɪnɪʃ]	Oberfläche(nbeschaffenheit)
	to **fabricate** ['fæbrɪkeɪt]	fertigen, herstellen
	feature ['fiːtʃə]	Teil, Sonderanfertigung
	circular ['sɜːkjələ]	kreisförmig
	cross section [ˌkrɒs 'sekʃn]	Querschnitt
	to **drive** [draɪv]	antreiben
	gear train ['gɪə treɪn]	Getriebe
	tailstock ['teɪlstɒk]	Reitstock
	centre ['sentə]	Reitstockspitze
	to **ream** [riːm]	reiben

	to **thread** [θred]	Gewinde schneiden
	taper ['teɪpə]	Kegel
31	**apron** ['eɪprən]	Schlosskasten
	bed slideways ['bed slaɪdweɪz]	Maschinenbett
	compound slide [ˌkɒmpaʊnd 'slaɪd]	Kreuzschlitten
	control unit [kən'trəʊl juːnɪt]	Steuergerät, Steuerung
	headstock ['hedstɒk]	Spindelkasten
	protective hood [prəˌtektɪv 'hʊd]	Schutzhaube
	rack [ræk]	Zahnstange
	tool holder ['tuːl həʊldə]	Werkzeughalter
	to **serve** [sɜːv]	dienen
	housing ['haʊzɪŋ]	Gehäuse
	driving pulley ['draɪvɪŋ pʊli]	Antriebsscheibe
	back gear [ˌbæk 'gɪə]	(Räder-)Vorgelege
	live centre [ˌlaɪv 'sentə]	verfahrbare Führungsspitze
	feed reverse gear [fiːd rɪˌvɜːs 'gɪə]	Vorschub rückwärts
	to **feed** [fiːd]	vorschieben
	lathe operator [leɪð 'ɒpəreɪtə]	Dreher/in
	flying chips [ˌflaɪɪŋ 'tʃɪps]	herumfliegende Späne
	coolant ['kuːlənt]	Kühlmittel
	to **slide** [slaɪd]	gleiten
	to **accommodate** [ə'kɒmədeɪt]	aufnehmen, unterbringen
	length [leŋθ]	Länge
	to **fasten sth to sth** ['fɑːsn tə]	etw an etw befestigen
	to **house** [haʊz]	beherbergen
	gears *pl* [gɪəz]	Gangschaltung
	clutch [klʌtʃ]	Kupplung
	lever ['liːvə]	Hebel
	cross slide ['krɒs slaɪd]	Querschlitten
	to **mount** [maʊnt]	befestigen, montieren, anbringen
	rugged ['rʌgɪd]	robust, stabil
	casting ['kɑːstɪŋ]	Gussstück
	carriage assembly ['kærɪdʒ əsembli]	Werkzeugschlitten
	gear [gɪə]	Zahnrad
	rotation [rəʊ'teɪʃn]	Rotation, Drehung
	compound rest ['kɒmpaʊnd rest]	Kreuzschlitten
	rigid(ly) ['rɪdʒɪd]	starr, fest
	to **clamp** [klæmp]	einspannen
	height [haɪt]	Höhe
	support [sə'pɔːt]	Träger, Halter
32	to **take care of sth** [ˌteɪk 'keər əv]	sich um etw kümmern, etw bearbeiten, etw erledigen
	enquiry [ɪn'kwaɪəri]	Anfrage
	to **appear** [ə'pɪə]	erscheinen, auftreten, vorkommen
	dot [dɒt]	Punkt

	hyphen ['haɪfn]	Bindestrich
	underscore ['ʌndəskɔː]	Unterstrich
	to **dictate** [dɪk'teɪt]	diktieren
	subject line ['sʌbdʒɪkt laɪn]	Betreffzeile
	indication [ˌɪndɪ'keɪʃn]	Hinweis, Anzeichen
	to **state** [steɪt]	angeben, erklären, sagen
	request (for sth) [rɪ'kwest]	Bitte (um etw)
	assistance [ə'sɪstəns]	Hilfe, Unterstützung
	to **announce** [ə'naʊns]	ankündigen
	covering letter ['kʌvərɪŋ letə]	Anschreiben, Begleitschreiben
	brochure ['brəʊʃə]	Broschüre
	venue ['venjuː]	Veranstaltungsort
	event [ɪ'vent]	Veranstaltung
	flyer ['flaɪə]	Faltblatt
	to **attach** [ə'tætʃ]	(*E-Mail:*) anhängen
	update (on sth) ['ʌpdeɪt]	aktuelle Informationen (zu etw)
	agenda [ə'dʒendə]	Tagesordnung
	application [ˌæplɪ'keɪʃn]	Antrag, Bewerbung
	stand [stænd]	(Messe-)Stand
	fair [feə]	Messe
	to **interview sb** ['ɪntəvjuː]	mit jdm ein Vorstellungsgespräch führen
33	**reply** [rɪ'plaɪ]	Antwort
	to **reply** [rɪ'plaɪ]	antworten
	catalogue ['kætəlɒg]	Katalog
	item ['aɪtəm]	Artikel
	in stock [ɪn 'stɒk]	auf Lager, verfügbar
	Yours faithfully [ˌjɔːz 'feɪθfəli]	... und verbleiben mit freundlichen Grüßen
	Ltd ['lɪmɪtɪd]	GmbH
	to **dispatch** [dɪ'spætʃ]	versenden
	to **do business with sb** [du 'bɪznəs wɪð]	mit jdm Geschäfte machen
	complimentary close [ˌkɒmplɪˌmentri 'kləʊz]	(*Brief:*) Schlussformel
	salutation [ˌsælju'teɪʃn]	(*Brief:*) Anrede
	sir [sɜː]	Herr
	madam ['mædəm]	Dame
	unknown [ˌʌn'nəʊn]	unbekannt
	(Best) Regards [rɪ'gɑːdz]	Mit freundlichen Grüßen
	Best wishes [best 'wɪʃɪz]	Mit freundlichen Grüßen
	Yours sincerely [ˌjɔːz sɪn'sɪəli]	Mit freundlichen Grüßen

UNIT 4

34	**trade fair** ['treɪd feə]	(Branchen-, Handels-)Messe
	to **classify** ['klæsɪfaɪ]	klassifizieren
	carbon fibre [ˌkɑːbən 'faɪbə]	Kohlefaser
	iron ['aɪən]	Eisen
	cast iron [ˌkɑːst 'aɪən]	Gusseisen
	glass fibre [ˌglɑːs 'faɪbə]	Glasfaser
	lead [led]	Blei
	titanium [tɪ'teɪniəm]	Titan
	zinc [zɪŋk]	Zink
	aluminium *BE* [ˌæljə'mɪniəm]	Aluminium
	aluminum *AE* [ə'luːmɪnəm]	Aluminium
	stress [stres]	Betonung
	syllable ['sɪləbl]	Silbe
	ferrous metals *pl* [ˌferəs 'metlz]	Eisenmetalle
	e.g. [ˌiː 'dʒiː]	z.B.
	non-ferrous metals *pl* [nɒn ˌferəs 'metlz]	Buntmetalle
	heavy metals *pl* [ˌhevi 'metlz]	Schwermetalle
	light metals *pl* [ˌlaɪt 'metlz]	Leichtmetalle
	non-metals *pl* [ˌnɒn 'metlz]	Nichtmetalle, Steine und Erden
	natural ['nætʃrəl]	natürlich
	artificial [ˌɑːtɪ'fɪʃl]	künstlich
	compound ['kɒmpaʊnd]	Verbundwerkstoff
35	**mechanical(ly)** [mɪ'kænɪkl]	mechanisch
	property ['prɒpəti]	Eigenschaft
	elastic(ally) [ɪ'læstɪk]	elastisch
	flexible ['fleksəbl]	biegsam
	hard-wearing [ˌhɑːd 'weərɪŋ]	strapazierfähig, verschleißfest
	light-weight ['laɪtweɪt]	leicht
	malleable ['mæliəbl]	formbar
	resilient [rɪ'zɪliənt]	federelastisch
	tough [tʌf]	zäh
	to **absorb** [əb'sɔːb]	absorbieren, aufnehmen
	to **deform** [dɪ'fɔːm]	verformen
	in response to [ɪn rɪ'spɒns tə]	als Reaktion auf
	to **apply sth** [ə'plaɪ]	etw anwenden
	force [fɔːs]	Kraft
	compressive stress [kəmˌpresɪv 'stres]	Druckbelastung, Druckspannung
	defect ['diːfekt]	Schaden, Fehler
	to **withstand sth** [wɪð'stænd]	etw aushalten, einer Sache widerstehen
	shock [ʃɒk]	Stoß, Stöße
	plastic(ally) ['plæstɪk]	plastisch
	to **fracture** ['fræktʃə]	brechen, zerbrechen
	to **rupture** ['rʌptʃə]	reißen, zerreißen
	indentation [ˌɪnden'teɪʃn]	Eindruck, Einkerbung
	scratching ['skrætʃɪŋ]	Verkratzen
	to **resist** [rɪ'zɪst]	einer Sache widerstehen
	distorting [dɪ'stɔːtɪŋ]	verformend, deformierend
	shape [ʃeɪp]	Form
	silvery-grey [ˌsɪlvəri 'greɪ]	silbrig-grau
	crash helmet ['kræʃ helmɪt]	Sturzhelm

	household goods *pl* ['haʊshəʊld gʊdz]	Haushaltsartikel
	rough [rʌf]	rau
	hand-out ['hændaʊt]	Arbeitsblatt, Informationsblatt, Merkblatt
	to **distribute** [dɪ'strɪbjuːt]	verteilen
	to **refer to sth** [rɪ'fɜː tə]	auf etw verweisen, sich auf etw beziehen
	conclusion [kən'kluːʒn]	Schluss
36	to **mediate** ['miːdieɪt]	vermitteln
	(printed) circuit board (PCB) ['sɜːkɪt bɔːd]	Leiterplatte, Platine
	to **insulate** ['ɪnsjuleɪt]	isolieren
	interconnection [ˌɪntəkə'nekʃn]	Verbindung, Verschaltung
	populated PCB [ˌpɒpjuleɪtɪd ˌpiː siː 'biː]	(mit Bauelementen) bestückte Leiterplatte
	layer ['leɪə]	Schicht
	multi-layer [ˌmʌlti 'leɪə]	Mehrschicht-, mehrschichtig
	to **enable sth to do sth** [ɪ'neɪbl]	etw in die Lage versetzen, etw zu tun
	to **function** ['fʌŋkʃn]	funktionieren
	conducting [kən'dʌktɪŋ]	leitend, leitfähig
	various ['veəriəs]	verschieden
	to **require** [rɪ'kwaɪə]	erfordern, benötigen
	multilayer structure [mʌltiˌleɪə 'strʌktʃə]	mehrschichtiger Aufbau
	conductor [kən'dʌktə]	Leiter
	conductor pattern [kən'dʌktə pætn]	Leiterbild, Leitermuster
	resistor [rɪ'zɪstə]	Widerstand
	capacitor [kə'pæsɪtə]	Kondensator
	integrated circuit [ˌɪntɪgreɪtɪd 'sɜːkɪt]	integrierter Schaltkreis
	surface-mounted ['sɜːfɪs maʊntɪd]	oberflächenmontiert
	surface-mount(ed) device (SMD) ['sɜːfɪs maʊnt dɪvaɪs]	SMD-Bauelement
	reflow soldering ['rɪfləʊ səʊldərɪŋ]	Reflow-Löten
	through-hole device ['θruː həʊl dɪvaɪs]	THT-Bauelement
	wave soldering ['weɪv səʊldərɪŋ]	Wellenlöten
	plated through hole (PTH) [ˌpleɪtɪd 'θruː həʊl]	Durchkontaktierung
	conductive layer [kənˌdʌktɪv 'leɪə]	leitfähige Schicht
	to **plate** [pleɪt]	galvanisieren, überziehen
	plated-through [ˌpleɪtɪd 'θruː]	durchkontaktiert
	via ['vaɪe]	Durchkontaktierung, Durchsteiger
	epoxy resin [ɪˌpɒksi 'rezɪn]	Kunstharz, Epoxidharz
	composite material [ˌkɒmpəzɪt mə'tɪəriəl]	Verbundwerkstoff
	reinforcement [ˌriːɪn'fɔːsmənt]	Verstärkung
	to **bond** [bɒnd]	verkleben, verbinden
	copper traces *pl* ['kɒpə treɪsɪz]	Leiterbahnen
	internal [ɪn'tɜːnl]	innere/r/s
	foil [fɔɪl]	Folie
	to **make up sth** [ˌmeɪk 'ʌp]	etw ausmachen
	external [ɪk'stɜːnl]	äußere/r/s, Außen-
	solder pad ['səʊldə pæd]	Lötpad
	to **cover** ['kʌvə]	bedecken
	solder mask ['səʊldə mɑːsk]	Lötmaske
	solder point ['səʊldə pɔɪnt]	Lötpunkt, Lötstelle
	polymer coating ['pɒlɪmə kəʊtɪŋ]	Kunststoffbeschichtung
	to **apply sth** [ə'plaɪ]	etw (*Beschichtung usw.*) auftragen
	protection [prə'tekʃn]	Schutz
	oxidation [ˌɒksɪ'deɪʃn]	Oxidation, Oxidierung
	to **prevent** [prɪ'vent]	verhindern, verhüten
	solder ['səʊldə]	Lot
	unwanted [ʌnwɒn'tɪd]	unerwünscht
	closely spaced [ˌkləʊsli 'speɪst]	eng nebeneinanderliegend
37	**application** [ˌæplɪ'keɪʃn]	Anwendung
	single-board (micro) computer [sɪŋgl ˌbɔːd kəm'pjuːtə]	Einplatinenrechner
	control computer [kən'trəʊl kəmpjuːtə]	Steuerrechner, Steuerungsrechner
	interface ['ɪntəfeɪs]	Schnittstelle
	power supply (unit) ['paʊə səplaɪ]	Stromversorgung, Netzteil
	input ['ɪnpʊt]	Eingang
	output ['aʊtpʊt]	Ausgang
	to **measure** ['meʒə]	messen, betragen
	programmable [prə'græməbl]	programmierbar
	button ['bʌtn]	Taste
	power port ['paʊə pɔːt]	Stromversorgungsbuchse, -anschluss
	ground port ['graʊnd pɔːt]	Erdungsbuchse, -anschluss
	accelerometer [əkˌselə'rɒmɪtə]	Beschleunigungssensor
	compass ['kʌmpəs]	Kompass
	antenna [æn'tenə]	Antenne
	I/O connector [ˌaɪ 'əʊ kənektə]	Anschluss (nutzbar als Eingang oder Ausgang)
	to **be capable of sth** [bi 'keɪpəbl əv]	zu etw in der Lage sein, etw können
	to **program** ['prəʊgræm]	programmieren
	magnetometer [mægnə'tɒmətə]	Magnetfeldsensor
	actor ['æktə]	Aktor

	to **drive** [draɪv]	steuern
38	**alloy** ['ælɔɪ]	Legierung
	leaded ['ledɪd]	bleihaltig
	solder alloy ['səʊldər ælɔɪ]	Lötlegierung
	tin [tɪn]	Zinn
	compositional ratio [kɒmpəˌzɪʃnl 'reɪʃiəʊ]	Zusammensetzungsverhältnis
	to **melt** [melt]	schmelzen
	approximately [ə'prɒksɪmətli]	zirka, ungefähr
	toxic ['tɒksɪk]	giftig, toxisch
	consequently ['kɒnsɪkwəntli]	folglich, infolgedessen
	widely used [ˌwaɪdli 'juːzd]	weit verbreitet
	bismuth ['bɪzməθ]	Bismut, Wismut
	antimony ['æntɪməni]	Antimon
	melting point ['meltɪŋ pɔɪnt]	Schmelzpunkt
T	**core element** [ˌkɔː 'elɪmənt]	Hauptbestandteil
	casing ['keɪsɪŋ]	Gehäuse
	insulator ['ɪnsjəleɪtə]	Isolator
	semi-conductor [ˌsemi kən'dʌktə]	Halbleiter
	electrical flow [ɪˌlektrɪkl 'fləʊ]	elektrischer Fluss, Stromfluss
	to **exhibit sth** [ɪg'zɪbɪt]	etw an den Tag legen, etw zeigen
	silicon ['sɪlɪkən]	Silizium
	boron ['bɔːrɒn]	Bor
	phosphorus ['fɒsfərəs]	Phosphor
	doping ['dəʊpɪŋ]	Dotierung
	doped [dəʊpt]	dotiert
	precious ['preʃəs]	wertvoll, kostbar, edel
	laminate material ['læmɪnət mətɪəriəl]	Verbundwerkstoff
	conformal coating [kənˌfɔːml 'kəʊtɪŋ]	Schutzbeschichtung
	precious metals *pl* [ˌpreʃəs 'metlz]	Edelmetalle
	platinum ['plætɪnəm]	Platin
	significant [sɪg'nɪfɪkənt]	erheblich
	transition [træn'zɪʃn]	Übergang, Umstellung
	directive [dɪ'rektɪv]	Richtlinie
	to **come into effect** [kʌm ɪntu ɪ'fekt]	in Kraft treten
	restriction [rɪ'strɪkʃn]	Beschränkung
	hazardous substance [ˌhæzədəs 'sʌbstəns]	Gefahrstoff
	to **prohibit sth** [prə'hɪbɪt]	etw verbieten
	replacement [rɪ'pleɪsmənt]	Ersatz
	disadvantage [ˌdɪsəd'vɑːntɪdʒ]	Nachteil
	altered ['ɔːltəd]	geändert, verändert
	corrosion [kə'rəʊʒn]	Korrosion
	affordable [ə'fɔːdəbl]	erschwinglich, bezahlbar
	to **destroy** [dɪ'strɔɪ]	zerströren
39	**specific** [spə'sɪfɪk]	speziell, bestimmt, konkret
	dimensions *pl* [dɪ'menʃnz]	Abmessungen, Dimensionen
T	to **sort out sth** [ˌsɔːt 'aʊt]	etw klären
	to **talk sb through sth** [ˌtɔːk 'θruː]	etw mit jdm durchgehen
	plate [pleɪt]	Platte
	chamfer ['tʃæmfə]	Fase
	convex ['kɒnveks]	konvex
	semicircle ['semisɜːkl]	Halbkreis
	radius, radii ['reɪdiəs, 'reɪdiaɪ]	Radius, Radien
	concave [kɒn'keɪv]	konkav
	base line ['beɪs laɪn]	Grundlinie
	groove [gruːv]	Nut
	borehole ['bɔːhəʊl]	Bohrloch
	bore [bɔː]	Bohrung
	feature ['fiːtʃə]	technisches Merkmal
	continuous line [kənˌtɪnjuəs 'laɪn]	durchgezogene Linie
	chain-dotted line ['tʃeɪn dɒtɪd laɪn]	strichpunktierte Linie
	dimension line [dɪ'menʃn laɪn]	Bemaßungslinie
	circumference [sə'kʌmfərəns]	Umfang
40	**rectangle** ['rektæŋgl]	Rechteck
	triangle ['traɪæŋgl]	Dreieck
	circle ['sɜːkl]	Kreis
	cube [kjuːb]	Würfel
	cubical ['kjuːbɪkl]	würfelförmig
	solid ['sɒlɪd]	(dreidimensionaler) Körper
	rectangular solid [rekˌtæŋgjələ 'sɒlɪd]	Quader
	sphere [sfɪə]	Kugel
	hemisphere ['hemɪsfɪə]	Halbkugel
	hemispherical [ˌhemɪ'sferɪkl]	halbkugelförmig
	cone [kəʊn]	Kegel, Konus
	bar [bɑː]	Barren
	block [blɒk]	Klotz, Block
	film [fɪlm]	Folie
	sheet [ʃiːt]	Blech
	strip [strɪp]	Leiste, Streifen
	tube [tjuːb]	Rohr
41	**rolled** [rəʊld]	gewalzt, Walz-
	cylindrical(ly) [sə'lɪndrɪkl]	zylindrisch
	conical ['kɒnɪkl]	konisch, kegelförmig
	L-shaped ['el ʃeɪpt]	L-förmig
	symmetrical [sɪ'metrɪkl]	symmetrisch
	edge [edʒ]	Kante
	back to back [ˌbæk tə 'bæk]	Rücken an Rücken
P	**saddle** ['sædl]	Sattel
	handwheel ['hændwiːl]	Handrad

42	**signpost** ['saɪnpəʊst]	*Hinweise zur Orientierung der Zuhörer in einer Präsentation*
	to **invite sth** [ɪn'vaɪt]	zu etw auffordern
	clarity ['klærəti]	Klarheit, Deutlichkeit
	correctness [kə'rektnəs]	Richtigkeit
	spelling ['spelɪŋ]	Rechtschreibung
	prompt card ['prɒmt kɑːd]	Moderationskarte
	either ['aɪðə]	eines (von mehreren)
	index card ['ɪndeks kɑːd]	Karteikarte
	to **divide** [dɪ'vaɪd]	teilen, unterteilen
43	**feedback** ['fiːdbæk]	Rückmeldung(en)
	improvement [ɪm'pruːvmənt]	Verbesserung
	to **support** [sə'pɔːt]	(*Argumentation*) untermauern
	to **deal with sth** ['diːl wɪð]	sich mit etw befassen
	manner ['mænə]	Art (und Weise)
	overall score [əʊvər,ɔːl 'skɔː]	Gesamtpunktzahl

UNIT 5

46	**manual** ['mænjuəl]	Handbuch
	safety instructions *pl* ['seɪfti ɪnstrʌkʃnz]	Sicherheitshinweise
	trolley ['trɒli]	Wagen
	platform trolley ['plætfɔːm trɒli]	Plattformwagen, Flachtransportwagen
	scaffold ['skæfəʊld]	Gerüst
	to **clarify** ['klærəfaɪ]	klären, abklären
	mathematical operation [mæθə,mætɪkl ,ɒpə'reɪʃn]	Rechenoperation
	degree [dɪ'griː]	Grad
	to **read out sth** [,riːd 'aʊt]	etw vorlesen
47	**rectilinear solid** [rektɪ,lɪniə 'sɒlɪd]	geradkantiger Körper
	reverse order [rɪ,vɜːs 'ɔːdə]	umgekehrte Reihenfolge
	alphabetical [,ælfə'betɪkl]	alphabetisch
	castor ['kɑːstə]	Laufrolle
	to **fit sth with sth** [fɪt]	etw mit etw ausstatten
	brake [breɪk]	Bremse
48	**installation instruction** [,ɪnstə'leɪʃn ɪnstrʌkʃn]	Montageanleitung
	ceiling ['siːlɪŋ]	(Zimmer-)Decke
	fan [fæn]	Lüfter
	heat source ['hiːt sɔːs]	Wärmequelle
	to **detect** [dɪ'tekt]	erkennen
	moving object [,muːvɪŋ 'ɒbdʒɪkt]	bewegtes Objekt
	detection zone [dɪ'tekʃn zəʊn]	Erfassungsbereich
	vehicle ['viːəkl]	Fahrzeug
	fork-lift truck [,fɔːklɪft 'trʌk]	Gabelstapler
49	**fuse box** ['fjuːz bɒks]	Sicherungskasten
	skylight ['skaɪlaɪt]	Dachluke, Oberlicht
T	**floor plan** ['flɔː plæn]	Grundriss, Lageplan
	to **calculate** ['kælkjuleɪt]	berechnen, ausrechnen
	in case [ɪn 'keɪs]	falls
	roof [ruːf]	Dach
	booklet ['bʊklət]	Broschüre
	floating ['fləʊtɪŋ]	potentialfrei
	switch contact ['swɪtʃ kɒntækt]	Schaltkontakt
	to **set** [set]	einstellen
	switching ['swɪtʃɪŋ]	Schaltung
	mains voltage ['meɪnz vəʊltɪdʒ]	Netzspannung
	coupler [kʌplə]	Koppler, Kupplung
	control line [kən'trəʊl laɪn]	Steuerleitung
50	to **extend sth** [ɪk'stend]	etw erweitern, etw ausbauen
	hardwired [,hɑːd'waɪəd]	festverdrahtet
	heat and smoke alarm system [,hiːt ənd sməʊk ə'lɑːm sɪstəm]	Hitze- und Rauchmeldeanlage
	storey ['stɔːri]	Geschoss, Etage
	to **expand** [ɪk'spænd]	expandieren, sich erweitern
	to **fit sth** [fɪt]	etw einbauen
	dust [dʌst]	Staub
	life span ['laɪf spæn]	Lebensdauer
	significance [sɪg'nɪfɪkəns]	Bedeutung
	flashing light [,flæʃɪŋ 'laɪt]	Blinklicht
	amber ['æmbə]	bernsteingelb
	interconnected [,ɪntəkə'nektɪd]	(untereinander) verbunden
	optical ['ɒptɪkl]	optisch
	fire alarm ['faɪə əlɑːm]	Brandmelder
	sensing element ['sensɪŋ elɪmənt]	Sensorelement
	to **respond to sth** [rɪ'spɒnd tə]	auf etw reagieren
	fast-flaming [,fɑːst 'fleɪmɪŋ]	schnell brennend
	false alarm [,fɔːls ə'lɑːm]	Fehlalarm
	unique [ju'niːk]	einzigartig
	compensation feature [,kɒmpən'seɪʃn fiːtʃə]	Ausgleichsfunktion
	to **adjust for sth** [ə'dʒʌst fə]	etw berücksichtigen, etw ausgleichen
	contamination [kən,tæmɪ'neɪʃn]	Verunreinigung, Kontamination
	sensor chamber ['sensə tʃeɪmbə]	Sensorkammer
	mains power ['meɪnz paʊə]	Netzstrom
	built-in [,bɪlt'ɪn]	eingebaut
	rechargeable [,riː'tʃɑːdʒəbl]	wiederaufladbar
	cell [sel]	Zelle

	back-up ['bækʌp]	*hier:* Notstromquelle
	in the event of [ɪn ði ɪ'vent əv]	für den Fall eine/r/s
	mains failure ['meɪnz feɪljə]	Netzausfall
	to **outlast sth** [ˌaʊt'lɑːst]	länger halten als etw
	operating life ['ɒpəreɪtɪŋ laɪf]	Lebensdauer, Betriebsdauer
	to **self-check** [ˌself 'tʃek]	einen Selbsttest durchführen
	internal [ɪn'tɜːnl]	intern, innere/r/s
	circuitry ['sɜːkɪtri]	Schaltung, Schaltkreise
	to **flash** [flæʃ]	blinken
	signal tone ['sɪgnəl təʊn]	Signalton
	to **beep** [biːp]	piepen
	to **simulate** ['sɪmjuleɪt]	simulieren
	horn [hɔːn]	Signalhorn
	to **sense** [sens]	wahrnehmen, erkennen
	add-on ['æd ɒn]	zusätzlich, Erweiterungs-
	radio link ['reɪdiəʊ lɪŋk]	Funkverbindung
	module ['mɒdjuːl]	Modul
	hybrid ['haɪbrɪd]	gemischt, mehrgleisig, Hybrid-
	communication [kəˌmjuːnɪ'keɪʃn]	Datenübermittlung, Verbindung
	hardwiring ['hɑːdwaɪərɪŋ]	Festverdrahtung
51	**theme** [θiːm]	Thema
	procedure [prə'siːdʒə]	Verfahren, Maßnahme
	warning sign ['wɔːnɪŋ saɪn]	Hinweisschild, Warnhinweis
	Caution! ['kɔːʃn]	Achtung! Vorsicht!
	buried cable [ˌberid 'keɪbl]	Erdkabel
	to **lock out sth** [ˌlɒk 'aʊt]	etw (dauerhaft) abschalten
	individual [ˌɪndɪ'vɪdʒuəl]	Person
	to **sign** [saɪn]	unterzeichnen
	reverse side [rɪ'vɜːs saɪd]	Rückseite
	tag [tæg]	Anhänger, Etikett
	remark [rɪ'mɑːk]	Bemerkung
	electrical fire [ɪˌlektrɪkl 'faɪə]	elektrischer Brand
	to **keep sth clear** [kiːp 'klɪə]	etw frei halten
	bare [beə]	(*Draht:*) blank
	live [laɪv]	unter Spannung
	underground ['ʌndəgraʊnd]	unterirdisch
	earthmoving machinery ['ɜːθmuːvɪŋ məʃiːnəri]	Erdbaumaschinen
	prohibition [ˌprəʊɪ'bɪʃn]	Verbot
	permission [pə'mɪʃn]	Erlaubnis
52	**throughout the company** [θruːˌaʊt ðə 'kʌmpəni]	in der ganzen Firma
	workmate ['wɜːkmeɪt]	Arbeitskollege/-in
	to **turn sth on/off** [ˌtɜːn 'ɒn/'ɒf]	etw ein-/ausschalten
	to **disconnect** [dɪskə'nekt]	trennen
	to **kill** [kɪl]	töten
	death [deθ]	Tod, Todesfall
	chest [tʃest]	Brust, Brustkorb
	strength [streŋθ]	Stärke
	amperage ['æmpərɪdʒ]	Stromstärke
	duration [dju'reɪʃn]	Dauer
	tingle ['tɪŋgl]	Kribbeln
	if anything [ɪf 'eniθɪŋ]	wenn überhaupt
	unpleasant [ʌn'pleznt]	unangenehm
	slightly ['slaɪtli]	geringfügig, etwas
	muscle ['mʌsl]	Muskel
	to **freeze** [friːz]	erstarren
	to **let go of sth** [ˌlet 'gəʊ əv]	etw loslassen
	greatly ['greɪtli]	sehr, in hohem Maße
	painful ['peɪnfl]	schmerzhaft
	to **disturb** [dɪ'stɜːb]	stören
	ventricular fibrillation [venˌtrɪkjələ faɪbrɪ'leɪʃn]	Herzkammerflimmern
	uncoordinated [ˌʌnkəʊ'ɔːdɪneɪtɪd]	unkoordiniert
	nerve damage ['nɜːv dæmɪdʒ]	Nervenschäden
	cardiac arrest [ˌkɑːdɪak ə'rest]	Herzstillstand
	burn [bɜːn]	Verbrennung
53	**mild** [maɪld]	leicht
	severe [sɪ'vɪə]	schwer, ernsthaft
	tumble dryer [ˌtʌmbl 'draɪə]	Wäschetrockner
	packaging ['pækɪdʒɪŋ]	Verpackung
	measures *pl* ['meʒəz]	Maßnahmen
T	**packaging line** ['pækɪdʒɪŋ laɪn]	Verpackungsstraße
	approaching device [ə'prəʊtʃɪŋ dɪvaɪs]	Näherungsvorrichtung
	to **be supposed to do sth** [bi sə'pəʊzd tə]	etw tun sollen
	approaching [ə'prəʊtʃɪŋ]	nahend, sich nähernd
	proximity sensor [prə'ksɪməti sensə]	Näherungssensor
	sporadic [spə'rædɪk]	gelegentlich, vereinzelt
	fault [fɔːlt]	Defekt
	uncommon [ʌn'kɒmən]	selten, ungewöhnlich
	to **fail** [feɪl]	versagen, ausfallen
	noise [nɔɪz]	Rauschen
	to **tag** [tæg]	markieren, kennzeichnen
	to **carry out sth** [ˌkæri 'aʊt]	etw durchführen
	dead [ded]	tot, ohne Strom
	probe [prəʊb]	Sonde, Fühler
	to **register sb** ['redʒɪstə]	etw anzeigen
	to **short-circuit** [ˌʃɔːt 'sɜːkɪt]	kurzschließen
	spark [spɑːk]	Funke
	crackling noise [ˌkræklɪŋ 'nɔɪz]	Knistern
	to **trip** [trɪp]	auslösen
	to **fence sth off** [ˌfens 'ɒf]	etw abschranken

54	**graph** [grɑːf]	Diagramm, Grafik
	union ['juːniən]	Gewerkschaft
	union representative [ˌjuːniən reprɪ'zentətɪv]	Gewerkschaftsvertreter/in
	conference ['kɒnfərəns]	Tagung, Konferenz
	to **refresh** [rɪ'freʃ]	auffrischen
	bar chart ['bɑː tʃɑːt]	Säulendiagramm
	line graph ['laɪn grɑːf]	Liniendiagramm
	pie chart ['paɪ tʃɑːt]	Tortendiagramm
	to **go up** [ˌgəʊ 'ʌp]	steigen
	to **go down** [ˌgəʊ 'daʊn]	sinken
	to **increase** [ɪn'kriːs]	zunehmen, ansteigen
	increase ['ɪŋkriːs]	Zunahme, Anstieg
	to **flatten out** [ˌflætn 'aʊt]	sich stabilisieren, sich einpendeln (bei)
	to **level off** [ˌlevl 'ɒf]	sich stabilisieren, sich einpendeln (bei)
	to **decrease** [dɪ'kriːs]	abnehmen, sinken
	decrease ['diːkriːs]	Abnahme, Sinken
	to **drop** [drɒp]	sinken, fallen
	drop [drɒp]	Fall, Sinken
	rise [raɪz]	Anstieg
	to **fluctuate** ['flʌktʃueɪt]	schwanken, sich ständig verändern
	fluctuation [ˌflʌktʃu'eɪʃn]	Schwankung(en), ständige Veränderung
	to **fall** [fɔːl]	abstürzen
	fall [fɔːl]	Absturz
	to **climb** [klaɪm]	steigen
	climb [klaɪm]	Anstieg
	to **peak** [piːk]	einen Spitzenwert erreichen
	peak [piːk]	Spitzenwert
	traffic ['træfɪk]	Verkehr
	traveller ['trævələ]	Fahrgast
P	**manufacturing output** [ˌmænju'fæktʃərɪŋ aʊtpʊt]	Produktionsleistung
55	**figures** *pl* ['fɪgəz]	Zahlen, Ziffern
	sales *pl* [seɪlz]	Umsatz, Umsätze, Verkaufszahlen
	financial year [faɪˌnænʃl 'jɪə]	Geschäftsjahr
	quarterly ['kwɔːtəli]	vierteljährlich, Quartals-
	quarter ['kwɔːtə]	Quartal
T	**drastic(ally)** ['dræstɪkli]	drastisch
T	to **recover** [rɪ'kʌvə]	sich erholen
T	**volume** ['vɒljuːm]	Volumen
T	**at a glance** [ət ə 'glɑːns]	auf einen Blick
	condition [kən'dɪʃn]	Bedingung
	blue collar workers *pl* [ˌbluː kɒlə 'wɜːkəz]	Arbeiter/innen
	white collar workers *pl* [ˌwaɪt kɒlə 'wɜːkəz]	Angestellte

UNIT 6

56	to **advise** [əd'vaɪz]	beraten
	medical equipment [ˌmedɪkl ɪ'kwɪpmənt]	medizinische Geräte, Medizintechnik
	portable ['pɔːtəbl]	tragbar, mobil
	X-ray ['eksreɪ]	Röntgen
	swimming pool attendant ['swɪmɪŋ puːl ətendənt]	Bademeister/in
	to **enquire about sth** [ɪn'kwaɪər əbaʊt]	sich nach etw erkundigen
	pulse [pʌls]	Puls
	blood pressure ['blʌd preʃə]	Blutdruck
	pulse and blood pressure monitor [ˌpʌls ənd 'blʌd preʃə mɒnɪtə]	Puls- und Blutdruckmessgerät
T	**swimming pool complex** ['swɪmɪŋ puːl kɒmpleks]	Bäderlandschaft, Schwimmbadanlage
T	**waterproof** ['wɔːtəpruːf]	wasserdicht
T	**lap** [læp]	Bahn (*im Schwimmbecken*)
T	**adjustable** [ə'dʒʌstəbl]	regelbar, einstellbar
T	**bright** [braɪt]	(*Licht:*) hell, gleißend
T	**sunlight** ['sʌnlaɪt]	Sonnenlicht
T	**beat per minute** [ˌbiːt pɜː 'mɪnɪt]	Schlag pro Minute
T	**by** [baɪ]	(*Abmessungen:*) mal
T	**cover** ['kʌvə]	Hülle, Tasche
T	**slip-on cover** [ˌslɪp ɒn 'kʌvə]	Einstecktasche
T	to **weigh** [weɪ]	wiegen
T	**gramme** *BE* [græm]	Gramm
T	to **place an order** [ˌpleɪs ən 'ɔːdə]	einen Auftrag erteilen, eine Bestellung aufgeben
T	**delivery terms** *pl* [dɪ'lɪvəri tɜːmz]	Lieferbedingungen
T	to **package** ['pækɪdʒ]	verpacken
T	**individual(ly)** [ˌɪndɪ'vɪdʒuəl]	einzeln
T	**case** [keɪs]	Schachtel, Hülle, Gehäuse
	accuracy ['ækjərəsi]	Genauigkeit
57	**darkroom** ['dɑːkruːm]	Dunkelkammer
	radiation [ˌreɪdi'eɪʃn]	Strahlung
	dose [dəʊs]	Dosis
	X-ray tube ['eksreɪ tjuːb]	Röntgenröhre
	power consumption [ˌpaʊə kən'sʌmpʃn]	Stromverbrauch
	net [net]	netto
	gross [grəʊs]	brutto
	carton ['kɑːtn]	Karton
	general practitioner (GP) [ˌdʒenrəl præk'tɪʃənə]	Allgemeinarzt/-ärztin, Hausarzt/-ärztin
	construction site [kən'strʌkʃn saɪt]	Baustelle
	to **perform sth** [pə'fɔːm]	(*Theater usw.:*) etw aufführen, etw spielen
	latest ['leɪtɪst]	neueste/r/s

	salesperson ['seɪlzpɜːsn]	Verkäufer/in, Vertriebsmitarbeiter/in
	to **reject** [rɪ'dʒekt]	ablehnen, zurückweisen
	to **have sth in mind** [həv ɪn 'maɪnd]	an etw denken, sich etw vorstellen
58	**door operating system** ['dɔːr ɒpəreɪtɪŋ sɪstəm]	Türanlage, Türsteuerung
	to **identify** [aɪ'dentɪfaɪ]	bestimmen, herausfinden, identifizieren
	requirement [rɪ'kwaɪəmənt]	Anforderung, Bedürfnis
	to **review** [rɪ'vjuː]	(*Text*) noch einmal durchgehen
	durable ['djʊərəbl]	strapazierfähig, langlebig
	insulated ['ɪnsjuleɪtɪd]	isoliert
	power-assisted ['pɒʊər əsɪstɪd]	Servo-
	sliding door [ˌslaɪdɪŋ 'dɔː]	Schiebetür
	cold storage [ˌkəʊld 'stɔːrɪdʒ]	Kühllager, Kühlhaus
	premium ['priːmiəm]	hochwertig, erstklassig
	non-corrosive [ˌnɒn kə'rəʊsɪv]	korrosionsbeständig
	performance [pə'fɔːməns]	Leistung
	efficiency [ɪ'fɪʃnsi]	Effizienz, Leistungsfähigkeit
	programmable logic controller (PLC) [ˌprəʊgræməbl ˌlɒdʒɪk kən'trəʊlə]	speicherprogrammierbare Steuerung (SPS)
	rollup door [rəʊlˌʌp 'dɔː]	Rolltor
	robust [rəʊ'bʌst]	widerstandsfähig
	space-saving ['speɪs seɪvɪŋ]	platzsparend
	transit ['trænzɪt]	Durchgangsverkehr
	tight [taɪt]	dicht
	seal [siːl]	Dichtung, Verschluss
	to **optimize** ['ɒptɪmaɪz]	optimieren
	inbuilt [ˌɪn'bɪlt]	eingebaut
	window panel ['wɪndəʊ pænl]	Fenster, Scheibe
	visibility [ˌvɪzə'bɪləti]	Sicht
	strip door ['strɪp dɔː]	Streifenvorhangtor
	secondary ['sekəndri]	sekundär
	barrier ['bæriə]	Barriere, Schranke
	cost-effective [ˌkɒstɪ'fektɪv]	kostengünstig
	refrigerated air [rɪˌfrɪdʒəreɪtɪd 'eə]	gekühlte Luft
	loss [lɒs]	Verlust
	cooler ['kuːlə]	Kühlanlage
	pollution [pə'luːʃn]	Verschmutzung
	pedestrian [pɪ'destriən]	Fußgänger
	swing door [ˌswɪŋ 'dɔː]	Schwenktür, Pendeltür
	bumper ['bʌmpə]	Stoßfänger, Stoßstange
	impact ['ɪmpækt]	Aufprall
	frozen food [ˌfrəʊzn 'fuːd]	Tiefkühlkost, Tiefkühlprodukte
	storage ['stɔːrɪdʒ]	Lagerung, Aufbewahrung
	frequent ['friːkwənt]	häufig
	narrow ['nærəʊ]	schmal
	doorway ['dɔːweɪ]	Durchgang, Türöffnung
59	to **convert** [kən'vɜːt]	umwandeln
	command [kə'mɑːnd]	Befehl
	central processing unit (CPU) [ˌsentrəl 'prəʊsesɪŋ juːnɪt]	Hauptprozessor
	actuator ['æktʃʊeɪtə]	Aktor
	to **access sth** ['ækses]	auf etw zugreifen
	port [pɔːt]	Schnittstelle
	non-volatile [ˌnɒn 'vɒlətaɪl]	nichtflüchtig
	memory ['meməri]	Speicher
	required [rɪ'kwaɪəd]	erforderlich
T	**manually operated** [ˌmænjuəli 'ɒpəreɪtɪd]	handbetrieben
	inefficient [ˌɪnɪ'fɪʃnt]	ineffizient
	attractive [ə'træktɪv]	ansprechend, attraktiv
	three-phase current [ˌθriː feɪz 'kʌrənt]	Drehstrom
	fruit processing ['fruːt prəʊsesɪŋ]	Obstverarbeitung
	to **pass through** ['pɑːs θruː]	hindurchfahren
	to **enter sth** ['entə]	etw betreten
	mechanism ['mekənɪzəm]	Mechanismus
60	**appearance** [ə'pɪərəns]	Aussehen, Erscheinungsbild
	flexibility [ˌfleksə'bɪləti]	Flexibilität
	ease of use [ˌiːz əv 'juːs]	Bedienungskomfort
	director [də'rektə]	Leiter/in, Direktor/in
	furniture ['fɜːnɪtʃə]	Möbel
61	to **estimate** ['estɪmeɪt]	schätzen
	control centre [kən'trəʊl sentə]	Steuerzentrale
	to **compress** [kəm'pres]	verdichten, komprimieren
	to **pump** [pʌmp]	pumpen
	pneumatic [njuː'mætɪk]	pneumatisch
62	**operating voltage** [ˌɒpəreɪtɪŋ 'vəʊltɪdʒ]	Betriebsspannung
	phase [feɪz]	Phase
	protective earth [prəˌtektɪv 'ɜːθ]	Schutzleiter, Schutzerde
	fuse [fjuːz]	Sicherung
	slow-blow fuse [ˌsləʊ bləʊ 'fjuːz]	träge Sicherung
	nominal current [ˌnɒmɪnl 'kʌrənt]	Nennstrom
	frequency ['friːkwənsi]	Frequenz
	nominal apparent power [nɒmɪnl əˌpærənt 'paʊə]	Nennscheinleistung
	conductor cross-section [kənˌdʌktə 'krɒs sekʃn]	Leiterquerschnitt
	test run ['test rʌn]	Probelauf
	oscillogram ['ɒsɪləgræm]	Oszillogramm
	waveform ['weɪvfɔːm]	Kurve
	peak [piːk]	Spitze, Wellenkamm

	spike [spaɪk]	Zacke
	trough [trɒf]	Wellental
	dip [dɪp]	Senke
	jagged ['dʒægɪd]	gezackt
	erratic [ɪ'rætɪk]	unregelmäßig, sprunghaft
	to **fix** [fɪks]	(*Problem:*) beheben, lösen
	power tuning ['paʊə tju:nɪŋ]	Leistungsabstimmung
	active dynamic filter (ADF) [,æktɪv daɪ,næmɪk 'fɪltə]	aktiver dynamischer Filter, Aktivfilter
63	**compensation** [,kɒmpən'seɪʃn]	Ausgleich, Kompensation
	compensation current [,kɒmpən'seɪʃn kʌrənt]	Ausgleichsstrom, Kompensationsstrom
	operational principle [ɒpə,reɪʃənl 'prɪnsəpl]	Funktionsprinzip
	ability [ə'bɪləti]	Fähigkeit
	simplified ['sɪmplɪfaɪd]	vereinfacht
	figure ['fɪgə]	Abbildung
	in parallel [ɪn 'pærəlel]	parallel geschaltet
	in shunt [ɪn 'ʃʌnt]	in Nebenschluss
	flow [fləʊ]	Fluss
	network ['netwɜ:k]	Netz
	to **analyse** ['ænəlaɪz]	analysieren
	to **determine** [dɪ'tɜ:mɪn]	bestimmen
	disturbance [dɪ'stɜ:bəns]	Störung
	reactive displacement [rɪ,æktɪv dɪs'pleɪsmənt]	Blindleistungsphasenverschiebung
	harmonics *pl* [hɑ:'mɒnɪks]	Oberschwingungen
	present ['preznt]	anwesend
	to **inject** [ɪn'dʒekt]	einspeisen
	load behaviour ['ləʊd bɪheɪvjə]	Lastverhalten
	arrangement [ə'reɪndʒmənt]	(Termin-)Vereinbarung, Vorbereitung
64	**ecological** [,i:kə'lɒdʒɪkl]	ökologisch, Öko-
	to **set up sth** [,set 'ʌp]	etw (*Treffen usw.*) vereinbaren
	to **get in touch with sb** [get ɪn 'tʌtʃ wɪð]	sich mit jdm in Verbindung setzen
	waste water [,weɪst 'wɔ:tə]	Abwasser
	filter press ['fɪltə pres]	Filterpresse
	to **book** [bʊk]	reservieren, buchen
	noon [nu:n]	Mittag
	timetable ['taɪmteɪbl]	Programm, Fahrplan, Flugplan
	by tomorrow [baɪ tə'mɒrəʊ]	bis morgen
65	to **reserve** [rɪ'zɜ:v]	reservieren
	with a room attached [wɪð ə ,ru:m ə'tætʃt]	mit einem Nebenraum
	to **postpone** [pə'spəʊn]	(nach hinten) verschieben
	business partner ['bɪznəs pɑ:tnə]	Geschäftspartner/in
	itinerary [aɪ'tɪnərəri]	Reiseplan

UNIT 7

68	to **communicate** [kə'mju:nɪkeɪt]	kommunizieren
	survey ['sɜ:veɪ]	Umfrage
	means of communication [,mi:nz əf kəmju:nɪ'keɪʃn]	Kommunikationmittel
	method ['meθəd]	Art (und Weise), Weg
	to **get sth across** [,get ə'krɒs]	etw (*Inhalt usw.*) verständlich machen
	construction mechanic [kən'strʌkʃn mɪkænɪk]	Konstruktionsmechaniker/in
	energy engineer ['enədʒi endʒɪnɪə]	Energieingenieur/in, Energietechniker/in
69	**face-to-face** [,feɪs tə 'feɪs]	persönlich
T	**in writing** [ɪn 'raɪtɪŋ]	schriftlich
	to **get at sth** ['get ət]	auf etw hinauswollen
	to **copy in sb** [,kɒpi 'ɪn]	jdn auf CC/in den Verteiler setzen
	all over the place [ɔ:l 'əʊvə ðə pleɪs]	überall
	access (to sth) ['ækses]	Zugriff (auf etw)
	cloud storage ['klaʊd stɔ:rɪdʒ]	Datenspeicherung in der Cloud
	to **synchronize** ['sɪŋkrənaɪz]	abgleichen, synchronisieren
	to **select** [sɪ'lekt]	auswählen
	to **bring up sth** [,brɪŋ 'ʌp]	etw zur Sprache bringen, etw ansprechen
	to **take up time** [,teɪk 'ʌp taɪm]	Zeit beanspruchen
	to **hate** [heɪt]	überhaupt nicht mögen, hassen
	waste of time [,weɪst əf 'taɪm]	Zeitverschwendung
	to **consider sth** [kən'sɪdə]	etw in Betracht ziehen, über etw nachdenken
	graphic image [,græfɪk 'ɪmɪdʒ]	Grafik, Schaubild
	quantity ['kwɒntəti]	Menge
	attachment [ə'tætʃmənt]	(*E-Mail:*) Anhang
70	**data sheet** ['deɪtə ʃi:t]	Datenblatt
	to **join sth** [dʒɔɪn]	einer Sache beitreten, bei einer Sache mitmachen
	bridge rectifier ['brɪdʒ rektɪfaɪə]	Brückengleichrichter
	full-wave bridge rectifier [,fʊl weɪv 'brɪdʒ rektɪfaɪə]	Vollwellenbrückengleichrichter
	glass fuse ['glɑ:s fju:z]	Glassicherung
	integrated voltage stabilizer [,ɪntɪgreɪtɪd 'vəʊltɪdʒ steɪbəlaɪzə]	integrierter Spannungsstabilisator
	mains input socket [,meɪnz 'ɪnpʊt sɒkɪt]	Netzanschlussbuchse

	tube *AE* [tjuːb]	(Elektronen-)Röhre
P	to **ring** [rɪŋ]	mit einem Kreis kennzeichnen
	square [skweə]	Feld
	amplifier ['æmplɪfaɪə]	Verstärker
	to **amplify** ['æmplɪfaɪ]	verstärken
	to **energize** ['enədʒaɪz]	mit Spannung versorgen, speisen
	to **raise** [reɪz]	erhöhen, anheben
	to **lower** ['ləʊə]	senken
	to **rectify** ['rektɪfaɪ]	gleichrichten
	to **smooth** [smuːð]	glätten
	to **stabilize** ['steɪbəlaɪz]	stabilisieren
	(electric) charge [tʃɑːdʒ]	(elektrische) Ladung
71	to **trace** [treɪs]	ausfindig machen, aufspüren
	host [həʊst]	Moderator/in (*einer Sendung*)
T	**guitar amp** [gɪ'tɑːr æmp]	Gitarrenverstärker
	mains lead ['meɪnz liːd]	Netzkabel
	control light [kən'trəʊl laɪt]	Kontrollampe
	ground fault circuit interrupter (GFCI) [ˌgraʊnd fɔːlt 'sɜːkɪt ɪntərʌptə]	FI-Schalter
	to **electrocute sb** [ɪ'lektrəkjuːt]	jdn durch Stromschlag töten
	No worries. [ˌnəʊ 'wʌriz]	Keine Sorge.
	to **come on** [ˌkʌm 'ɒn]	angehen
	to **illuminate** [ɪ'luːmɪneɪt]	beleuchten
	back panel [ˌbæk 'pænl]	Rückplatte
	sensory ['sensəri]	sensorisch
	smell of burning [ˌsmel əv 'bɜːnɪŋ]	Brandgeruch
	charred [tʃɑːd]	verkohlt
	to **be in luck** [bi ɪn 'lʌk]	Glück haben
	to **power sth** ['paʊə]	etw mit Strom versorgen
	to **change sth into sth** ['tʃeɪndʒ ɪntə]	etw in etw umwandeln
	You're welcome. [jɔː 'welkəm]	Bitte. Gern geschehen.
	safety precautions *pl* ['seɪfti prɪkɔːʃnz]	Sicherheitsvorkehrungen, Sicherheitsmaßnahmen
	optimistic [ˌɒptɪ'mɪstɪk]	optimistisch
	to **draw a conclusion** [drɔː ə kən'kluːʒn]	eine Schlussfolgerung ziehen
72	to **handle sth** ['hændl]	mit etw umgehen
	peak forward surge current [piːk ˌfɔːwəd 'sɜːdʒ kʌrənt]	Spitzendurchlassstrom
	half sine wave [ˌhɑːf 'saɪn weɪv]	Sinushalbwelle
	forward current [ˌfɔːwəd 'kʌrənt]	Durchlassstrom
	repetitive peak reverse voltage [ˌrɪpetətɪv piːk rɪˌvɜːs 'voltage]	wiederkehrende Spitzensperrspannung
	Good luck! [ˌgʊd 'lʌk]	Viel Glück!
	to **download** [ˌdaʊn'ləʊd]	herunterladen
	characteristics *pl* [ˌkærəktə'rɪstɪks]	Eigenschaften, Merkmale
	avalanche diode ['ævəlɑːnʃ daɪəʊd]	Lawinendiode
	sinterglass ['sɪntəglɑːs]	Sinterglas
	glass passivated ['glɑːs pæsɪveɪtɪd]	glaspassiviert
	junction ['dʒʌŋkʃn]	P-N-Übergang (*in Halbleitern*)
	hermetically sealed [hɜː'metɪkli siːld]	hermetisch abgedichtet
	package ['pækɪdʒ]	hier: Gehäuse
	surge current loading ['sɜːdʒ kʌrənt ləʊdɪŋ]	Stoßstrom-Grenzwert
	rectification [ˌrektɪfɪ'keɪʃn]	Gleichrichtung
	plated ['pleɪtɪd]	metallüberzogen
	axial ['æksɪəl]	axial
	polarity [pə'lærəti]	Polung, Polarität
	color band *AE* ['kʌlə bænd]	Farbring
	to **denote** [dɪ'nəʊt]	bezeichnen, kennzeichnen
	cathode ['kæθəʊd]	Kathode
	absolute maximum ratings *pl* [ˌæbsəluːt ˌmæksɪməm 'reɪtɪŋz]	absolute Grenzdaten
	to **specify** ['spesɪfaɪ]	angeben
	sub type ['sʌb taɪp]	Untertyp, Subtyp
	repetitive peak forward current [rɪˌpetətɪv piːk ˌfɔːwəd 'kʌrənt]	wiederkehrender Spitzendurchlassstrom
	pulse avalanche peak power [ˌpʌls ævəlɑːnʃ ˌpiːk 'paʊə]	Spitzenleistung bei Pulsbelastung
73	**relocation** [ˌriːləʊ'keɪʃn]	Verlegung, Verlagerung
	to **relocate sth** [riːləʊ'keɪt]	etw verlegen, etw verlagern
	thermal (cutoff) fuse [ˌθɜːml 'fjuːz]	Thermosicherung
	memo ['meməʊ]	Notiz, Kurzmitteilung, Aktenvermerk
	thermal cutoff [ˌθɜːml 'kʌtɒf]	thermische Abschaltung
	to **skim** [skɪm]	(*Text*) überfliegen
	to **integrate** ['ɪntɪgreɪt]	integrieren, einbauen
	to **overheat** [ˌəʊvə'hiːt]	sich überhitzen, zu heiß werden
	to **catch fire** [ˌkætʃ 'faɪə]	in Brand geraten, Feuer fangen
	thermal pellet [ˌθɜːml 'pelɪt]	thermisch geschütztes Gehäuse
	fusible alloy [ˌfjuːzɪbl 'ælɔɪ]	Schmelzlegierung
	hermetic sealing [həˌmetɪk 'siːlɪŋ]	hermetische Abdichtung
	resin ['rezɪn]	Harz

	resin-sealed ['rezɪn siːld]	mit Gießharz vergossen
	ambient temperature [ˌæmbiənt 'temprətʃə]	Umgebungstemperatur
	to **interrupt** [ˌɪntə'rʌpt]	unterbrechen
	a broad range of [ə ˌbrɔːd 'reɪndʒ əv]	eine große Auswahl von
	to suit sth [suːt]	für etw passen
	operating temperature [ˌɒpəreɪtɪŋ 'temprətʃə]	Betriebstemperatur
	rated current [ˌreɪtɪd 'kʌrənt]	Nennstrom
	to **conform to sth** [kən'fɔːm tə]	einer Sache entprechen
	environmental standard [ɪnvaɪrənˌmentl 'stændəd]	Umweltnorm
	regulations *pl* [ˌregju'leɪʃnz]	Vorschriften
	to **be sensitive to sth** [bi 'sensətɪv tə]	empfindlich auf etw reagieren
	abnormal [æb'nɔːml]	ungewöhnlich, anormal
	range [reɪndʒ]	Bereich, Umfang
	version ['vɜːʃn]	Ausführung, Modell
	resin-seal ['rezɪn siːl]	Gießharzverguss
	reliability [rɪˌlaɪə'bɪləti]	Zuverlässigkeit
	domestic [də'mestɪk]	Haushalts-
	iron ['aɪən]	Bügeleisen
	air conditioner ['eə kəndɪʃnə]	Klimaanlage
	ventilation fan [ˌventɪ'leɪʃn fæn]	Ventilator
	gas boiler ['gæs bɔɪlə]	Gaskessel
	transformer [træns'fɔːmə]	Transformator
	adaptor [ə'dæptə]	Adapter
	charger ['tʃɑːdʒə]	Ladegerät
	battery pack ['bætəri pæk]	Akku
	copier ['kɒpiə]	Kopiergerät
	laser beam printer ['leɪzə biːm prɪntə]	Laserdrucker
74	**airtight** ['eətaɪt]	luftdicht
	resin-sealing unit ['rezɪn siːlɪŋ juːnɪt]	Versiegelungsanlage
	crate [kreɪt]	Kiste
	drill bit ['drɪl bɪt]	Bohrer, Bohrspitze
	glue [gluː]	Klebstoff
	data cable ['deɪtə keɪbl]	Datenkabel, Datenleitung
	power cable ['paʊə keɪbl]	Stromkabel, Stromleitung
	cable trunk ['keɪbl trʌŋk]	Kabelkanal
	flooring ['flɔːrɪŋ]	Fußboden
	pneumatic hose [njuːˌmætɪk 'həʊz]	Druckluftschlauch, Pneumatikschlauch
	temperature detection ['temprətʃə dɪtekʃn]	Temperaturmessung, -erfassung
T	to **unpack** [ʌn'pæk]	auspacken
	to **handle sth** ['hændl]	etw behandeln
	transportation [ˌtrænspɔː'teɪʃn]	Beförderung, Transport
	nearby ['nɪəbaɪ]	in der Nähe
	to **fix** [fɪks]	befestigen
	to **lay cables** [ˌleɪ 'keɪblz]	Kabel/Leitungen verlegen
	up and running [ˌʌp ən 'rʌnɪŋ]	betriebsbereit
	on time [ɒn 'taɪm]	rechtzeitig, pünktlich
75	**specifically** [spə'sɪfɪkli]	ausdrücklich
	resin-sealer ['rezɪn siːlə]	Versiegelungsanlage
	report update [rɪ'pɔːt ʌpdeɪt]	aktueller Bericht
76	**incident** ['ɪnsɪdənt]	Vorfall
	notice ['nəʊtɪs]	Warnhinweis, Hinweisschild
	fire damage ['faɪə dæmɪdʒ]	Brandschaden
	to **report to sb** [rɪ'pɔːt tə]	sich bei jdm melden
	statement ['steɪtmənt]	Aussage, Schilderung
	first-aider [ˌfɜːst 'eɪdə]	Sanitäter/in
	welder ['weldə]	Schweißer/in
	shouting ['ʃaʊtɪŋ]	Geschrei
	next door [ˌnekst 'dɔː]	nebenan
	to **put out a fire** [pʊt ˌaʊt ə 'faɪə]	einen Brand löschen
	to **spread** [spred]	sich ausbreiten
	to **set off the alarm** [set ˌɒf ði ə'lɑːm]	Alarm auslösen
	assembly point [ə'sembli pɔɪnt]	Sammelplatz
	crash [kræʃ]	Krach, Schlag, Rums
	acetone ['æsɪtəʊn]	Aceton
	flash [flæʃ]	Stichflamme
	to **stomp** [stɒmp]	trampeln, treten
	flame [fleɪm]	Flamme
	to **light** [laɪt]	sich entzünden
77	to **go off** [ˌgəʊ 'ɒf]	(*Alarm:*) losgehen
	fire brigade ['faɪə brɪgeɪd]	Feuerwehr
	to **administer sth** [əd'mɪnɪstə]	etw geben, etw erteilen
	ambulance ['æmbjələns]	Rettungswagen
	burn [bɜːn]	Verbrennung
	to **be in shock** [bi ɪn 'ʃɒk]	unter Schock stehen
	emergency services *pl* [ɪ'mɜːdʒənsi sɜːvɪsɪz]	Einsatzkräfte, Rettungsdienste
	to **extinguish** [ɪk'stɪŋgwɪʃ]	löschen
	to **reach (over)** [riːtʃ]	greifen
	to **knock over sth** [ˌnɒk 'əʊvə]	etw umstoßen
	to **realise sth** ['rɪəlaɪz]	etw (be)merken
	bench [bentʃ]	Werkbank
	to **spill** [spɪl]	(*Flüssigkeit:*) laufen, auslaufen
	to **trickle** ['trɪkl]	rinnen, (in einem Rinnsal) laufen
	chronological(ly) [ˌkrɒnə'lɒdʒɪkl]	chronologisch

	administration [əd,mɪnɪ'streɪʃn]	Verwaltung
	record ['rekɔːd]	Aufzeichnung(en)
	involved (in sth) [ɪn'vɒlvd]	(an etw) beteiligt
	background ['bækgraʊnd]	Hintergrund

UNIT 8

78	to **regulate** ['regjuleɪt]	regeln
	charging cable ['tʃɑːdʒɪŋ keɪbl]	Ladekabel
	to **define** [dɪ'faɪn]	definieren
	more closely [,mɔː 'kləʊsli]	näher, genauer
	to **invent** [ɪn'vent]	erfinden
	everyday ['evrideɪ]	Alltags-
	aspect ['æspekt]	Gesichtspunkt, Aspekt
79	**standardization** [,stændədaɪ'zeɪʃn]	Normung
	currently ['kʌrəntli]	zur Zeit, gegenwärtig, momentan
	manufacturing company [,mænjʊ'fæktʃərɪŋ kʌmpəni]	Fertigungsbetrieb, Produktionsunternehmen
	to **compete** [kəm'piːt]	konkurrieren
	quality management ['kwɒləti mænɪdʒmənt]	Qualitätsmanagement, Qualitätssicherung
	labour ['leɪbə]	Arbeit
	output ['aʊtpʊt]	Produktion
	fire safety ['faɪə seɪfti]	Brandschutz
	fire risk assessment ['faɪə rɪsk əsesmənt]	Brandrisikobewertung, -analyse
	consultancy [kən'sʌltənsi]	Beratung
	to **take over sth** [,teɪk 'əʊvə]	etw übernehmen
	to **set up standards** [set ,ʌp 'stændədz]	Normen aufstellen
	proof [pruːf]	Nachweis(e), Beleg(e)
	fire protection ['faɪə prətekʃn]	Brandschutz
	certified ['sɜːtɪfaɪd]	geprüft, zertifiziert
	to **cover** ['kʌvə]	absichern, erfassen
	satisfied ['sætɪsfaɪd]	zufrieden
	to **insist on sth** [ɪn'sɪst ɒn]	auf etw bestehen
	to **research sth** [rɪ'sɜːtʃ]	etw recherchieren, sich über etw informieren
	to **draw up** [,drɔː 'ʌp]	(*Text*) erstellen, (*Liste*) aufstellen
80	**automated** ['ɔːtəmeɪtɪd]	automatisch
	washing system ['wɒʃɪŋ sɪstəm]	Waschanlage
	mat [mæt]	Matte
	abrasive sand [ə,breɪsɪv 'sænd]	Abrasivsand
	to **wash off sth** [,wɒʃ 'ɒf]	etw abwaschen
	manually ['mænjuəli]	von Hand
	air conditioned ['eə kəndɪʃənd]	klimatisiert
	conveyor [kən'veɪə]	Förderband, Förderer, Fördersystem
	legislation [,ledʒɪs'leɪʃn]	Gesetze, Gesetzgebung
	palletizer ['pælitaɪzə]	Palettierer
	item ['aɪtəm]	Gegenstand
	to **transport** [træn'spɔːt]	befördern, transportieren
	strict [strɪkt]	streng
T	**contract** ['kɒntrækt]	Vertrag
	to **mix** [mɪks]	mischen
	to **wash down sth** [,wɒʃ 'daʊn]	etw abwaschen
	plant [plɑːnt]	Werk, Betrieb
	heat [hiːt]	Hitze
	washing machine ['wɒʃɪŋ məʃiːn]	Waschmaschine
	to **palletize** ['pælitaɪz]	palettieren
	to **come up with sth** [,kʌm 'ʌp wɪð]	sich etw ausdenken, sich etw einfallen lassen
	to **pollute** [pə'luːt]	verschmutzen
	to **filter** ['fɪltə]	filtern
	to **reuse** [,riː'juːs]	wiederverwenden
81	**hot air blower** [hɒt 'eə bləʊə]	Heißluftgebläse
	to **construct** [kən'strʌkt]	bauen, konstruieren
	roller ['rəʊlə]	Rolle, Walze
	upwards ['ʌpwədz]	aufwärts, nach oben
	downwards ['daʊnwədz]	abwärts, nach unten
	to **drip off** [,drɪp 'ɒf]	abtropfen
	to **position** [pə'zɪʃn]	platzieren
	to **sketch** [sketʃ]	skizzieren
	draft [drɑːft]	Entwurf
	mixture ['mɪkstʃə]	Mischung, Gemisch
82	to **separate** ['sepəreɪt]	trennen
83	to **train sb** [treɪn]	jdn schulen
	feeding system ['fiːdɪŋ sɪstəm]	Einzug
	pushbutton ['pʊʃbʌtn]	Drucktaster, Taster
	interior [ɪn'tɪəriə]	Innen-
	ultrasonic sensor [ʌltrə,sɒnɪk 'sensə]	Ultraschallsensor
	to **activate** ['æktɪveɪt]	aktivieren, betätigen
	floor tray ['flɔː treɪ]	Bodenwanne
84	**nozzle** ['nɒzl]	Düse
	high-pressure nozzle [,haɪ preʃə 'nɒzl]	Hochdruckdüse
	pressure ['preʃə]	Druck
	usage ['juːsɪdʒ]	Verwendung
	nominal pressure [,nɒmɪnl 'preʃə]	Nenndruck
	capacity [kə'pæsəti]	Leistung
	knock [nɒk]	Stoß, Schlag
	to **limit** ['lɪmɪt]	begrenzen, beschränken
	to **overload** [,əʊvə'ləʊd]	überlasten
	alternating current (AC) [,ɔːltəneɪtɪŋ 'kʌrənt]	Wechselstrom

	chemicals *pl* ['kemɪklz]	Chemikalien
	coupling ['kʌplɪŋ]	Kupplung
	plunger pump ['plʌndʒə pʌmp]	Kolbenpumpe, Plungerpumpe
	valve [vælv]	Ventil
	feed [fiːd]	Einzug
	light barrier ['laɪt bæriə]	Lichtschranke
	time lag ['taɪm læg]	Zeitverzögerung
	to **waste** [weɪst]	verschwenden, vergeuden
85	**stacking system** ['stækɪŋ sɪstəm]	Stapeleinheit
	air-flow rate ['eə fləʊ reɪt]	Luftdurchsatz
	vibration-cushioned [vaɪ'breɪʃn kʊʃnd]	schwingungsgedämpft
	to **suck in** [ˌsʌk 'ɪn]	ansaugen
	to **blow** [bləʊ]	blasen
	optimum ['ɒptɪməm]	optimal
	endstop [endstɒp]	Endanschlag
	to **fold** [fəʊld]	klappen
	force of gravity [ˌfɔːs əv 'grævəti]	Schwerkraft
	gripper ['grɪpə]	Greifer
	to **grab** [græb]	greifen
	end switch ['end swɪtʃ]	Endschalter
	linear unit ['lɪniə juːnɪt]	Lineareinheit
	to **force** [fɔːs]	zwingen, *hier:* drücken
	key word ['kiː wɜːd]	Schlagwort, Stichwort
	eye contact ['aɪ kɒntækt]	Blickkontakt
	to **be prepared to do sth** [bi prɪ'peəd tə duː]	bereit sein, etw zu tun
86	**business trip** ['bɪznəs trɪp]	Geschäftsreise
	award [ə'wɔːd]	Auszeichnung, Preis
	prize-giving ceremony [ˌpraɪz gɪvɪŋ 'serəməni]	Preisverleihung
	receptionist [rɪ'sepʃənɪst]	Empfangsmitarbeiter/in
	to **check in** [ˌtʃek 'ɪn]	sich anmelden, einchecken
T	**reservation** [ˌrezə'veɪʃn]	Reservierung
	to **serve** [sɜːv]	servieren
	buffet breakfast ['bʌfeɪ brekfəst]	Frühstücksbüfett
	dining room ['daɪnɪŋ ruːm]	(*Hotel:*) Speisesaal
	ground floor [ˌgraʊnd 'flɔː]	Erdgeschoss
	wheelchair ['wiːltʃeə]	Rollstuhl
	access ['ækses]	Zugang
	facilities *pl* [fə'sɪlətiz]	Einrichtungen
	secure [sɪ'kjuə]	sicher, bewacht
	gate [geɪt]	Tor, Einfahrt
	to **check out** [ˌtʃek 'aʊt]	sich abmelden, auschecken
87	**Pleased to meet you.** [ˌpliːzd tə 'miːt ju]	Schön, Sie kennenzulernen.
	to **get ready** [get 'redi]	sich bereit machen, sich fertig machen
	Is this seat taken? [ɪz ðɪs ˌsiːt 'teɪkən]	Ist hier besetzt?
	cultural awareness [ˌkʌltʃərəl ə'weənəs]	Kulturbewusstsein, kulturelle Sensibilität
	to **bow** [baʊ]	sich verbeugen
	to **shake hands with sb** [ˌʃeɪk 'hændz wɪð]	jdm die Hand geben
	to **respect** [rɪ'spekt]	respektieren, achten
	aggressive [ə'gresɪv]	aggressiv
	dominant ['dɒmɪnənt]	dominant
	powerful ['paʊəfl]	mächtig
	to **pin sth to sth** [pɪn]	etw an etw befestigen

UNIT 9

90	**video conferencing** ['vɪdiəʊ kɒnfərənsɪŋ]	Videokonferenz
	item ['aɪtəm]	Punkt
	to **re-play** [ˌriː'pleɪ]	erneut abspielen
	session ['seʃn]	Sitzung
	integration [ˌɪntɪ'greɪʃn]	Einbindung, Integrierung
	trial ['traɪəl]	Test, Probe
	support [sə'pɔːt]	Unterstützung
	recording [rɪ'kɔːdɪŋ]	Aufzeichnung, Aufnahme
T	**Never mind.** [ˌnevə 'maɪnd]	Macht nichts.
	to **supply sth** [sə'plaɪ]	etw zur Verfügung stellen, etw liefern
	to **schedule** ['ʃedjuːl]	planen, (*Termin*) ansetzen
91	to **argue against/for sth** ['ɑːgjuː əgenst/fə]	sich gegen/für etw aussprechen, gegen/für etw argumentieren
	to **assist** [ə'sɪst]	assistieren, helfen, unterstützen
	research [rɪ'sɜːtʃ]	Recherche
	to **feature** ['fiːtʃə]	(*Merkmal*) aufweisen
	to **sum up** [ˌsʌm 'ʌp]	zusammenfassen
	recommendation [ˌrekəmen'deɪʃn]	Empfehlung
	in conclusion [ɪn kən'kluːʒn]	abschließend
92	**linear drive** ['lɪniə draɪv]	Linearantrieb
	quality assurance ['kwɒləti əʃʊərəns]	Qualitätssicherung
	measuring equipment ['meʒərɪŋ ɪkwɪpmənt]	Messgeräte
	custom-made ['kʌstəm meɪd]	speziell angefertigt, individuell gefertigt
	HGV (heavy goods vehicle) [ˌeɪtʃ dʒiː 'viː]	Lkw
	deviation [ˌdiːvi'eɪʃn]	Abweichung
	repetitive [rɪ'petətɪv]	(sich) wiederholend
	stationary ['steɪʃənri]	ortsfest, stationär
	surface roughness ['sɜːfɪs rʌfnəs]	Oberflächenrauigkeit
	coordinates *pl* [kəʊ'ɔːdɪnəts]	Koordinaten

	measurement run ['meʒəmənt rʌn]	Messfahrt
	to **detect** [dɪ'tekt]	erfassen
	versatile ['vɜːsətaɪl]	vielseitig verwendbar
	to **configure** [kən'fɪgə]	einrichten, konfigurieren
	measuring station ['meʒərɪŋ steɪʃn]	Messplatz, Messstation
	to **meet** [miːt]	(*Anforderungen usw.*) erfüllen
93	**guiding rail** ['gaɪdɪŋ reɪl]	Führungsschiene
	motion ['məʊʃn]	Bewegung
	ball bearing [ˌbɔːl 'beərɪŋ]	Kugellager
	rail [reɪl]	Schiene
	coefficient [ˌkəʊɪ'fɪʃnt]	Koeffizient
	friction ['frɪkʃn]	Reibung
	conventional [kən'venʃənl]	herkömmlich, konventionell
	rigidity [rɪ'dʒɪtəti]	Steifigkeit
	guidance ['gaɪdəns]	Führung
	automation system [ˌɔːtə'meɪʃn sɪstəm]	Automatisierungssystem, -anlage
	laser engraving ['leɪzər ɪngreɪvɪŋ]	Lasergravur
	lifting equipment ['lɪftɪŋ ɪkwɪpmənt]	Hebegeräte, Hebezeuge
	compound ['kɒmpaʊnd]	Verbindung
	gearing ['gɪərɪŋ]	Verzahnung
	drive unit ['draɪv juːnɪt]	Antriebseinheit, -aggregat
94	**permissible load** [pəˌmɪsɪbl 'ləʊd]	zulässige Last
	to **pre-load** [ˌpriː 'ləʊd]	vorspannen
	order code ['ɔːdə kəʊd]	Bestellcode, Bestellschlüssel
	quotation [kwəʊ'teɪʃn]	Preisangebot, Kostenvoranschlag
	regular customer [ˌregjələ 'kʌstəmə]	Stammkunde/-kundin
	to **request sth** [rɪ'kwest]	um etw bitten
	discount ['dɪskaʊnt]	Rabatt
	date of delivery [ˌdeɪt əv dɪ'lɪvəri]	Lieferdatum
95	**desktop machine** ['desktɒp məʃiːn]	Tischgerät
	hydraulic power unit [haɪˌdrɔːlɪk 'paʊə juːnɪt]	Hydraulikaggregat
	pneumatic controller [njuːˌmætɪk kən'trəʊlə]	pneumatischer Regler
	labelling plate ['leɪbəlɪŋ pleɪt]	Typenschild
	aggregate ['ægrɪgət]	Aggregat
T	to **engrave** [ɪn'greɪv]	(ein)gravieren
	to **come off** [ˌkʌm 'ɒf]	sich lösen, abgehen
	independent [ˌɪndɪ'pendənt]	unabhängig
	model-maker ['mɒdlmeɪkə]	Modellbauer/in
	gantry ['gæntri]	Portal
	stepper motor ['stepə məʊtə]	Schrittmotor
	DIY kit [ˌdiː aɪ 'waɪ kɪt]	Bausatz
96	to **customize** ['kʌstəmaɪz]	individuell anpassen
	to **create** [kri'eɪt]	(*Datei*) anlegen
	work file ['wɜːk faɪl]	Arbeitsdatei
	to **process** ['prəʊses]	verarbeiten
	to **reproduce** [ˌriːprə'djuːs]	kopieren, reproduzieren
	virtually ['vɜːtʃuəli]	praktisch
	unlimited [ʌn'lɪmɪtɪd]	unbegrenzt
	thermoplastic *pl* [ˌθɜːməʊ'plæstɪk]	Thermoplaste
	stability [stə'bɪləti]	Stabilität
	linear track profile [ˌlɪniə 'træk prəʊfaɪl]	Linearachsprofil
	cover profile ['kʌvə prəʊfaɪl]	Abdeckungsprofil
	stainless steel [ˌsteɪnləs 'stiːl]	Edelstahl
	profiled ['prəʊfaɪld]	profiliert
	specifically [spə'sɪfɪkli]	eigens, speziell
	to **adapt** [ə'dæpt]	anpassen
	reliable [rɪ'laɪəbl]	zuverlässig
	ready built ['redi bɪlt]	fertig montiert
	directly operational [dəˌrektli ɒpə'reɪʃənl]	direkt einsatzbereit
	to **opt for sth** ['ɒpt fə]	sich für etw entscheiden
	to **screw** [skruː]	schrauben
	to **base** [beɪs]	basieren, fußen
	intermediate [ˌɪntə'miːdiət]	Zwischen-
	compatibility [kəmˌpætə'bɪləti]	Kompatibilität
	collar ['kɒlə]	Spannhals
	power limit ['paʊə lɪmɪt]	Leistungsobergrenze
	system-guided ['sɪstəm gaɪdɪd]	systemgeführt
	drag knife ['dræg naɪf]	Schleppmesser
	engraving needle [ɪn'greɪvɪŋ niːdl]	Graviernadel
	hot cutting system ['hɒt kʌtɪŋ sɪstəm]	Heißschneidesystem
97	**6-point ball bearing cage** [ˌsɪks pɔɪnt 'bɔːl beərɪŋ keɪdʒ]	sechsfach kugelgelagerter Laufwagen
T	**play-free** ['pleɪ friː]	spielfrei
	carriage ['kærɪdʒ]	Schlitten
	continuously [kən'tɪnjuəsli]	fortwährend, ständig, kontinuierlich
	freely accessible [ˌfriːli ək'sesəbl]	frei zugänglich
	disassembly [ˌdɪsə'sembli]	Zerlegen, Demontage
	to **dismantle** [dɪs'mæntl]	demontieren, zerlegen
	feed rate ['fiːd reɪt]	Vorschub
	connecting cable [kə'nektɪŋ keɪbl]	Anschlusskabel

P

clamping surface ['klæmpɪŋ sɜːfɪs] — Aufspannfläche
working space ['wɜːkɪŋ speɪs] — Arbeitsraum
overall size [əʊvər,ɔːl 'saɪz] — Gesamtmaße

98 **body** ['bɒdi] — *(Brief:)* Haupttext
enclosure [ɪn'kləʊʒə] — *(Brief:)* Anlage
inside address [,ɪnsaɪd ə'dres] — Innenadresse
reference initials *pl* ['refərəns ɪnɪʃlz] — *(Brief:)* Zeichen
signature ['sɪgnətʃə] — Unterschrift
surgery light ['sɜːdʒəri laɪt] — Operationslampe, -leuchte
edition [ɪ'dɪʃn] — *(Zeitschrift etc.:)* Ausgabe
trade magazine ['treɪd mægəziːn] — Fachzeitschrift
outpatient clinic ['aʊtpeɪʃnt klɪnɪk] — Ambulanz
operating theatre ['ɒpəreɪtɪŋ θɪətə] — Operationssaal
trial order [,traɪəl 'ɔːdə] — Probebestellung
payment ['peɪmənt] — Zahlung
terms of payment *pl* [,tɜːmz əf 'peɪmənt] — Zahlungsbedingungen
to **protect** [prə'tekt] — schützen
reference ['refərəns] — Referenz
attention [ə'tenʃn] — Aufmerksamkeit
confirmation [,kɒnfə'meɪʃn] — Bestätigung
to **enclose** [ɪn'kləʊz] — *(Brief:)* beifügen
to **guarantee** [,gærən'tiː] — garantieren
to **pack** [pæk] — verpacken
surgical light [,sɜːdʒɪkl 'laɪt] — Operationslampe, -leuchte
wooden ['wʊdn] — Holz-
packing crate ['pækɪŋ kreɪt] — Packkiste
price list ['praɪs lɪst] — Preisliste

UNIT 10

100 **container** [kən'teɪnə] — Behälter, Box, Container
stackable ['stækəbl] — stapelbar
snap fastener ['snæp fɑːsnə] — Schnappverschluss
padlock ['pædlɒk] — Vorhängeschloss
to **stack** [stæk] — stapeln

101 **guarantee period** [,gærən'tiː pɪəriəd] — Garantiezeit
prospective customer [prə,spektɪv 'kʌstəmə] — potenzielle/r Kunde/Kundin

P

light [laɪt] — Scheinwerfer
microphone ['maɪkrəfəʊn] — Mikrofon
speaker ['spiːkə] — Lautsprecher

with reference to [wɪð 'refrəns tə] — mit Bezug auf, bezüglich
to **attach** [ə'tætʃ] — *(Brief:)* etw beifügen
to **establish** [ɪ'stæblɪʃ] — etablieren, schaffen, aufbauen

102 **electric motor** [ɪ,lektrɪk 'məʊtə] — Elektromotor
conveyor belt [kən'veɪə belt] — Förderband
food processing ['fuːd prəʊsesɪŋ] — Lebensmittelverarbeitung
magnetic field [mæg,netɪk 'fiːld] — Magnetfeld
pole [pəʊl] — Pol
permanent magnet ['pɜːmənənt magnɪt] — Permanentmagnet
to **interact** [,ɪntər'ækt] — aufeinander einwirken
to **attract** [ə'trækt] — anziehen
to **repel** [rɪ'pel] — abstoßen
loop [luːp] — Schleife
armature ['ɑːmətʃʊə] — Anker
axle ['æksl] — Achse
attraction [ə'trækʃn] — Anziehung
repulsion [rɪ'pʌlʃn] — Abstoßung
arrow ['ærəʊ] — Pfeil
turn [tɜːn] — Umdrehung
to **reverse** [rɪ'vɜːs] — umkehren
split-ring commutator [,splɪt rɪŋ 'kɒmjuteɪtə] — Stromwender mit Stromwenderlamellen
brush [brʌʃ] — Bürste
alternating ['ɔːltɜːneɪtɪŋ] — wechselnd, alternierend
rotor ['rəʊtə] — Anker, Rotor
stator ['steɪtə] — Ständer, Stator
thumb [θʌm] — Daumen

103 **continuous use** [kən,tɪnjuəs 'juːs] — Dauerbetrieb
wear and tear [,weər ən 'teə] — Verschleiß, Abnutzung
drive [draɪv] — Laufwerk
battery-powered ['bætəri paʊəd] — batteriebetrieben
to **wear out** [,weər 'aʊt] — sich abnutzen, verschleißen
vacuum cleaner ['vækjuəm kliːnə] — Staubsauger
food mixer ['fuːd mɪksə] — Küchenmaschine
crane [kreɪn] — Kran
hoist [hɔɪst] — Winde
field coil ['fiːld kɔɪl] — Feldspule
self-starting [,self 'stɑːtɪŋ] — selbstanlaufend
air conditioning ['eə kəndɪʃnɪŋ] — Klimatisierung, Klimaanlage
hair dryer ['heə draɪə] — Föhn
refrigerator [rɪ'frɪdʒəreɪtə] — Kühlschrank
pump [pʌmp] — Pumpe

104	**brushed DC motor** [ˌbrʌʃt diː ˌsiː 'məʊtə]	bürstenbehafteter Gleichstrommotor
	revolving [rɪ'vɒlvɪŋ]	drehbar, sich drehend, Dreh-
	brushless DC motor [ˌbrʌʃləs diː ˌsiː 'məʊtə]	bürstenloser Gleichstrommotor
	shaded pole motor [ˌʃeɪdɪd pəʊlː 'məʊtə]	Spaltpolmotor
	cylinder ['sɪlɪndə]	Zylinder
	spontaneous [spɒn'teɪniəs]	spontan
	induction motor [ɪn'dʌkʃn məʊtə]	Asychron-Motor
	squirrel cage motor [ˌskwɪrəl keɪdʒ 'məʊtə]	Käfigläufermotor
	electromagnet [ɪˌlektrəʊ'magnɪt]	Elektromagnet
	synchronously ['sɪŋkrənəsli]	gleichzeitig
T	**monodirectional** [ˌmɒnədə'rekʃnl]	in einer Richtung laufend, monodirektional
	reversible [rɪ'vɜːsəbl]	reversierbar
	variable ['veəriəbl]	variabel, regelbar
	enclosure [ɪn'kləʊʒə]	Gehäuse
	drip-proof ['drɪp pruːf]	tropfwassergeschützt
	to **splash** [splæʃ]	spritzen
	enclosed [ɪn'kləʊzd]	umschlossen
	blower cooled ['bləʊə kuːld]	gebläsegekühlt
	to **vary** ['veəri]	variieren, regeln
	variable frequency drive [ˌveəriəbl 'friːkwənsi draɪv]	frequenzgeregelter Antrieb
	raw [rɔː]	roh
	to **load** [ləʊd]	beladen
	to **unload** [ˌʌn'ləʊd]	entladen
	to **give reasons for sth** [ˌgɪv 'riːznz fə]	etw begründen
105	**nameplate** ['neɪmpleɪt]	Typenschild
	association [əˌsəʊsi'eɪʃn]	Verband, Vereinigung
	duty ['djuːti]	Betriebsart
	severe duty [sɪˌvɪə 'djuːti]	Einsatz unter härtesten Bedingungen
	frame [freɪm]	Rahmen, Gestell
	lube [luːb]	Schmiermittel
	serial number (S/N) ['sɪəriəl nʌmbə]	Seriennummer
	full load [ˌfʊl 'ləʊd]	Volllast
	torque [tɔːk]	Drehmoment
	power rating ['paʊə reɪtɪŋ]	Leistung, Nennleistung
	horsepower ['hɔːspaʊə]	PS
	revolutions *pl* **per minute (RPM)** [revəˌluːʃnz pɜː 'mɪnɪt]	Umdrehungen pro Minute (U/min)
	service factor ['sɜːvɪs fæktə]	Betriebsfaktor
	insulation class [ˌɪnsju'leɪʃn klɑːs]	Isolationsklasse, Schutzgrad
	to **rate** [reɪt]	klassifizieren, einstufen
106	**classification** [ˌklæsɪfɪ'keɪʃn]	Klassifikation
	numeral ['njuːmərəl]	Ziffer
	solid object [ˌsɒlɪd 'ɒbdʒɪkt]	Fremdkörper
	liquid ['lɪkwɪd]	Flüssigkeit
	dripping water [ˌdrɪpɪŋ 'wɔːtə]	Tropfwasser
	vertical ['vɜːtɪkl]	senkrecht, vertikal
	drop [drɒp]	Tropfen
	spraying water [ˌspreɪɪŋ 'wɔːtə]	Sprühwasser
	splashing water [ˌsplæʃɪŋ 'wɔːtə]	Spritzwasser
	water jet ['wɔːtə dʒet]	Strahlwasser
	to **spray** [spreɪ]	sprühen
	non-ventilated [ˌnɒn 'ventɪleɪtɪd]	unbelüftet
	damp [dæmp]	feucht
107	**salesman** ['seɪlzmən]	Verkäufer, Vertriebsmitarbeiter
	necessity [nə'sesəti]	Notwendigkeit
	retrofit ['retrəʊfɪt]	Nachrüstung, nachträglicher Einbau
	brushwear detection ['brʌʃweə dɪtekʃn]	Abnutzungserkennung an den Bürsten
	intermittent use [ɪntəˌmɪtənt 'juːs]	Kurzzeitbetrieb
	dusty ['dʌsti]	staubig
T	to **near** [nɪə]	sich nähern
	working life [ˌwɜːkɪŋ 'laɪf]	Lebensdauer
	in good time [ɪn ˌgʊd 'taɪm]	rechtzeitig
	to **lift** [lɪft]	heben
	to **vary** ['veəri]	sich ändern, unterschiedlich sein
	immediate [ɪ'miːdiət]	unverzüglich, sorfortig
108	**calibration equipment** [kalɪ'breɪʃn ɪkwɪpmənt]	Kalibriergerät(e)
	Documentary Letter of Credit [dɒkjuˌmentri ˌletər əf 'kredɪt]	Dokumentenakkreditiv
109	**scheme** [skiːm]	Schema
	re [riː]	bezüglich, betreffs
	bulk order [ˌbʌlk 'ɔːdə]	Großbestellung, Großauftrag
	as requested [əz rɪ'kwestɪd]	wie gewünscht

UNIT 11

112 **complaint** [kəm'pleɪnt]	Beschwerde, Reklamation
issue ['ɪʃuː]	Frage, Problem
to **attend sth** [ə'tend]	an etw teilnehmen
to **reverse** [rɪ'vɜːs]	umkehren, rückgängig machen
mining ['maɪnɪŋ]	Bergbau, Abbau, Förderung
study ['stʌdi]	Untersuchung, Studie
impact ['ɪmpækt]	Auswirkung(en), Folge(n)
soil erosion [ˌsɔɪl ɪ'rəʊʒn]	Bodenerosion
formation [fɔː'meɪʃn]	Bildung
sinkhole ['sɪŋkhəʊl]	Erdfall, Doline
biodiversity [ˌbaɪədaɪ'vɜːsɪti]	Artenvielfalt
to **contaminate** [kən'tæmɪneɪt]	verunreinigen, kontaminieren
groundwater ['graʊndwɔːtə]	Grundwasser
surface water ['sɜːfɪs wɔːtə]	Oberflächenwasser
to **cut down** [ˌkʌt 'daʊn]	(*Baum*) fällen
to **clear space** [ˌklɪə 'speɪs]	Platz schaffen
rock [rɒk]	Fels, Stein
hillside ['hɪlsaɪd]	Hang
waste dump ['weɪst dʌmp]	Müllhalde
surrounding area [səˌraʊndɪŋ 'eərɪə]	Umgebung
wilderness ['wɪldənəs]	Wildnis
destruction [dɪ'strʌkʃn]	Zerstörung
ecosystem ['iːkəʊsɪstəm]	Ökosystem
habitat ['hæbɪtæt]	(natürlicher) Lebensraum
farming area ['fɑːmɪŋ eəriə]	Landwirtschaftsfläche(n)
grazing ['greɪzɪŋ]	Weideland
cropland ['krɒplænd]	Anbaufläche
urban environment [ˌɜːbən ɪn'vaɪrənmənt]	städtischer Raum
to **affect sb/sth** [ə'fekt]	sich auf jdn/etw auswirken, negative Auswirkungen auf jdn/etw haben
leakage ['liːkɪdʒ]	Austreten, Versickern
population [ˌpɒpju'leɪʃn]	Bevölkerung
government ['gʌvənmənt]	Regierung
to **clean up** [ˌkliːn 'ʌp]	reinigen, saubermachen, aufräumen
surroundings [sə'raʊndɪŋz]	Umgebung
to **restore** [rɪ'stɔː]	wiederherstellen, wieder in den ursprünglichen Zustand versetzen
fixed amount [ˌfɪkst ə'maʊnt]	Pauschalbetrag
account [ə'kaʊnt]	Konto
third party [ˌθɜːd 'pɑːti]	Dritte/r
to **reclaim** [rɪ'kleɪm]	(*Land*) zurückgewinnen, rekultivieren
acre ['eɪkə]	Morgen (*Flächenmaß*)
wildlife ['waɪldlaɪf]	Tier- und Pflanzenwelt, Natur
to **breed** [briːd]	sich vermehren
ranching ['rɑːntʃɪŋ]	Viehwirtschaft
113 **in relation to** [ɪn rɪ'leɪʃn tə]	in Bezug auf
carbon footprint [ˌkɑːbən 'fʊtprɪnt]	CO_2-Fußabdruck
to **dissolve** [dɪ'zɒlv]	auflösen
to **glue** [gluː]	kleben
greenhouse gas [ˌgriːnhaʊs 'gæs]	Treibhausgas
incinerator [ɪn'sɪnəreɪtə]	Müllverbrennungsanlage
to **conduct sth** [kən'dʌkt]	etw durchführen
to **eliminate** [ɪ'lɪmɪneɪt]	entfernen, eliminieren
hazardous ['hæzədəs]	gefährlich, schädlich
CO_2 equivalent [siː əʊ ˌtuː ɪ'kwɪvələnt]	CO_2-Äquivalent
emission [ɪ'mɪʃn]	Ausstoß, Emission
mercury ['mɜːkjəri]	Quecksilber
T to **aim** [eɪm]	darauf abzielen, wollen
aim [eɪm]	Ziel
to **gather** ['gæðə]	sammeln, zusammentragen
to **persuade** [pə'sweɪd]	überzeugen
substance ['sʌbstəns]	Stoff, Substanz
climate ['klaɪmət]	Klima
to **harm** [hɑːm]	schaden, Schaden zufügen
carbon ['kɑːbən]	Kohlenstoff
consumer [kən'sjuːmə]	Verbraucher/in
poisonous ['pɔɪzənəs]	giftig
chromium ['krəʊmiəm]	Chrom
to **disappear** [ˌdɪsə'pɪə]	verschwinden
to **end up** [ˌend 'ʌp]	(irgendwo) landen
landfill ['lændfɪl]	Mülldeponie
to **release** [rɪ'liːs]	freisetzen
to **link** [lɪŋk]	in Verbindung bringen
to **dump** [dʌmp]	(*Müll*) abladen, verfrachten
profitable ['prɒfɪtəbl]	einträglich, profitabel
dead [ded]	(*Akku:*) leer
guide [gaɪd]	Anleitung
record [rɪ'kɔːd]	Bilanz, Ergebnis(se)
to **expand on sth** [ɪk'spænd ɒn]	ausführlich über etw sprechen
manufacture [ˌmænju'fæktʃə]	Herstellung, Fertigung
to **deal with sth** ['diːl wɪð]	mit etw fertig werden, etw bewältigen
to **extract** [ɪk'strækt]	(*Rohstoffe*) gewinnen
contract length ['kɒntrækt leŋθ]	Vertragsdauer

	to **cut down on sth** [ˌkʌt 'daʊn ɒn]	etw reduzieren
	comment ['kɒment]	Kommentar
	to **point out sth** [ˌpɔɪnt 'aʊt]	auf etw hinweisen
	to **damage** ['dæmɪdʒ]	schädigen
	to **illustrate** ['ɪləstreɪt]	veranschaulichen
114	**robot** ['rəʊbɒt]	Roboter
	assembly robot [ə'sembli rəʊbɒt]	Montageroboter
	widespread ['waɪdspred]	verbreitet
	to **perform** [pə'fɔːm]	(*Tätigkeit*) ausführen
	arc welding ['ɑːk weldɪŋ]	Lichtbogenschweißen
	assembly system [ə'sembli sɪstəm]	Montageanlage
	material handling [mə'tɪəriəl hændlɪŋ]	Materialtransport, Fördertechnik
	to **collaborate** [kə'læbəreɪt]	zusammenarbeiten
	collaboration [kəˌlæbə'reɪʃn]	Zusammenarbeit
	to **take delivery** [ˌteɪk dɪ'lɪvəri]	Ware entgegennehmen, eine Lieferung in Empfang nehmen
	delivery note [dɪ'lɪvəri nəʊt]	Lieferschein
	extent [ɪk'stent]	Ausdehnung
	heaviness [hevɪnəs]	Gewicht
	mass [mæs]	Masse
	overhead ['əʊvəhed]	Überkopf-, obere/r/s
	to **assign** [ə'saɪn]	zuweisen, vergeben
	to **communicate sth** [kə'mjuːnɪkeɪt]	etw übermitteln
	payload ['peɪləʊd]	Nutzlast
	working envelope ['wɜːkɪŋ envələʊp]	Arbeitsraum
	reach [riːtʃ]	Reichweite
	controller [kən'trəʊlə]	Steuerung, Steuereinheit, Controller
	protection class [prə'tekʃn klɑːs]	Schutzklasse
115	**total price** [ˌtəʊtl 'praɪs]	Gesamtpreis
	power supply cable ['pauə səplaɪ keɪbl]	Netzkabel
	labelling plate ['leɪbəliŋ pleɪt]	Beschriftungsplatte
	contents ['kɒntents]	Inhalt
T	**gantry crane** ['gæntri kreɪn]	Portalkran
	type plate ['taɪp pleɪt]	Typenschild
	Hold on. [ˌhəʊld 'ɒn]	Moment mal!
	handbook ['hændbʊk]	Handbuch
	documentation [ˌdɒkjumen'teɪʃn]	Unterlagen, Dokumentation
	to **be up and running** [bi ˌʌp ən 'rʌnɪŋ]	laufen, im Einsatz sein
	error ['erə]	Fehler, Irrtum
116	**sales department** ['seɪlz dɪpɑːtmənt]	Verkauf(sabteilung), Vertrieb
	sales representative ['seɪlz reprɪzentətɪv]	Vertreter/in
117	**gap** [gæp]	Lücke
	stringing ['strɪŋɪŋ]	Fadenzug
	string [strɪŋ]	Faden
	to **ooze** [uːz]	tropfen, quellen
	overheating [ˌəʊvə'hiːtɪŋ]	Überhitzung
	shifting ['ʃɪftɪŋ]	Verschiebung
	misaligned [ˌmɪsə'laɪnd]	falsch ausgerichtet
	to **shift** [ʃɪft]	sich verschieben
	layer separation ['leɪə sepəreɪʃn]	Schichttrennung
	to **split** [splɪt]	reißen, springen
	filament ['fɪləmnt]	Filament (*drahtförmige thermoplastische Kunststoffe*)
	to **grind** [graɪnd]	schleifen
	clogged [klɒgd]	verstopft
	extruder [ɪk'struːdə]	Extruder
	jammed [jæmd]	blockiert, verstopft
	to **extrude** [ɪk'struːd]	herauspressen, herausdrücken, extrudieren
	nozzle tip ['nɒzl tɪp]	Düsenspitze
	randomly ['rændəmli]	willkürlich
118	**reproduction** [ˌriːprə'dʌkʃn]	Wiedergabe
	extrusion [ɪk'struːʃn]	Extrusion
	to **interact** [ˌɪntər'ækt]	zusammenspielen
	printer resin ['prɪntə rezɪn]	geschmolzener Filamentkunststoff
	settings *pl* ['setɪŋz]	Voreinstellungen
	to **resolve** [rɪ'zɒlv]	lösen
	multiplier ['mʌltɪplaɪə]	Multiplikator
	to **increase** [ɪn'kriːs]	erhöhen, vergrößern
	to **decrease** [dɪ'kriːs]	verkleinern, verringern
	hairy ['heəri]	haarig
	to **deposit** [dɪ'pɒzɪt]	ablagern
	to **be due to sth** [bi 'djuː tə]	an etw liegen
	typically ['tɪpɪkli]	normalerweise, üblicherweise
	retraction [rɪ'trækʃn]	Rücksaugung
	to **enable** [ɪ'neɪbl]	einschalten
	to **edit** ['edɪt]	bearbeiten, editieren
	tab [tæb]	Reiter
	printer head ['prɪntə hed]	Druckkopf
	course [kɔːs]	Verlauf
	jam [dʒæm]	Stau
	clog [klɒg]	Verstopfung
	to **heat** [hiːt]	erhitzen
	to **jam** [dʒæm]	blockieren, verstopfen
	wavy ['weɪvi]	wellenförmig
	pattern ['pætn]	Muster
	wobble ['wɒbl]	Wackeln
	sudden ['sʌdn]	plötzlich
	sharp [ʃɑːp]	scharf

	inertia [ɪ'nɜːʃə]	Trägheit
	visible ['vɪzəbl]	sichtbar
	print [prɪnt]	Ausdruck
	bracket ['brækɪt]	Halterung
	vibration [vaɪ'breɪʃn]	Vibration
	to **suffer from** ['sʌfə frəm]	unter etw leiden
119	**fail** [feɪl]	Fehldruck
	prototype ['prəʊtətaɪp]	Prototyp
	in the beginning [ɪn ðə bɪ'gɪnɪŋ]	anfangs
	satisfactory [ˌsætɪs'fæktəri]	zufriedenstellend
	to **inform** [ɪn'fɔːm]	informieren, mitteilen
	inspection [ɪn'spekʃn]	Überprüfung, Kontrolle
	early ['ɜːli]	schnell, baldig
	unsatisfactory [ˌʌnˌsætɪs'fæktəri]	unzureichend, unbefriedigend
T	**customer service** [ˌkʌstəmə 'sɜːvɪs]	Kundendienst
	to **forward** ['fɔːwəd]	weiterleiten
	terrible ['terəbl]	furchtbar, fürchterlich
	desert ['dezət]	Wüste
	to **harden** ['hɑːdn]	aushärten
	filament coil ['fɪləmnt kɔɪl]	Filamentspule
	to **exit sth** ['eksɪt]	aus etw treten
	to **cool** [kuːl]	abkühlen
	to **retain** [rɪ'teɪn]	behalten
	to **solidify** [sə'lɪdɪfaɪ]	fest werden
	to **exceed** [ɪk'siːd]	überschreiten
120	to **apologize** [ə'pɒlədʒaɪz]	sich entschuldigen
	to **react to sth** [ri'ækt tə]	auf etw reagieren
	action ['ækʃn]	Maßnahmen
	at one's expense [ət wʌnz ɪk'spens]	auf jds Kosten
	X-ray machine ['eks reɪ məʃiːn]	Röntgengerät
T	**dental clinic** [ˌdentl 'klɪnɪk]	Zahnklinik
	scratched [skrætʃt]	verkratzt
	dented ['dentɪd]	verbeult
	to **get sth sorted** [ˌget 'sɔːtɪd]	etw klären, sich um etw kümmern
	business ['bɪznəs]	Angelegenheit, Sache
	superior [suː'pɪəriə]	Vorgesetzte/r
	spelling ['spelɪŋ]	Schreibweise
	consignment [kən'saɪnmənt]	Warensendung
	to **fulfil an order** [fʊlˌfɪl ən 'ɔːdə]	einen Auftrag abwickeln, eine Bestellung ausführen
121	**transcript** ['trænskrɪpt]	Mitschrift
	record ['rekɔːd]	Datensatz
	I realize that. [aɪ 'rɪəlaɪz ðæt]	Das ist mir bewusst.

UNIT 12

122	**(job) application** [ˌæplɪ'keɪʃn]	Bewerbung
	to **apply for a job** [əˌplaɪ fər ə 'dʒɒb]	sich um eine Stelle bewerben
	job agency ['dʒɒb eɪdʒənsi]	Arbeitsagentur, Arbeitsvermittlung
	newly-qualified [ˌnjuːli 'kwɒlɪfaɪd]	frisch gebacken
	panel building electrician ['pænl bɪldɪŋ ɪlektrɪʃn]	Schaltschrankverdrahter/in
T	**listener** ['lɪsnə]	Hörer/in
	computer aided [kəm'pjuːtər eɪdɪd]	computerunterstützt
	experienced [ɪk'spɪəriənst]	erfahren
	construction [kən'strʌkʃn]	Baugewerbe
	transmitter [træns'mɪtə]	Sender
	ideally [aɪ'diːəli]	idealerweise
123	**soldering** [səʊldərɪŋ]	Weichlöten
	job opportunities *pl* [dʒɒb ˌɒpə'tjuːnətiz]	Arbeitsmöglichkeiten
	career prospects *pl* [kə'rɪə prɒspekts]	berufliche Perspektiven
	job offer ['dʒɒb ɒfə]	Stellenangebot
	to **come across sth** [ˌkʌm ə'krɒs]	auf etw stoßen
	CV (curriculum vitae) [ˌsiː 'viː, kəˌrɪkjələm 'viːtaɪ]	Lebenslauf
	agent ['eɪdʒənt]	*hier:* zuständige/r Mitarbeiter/in
	standardized ['stændədaɪzd]	genormt
	potential [pə'tenʃl]	möglich, potenziell
	particular [pə'tɪkjələ]	besondere/r/s, speziell
	self-assessment [ˌself ə'sesmənt]	Selbsteinstufung
	mobility [məʊ'bɪləti]	Freizügigkeit, Mobilität
	to **acquire** [ə'kwaɪə]	erlangen, erwerben
	supplement ['sʌplɪmənt]	Zusatz, Ergänzung
	holder ['həʊldə]	Inhaber/in
124	**job advert(isement)** ['dʒɒb ædvɜːt, ədvɜːtɪsmənt]	Stellenanzeige
	requirement [rɪ'kwaɪəmənt]	Voraussetzung, Bedingung
	benefits *pl* ['benɪfɪts]	Zusatzleistungen, Sozialleistungen
	recruitment agency [rɪ'kruːtmənt eɪdʒənsi]	Personalvermittlung
	metalwork ['metlwɜːk]	Metallbau
	salary ['sæləri]	Gehalt
	negotiable [nɪ'gəʊʃiəbl]	verhandelbar
	renewable [rɪ'njuːəbl]	verlängerbar
	to **face sth** [feɪs]	mit etw konfrontiert sein

	chronic ['krɒnɪk]	dauerhaft
	skills shortage ['skɪlz ʃɔːtɪdʒ]	Fachkräftemangel
	in high demand [ɪn ˌhaɪ dɪ'mɑːnd]	sehr gefragt
	commitment [kə'mɪtmənt]	Engagement
	willingness ['wɪlɪŋnəs]	Bereitschaft
	drive [draɪv]	Tatendrang, Motivation
	starting salary ['stɑːtɪŋ sæləri]	Einstiegsgehalt
	opportunity [ˌɒpə'tjuːnəti]	Gelegenheit, Möglichkeit
	initial [ɪ'nɪʃl]	erste/r/s
	overtime ['əʊvətaɪm]	Überstunden
125	**electrician's mate** [ɪlekˌtrɪʃnz 'meɪt]	Elektro-Gehilfe
	vacancy ['veɪkənsi]	freie/offene Stelle
	valuable ['væljuəbl]	wertvoll
	to **upgrade** [ˌʌp'greɪd]	höherstufen, (sich) verbessern
	driving licence ['draɪvɪŋ laɪsns]	Führerschein
	site work ['saɪt wɜːk]	Arbeit vor Ort
	full-time [ˌfʊl 'taɪm]	Vollzeit-
	annual(ly) ['ænjuəli]	jährlich
	paid holiday [ˌpeɪd 'hɒlədeɪ]	bezahlter Urlaub
	public holiday [ˌpʌblɪk 'hɒlədeɪ]	gesetzlicher Feiertag
	equivalent [ɪ'kwɪvələnt]	gleichwertig
P	to **inspect** [ɪn'spekt]	kontrollieren, prüfen, inspizieren
	in accordance with [ɪn ə'kɔːdəns wɪð]	in Übereinstimmung mit
	emergency duty [ɪ'mɜːdʒənsi djuːti]	Notdienst, Notfalleinsatz
	candidate ['kændɪdət]	Bewerber/in
	preliminary [prɪ'lɪmɪnəri]	vorläufig, Vor-
	control panel wirer [kən'trəʊl pænl waɪərə]	Schaltschrankverdrahter/in
	vocational school [vəʊˌkeɪʃənl 'skuːl]	Berufsschule
	to **assume** [ə'sjuːm]	davon ausgehen
	occasion [ə'keɪʒn]	Gelegenheit
	to **arise** [ə'raɪz]	sich ergeben
	appropriate [ə'prəʊpriət]	entsprechend, passend, geeignet
126	to **be shortlisted** [bi 'ʃɔːtlɪstɪd]	in die engere Auswahl kommen
	interviewer ['ɪntəvjuːə]	*Person, die ein Vorstellungsgespräch führt*
	weakness ['wiːknəs]	Schwäche
	to **irritate** ['ɪrɪteɪt]	stören, irritieren
	to **flick through** ['flɪk θruː]	durchblättern
	landline ['lændlaɪn]	Festnetz(telefon)
	to **get disconnected** [get ˌdɪskə'nektɪd]	(*Telefonverbindung:*) unterbrochen werden
	to **dress** [dres]	sich kleiden
	strange [streɪndʒ]	seltsam
	bored [bɔːd]	gelangweilt
	uninterested [ʌn'ɪntrəstɪd]	uninteressiert
	to **focus** ['fəʊkəs]	sich konzentrieren
	professional [prə'feʃənl]	professionell
	to **hang on** [ˌhæŋ 'ɒn]	warten
	impression [ɪm'preʃn]	Eindruck
	to **swallow** ['swɒləʊ]	schlucken
	to **look the part** [ˌlʊk ðə 'pɑːt]	entsprechend (rollengerecht) aussehen
127	**clarification** [ˌklærɪfɪ'keɪʃn]	Klarstellung, Klärung
T	to **calm down** [ˌkɑːm 'daʊn]	sich beruhigen
	Not particularly. [ˌnɒt pə'tɪkjələli]	Eigentlich nicht.
	smart [smɑːt]	(*Kleidung:*) schick
	confident(ly) ['kɒnfɪdənt]	selbstbewusst
	shy [ʃaɪ]	schüchtern
	habit ['hæbɪt]	Gewohnheit
	to **get into the habit of doing sth** [ˌget ɪntə ðə 'hæbɪt əv]	sich daran gewöhnen, etw zu tun
	panel ['pænl]	Gremium
	to **relate sth to sth** [rɪ'leɪt tə]	etw auf etw beziehen
	to **occur to sb** [ə'kɜː tə]	jdm in den Sinn kommen
	firm handshake [ˌfɜːm 'hændʃeɪk]	fester Händedruck
P	to **indicate** ['ɪndɪkeɪt]	andeuten, darauf hinweisen
	to **keep in mind** [ˌkiːp ɪn 'maɪnd]	daran denken
	to **stress** [stres]	betonen
	to **progress with sth** [prə'gres wɪð]	mit etw vorankommen
	selection process [sɪ'lekʃn prəʊses]	Auswahlverfahren
128	**set** [set]	vorgegeben, starr, fest
	to **grab sb's attention** [ˌgræb ə'tenʃn]	jds Aufmerksamkeit fesseln
	duty ['djuːti]	Aufgabe, Pflicht
	achievement [ə'tʃiːvmənt]	Leistung
	academic [ˌækə'demɪk]	universitär
	professional [prə'feʃənl]	beruflich
	socializing ['səʊʃəlaɪzɪŋ]	Ausgehen
	date of birth [ˌdeɪt əv 'bɜːθ]	Geburtsdatum
	marital status [ˌmærɪtl 'steɪtəs]	Familienstand

	married ['mærid]	verheiratet
	divorced [dɪ'vɔːst]	geschieden
	separated ['sepəreɪtɪd]	getrennt lebend
	data protection ['deɪtə prətekʃn]	Datenschutz
	referee [ˌrefə'riː]	Referenz(geber/in)
	on request [ɒn rɪ'kwest]	auf Anfrage
129	to **seek** [siːk]	suchen
130	**reference (to sth)** ['refrəns]	Bezug (auf etw), Erwähnung (von etw)
	applicant ['æplɪkənt]	Bewerber/in
	to **refer to sth** [rɪ'fɜː tə]	etw erwähnen
	capital letter [ˌkæpɪtl 'letə]	Großbuchstabe
131	**Attn.** [ə'tenʃn]	z. Hdn.
	particularly [pə'tɪkjələli]	insbesondere
	to **be keen to do sth** [bi 'kiːn]	jdm liegt sehr daran, etw zu tun
	on a daily basis [ɒn ə ˌdeɪli 'beɪsɪs]	jeden Tag, täglich
	fluent ['fluːənt]	(*Sprache:*) fließend
	to **benefit sb/sth** ['benɪfɪt]	jdm/etw nützen
	at short notice [ət ˌʃɔːt 'nəʊtɪs]	kurzfristig
	to **appreciate** [ə'priːʃieɪt]	schätzen, zu schätzen wissen

A–Z word list

Dieses Wörterverzeichnis enthält alle neuen Wörter aus *Mechatronics Matters – 2nd Edition* in alphabetischer Reihenfolge. Nicht angeführt sind Wörter, die zum Grundwortschatz (*Basic word list*) gehören. Die Zahl nach dem Stichwort bezieht sich auf die Seite, auf der das Wort zum ersten Mal erscheint. Wörter aus den Hörverständnisübungen sind zusätzlich mit einem **T** (Transkript) und Wörter aus den *Partner files* mit einem **P** gekennzeichnet.

0–9

24/7 *10* rund um die Uhr
6-point ball bearing cage *97T* sechsfach kugelgelagerter Laufwagen

A

ability *63* Fähigkeit
abnormal *73* ungewöhnlich, anormal
abrasive sand *80* Abrasivsand
absolute maximum ratings *pl* *72* absolute Grenzdaten
to **absorb** *35* absorbieren, aufnehmen
academic *128* universitär
accelerometer *37* Beschleunigungssensor
access *86T* Zugang; **~ (to sth)** *69T* Zugriff (auf etw)
to **access sth** *59* auf etw zugreifen
to **accommodate** *31* aufnehmen, unterbringen
to **accompany** *17* begleiten
accordance, in ~ with *125F* in Übereinstimmung mit
according to *7* gemäß, entsprechend, zufolge
account *112* Konto; **key ~ management** *9F* Großkundenbetreuung
accuracy *56* Genauigkeit
accurate(ly) *24* genau
acetone *76* Aceton
achievement *128* Leistung
acid *15* Säure
to **acquire** *123* erlangen, erwerben
acre *112* Morgen *(Flächenmaß)*
to **act out** *28* spielen
action *120* Maßnahmen
to **activate** *83* aktivieren, betätigen
active dynamic filter (ADF) *62* aktiver dynamischer Filter, Aktivfilter
actor *37* Aktor
actuator *59* Aktor
to **adapt** *96* anpassen
adaptor *73* Adapter
add-on *50* zusätzlich, Erweiterungs-
address, inside ~ *98* Innenadresse
to **adjust** *27T* einstellen, regeln; **~ for sth** *50* etw berücksichtigen, etw ausgleichen
adjustable *56T* regelbar, einstellbar
to **administer sth** *77* etw geben, etw erteilen
administration *77* Verwaltung
advanced *24* fortschrittlich, modern, hoch entwickelt
advert(isment), job ~ *124* Stellenanzeige
to **advise** *56* beraten
to **affect sb/sth** *112* sich auf jdn/etw auswirken, negative Auswirkungen auf jdn/etw haben
affordable *38T* erschwinglich, bezahlbar
agency, job ~ *122* Arbeitsagentur, Arbeitsvermittlung; **recruitment ~** *124* Personalvermittlung
agenda *32* Tagesordnung
agent *123* *hier:* zuständige/r Mitarbeiter/in
aggregate *95* Aggregat
aggressive *87* aggressiv
aid, first ~ *15* Erste Hilfe
aim *113T* Ziel
to **aim** *113T* darauf abzielen, wollen
air, hot ~ blower *81* Heißluftgebläse; **refrigerated ~** *58* gekühlte Luft
air conditioned *80* klimatisiert
air conditioner *73* Klimaanlage
air conditioning *103* Klimatisierung, Klimaanlage; **~ system** *16* Klimasteuerung, Klimaanlage
air-flow rate *85* Luftdurchsatz
airtight *74* luftdicht
alarm, false ~ *50* Fehlalarm; **fire ~** *50* Brandmelder; **heat and smoke ~ system** *50* Hitze- und Rauchmeldeanlage; to **set off the ~** *76* Alarm auslösen
Allen key *26* Inbusschlüssel, Innensechskantschlüssel
all over the place *69T* überall
alloy *38* Legierung; **fusible ~** *73* Schmelzlegierung; **solder ~** *38* Lötlegierung
alphabetical *47* alphabetisch
altered *38T* geändert, verändert
alternating *102* wechselnd, alternierend; **~ current (AC)** *84* Wechselstrom
alternative *21* Alternative
aluminium *BE* *34* Aluminium
aluminum *AE* *34* Aluminium
amber *50* bernsteingelb
ambient temperature *73* Umgebungstemperatur
ambulance *77* Rettungswagen
amperage *52* Stromstärke
amp, guitar ~ *71T* Gitarrenverstärker
amplifier *70F* Verstärker
to **amplify** *70* verstärken
to **analyse** *63* analysieren
and so on *8T* und so weiter
angle grinder *26* Winkelschleifer, Trennschleifer
to **announce** *32* ankündigen
annoying *27T* ärgerlich, nervend
annual(ly) *125* jährlich
antenna *37* Antenne
antimony *38* Antimon
apartment block *11T* Mietshaus, Wohnblock
to **apologize** *120* sich entschuldigen
apparent, nominal ~ power *62* Nennscheinleistung
to **appear** *32* erscheinen, auftreten, vorkommen
appearance *60* Aussehen, Erscheinungsbild
appliance, electrical ~ *15* Elektrogerät
applicant *130* Bewerber/in
application *32* Antrag, Bewerbung; **~** *37* Anwendung; **job ~** *122* Bewerbung
to **apply: ~ sth** *35* etw anwenden; *36* etw *(Beschichtung usw.)* auftragen; **~ for a job** *122* sich um eine Stelle bewerben
to **appreciate** *131* schätzen, zu schätzen wissen
apprentice *6* Auszubildende/r, Lehrling
apprenticeship *6* Lehre, Ausbildung
approaching *53T* nahend, sich nähernd; **~ device** *53T* Näherungsvorrichtung
appropriate *125* entsprechend, passend, geeignet
approximately *38* zirka, ungefähr
apron *31* Schlosskasten
arc welding *114* Lichtbogenschweißen
to **argue against/for sth** *91* sich gegen/für etw aussprechen, gegen/für etw argumentieren
to **arise** *125F* sich ergeben
armature *102* Anker
arrangement *63* (Termin-)Vereinbarung, Vorbereitung
arrest, cardiac ~ *52* Herzstillstand
arrow *102* Pfeil
artificial *34* künstlich

aspect *78* Gesichtspunkt, Aspekt
to **assemble** *11T* montieren, zusammenbauen
assembly *11* Montage; **carriage ~** *31* Werkzeugschlitten; **final ~** *11* Endmontage; **pre-~** *11* Vormontage; **~ point** *76* Sammelplatz; **~ robot** *114* Montageroboter; **~ system** *114* Montageanlage
assessment, fire risk ~ *79* Brandrisikobewertung, -analyse; **self-~** *123* Selbsteinstufung
to **assign** *114* zuweisen, vergeben
to **assist** *91* assistieren, helfen, unterstützen
assistance *32* Hilfe, Unterstützung
association *105* Verband, Vereinigung
to **assume** *125F* davon ausgehen
assurance, quality ~ *92* Qualitätssicherung
to **attach** *17* anbringen, befestigen; *32* *(E-Mail:)* anhängen; *101* *(Brief:)* etw beifügen; **~ sth to sth** *14* etw mit etw verbinden, etw an etw anschließen
attached, with a room ~ *65* mit einem Nebenraum
attachment *69* *(E-Mail:)* Anhang
to **attend** *18* *(Schule)* besuchen; **~ sth** *112* an etw teilnehmen
attendant, swimming pool ~ *56* Bademeister/in
attention *98* Aufmerksamkeit; to **grab sb's ~** *128* jds Aufmerksamkeit fesseln
Attn. *131* z. Hdn.
to **attract** *102* anziehen
attraction *102* Anziehung
attractive *59T* ansprechend, attraktiv
audience *7* Publikum
automated *80* automatisch
automation *6* Automatisierung, Automation; **~ system** *93* Automatisierungssystem, -anlage
automative *7T* Automations-
available *10* lieferbar, verfügbar
avalanche: ~ diode *72* Lawinendiode; **pulse ~ peak power** *72* Spitzenleistung bei Pulsbelastung
to **avoid** *13* vermeiden
award *86* Auszeichnung, Preis
awareness, cultural ~ *87* Kulturbewusstsein, kulturelle Sensibilität
axial *72* axial
axle *102* Achse

B

back: ~ gear *31* (Räder-)Vorgelege; **~ panel** *71T* Rückplatte; **~ to ~** *41* Rücken an Rücken
back-up *50* *hier:* Notstromquelle
background *77* Hintergrund
ball bearing *93* Kugellager; **6-point ~ cage** *97T* sechsfach kugelgelagerter Laufwagen
band, color ~ *AE* *72* Farbring
bandsaw *29* Bandsäge
bar *40* Barren; **~ chart** *54* Säulendiagramm
bare *51* *(Draht:)* blank
barrier *58* Barriere, Schranke; **light ~** *84* Lichtschranke
to **base** *96* basieren, fußen
base *29* Basis, Sockel; **~ line** *39T* Grundlinie
based, to **be ~ in ...** *13* seinen Sitz in ... haben, in ... sein
batch *9* Charge, Los
battery pack *73* Akku
battery-powered *103* batteriebetrieben
bay, welding ~ *11T* Schweißplatz
bearing, 6-point ball ~ cage *97T* sechsfach kugelgelagerter Laufwagen; **ball ~** *93* Kugellager
beat per minute *56T* Schlag pro Minute
bed slideways *31* Maschinenbett
to **beep** *50* piepen
beginning, in the ~ *119* anfangs
behalf, on ~ of sb *20* für jdn, in jds Namen
behaviour, load ~ *63* Lastverhalten
belt, conveyor ~ *102* Förderband
bench *77* Werkbank
to **bend** *11T* biegen
to **benefit** *18* (davon) profitieren; **~ sb/sth** *131* jdm/etw nützen
benefits *pl* *124* Zusatzleistungen, Sozialleistungen
best: B~ regards *33* Mit freundlichen Grüßen; **B~ wishes** *33* Mit freundlichen Grüßen
biodiversity *112* Artenvielfalt
birth, date of ~ *128* Geburtsdatum; **place of ~** *12* Geburtsort
bismuth *38* Bismut, Wismut
bit, drill ~ *74* Bohrer, Bohrspitze
blade, cutting ~ *27T* Trennscheibe
block *40* Klotz, Block
to **block** *14T* versperren, blockieren
blood pressure *56* Blutdruck; **pulse and ~ monitor** *56* Puls- und Blutdruckmessgerät
to **blow** *85* blasen
blower, hot air ~ *81* Heißluftgebläse; **~ cooled** *104T* gebläsegekühlt
blue collar workers *pl* *55* Arbeiter/innen
board *6* Aufsichtsrat; **circuit ~** *16* Leiterplatte, Platine; **installation ~** *11T* Installationsplatte; **printed circuit ~ (PCB)** *36* Leiterplatte, Platine; **single-~ (micro)computer** *37* Einplatinenrechner
body *98* *(Brief:)* Haupttext
boiler, gas ~ *73* Gaskessel
bolt *26* Schraube *(ohne Spitze),* Bolzen
to **bond** *36* verkleben, verbinden
to **book** *64* reservieren, buchen
booklet *49T* Broschüre
to **bore** *30* innendrehen
bore *39T* Bohrung
bored *126* gelangweilt
borehole *39T* Bohrloch
boron *38T* Bor
to **bow** *87* sich verbeugen
bracket *118* Halterung
to **brainstorm** *14T* Ideen sammeln
brake *47* Bremse
branch *8* Niederlassung; *19* Ast, Zweig
brand new *17T* brandneu
to **break down** *17T* kaputtgehen
breaker, circuit ~ *10* Leitungsschutzschalter, Sicherungsautomat
to **breed** *112* sich vermehren
brick *27* Ziegel, Backstein
bridge rectifier *70* Brückengleichrichter; **full-wave ~** *70* Vollwellenbrückengleichrichter
brief *10* kurz, knapp
brigade, fire ~ *77* Feuerwehr
bright *56T* *(Licht:)* hell, gleißend
to **bring up sth** *69T* etw zur Sprache bringen, etw ansprechen
broad, a ~ range of *73* eine große Auswahl von
brochure *32* Broschüre
brush *102* Bürste
brushed DC motor *104* bürstenbehafteter Gleichstrommotor
brushless DC motor *104* bürstenloser Gleichstrommotor
brushwear detection *107* Abnutzungserkennung an den Bürsten
bubble, speech ~ *16* Sprechblase
buddy *26* Kumpel
buffet breakfast *86T* Frühstücksbüfett
builder, machine ~ *24* Maschinenbauer/in; **panel ~** *16* Schaltanlagenbauer/in
building *7* Bauwesen
building site *27* Baustelle
built, ready ~ *96* fertig montiert
built-in *50* eingebaut
bulk order *109* Großbestellung, Großauftrag
to **bump into sth** *15* gegen etw stoßen
bumper *58* Stoßfänger, Stoßstange
buried cable *51* Erdkabel
burn *52* Verbrennung
burning, smell of ~ *71T* Brandgeruch

business *120T* Angelegenheit, Sache; **~ partner** *65* Geschäftspartner/in; **~ trip** *86* Geschäftsreise; to **do ~ with sb** *33* mit jdm Geschäfte machen
button *37* Taste; **emergency stop ~** *15* Not-Aus-Taster
by *56T* *(Abmessungen:)* mal

C

cabin, lift ~ *9* Aufzugskabine
cable *6* Kabel; **buried ~** *51* Erdkabel; **charging ~** *78* Ladekabel; **connecting ~** *97T* Anschlusskabel; **data ~** *74* Datenkabel, Datenleitung; **overhead power ~** *17* Freileitung, Überlandleitung; **power ~** *14* Elektrowerkzeug; **power ~** *74* Stromkabel, Stromleitung; **power supply ~** *115* Netzkabel; **underground ~** *17* Erdleitung; to **lay ~s** *74T* Kabel/Leitungen verlegen; **~ duct** *27* Kabelkanal; **~ sleeve** *10* Kabeltülle, Kabelmuffe; **~ trunk** *74* Kabelkanal; **~ trunking** *10* Leitungsführung
CAD engineer *8* Technische/r Zeichner/in
cage, 6-point ball bearing ~ *97T* sechsfach kugelgelagerter Laufwagen; **squirrel ~ motor** *104* Käfigläufermotor
to **calculate** *49T* berechnen, ausrechnen
calibration equipment *108* Kalibriergerät(e)
to **call back** *20* zurückrufen
callipers *pl*, **vernier ~** *24* Messschieber
to **calm down** *126T* sich beruhigen
candidate *125F* Bewerber/in
canteen *19* Kantine
capable, to **be ~ of sth** *37* zu etw in der Lage sein, etw können
capacitance *24* Kapazität
capacitor *36* Kondensator
capacity *84* Leistung
capital letter *130* Großbuchstabe
carbon *113T* Kohlenstoff; **~ fibre** *34* Kohlefaser; **~ footprint** *113* CO_2-Fußabdruck
cardiac arrest *52* Herzstillstand
care, to **take ~ of sth** *32* sich um etw kümmern, etw bearbeiten, etw erledigen
career prospects *pl* *123* berufliche Perspektiven
carriage *97T* Schlitten; **~ assembly** *31* Werkzeugschlitten
to **carry: ~ sth** *25* etw mit sich führen; **~ out sth** *53T* etw durchführen
carton *57* Karton
case *56T* Schachtel, Hülle, Gehäuse; **in ~** *49T* falls
casing *38T* Gehäuse
cast iron *34* Gusseisen
casting *31* Gussstück
castor *47* Laufrolle
catalogue *33* Katalog
to **catch fire** *73* in Brand geraten, Feuer fangen
category *15* Kategorie
cathode *72* Kathode
Caution! *51* Achtung! Vorsicht!
ceiling *48* (Zimmer-)Decke
cell *50* Zelle
central processing unit (CPU) *59* Hauptprozessor
centre *30* Reitstockspitze; **data ~** *10* Rechenzentrum; **live ~** *31* verfahrbare Führungsspitze; **~ punch** *24* Körner
ceremony, prize-giving ~ *86* Preisverleihung
certification *10* Zulassung, Abnahme, Zertifizierung
certified *79* geprüft, zertifiziert
chain-dotted line *39* strichpunktierte Linie
chairman *6* Vorsitzende/r
chamber, sensor ~ *50* Sensorkammer
chamfer *39T* Fase
change, to **make ~s** *9* Änderungen vornehmen
to **change sth into sth** *71T* etw in etw umwandeln
changing room *11* Umkleide
channel *27* Kanal
characteristics *pl* *72* Eigenschaften, Merkmale
charge *70* (elektrische) Ladung; to **be in ~ of sth** *8T* für etw zuständig/verantwortlich sein
charger *73* Ladegerät
charging cable *78* Ladekabel
charred *71T* verkohlt
chart *8* Diagramm, Tabelle; **bar ~** *54* Säulendiagramm; **organization ~** *8* Organigramm; **pie ~** *54* Tortendiagramm
chaser, wall ~ *27T* Mauerfräser
to **check: ~ in** *86* sich anmelden, einchecken; **~ out** *86* sich abmelden, auschecken
chemical *10* chemisch, Chemie-
chemicals *pl* *84* Chemikalien
chest *52* Brust, Brustkorb
chip, flying ~s *31* herumfliegende Späne
chisel *27* Meißel
chromium *113T* Chrom
chronic *124* dauerhaft
chronological(ly) *77* chronologisch
chuck *29* Spannfutter, Bohrfutter
circle *40* Kreis
circuit *27* Stromkreis, Schaltkreis; **integrated ~** *36* integrierter Schaltkreis; **~ board** *16* Leiterplatte, Platine; **printed ~ board (PCB)** *36* Leiterplatte, Platine; **~ breaker** *10* Leitungsschutzschalter, Sicherungsautomat
circuitry *50* Schaltung, Schaltkreise
circular *30* kreisförmig
circumference *39* Umfang
to **clamp** *31* einspannen
clamp, hold down ~ *29* Niederhalter; **~ meter** *26* Zangenamperemeter
clamping surface *97F* Aufspannfläche
clarification *126* Klarstellung, Klärung
to **clarify** *46* klären, abklären
clarity *42* Klarheit, Deutlichkeit
classification *106* Klassifikation
to **classify** *34* klassifizieren
to **clean up** *112* reinigen, saubermachen, aufräumen
clear, to **keep sth ~** *51* etw frei halten
to **clear space** *112* Platz schaffen
client *20* Kunde/Kundin
climate *113T* Klima
climb *54* Anstieg
to **climb** *54* steigen
clinic, dental ~ *120T* Zahnklinik; **outpatient ~** *98* Ambulanz
clog *118* Verstopfung
clogged *117* verstopft
close-up photo *25* Nahaufnahme
closely, more ~ *78* näher, genauer; **~ spaced** *36* eng nebeneinanderliegend
clothing, protective ~ *14T* Schutzkleidung
cloud storage *69T* Datenspeicherung in der Cloud
clutch *31* Kupplung
CO_2 equivalent *113* CO_2-Äquivalent
coating, conformal ~ *38T* Schutzbeschichtung; **polymer ~** *36* Kunststoffbeschichtung
coefficient *93* Koeffizient
cold storage *58* Kühllager, Kühlhaus
coil, field ~ *103* Feldspule; **filament ~** *119T* Filamentspule
to **collaborate** *114* zusammenarbeiten
collaboration *114* Zusammenarbeit
collar *96* Spannhals
colleague *8T* Kollege/-in
color band *AE* *72* Farbring
column *25* *(Text:)* Spalte; *29* Säule
combination pliers *pl* *26* Kombizange
to **combine** *18* verknüpfen, kombinieren
to **come: ~ off** *95T* sich lösen, abgehen; **~ on** *71T* angehen; **~ across sth** *123* auf etw stoßen; **~ up with sth** *80T* sich etw ausdenken, sich etw einfallen lassen; **~ into effect** *38T* in Kraft treten
command *59* Befehl

comment *113* Kommentar
commercial *16* gewerblich
commitment *124* Engagement
common sense *14T* gesunder Menschenverstand
to **communicate** *68* kommunizieren; **~ sth** *114* etw übermitteln
communication *50* Datenübermittlung, Verbindung; **industrial ~** *10* industrielle Kommunikation
commutator, split-ring ~ *102* Stromwender mit Stromwenderlamellen
compact construction *10* kompakte Bauweise
compass *37* Kompass
company, in-~ *18* innerbetrieblich
compatibility *96* Kompatibilität
compensation *63* Ausgleich, Kompensation; **~ current** *63* Ausgleichsstrom, Kompensationsstrom; **~ feature** *50* Ausgleichsfunktion
to **compete** *79* konkurrieren
competition *11T* Konkurrenz, Wettbewerb
competitor *7* Wettbewerber/in, Konkurrent/in
complaint *112* Beschwerde, Reklamation
complimentary close *33* *(Brief:)* Schlussformel
component *10* Element, Bestandteil; *11T* Bauteil
composed, to **be ~ of sth** *29* aus etw bestehen
composite material *36* Verbundwerkstoff
compositional ratio *38* Zusammensetzungsverhältnis
compound *34* Verbundwerkstoff; *93* Verbindung; **~ rest** *31* Kreuzschlitten; **~ slide** *31* Kreuzschlitten
to **compress** *61* verdichten, komprimieren
compressive stress *35* Druckbelastung, Druckspannung
computer aided *122T* computerunterstützt
computerized *12* Computer-
concave *39T* konkav
to **concern sth** *9* etw betreffen
conclusion *35* Schluss; **in ~** *91* abschließend; to **draw a ~** *71* eine Schlussfolgerung ziehen
concrete *27* Beton
condition *55* Bedingung
to **conduct sth** *113* etw durchführen
conducting *36* leitend, leitfähig
conductive layer *36* leitfähige Schicht
conductor *36* Leiter; **semi-~** *38T* Halbleiter; **~ cross-section** *62* Leiterquerschnitt; **~ pattern** *36* Leiterbild, Leitermuster
conduit *17* Kabelkanal
cone *40* Kegel, Konus
conference *54* Tagung, Konferenz; **~ room** *11* Tagungsraum, Besprechungsraum
confident(ly) *126T* selbstbewusst
to **configure** *92* einrichten, konfigurieren
to **confirm** *20* bestätigen
confirmation *98* Bestätigung
to **conform to sth** *73* einer Sache entprechen
conformal coating *38T* Schutzbeschichtung
conical *41* konisch, kegelförmig
to **connect** *17* verbinden, anschließen
connecting: ~ cable *97T* Anschlusskabel; **~ pipe** *9* Verbindungsrohr, -leitung
connector *6* Verbinder, Stecker; **I/O ~** *37* Anschluss (nutzbar als Eingang oder Ausgang)
consequently *38* folglich, infolgedessen
to **consider sth** *69T* etw in Betracht ziehen, über etw nachdenken
consignment *120* Warensendung
to **consist of sth** *11* aus etw bestehen
to **construct** *81* bauen, konstruieren
construction *7* Bau; *122T* Baugewerbe; **compact ~** *10* kompakte Bauweise; **~ mechanic** *68* Konstruktionsmechaniker/in; **~ site** *57F* Baustelle
consultancy *79* Beratung
consumer *113T* Verbraucher/in
consumption, power ~ *57* Stromverbrauch
contact details *pl* *21F* Kontaktdaten
to **contain** *29* enthalten
container *100* Behälter, Box, Container
to **contaminate** *112* verunreinigen, kontaminieren
contamination *50* Verunreinigung, Kontamination
contents *115* Inhalt
to **continue to do sth** *19* mit etw weitermachen
continuous: ~ line *39* durchgezogene Linie; **~ use** *103* Dauerbetrieb
continuously *97T* fortwährend, ständig, kontinuierlich
contract *80T* Vertrag; **~ length** *113* Vertragsdauer
control: ~ centre *61* Steuerzentrale; **~ computer** *37* Steuerrechner, Steuerungsrechner; **~ dial** *29* Drehregler; **~ light** *71T* Kontrolllampe; **~ line** *49* Steuerleitung; **~ panel** *16* Steuertafel, Schaltschrank; **~ panel wirer** *125F* Schaltschrankverdrahter/in; **~ system** *11T* Steuerung, Steuer-/Regelsystem; **~ technology** *10* Leittechnik; **~ unit** *31* Steuergerät, Steuerung
controller *114* Steuerung, Steuereinheit, Controller; **pneumatic ~** *95* pneumatischer Regler; **programmable logic ~ (PLC)** *58* speicherprogrammierbare Steuerung (SPS)
conventional *93* herkömmlich, konventionell
to **convert** *59* umwandeln
convex *39T* konvex
conveyor *80* Förderband, Förderer, Fördersystem; **~ belt** *102* Förderband
cooker *17* Herd
to **cool** *119T* abkühlen
coolant *31* Kühlmittel
cooler *58* Kühlanlage
cooperation *9* Zusammenarbeit
coordinates *pl* *92* Koordinaten
copier *73* Kopiergerät
copper *11* Kupfer; **~ traces** *pl* *36* Leiterbahnen
to **copy in sb** *69T* jdn auf CC/in den Verteiler setzen
core element *38T* Hauptbestandteil
corporation *16* Unternehmen, Konzern
correctness *42* Richtigkeit
corridor *11T* Flur, Gang
corrosion *38T* Korrosion
corrosive, non-~ *58* korrosionsbeständig
cost-effective *58* kostengünstig
coupler *49* Koppler, Kupplung
coupling *84* Kupplung
course *118* Verlauf
to **cover** *7* *(Thema)* behandeln; *14T* verdecken, abdecken; *36* bedecken; *79* absichern, erfassen
cover *56T* Hülle, Tasche; **~ profile** *96* Abdeckungsprofil
covering letter *32* Anschreiben, Begleitschreiben
crackling noise *53T* Knistern
crane *103* Kran; **gantry ~** *115T* Portalkran
crash *76* Krach, Schlag, Rums; **~ helmet** *35* Sturzhelm
crate *74* Kiste; **packing ~** *98* Packkiste
to **create** *96* *(Datei)* anlegen
crimping pliers *pl* *26* Kabelschuhzange, Crimpzange
cropland *112* Anbaufläche
cross: ~ section *30* Querschnitt; **~ slide** *31* Querschlitten
cube *40* Würfel
cubical *40* würfelförmig

cultural awareness *87* Kulturbewusstsein, kulturelle Sensibilität

current *10* Strom; **alternating ~ (AC)** *84* Wechselstrom; **compensation ~** *63* Ausgleichsstrom, Kompensationsstrom; **direct ~ (DC)** *52* Gleichstrom; **forward ~** *72* Durchlassstrom; **high-~** *10* Hochstrom-; **nominal ~** *62* Nennstrom; **peak forward surge ~** *72* Spitzendurchlassstrom; **rated ~** *73* Nennstrom; **repetitive peak forward ~** *72* wiederkehrender Spitzendurchlassstrom; **surge ~ loading** *72* Stoßstrom-Grenzwert; **three-phase ~** *59T* Drehstrom; **~ gain** *24* Stromverstärkung

currently *79* zur Zeit, gegenwärtig, momentan

custom-made *92* speziell angefertigt, individuell gefertigt

customer service *119T* Kundendienst

to **customize** *96* individuell anpassen

customized *10* maßgeschneidert, individuell

to **cut: ~ down** *112* *(Baum)* fällen; **~ on sth** *113* etw reduzieren

cut out switch, emergency ~ *14T* Not-Aus-Schalter

cutoff, thermal ~ *73* thermische Abschaltung

cutter, multi-toothed ~ *30* mehrzahniges Fräswerkzeug

cutting: ~ blade *27T* Trennscheibe; **~ tool** *29* Schneidwerkzeug; **hot ~ system** *96* Heißschneidesystem

CV (curriculum vitae) *123* Lebenslauf

cylinder *104* Zylinder

cylindrical(ly) *41* zylindrisch

D

daily, on a ~ basis *131* jeden Tag, täglich

damage, fire ~ *76* Brandschaden; **nerve ~** *52* Nervenschäden

to **damage** *113* schädigen

damaged *14T* beschädigt, defekt

damp *106* feucht

darkroom *57* Dunkelkammer

data: ~ cable *74* Datenkabel, Datenleitung; **~ centre** *10* Rechenzentrum; **~ protection** *128* Datenschutz; **~ sheet** *70* Datenblatt

date: ~ of birth *128* Geburtsdatum; **~ of delivery** *94* Lieferdatum

day, at the end of the ~ *18* letzten Endes

dead *53T* tot, ohne Strom; *113T* *(Akku:)* leer

to **deal with sth** *17T* sich um etw kümmern, mit etw umgehen; *43* sich mit etw befassen; *113* mit etw fertig werden, etw bewältigen

dealer *7T* Händler/in

death *52* Tod, Todesfall

decrease *54* Abnahme, Sinken

to **decrease** *54* abnehmen, sinken; *118* verkleinern, verringern

deep *18* tief, vertieft

defect *35* Schaden, Fehler

to **define** *78* definieren

to **deform** *35* verformen

degree *18* Abschluss; *46* Grad

delighted, to **be ~ to do sth** *10* etw sehr gerne tun

delivery, to **take ~** *114* Ware entgegennehmen, eine Lieferung in Empfang nehmen; **date of ~** *94* Lieferdatum; **~ terms** *pl* *56T* Lieferbedingungen; **~ note** *114* Lieferschein

demand, in high ~ *124* sehr gefragt

to **denote** *72* bezeichnen, kennzeichnen

dent *24* Vertiefung

dental clinic *120T* Zahnklinik

dented *120T* verbeult

to **deposit** *118* ablagern

depth *24* Tiefe

description, job ~ *12* Stellenbeschreibung

desert *119T* Wüste

design, electrical ~ *11* Elektroplanung

desktop machine *95* Tischgerät

to **destroy** *38T* zerströren

destruction *112* Zerstörung

detail, in ~ *10* genau, detailliert

to **detect** *48* erkennen; *92* erfassen

detection, brushwear ~ *107* Abnutzungserkennung an den Bürsten; **temperature ~** *74* Temperaturmessung, -erfassung; **~ zone** *48* Erfassungsbereich

to **determine** *63* bestimmen

to **develop** *6* entwickeln

deviation *92* Abweichung

device *10* Gerät, Element; **approaching ~** *53T* Näherungsvorrichtung

to **diagnose** *24* diagnostizieren, feststellen

dial *29* Anzeige, Regler; **control ~** *29* Drehregler

diameter *9* Durchmesser; **inside ~** *24* Innendurchmesser; **outside ~** *24* Außendurchmesser

to **dictate** *32* diktieren

digit *21* Ziffer

dimension line *39* Bemaßungslinie

dimensions *pl* *39* Abmessungen, Dimensionen

dining room *86T* *(Hotel:)* Speisesaal

diode, avalanche ~ *72* Lawinendiode

dip *62* Senke

directive *38T* Richtlinie

directly operational *96* direkt einsatzbereit

director *60* Leiter/in, Direktor/in

dirt *14T* Schmutz, Dreck

disadvantage *38T* Nachteil

to **disappear** *113T* verschwinden

disassembly *97T* Zerlegen, Demontage

to **disconnect** *52* trennen

disconnected, to **get ~** *126* *(Telefonverbindung:)* unterbrochen werden

discount *94* Rabatt

to **discuss** *14* diskutieren, besprechen, (über etw) sprechen

to **dismantle** *97T* demontieren, zerlegen

to **dispatch** *33* versenden

displacement, reactive ~ *63* Blindleistungsphasenverschiebung

to **dissolve** *113* auflösen

distance *27* Entfernung, Strecke, Abstand

distorting *35* verformend, deformierend

to **distract** *15* ablenken

to **distribute** *35* verteilen

distribution, power ~ *6* Stromverteilung

to **disturb** *52* stören

disturbance *63* Störung

to **divide** *42* teilen, unterteilen

division *8* Geschäftsbereich, Division, Sparte; **head of ~** *8* Bereichsleiter/in

divorced *128* geschieden

DIY kit *95* Bausatz

to **do business with sb** *33* mit jdm Geschäfte machen

Documentary Letter of Credit *108* Dokumentenakkreditiv

documentation *115T* Unterlagen, Dokumentation

domestic *10* häuslich, Haus-, Haushalts-

domestic *73* Haushalts-

dominant *87* dominant

door, next ~ *76* nebenan; **next ~ to** *11T* neben; **rollup ~** *58* Rolltor; **sliding ~** *58* Schiebetür; **strip ~** *58* Streifenvorhangtor; **swing ~** *58* Schwenktür, Pendeltür; **~ operating system** *58* Türanlage, Türsteuerung

doorway *58* Durchgang, Türöffnung

doped *38T* dotiert

doping *38T* Dotierung

dose *57* Dosis

dot *32* Punkt

to **download** *72* herunterladen

downtime *17T* Ausfallzeiten

downwards *81* abwärts, nach unten

draft *81* Entwurf

drag knife *96* Schleppmesser

drastic(ally) *55T* drastisch

to **draw:** ~ **up** *79* *(Text)* erstellen, *(Liste)* aufstellen; ~ **a conclusion** *71* eine Schlussfolgerung ziehen
to **dress** *126* sich kleiden
to **drill** *9* bohren
drill *21* Bohrer; **electric** ~ *26* Bohrmaschine; **power** ~ *26* Bohrmaschine; ~ **bit** *74* Bohrer, Bohrspitze
to **drip off** *81* abtropfen
drip-proof *104T* tropfwassergeschützt
dripping water *106* Tropfwasser
to **drive** *30* antreiben; *37* steuern
drive *103* Laufwerk; *124* Tatendrang, Motivation; **linear** ~ *92* Linearantrieb; **variable frequency** ~ *104T* frequenzgeregelter Antrieb; ~ **unit** *93* Antriebseinheit, -aggregat
driving: ~ **licence** *125* Führerschein; ~ **pulley** *31* Antriebsscheibe
to **drop** *54* sinken, fallen
drop *54* Fall, Sinken; *106* Tropfen
dryer, hair ~ *103* Föhn; **tumble** ~ *53* Wäschetrockner
dual system *18* duales System
duct, cable ~ *27* Kabelkanal
due to *15* aufgrund von, wegen; to **be** ~ **sth** *118* an etw liegen
to **dump** *113T* *(Müll)* abladen, verfrachten
dump, waste ~ *112* Müllhalde
durable *58* strapazierfähig, langlebig
duration *52* Dauer
dust *50* Staub
dusty *107* staubig
duty *105* Betriebsart; *128* Aufgabe, Pflicht; **emergency** ~ *125F* Notdienst, Notfalleinsatz; **on** ~ *17T* im Dienst; **severe** ~ *105* Einsatz unter härtesten Bedingungen

E

early *119* schnell, baldig
earth, protective ~ *62* Schutzleiter, Schutzerde
earthmoving machinery *51* Erdbaumaschinen
ease of use *60* Bedienungskomfort
ecological *64* ökologisch, Öko-
ecosystem *112* Ökosystem
edge *41* Kante
to **edit** *118* bearbeiten, editieren
edition *98* *(Zeitschrift etc.:)* Ausgabe
education system *18* Bildungssystem, Schulsystem
effect, overall ~ *15* Gesamteindruck, Gesamtwirkung; to **come into** ~ *38T* in Kraft treten
efficiency *58* Effizienz, Leistungsfähigkeit

e.g. *34* z.B.
either *42* eines (von mehreren)
elastic(ally) *35* elastisch
electric: ~ **charge** *70* (elektrische) Ladung; ~ **drill** *26* Bohrmaschine; ~ **motor** *102* Elektromotor; ~ **shock** *14* Stromschlag; ~ **appliance** *15* Elektrogerät; ~ **design** *11* Elektroplanung; ~ **fire** *51* elektrischer Brand; ~ **flow** *38T* elektrischer Fluss, Stromfluss
electrical: ~ **engineer** *12T* Elektroingenieur/in, Elektrotechniker/in; ~ **panel** *10* Schaltanlage, Schalttafel
electrician, installation ~ *16* Elektroinstallateur/in
electrician's mate *125* Elektro-Gehilfe
to **electrocute sb** *71T* jdn durch Stromschlag töten
electromagnet *104* Elektromagnet
electronics, industrial ~ *6* Industrieelektronik
to **eliminate** *113* entfernen, eliminieren
emergency: ~ **cut out switch** *14T* Not-Aus-Schalter; ~ **duty** *125F* Notdienst, Notfalleinsatz; ~ **exit** *15* Notausgang; ~ **service** *10* Notdienst; ~ **services** *pl* *77* Einsatzkräfte, Rettungsdienste; ~ **stop button** *15* Not-Aus-Taster
emission *113* Ausstoß, Emission
to **employ sb** *6* jdn beschäftigen
employee *7* Angestellte/r, Beschäftigte/r
to **enable** *118* einschalten; ~ **sth to do sth** *36* etw in die Lage versetzen, etw zu tun
to **enclose** *98* *(Brief:)* beifügen
enclosed *104T* umschlossen
enclosure *98* *(Brief:)* Anlage; *104T* Gehäuse
end: ~ **switch** *85* Endschalter; **at the** ~ **of the day** *18* letzten Endes
to **end up** *113T* (irgendwo) landen
endstop *85* Endanschlag
to **energize** *70* mit Spannung versorgen, speisen
energy engineer *68* Energieingenieur/in, Energietechniker/in
engaged *20* *(Telefon:)* besetzt
engineering, mechanical ~ *6* Maschinenbau
to **engrave** *95T* (ein)gravieren
engraving, laser ~ *93* Lasergravur; ~ **needle** *96* Graviernadel
to **enquire about sth** *56* sich nach etw erkundigen
enquiry *32* Anfrage

to **enter sth** *18* etw *(Ausbildung usw.)* beginnen, mit etw anfangen; *59T* etw betreten
entrance *11* Eingang, Einfahrt; **staff** ~ *11T* Personaleingang
entry, no ~ *15* Einfahrt verboten
envelope, working ~ *114* Arbeitsraum
environment, urban ~ *112* städtischer Raum
environmental standard *73* Umweltnorm
epoxy resin *36* Kunstharz, Epoxidharz
equipment *7T* Geräte, Ausstattung
equipped, well-~ *16* gut ausgestattet; ~ **with sth** *30* mit etw ausgestattet
equivalent *20* Entsprechung, Übersetzung; *125* gleichwertig
erosion, soil ~ *112* Bodenerosion
erratic *62* unregelmäßig, sprunghaft
error *115T* Fehler, Irrtum
to **establish** *101* etablieren, schaffen, aufbauen
to **estimate** *61* schätzen
event *32* Veranstaltung; **in the** ~ **of** *50* für den Fall eine/r/s
everyday *78* Alltags-
exam, to **pass an** ~ *19* eine Prüfung bestehen
examination, goods inwards ~ *11* Wareneingangskontrolle
to **exceed** *119T* überschreiten
except for *21* außer
excerpt *9* Auszug
exchange *26* Austausch
Excuse me. *13* Verzeihung. Entschuldigung
to **exhibit sth** *38T* etw an den Tag legen, etw zeigen
to **exit sth** *119T* aus etw treten
exit, emergency ~ *15* Notausgang; **fire** ~ *15* Notausgang
to **expand** *50* expandieren, sich erweitern; ~ **on sth** *113* ausführlich über etw sprechen
expense, at one's ~ *120* auf jds Kosten
experience, job ~ *18* Berufserfahrung
experienced *122T* erfahren
expert staff *18* Fachpersonal
expression *24* Ausdruck
to **extend sth** *50* etw erweitern, etw ausbauen
extension *21* Durchwahl; ~ **reel** *26* Verlängerungskabel
extent *114* Ausdehnung
external *11T* extern, von außen; *36* äußere/r/s, Außen-
to **extinguish** *77* löschen
extinguisher, fire ~ *15* Feuerlöscher
to **extract** *113* *(Rohstoffe)* gewinnen

to **extrude** *117* herauspressen, herausdrücken, extrudieren
extruder *117* Extruder
extrusion *118* Extrusion
eye contact *85* Blickkontakt

F

to **fabricate** *30* fertigen, herstellen
to **face sth** *124* mit etw konfrontiert sein
face-to-face *69T* persönlich
facilities *pl 86T* Einrichtungen
fact, in ~ *13* tatsächlich, eigentlich
factory *6* Fabrik, Werk; **~ floor** *24* Fertigungsbereich, Werkshalle; **~ manager** *20* Betriebsleiter/in, Werksleiter/in
fail *119* Fehldruck
to **fail** *53T* versagen, ausfallen
failure, mains ~ *50* Netzausfall
fair *32* Messe; **trade ~** *34* (Branchen-, Handels-)Messe
fall *54* Absturz
to **fall** *54* abstürzen; **~ off** *15* herunterfallen
faithfully, Yours ~ *33* ... und verbleiben mit freundlichen Grüßen
false alarm *50* Fehlalarm
fan *48* Lüfter; **ventilation ~** *73* Ventilator
far, as ~ as *9* soweit
farming area *112* Landwirtschaftsfläche(n)
fast-flaming *50* schnell brennend
to **fasten sth to sth** *31* etw an etw befestigen
fastener, snap ~ *100* Schnappverschluss
fault *53T* Defekt; **ground ~ circuit interrupter (GFCI)** *71T* FI-Schalter
faulty *14* defekt, fehlerhaft, schadhaft
feature *30* Teil, Sonderanfertigung; *39T* technisches Merkmal; **compensation ~** *50* Ausgleichsfunktion
to **feature** *91* *(Merkmal)* aufweisen
feed *84* Einzug; **manual ~** *30* manueller Vorschub; **power ~** *30* automatischer Vorschub; **~ rate** *97T* Vorschub; **~ reverse gear** *31* Vorschub rückwärts
feedback *43* Rückmeldung(en)
feeding system *83* Einzug
to **feed** *31* vorschieben
to **fence sth off** *53T* etw abschranken
ferrous: ~ metals *pl 34* Eisenmetalle; **non-~ metals** *pl 34* Buntmetalle
fibre, carbon ~ *34* Kohlefaser; **glass ~** *34* Glasfaser
fibrillation, ventricular ~ *52* Herzkammerflimmern
field *10* Bereich, Gebiet; **magnetic ~** *102* Magnetfeld; **~ coil** *103* Feldspule
figure *63* Abbildung
figures *pl 55* Zahlen, Ziffern
filament *117* Filament *(drahtförmige thermoplastische Kunststoffe)*; **~ coil** *119T* Filamentspule
file, personnel ~ *12* Personalakte
to **fill** *14T* *(Regal)* befüllen
film *40* Folie
to **filter** *80T* filtern
filter, active dynamic ~ (ADF) *62* aktiver dynamischer Filter, Aktivfilter; **~ press** *64* Filterpresse
final assembly *11* Endmontage
finance *6* Finanz, Finanzen
financial year *55* Geschäftsjahr
finish, surface ~ *30* Oberfläche(nbeschaffenheit)
fire: electrical ~ *51* elektrischer Brand; to **catch ~** *73* in Brand geraten, Feuer fangen; to **put out a ~** *76* einen Brand löschen; **~ alarm** *50* Brandmelder; **~ brigade** *77* Feuerwehr; **~ damage** *76* Brandschaden; **~ exit** *15* Notausgang; **~ extinguisher** *15* Feuerlöscher; **~ protection** *79* Brandschutz; **~ risk assessment** *79* Brandrisikobewertung, -analyse; **~ safety** *79* Brandschutz
firm handshake *126T* fester Händedruck
first: ~ aid *15* Erste Hilfe; **~ of all** *8* zunächst, zuallererst
first-aider *76* Sanitäter/in
to **fit** *9* passen; **~ sth** *50* etw einbauen; **~ sth with sth** *47* etw mit etw ausstatten
fitter *8* Monteur/in
fitting *8* Montage
to **fix** *62* *(Problem:)* beheben, lösen; *74T* befestigen
fixed amount *112* Pauschalbetrag
flame *76* Flamme
flammable, highly ~ *15* leicht entzündlich
flange *9* Flansch
to **flash** *50* blinken
flash *76* Stichflamme
flashing light *50* Blinklicht
flat *BE 16* Wohnung; *30* eben; **~-bladed screwdriver** *26* Schlitzschraubenzieher/-dreher
to **flatten out** *54* sich stabilisieren, sich einpendeln (bei)
flexibility *60* Flexibilität
flexible *35* biegsam
to **flick through** *126* durchblättern
floating *49* potentialfrei
floor: ~ plan *49T* Grundriss, Lageplan; **~ tray** *83* Bodenwanne
flooring *74* Fußboden
flow *63* Fluss; **electrical ~** *38T* elektrischer Fluss, Stromfluss
to **fluctuate** *54* schwanken, sich ständig verändern
fluctuation *54* Schwankung(en), ständige Veränderung
fluent *131* *(Sprache:)* fließend
flyer *32* Faltblatt
flying chips *31* herumfliegende Späne
flywheel *9* Schwungrad
to **focus** *126* sich konzentrieren
foil *36* Folie
to **fold** *85* klappen
food: frozen ~ *58* Tiefkühlkost, Tiefkühlprodukte; **~ processing** *102* Lebensmittelverarbeitung; **~ mixer** *103* Küchenmaschine
footprint, carbon ~ *113* CO_2-Fußabdruck
force *35* Kraft; **~ of gravity** *85* Schwerkraft
to **force** *85* zwingen, *hier:* drücken
foreman/-woman *8* Vorarbeiter/in, Meister/in
fork-lift truck *48* Gabelstapler
to **form** *24* formen, bilden
formal *13* formell, förmlich
formation *112* Bildung
to **forward** *119T* weiterleiten
forward: ~ current *72* Durchlassstrom; **peak ~ surge current** *72* Spitzendurchlassstrom; **repetitive peak ~ current** *72* wiederkehrender Spitzendurchlassstrom
to **found** *6* gründen
foundation *6* Grundlage
to **fracture** *35* brechen, zerbrechen
frame *105* Rahmen, Gestell
freely accessible *97T* frei zugänglich
to **freeze** *52* erstarren
frequency *62* Frequenz; **variable ~ drive** *104T* frequenzgeregelter Antrieb
frequent *58* häufig
frequently *28* oft, häufig
fresh *17* frisch
friction *93* Reibung
frozen food *58* Tiefkühlkost, Tiefkühlprodukte
fruit processing *59T* Obstverarbeitung
to **fulfil an order** *120* einen Auftrag abwickeln, eine Bestellung ausführen
full load *105* Volllast
full-time *125* Vollzeit-
full-wave bridge rectifier *70* Vollwellenbrückengleichrichter
to **function** *36* funktionieren

household: ~ goods *pl* *35* Haushaltsartikel; **~ name** *10* (allgemein) bekannter Name
housing *31* Gehäuse
hybrid *50* gemischt, mehrgleisig, Hybrid-
hydraulic *9* hydraulisch, Hydraulik-; **~ power unit** *95* Hydraulikaggregat
hyphen *32* Bindestrich

I
ideally *122T* idealerweise
to **identify** *58* bestimmen, herausfinden, identifizieren
if anything *52* wenn überhaupt
illness *13* Krankheit
to **illuminate** *71T* beleuchten
to **illustrate** *113* veranschaulichen
immediate *107T* unverzüglich, sorfortig
impact *112* Auswirkung(en), Folge(n)
impact *58* Aufprall
impression *126* Eindruck
impressive *11T* beeindruckend, eindrucksvoll
improvement *43* Verbesserung
inbuilt *58* eingebaut
incident *76* Vorfall
incinerator *113* Müllverbrennungsanlage
to **include** *9* einbeziehen, aufnehmen
including *6* einschließlich
in-company *18* innerbetrieblich
increase *54* Zunahme, Anstieg
to **increase** *54* zunehmen, ansteigen; *118* erhöhen, vergrößern
indentation *35* Eindruck, Einkerbung
independent *95T* unabhängig
index card *42* Karteikarte
to **indicate** *126F* andeuten, darauf hinweisen
indication *32* Hinweis, Anzeichen
individual *51* Person
individual(ly) *56T* einzeln
inductance *24* Induktivität
induction motor *104* Asychron-Motor
industrial *10* Industrie-, industriell; **~ communication** *10* industrielle Kommunikation; **~ electronics** *6* Industrieelektronik
industry, heavy ~ *10* Schwerindustrie
inefficient *59T* ineffizient
inertia *118* Trägheit
to **inform** *119* informieren, mitteilen
infrared camera *26* Infrarotkamera
initial *124* erste/r/s
initials *pl*, **reference ~** *98* *(Brief:)* Zeichen
to **inject** *63* einspeisen
input *37* Eingang; **mains ~ socket** *70* Netzanschlussbuchse

inside: ~ address *98* Innenadresse; **~ diameter** *24* Innendurchmesser
to **insist on sth** *79* auf etw bestehen
to **inspect** *125F* kontrollieren, prüfen, inspizieren
inspection *119* Überprüfung, Kontrolle; **~ mirror** *24* Kontrollspiegel
installation: ~ board *11T* Installationsplatte; **~ electrician** *16* Elektroinstallateur/in; **~ instruction** *48* Montageanleitung
instruction, installation ~ *48* Montageanleitung
instructions *pl*, **safety ~** *46* Sicherheitshinweise
to **insulate** *36* isolieren
insulated *58* isoliert
insulation class *105* Isolationsklasse, Schutzgrad
insulator *38T* Isolator
to **integrate** *73* integrieren, einbauen
integrated: ~ circuit *36* integrierter Schaltkreis; **~ voltage stabilizer** *70* integrierter Spannungsstabilisator
integration *90* Einbindung, Integrierung
to **interact** *102* aufeinander einwirken; *118* zusammenspielen
interconnected *50* (untereinander) verbunden
interconnection *36* Verbindung, Verschaltung
interface *37* Schnittstelle
interior *83* Innen-
intermediate *96* Zwischen-
intermittent use *107* Kurzzeitbetrieb
internal *36* innere/r/s; *50* intern
to **interrupt** *73* unterbrechen
interrupter, ground fault circuit ~ (GFCI) *71T* FI-Schalter
to **interview sb** *32* mit jdm ein Vorstellungsgespräch führen
interviewer *126* *Person, die ein Vorstellungsgespräch führt*
introductions *pl* *12* Bekanntmachen, Vorstellen
to **invent** *78* erfinden
to **invite sth** *42* zu etw auffordern
to **involve** *16* beinhalten, mit sich bringen, einbeziehen
involved (in sth) *77* (an etw) beteiligt
inwards, goods ~ examination *11* Wareneingangskontrolle
I/O connector *37* Anschluss (nutzbar als Eingang oder Ausgang)
iron *34* Eisen; *73* Bügeleisen; **cast ~** *34* Gusseisen; **soldering ~** *24* Lötkolben
irregular *30* uneben
to **irritate** *126* stören, irritieren
issue *112* Frage, Problem

item *33* Artikel; *80* Gegenstand; *90* Punkt
itinerary *65* Reiseplan

J
jagged *62* gezackt
jam *118* Stau
to **jam** *118* blockieren, verstopfen
jammed *117* blockiert, verstopft
jewellery *15* Schmuck
jet, water ~ *106* Strahlwasser
job: ~ advert(isement) *124* Stellenanzeige; **~ agency** *122* Arbeitsagentur, Arbeitsvermittlung; **~ application** *122* Bewerbung; **~ description** *12* Stellenbeschreibung; **~ experience** *18* Berufserfahrung; **~ offer** *123* Stellenangebot; **~ opportunities** *pl* *123* Arbeitsmöglichkeiten
to **join** *11T* (miteinander) verbinden; **~ sth** *70* einer Sache beitreten, bei einer Sache mitmachen; **~ a company** *19* bei einem Unternehmen anfangen
journey *13* Fahrt, Anreise
junction *72* P-N-Übergang *(in Halbleitern)*; **~ box** *27T* Abzweigdose, Verteilerdose

K
keen, to **be ~ to do sth** *131* jdm liegt sehr daran, etw zu tun
to **keep: ~ on sb** *18* jdn behalten; **~ up sth** *8T* etw aufrecht erhalten; **~ in mind** *126F* daran denken; **sb safe** *14T* jdn schützen
key: Allen ~ *26* Inbusschlüssel, Innensechskantschlüssel; **~ account management** *9F* Großkundenbetreuung; **~ word** *85* Schlagwort, Stichwort
to **kill** *52* töten
knife, drag ~ *96* Schleppmesser
knock *84* Stoß, Schlag
to **knock: ~ out sth** *27T* etw herausschlagen; **~ over sth** *77* etw umstoßen
known, well-~ *7* bekannt

L
L-shaped *41* L-förmig
to **label** *11* bezeichnen, etikettieren
label *9* Etikett, Siegel
labelling plate *95* Typenschild; *115* Beschriftungsplatte
labour *79* Arbeit
ladder *15* Leiter
lag, time ~ *84* Zeitverzögerung
laminate material *38T* Verbundwerkstoff
landfill *113T* Mülldeponie

landline *126* Festnetz(telefon)
lap *56T* Bahn *(im Schwimmbecken)*
laser: ~ beam printer *73* Laserdrucker; **~ engraving** *93* Lasergravur
latest *57* neueste/r/s
lathe *11* Drehbank; **~ operator** *31* Dreher/in
to **lay** *17* legen; **~ cables** *74T* Kabel/Leitungen verlegen
layer *36* Schicht; **conductive ~** *36* leitfähige Schicht; **~ separation** *117* Schichttrennung
layout *11* Raumaufteilung, Plan
lead *34* Blei; **mains ~** *71T* Netzkabel
leaded *38* bleihaltig
leakage *112* Austreten, Versickern
least, last but not ~ *8T* zu guter Letzt
to **leave a message** *20* eine Nachricht hinterlassen
legislation *80* Gesetze, Gesetzgebung
length *31* Länge; **contract ~** *113* Vertragsdauer
to **let go of sth** *52* etw loslassen
Letter of Credit, Documentary ~ *108* Dokumentenakkreditiv
to **level off** *54* sich stabilisieren, sich einpendeln (bei)
lever *31* Hebel
licence, driving ~ *125* Führerschein
life, operating ~ *50* Lebendauer, Betriebsdauer; **working ~** *107T* Lebensdauer; **~ span** *50* Lebensdauer
to **lift** *107T* heben
lift: ~ cabin *9* Aufzugskabine; **~ shaft** *9* Aufzugsschacht
lifting: ~ equipment *93* Hebegeräte, Hebezeuge; **~ system** *9* Hubsystem
to **light** *76* sich entzünden
light *101F* Scheinwerfer; **naked ~s** *pl* *15* offene Flammen; **~ barrier** *84* Lichtschranke
light metals *pl* *34* Leichtmetalle
light-weight *35* leicht
to **limit** *84* begrenzen, beschränken
limit, power ~ *96* Leistungsobergrenze
line, base ~ *39T* Grundlinie; **chain-dotted ~** *39* strichpunktierte Linie; **continuous ~** *39* durchgezogene Linie; **control ~** *49* Steuerleitung; **dimension ~** *39* Bemaßungslinie; **packaging ~** *53T* Verpackungsstraße; **subject ~** *32* Betreffzeile; to **hold the ~** *20* *(Telefon:)* am Apparat bleiben; **~ graph** *54* Liniendiagramm; **~ manager** *8* direkte/r Vorgesetzte/r
to **line up sth** *27T* etw ausrichten
linear: ~ drive *92* Linearantrieb; **~ track profile** *96* Linearachsprofil; **~ unit** *85* Lineareinheit
to **link** *113T* in Verbindung bringen

liquid *106* Flüssigkeit
to **list** *8T* *(in einer Liste)* aufführen
listener *122T* Hörer/in
live *51* unter Spannung; **~ centre** *31* verfahrbare Führungsspitze
to **load** *104* beladen
load, permissible ~ *94* zulässige Last; **~ behaviour** *63* Lastverhalten
loading, surge current ~ *72* Stoßstrom-Grenzwert
to **lock out sth** *51* etw (dauerhaft) abschalten
long-time *19* langfristig
to **look the part** *126* entsprechend (rollengerecht) aussehen
loop *102* Schleife
loose *24* locker
to **loosen** *26* lockern, lösen
loss *58* Verlust
low maintenance *10* wartungsfreundlich
to **lower** *70* senken
Ltd *33* GmbH
lube *105* Schmiermittel
luck, to **be in ~** *71T* Glück haben; **Good ~!** *72* Viel Glück!

M

to **machine** *30* (maschinell) bearbeiten
machine: ~ builder *24* Maschinenbauer/in; **~ maintenance technician** *16* Maschinenwartungstechniker/in; **~ tool** *29* Werkzeugmaschine
machinery *14* Maschinen
madam *33* Dame
magnet, permanent ~ *102* Permanentmagnet
magnetic field *102* Magnetfeld
magnetometer *37* Magnetfeldsensor
mains: ~ failure *50* Netzausfall; **~ input socket** *70* Netzanschlussbuchse; **~ lead** *71T* Netzkabel; **~ power** *50* Netzstrom; **~ voltage** *49* Netzspannung
to **maintain** *16* warten, instand halten
maintenance *10* Wartung, Instandhaltung; **low ~** *10* wartungsfreundlich; **machine ~ technician** *16* Maschinenwartungstechniker/in
to **make up sth** *21F* sich etw ausdenken; *36* etw ausmachen
malleable *35* formbar
manner *43* Art (und Weise)
manual *46* Handbuch; **~ feed** *30* manueller Vorschub
manually *80* von Hand; **~ operated** *59T* handbetrieben
to **manufacture** *6* fertigen, herstellen
manufacture *113* Herstellung, Fertigung

manufacturing: ~ company *79* Fertigungsbetrieb, Produktionsunternehmen; **~ output** *54F* Produktionsleistung
marital status *128* Familienstand
to **mark** *24* kennzeichnen, markieren
marking *27T* Markierung
married *128* verheiratet
mask, solder ~ *36* Lötmaske
mass *114* Masse
mat *80* Matte
mate, electrician's ~ *125* Elektro-Gehilfe
material handling *114* Materialtransport, Fördertechnik
mathematical operation *46* Rechenoperation
means of communication *68* Kommunikationmittel
to **measure** *24* messen; *37* betragen
measurement run *92* Messfahrt
measures *pl* *53* Maßnahmen
measuring: ~ equipment *92* Messgeräte; **~ station** *92* Messplatz, Messstation; **~ tool** *24* Messwerkzeug
mechanic, precision ~ *24* Feinwerkmechaniker/in
mechanical engineering *6* Maschinenbau
mechanical(ly) *35* mechanisch
mechanics *18* Mechanik
mechanism *59T* Mechanismus
mechatronics *18* Mechatronik; **~ technician** *24* Mechatroniker/in
to **mediate** *36* vermitteln
medical *7T* medizinisch; **~ equipment** *56* medizinische Geräte, Medizintechnik
medium-sized *7* mittelgroß, mittelständisch
to **meet** *92* *(Anforderungen usw.)* erfüllen
to **melt** *38* schmelzen
melting point *38* Schmelzpunkt
member *11* Mitglied
memo *73* Notiz, Kurzmitteilung, Aktenvermerk
memory *59* Speicher
to **mention** *9* erwähnen, nennen
mercury *113* Quecksilber
message, to **leave a ~** *20* eine Nachricht hinterlassen; to **take a ~** *20* etw ausrichten
messiness *14T* Unordnung, Unsauberkeit
metals *pl*, **heavy ~** *34* Schwermetalle; **light ~** *34* Leichtmetalle; **non-~** *34* Nichtmetalle, Steine und Erden; **non-ferrous ~** *34* Buntmetalle; **precious ~** *38T* Edelmetalle
metalwork *124* Metallbau

meter, clamp ~ *26* Zangenamperemeter
method *68* Art (und Weise), Weg
micrometre *9* Mikrometer
microphone *101F* Mikrofon
mild *53* leicht
milling machine *29* Fräsmaschine
to **mind: Never ~.** *90T* Macht nichts.
mind, to **have sth in ~** *57* an etw denken, sich etw vorstellen; to **keep in ~** *126F* daran denken
mind map *19* Mindmap
to **minimize** *17T* gering halten, minimieren
mining *112* Bergbau, Abbau, Förderung
minor *14T* klein(er/e/s), geringfügig
mirror, inspection ~ *24* Kontrollspiegel
misaligned *117* falsch ausgerichtet
to **mix** *80T* mischen
mixer, food ~ *103* Küchenmaschine
mixture *81* Mischung, Gemisch
mobile *10* mobil; *20* Handy, Mobiltelefon
mobility *123* Freizügigkeit, Mobilität
model-maker *95T* Modellbauer/in
module *50* Modul
monodirectional *104T* in einer Richtung laufend, monodirektional
motion *93* Bewegung
motor *29* Motor; **brushed DC ~** *104* bürstenbehafteter Gleichstrommotor; **brushless DC ~** *104* bürstenloser Gleichstrommotor; **electric ~** *102* Elektromotor; **electric** *102* Elektromotor; **induction ~** *104* Asychron-Motor; **shaded pole ~** *104* Spaltpolmotor; **squirrel cage ~** *104* Käfigläufermotor; **stepper ~** *95* Schrittmotor
to **mount** *31* befestigen, montieren, anbringen
moving object *48* bewegtes Objekt
multi-layer *36* Mehrschicht-, mehrschichtig; **~ structure** *36* mehrschichtiger Aufbau
multi-toothed cutter *30* mehrzahniges Fräswerkzeug
multimeter *24* Multimeter
multinational (company) *7* internationaler Konzern
multiplier *118* Multiplikator
muscle *52* Muskel

N

naked lights *pl* *15* offene Flammen
nameplate *105* Typenschild
narrow *58* schmal
national grid *16* Stromnetz
natural *34* natürlich
to **near** *107T* sich nähern
nearby *74T* in der Nähe
necessity *107* Notwendigkeit
needle, engraving ~ *96* Graviernadel
negotiable *124* verhandelbar
nerve damage *52* Nervenschäden
net *57* netto
network *63* Netz
newly-qualified *122* frisch gebacken
next door *76* nebenan; **~ to** *11T* neben
noise *19* Lärm; *53T* Rauschen; **crackling ~** *53T* Knistern; **delivery ~** *114* Lieferschein
nominal: ~ apparent power *62* Nennscheinleistung; **~ current** *62* Nennstrom; **~ pressure** *84* Nenndruck
non-corrosive *58* korrosionsbeständig
non-ferrous metals *pl* *34* Buntmetalle
non-metals *pl* *34* Nichtmetalle, Steine und Erden
non-ventilated *106* unbelüftet
non-volatile *59* nichtflüchtig
noon *64* Mittag
notice *76* Warnhinweis, Hinweisschild; **at short ~** *131* kurzfristig
nozzle *84* Düse; **high-pressure ~** *84* Hochdruckdüse; **~ tip** *117* Düsenspitze
numeral *106* Ziffer
nut *26* Mutter

O

occasion *125F* Gelegenheit
occasional(ly) *27* gelegentlich
to **occur to sb** *126T* jdm in den Sinn kommen
off-hand grinder *29* Handschleifmaschine
offer, job ~ *123* Stellenangebot
official *10* amtlich, offiziell
on, and so ~ *8T* und so weiter
to **ooze** *117* tropfen, quellen
open ended spanner *26* Maulschlüssel
to **operate** *10* geschäftlich tätig sein; *17T* in Betrieb sein; *24* funktionieren, arbeiten
operating: ~ life *50* Lebensdauer, Betriebsdauer; **~ temperature** *73* Betriebstemperatur; **~ theatre** *98* Operationssaal; **~ voltage** *62* Betriebsspannung
operation *10* Betrieb; **mathematical ~** *46* Rechenoperation
operational, directly ~ *96* direkt einsatzbereit; **~ principle** *63* Funktionsprinzip
opportunity *124* Gelegenheit, Möglichkeit; **, job ~ies** *pl* *123* Arbeitsmöglichkeiten
to **opt for sth** *96* sich für etw entscheiden
optical *50* optisch
optimistic *71* optimistisch
to **optimize** *58* optimieren
optimum *85* optimal
order *15* Befehl; **bulk ~** *109* Großbestellung, Großauftrag; **reverse ~** *47* umgekehrte Reihenfolge; **trial ~** *98* Probebestellung; to **fulfil an ~** *120* einen Auftrag abwickeln, eine Bestellung ausführen; **~ code** *94* Bestellcode, Bestellschlüssel
organization chart *8* Organigramm
oscillogram *62* Oszillogramm
oscilloscope, portable digital ~ *26* tragbares Digital-Oszilloskop
outer ring *9* Außenring
to **outlast sth** *50* länger halten als etw
outpatient clinic *98* Ambulanz
output *37* Ausgang; *79* Produktion; **manufacturing ~** *54F* Produktionsleistung
outside diameter *24* Außendurchmesser
overall *14T* Schutzanzug; **~ effect** *15* Gesamteindruck, Gesamtwirkung; **~ score** *43* Gesamtpunktzahl; **~ size** *97F* Gesamtmaße
overhead *114* Überkopf-, obere/r/s; **~ power cable** *17* Freileitung, Überlandleitung
to **overheat** *73* sich überhitzen, zu heiß werden
overheating *117* Überhitzung
to **overload** *84* überlasten
overtime *124* Überstunden; to **work ~** *19* Überstunden machen; **~ work** *19* Überstunden
overview *10* Überblick, Übersicht
own, on one's ~ *7* alleine
oxidation *36* Oxidation, Oxidierung

P

to **pack** *98* verpacken
to **package** *56T* verpacken
package *72* Gehäuse
packaging *53* Verpackung; **~ line** *53T* Verpackungsstraße
packing crate *98* Packkiste
pad, solder ~ *36* Lötpad
padlock *100* Vorhängeschloss
paid holiday *125* bezahlter Urlaub
painful *52* schmerzhaft
to **pair** *16* koppeln, zuordnen
to **palletize** *80T* palettieren
palletizer *80* Palettierer
panel *10* Schaltanlage, Schalttafel; *11T* Blech, Tafel; *126T* Gremium; **back ~** *71T* Rückplatte; **control ~** *16* Steuertafel, Schaltschrank; **control ~ wirer** *125F* Schaltschrankverdrahter/in; **window ~** *58* Fenster, Scheibe; **~ builder** *16* Schaltanlagenbauer/in; **~ building** *14* Schalt-

anlagenbau; ~ **building electrician** 122 Schaltschrankverdrahter/in
parallel, in ~ 63 parallel geschaltet
part, to **look the ~** 126 entsprechend (rollengerecht) aussehen
particular 19 speziell; 123 besondere/r/s
particularly 131 insbesondere; **Not ~.** 126T Eigentlich nicht.
partner 6 Gesellschafter/in
party, third ~ 112 Dritte/r
to **pass: ~ on sth** 21F etw weiterleiten, etw weitergeben; **~ through** 59T hindurchfahren; **~ an exam** 19 eine Prüfung bestehen
passivated, glass ~ 72 glaspassiviert
past sth 11T an etw vorbei
pattern 118 Muster; **conductor ~** 36 Leiterbild, Leitermuster
pay 13 Bezahlung, Gehalt
payload 114 Nutzlast
payment 98 Zahlung; **terms** *pl* **of ~** 98 Zahlungsbedingungen
to **peak** 54 einen Spitzenwert erreichen
peak 54 Spitzenwert; 62 Spitze, Wellenkamm; **~ forward surge current** 72 Spitzendurchlassstrom; **pulse avalanche ~ power** 72 Spitzenleistung bei Pulsbelastung; **repetitive ~ forward current** 72 wiederkehrender Spitzendurchlassstrom; **repetitive ~ reverse voltage** 72 wiederkehrende Spitzensperrspannung
pedestrian 58 Fußgänger
pellet, thermal ~ 73 thermisch geschütztes Gehäuse
to **perform** 114 *(Tätigkeit)* ausführen; **~ sth** 57 *(Theater usw.:)* etw aufführen, etw spielen
performance 58 Leistung
period, guarantee ~ 101 Garantiezeit
permanent 18 unbefristet; **~ magnet** 102 Permanentmagnet
permissible load 94 zulässige Last
permission 51 Erlaubnis
personnel 12 Personal; **~ file** 12 Personalakte
to **persuade** 113T überzeugen
phase 62 Phase
Phillips screwdriver 26 Kreuzschlitzschraubenzieher/-dreher
phosphorus 38T Phosphor
pie chart 54 Tortendiagramm
pile 14T Stapel
to **pin** 15 befestigen, anheften
pipe, connecting ~ 9 Verbindungsrohr, -leitung
piston 9 Kolben
place, all over the ~ 69T überall; **~ of birth** 12 Geburtsort
to **place an order** 56T einen Auftrag erteilen, eine Bestellung aufgeben
plant 80T Werk, Betrieb
plastic(ally) 35 plastisch
to **plate** 36 galvanisieren, überziehen
plate 39T Platte; **type ~** 115T Typenschild
plated 72 metallüberzogen
plated-through 36 durchkontaktiert; **~ hole (PTH)** 36 Durchkontaktierung
platform trolley 46 Plattformwagen, Flachtransportwagen
platinum 38T Platin
play-free 97T spielfrei
pleased, P~ to meet you. 87 Schön, Sie kennenzulernen.
pliers *pl*, **combination ~** 26 Kombizange; **crimping ~** 26 Kabelschuhzange, Crimpzange
to **plug in** 15 einstecken, anschließen
plunger pump 84 Kolbenpumpe, Plungerpumpe
pneumatic 61 pneumatisch; **~ controller** 95 pneumatischer Regler; **~ hose** 74 Druckluftschlauch, Pneumatikschlauch
point, assembly ~ 76 Sammelplatz; **melting ~** 38 Schmelzpunkt; **solder ~** 36 Lötpunkt, Lötstelle
to **point out sth** 113 auf etw hinweisen
poisonous 113T giftig
polarity 72 Polung, Polarität
pole 102 Pol; **shaded ~ motor** 104 Spaltpolmotor
polite(ly) 21F höflich
politics 13 Politik
to **pollute** 80T verschmutzen
pollution 58 Verschmutzung
polymer coating 36 Kunststoffbeschichtung
populated PCB 36 (mit Bauelementen) bestückte Leiterplatte
population 112 Bevölkerung
port 59 Schnittstelle; **ground ~** 37 Erdungsbuchse, -anschluss; **power ~** 37 Stromversorgungsbuchse, -anschluss
portable 56 tragbar, mobil; **~ digital oscilloscope** 26 tragbares Digital-Oszilloskop
to **position** 81 platzieren
to **postpone** 65 (nach hinten) verschieben
potential 123 möglich, potenziell
to **power sth** 71T etw mit Strom versorgen
power: mains ~ 50 Netzstrom; **nominal apparent ~** 62 Nennscheinleistung; **overhead ~ cable** 17 Freileitung, Überlandleitung; **pulse avalanche peak ~** 72 Spitzenleistung bei Pulsbelastung; **~ cable** 74 Stromkabel, Stromleitung; **~ consumption** 57 Stromverbrauch; **~ distribution** 6 Stromverteilung; **~ drill** 26 Bohrmaschine; **~ feed** 30 automatischer Vorschub; **~ generation** 6 Stromerzeugung; **~ hacksaw** 29 Maschinenbügelsäge; **~ limit** 96 Leistungsobergrenze; **~ port** 37 Stromversorgungsbuchse, -anschluss; **~ rating** 105 Leistung, Nennleistung; **~ station** 10 Elektrizitätswerk; **~ supply (unit)** 37 Stromversorgung, Netzteil; **~ supply cable** 115 Netzkabel; **~ tool** 14 Elektrowerkzeug; **~ tuning** 62 Leistungsabstimmung; **~-assisted** 58 Servo-
powerful 87 mächtig
powerline technician 16 *Elektriker/in, der/die am öffentlichen Stromnetz arbeitet*
practitioner, General P~ (GP) 57F Allgemeinarzt/-ärztin, Hausarzt/-ärztin
pre-assembly 11 Vormontage
to **pre-load** 94 vorspannen
precautions *pl*, **safety ~** 71 Sicherheitsvorkehrungen, Sicherheitsmaßnahmen
precious 38T wertvoll, kostbar, edel; **~ metals** *pl* 38T Edelmetalle
precision mechanic 24 Feinwerkmechaniker/in
preliminary 125F vorläufig, Vor-
premium 58 hochwertig, erstklassig
prepared 7 bereit, vorbereitet; to **be ~ to do sth** 85 bereit sein, etw zu tun
present 63 anwesend
presentation 10 Vortrag, Präsentation
pressure 84 Druck; **blood ~** 56 Blutdruck; **nominal ~** 84 Nenndruck
to **prevent** 36 verhindern, verhüten
price list 98 Preisliste
principle, operational ~ 63 Funktionsprinzip
print 118 Ausdruck
printed circuit board (PCB) 36 Leiterplatte, Platine
printer: ~ head 118 Druckkopf; **~ resin** 118 geschmolzener Filamentkunststoff
prize-giving ceremony 86 Preisverleihung
probe 53T Sonde, Fühler
procedure 51 Verfahren, Maßnahme
to **process** 96 verarbeiten
process 8T Ablauf, Prozess, Verfahren; **selection ~** 126F Auswahlverfahren; **~ visualization** 10 Prozessvisualisierung

processing, food ~ *102* Lebensmittelverarbeitung; **fruit ~** *59T* Obstverarbeitung; **central ~ unit (CPU)** *59* Hauptprozessor
producer *6* Hersteller, Produzent
production *7* Produktion, Fertigung, Herstellung
profession *16* Beruf
professional *126* professionell; *128* beruflich
profile *6* Porträt, Beschreibung, Profil; **cover ~** *96* Abdeckungsprofil; **linear track ~** *96* Linearachsprofil
profiled *96* profiliert
profitable *113T* einträglich, profitabel
to **program** *37* programmieren
programmable *37* programmierbar; **~ logic controller (PLC)** *58* speicherprogrammierbare Steuerung (SPS)
to **progress with sth** *126F* mit etw vorankommen
to **prohibit sth** *38T* etw verbieten
prohibition *51* Verbot
promotion *17T* Beförderung
prompt *28* Stichwort; **~ card** *42* Moderationskarte
proof *79* Nachweis(e), Beleg(e)
properly *9* richtig, genau
property *35* Eigenschaft
prospective customer *101* potenzielle/r Kunde/Kundin
prospects *pl*, **career ~** *123* berufliche Perspektiven
to **protect** *98* schützen
protection *36* Schutz; **data ~** *128* Datenschutz; **fire ~** *79* Brandschutz; **~ class** *114* Schutzklasse; **~ clothing** *14T* Schutzkleidung; **~ earth** *62* Schutzleiter, Schutzerde; **~ hood** *31* Schutzhaube
prototype *119* Prototyp
proximity sensor *53T* Näherungssensor
public holiday *125* gesetzlicher Feiertag
pulley, driving ~ *31* Antriebsscheibe
pulse *56* Puls; **~ and blood pressure monitor** *56* Puls- und Blutdruckmessgerät; **~ avalanche peak power** *72* Spitzenleistung bei Pulsbelastung
pump *103* Pumpe; **plunger ~** *84* Kolbenpumpe, Plungerpumpe
to **pump** *61* pumpen
punch, centre ~ *24* Körner
purchasing *6* Einkauf
purpose *9* Zweck, Absicht
pushbutton *83* Drucktaster, Taster
to **put: ~ sb through** *20* *(Telefon:)* jdn durchstellen; **~ out a fire** *76* einen Brand löschen
pylon *17* Strommast

Q
qualification *18* Abschluss, Qualifikation
qualified *18* Fach-, mit Abschluss, qualifiziert
quality: ~ assurance *92* Qualitätssicherung; **~ control** *8* Qualitätskontrolle; **~ management** *79* Qualitätsmanagement, Qualitätssicherung
quantity *69* Menge
quarter *55* Quartal
quarterly *55* vierteljährlich, Quartals-
quotation *94* Preisangebot, Kostenvoranschlag

R
rack *31* Zahnstange
radiation *57* Strahlung
radio link *50* Funkverbindung
radius, radii *39T* Radius, Radien
rail *93* Schiene; **guiding ~** *93* Führungsschiene; **~ technology** *10* Eisenbahntechnik
to **raise** *70* erhöhen, anheben
ranching *112* Viehwirtschaft
randomly *117* willkürlich
range *10* Angebot(spalette), Sortiment; *73* Bereich, Umfang; **a broad ~ of** *73* eine große Auswahl von
to **rank** *15* einstufen, (in einer Rangliste) bewerten
to **rate** *105* klassifizieren, einstufen
rate, air-flow ~ *85* Luftdurchsatz; **feed ~** *97T* Vorschub
rated current *73* Nennstrom
rating, power ~ *105* Leistung, Nennleistung; **absolute maximum ~s** *pl* *72* absolute Grenzdaten
ratio, compositional ~ *38* Zusammensetzungsverhältnis
raw *104* roh
re *109* bezüglich, betreffs
reach *114* Reichweite
to **reach (over)** *77* greifen
to **react to sth** *120* auf etw reagieren
reactive displacement *63* Blindleistungsphasenverschiebung
to **read out sth** *46* etw vorlesen
ready, to **get ~** *87* sich bereit machen, sich fertig machen; **~ built** *96* fertig montiert
to **realise: ~ sth** *77* etw (be)merken; **I ~ that.** *121* Das ist mir bewusst.
to **ream** *30* reiben
reason, to **give ~s for sth** *104* etw begründen
receptionist *86* Empfangsmitarbeiter/in
rechargeable *50* wiederaufladbar
to **reclaim** *112* *(Land)* zurückgewinnen, rekultivieren

to **recognize** *15* erkennen; *18* anerkennen
recommendation *91* Empfehlung
to **record** *17* aufzeichnen, aufnehmen
record *77* Aufzeichnung(en); *113* Bilanz, Ergebnis(se); *121* Datensatz
recording *90* Aufzeichnung, Aufnahme
to **recover** *55T* sich erholen
to **recruit** *16* *(Personal)* anwerben, einstellen
recruitment *18* Einstellung, Anwerbung (von Personal); **~ agency** *124* Personalvermittlung
rectangle *40* Rechteck
rectangular solid *40* Quader
rectification *72* Gleichrichtung
rectifier, bridge ~ *70* Brückengleichrichter; **full-wave bridge ~** *70* Vollwellenbrückengleichrichter
to **rectify** *70* gleichrichten
rectilinear solid *47* geradkantiger Körper
to **reduce** *9* senken, reduzieren, verringern
reel, extension ~ *26* Verlängerungskabel
to **refer to sth** *35* auf etw verweisen, sich auf etw beziehen; *130* etw erwähnen
referee *128* Referenz(geber/in)
reference *98* Referenz; **~ (to sth)** *130* Bezug (auf etw), Erwähnung (von etw); **with ~ to** *101* mit Bezug auf, bezüglich; **~ initials** *pl* *98* *(Brief:)* Zeichen
reflow soldering *36* Reflow-Löten
to **refresh** *54* auffrischen
refreshment *13* Erfrischung
refrigerated air *58* gekühlte Luft
refrigerator *103* Kühlschrank
regard, Best ~s *33* Mit freundlichen Grüßen; **R~s** *33* Mit freundlichen Grüßen
to **register sb** *53T* etw anzeigen
regular customer *94* Stammkunde/-kundin
to **regulate** *78* regeln
regulations *pl* *73* Vorschriften
reinforcement *36* Verstärkung
to **reject** *57* ablehnen, zurückweisen
to **relate sth to sth** *126T* etw auf etw beziehen
related to sth *14* bezüglich etw
relation, in ~ to *113* in Bezug auf
to **release** *113T* freisetzen
reliability *73* Zuverlässigkeit
reliable *96* zuverlässig
to **relocate sth** *73* etw verlegen, etw verlagern
relocation *73* Verlegung, Verlagerung
remark *51* Bemerkung

sector 7 Bereich, Branche, Sektor
secure 86T sicher, bewacht
to **seek** 129 suchen
to **select** 69T auswählen
selection process 126F Auswahlverfahren
self-assessment 123 Selbsteinstufung
to **self-check** 50 einen Selbsttest durchführen
self-starting 103 selbstanlaufend
semi-conductor 38T Halbleiter
semicircle 39T Halbkreis
to **sense** 50 wahrnehmen, erkennen
sense, common ~ 14T gesunder Menschenverstand
sensing element 50 Sensorelement
sensitive, to **be ~ to sth** 73 empfindlich auf etw reagieren
sensor chamber 50 Sensorkammer
sensory 71T sensorisch
separate 11T eigen, separat, getrennt
to **separate** 82 trennen
separated 128 getrennt lebend
separately 21 einzeln
separation, layer ~ 117 Schichttrennung
serial number (S/N) 105 Seriennummer
to **serve** 31 dienen; 86T servieren
service 7 Dienst, Dienstleistung; **~ check** 20 Wartung, (routinemäßige) Überprüfung, Inspektion; **~ factor** 105 Betriebsfaktor
session 90 Sitzung
set 128 vorgegeben, starr, fest
to **set** 49 einstellen; **~ up sth** 64 etw *(Treffen usw.)* vereinbaren; **~ off the alarm** 76 Alarm auslösen; **~ up standards** 79 Normen aufstellen
settings *pl* 118 Voreinstellungen
severe 53 schwer, ernsthaft; **~ duty** 105 Einsatz unter härtesten Bedingungen
shaded pole motor 104 Spaltpolmotor
shaft 9 Welle; **lift ~** 9 Aufzugsschacht
to **shake hands with sb** 87 jdm die Hand geben
shape 35 Form
shaped 24 geformt
sharp 118 scharf
sheet 40 Blech; **data ~** 70 Datenblatt
shelf, shelves 14T Regal, Regale
shelving 14T Regale
shift 17T Schicht
to **shift** 117 sich verschieben
shifting 117 Verschiebung
shock 35 Stoß, Stöße; **electric ~** 14 Stromschlag; to **be in ~** 77 unter Schock stehen
shortage, skills ~ 124 Fachkräftemangel
to **short-circuit** 53T kurzschließen
shortlisted, to **be ~** 126 in die engere Auswahl kommen
shouting 76 Geschrei
showroom 11 Ausstellungsraum
shunt, in ~ 63 in Nebenschluss
to **shut down sth** 15 etw ausschalten
shy 126T schüchtern
side-cutters *pl* 26 Seitenschneider
to **sign** 51 unterzeichnen
sign, warning ~ 51 Hinweisschild, Warnhinweis
signal tone 50 Signalton
signature 98 Unterschrift
significance 50 Bedeutung
significant 38T erheblich
signpost 42 *Hinweis(e) zur Orientierung der Zuhörer in einer Präsentation*
silicon 38T Silizium
silvery-grey 35 silbrig-grau
simplified 63 vereinfacht
to **simulate** 50 simulieren
sincerely, Yours ~ 33 Mit freundlichen Grüßen
sine wave, half ~ 72 Sinushalbwelle
single-board (micro)computer 37 Einplatinenrechner
sinkhole 112 Erdfall, Doline
sinterglass 72 Sinterglas
sir 33 Herr
site, building ~ 27 Baustelle; **construction ~** 57F Baustelle; **~ work** 125 Arbeit vor Ort
size 7 Größe; **overall ~** 97F Gesamtmaße
to **sketch** 81 skizzieren
skilled worker 8 Facharbeiter/in
skills shortage 124 Fachkräftemangel
to **skim** 73 *(Text)* überfliegen
skylight 49 Dachluke, Oberlicht
sleeve 10 Kabeltülle, Kabelmuffe
to **slide** 31 gleiten
slide 10 *(Präsentation:)* Folie; **compound ~** 31 Kreuzschlitten; **cross ~** 31 Querschlitten
slideways, bed ~ 31 Maschinenbett
sliding door 58 Schiebetür
slightly 52 geringfügig, etwas
slip-on cover 56T Einstecktasche
slit 27T Schlitz
slow-blow fuse 62 träge Sicherung
smart 126T *(Kleidung:)* schick
smell of burning 71T Brandgeruch
smoke, heat and ~ alarm system 50 Hitze- und Rauchmeldeanlage
smooth 30 glatt, ruhig
to **smooth** 70 glätten
snap fastener 100 Schnappverschluss
socializing 128 Ausgehen
socket, mains input ~ 70 Netzanschlussbuchse
soil erosion 112 Bodenerosion
to **solder** 16 löten
solder 36 Lot; **~ alloy** 38 Lötlegierung; **~ mask** 36 Lötmaske; **~ pad** 36 Lötpad; **~ point** 36 Lötpunkt, Lötstelle
soldering 123 Weichlöten; **reflow ~** 36 Reflow-Löten; **wave ~** 36 Wellenlöten; **~ iron** 24 Lötkolben
solid 40 (dreidimensionaler) Körper; **rectangular ~** 40 Quader; **rectilinear ~** 47 geradkantiger Körper; **~ object** 106 Fremdkörper
to **solidify** 119T fest werden
solution 7 Lösung
to **sort out sth** 39T etw klären
sorted, to **get sth ~** 120T etw klären, sich um etw kümmern
source, heat ~ 48 Wärmequelle
space, to **clear ~** 112 Platz schaffen; **working ~** 97F Arbeitsraum; **~-saving** 58 platzsparend
spaced, closely ~ 36 eng nebeneinanderliegend
span, life ~ 50 Lebensdauer
spanner 26 Schraubenschlüssel; **open ended ~** 26 Maulschlüssel; **ring ~** 26 Ringschlüssel
spark 53T Funke
to **speak: Speaking.** 21 *(Telefon:)* Am Apparat.
speaker 101F Lautsprecher
to **specialize in sth** 10 sich auf etw spezialisieren
specific 39 speziell, bestimmt, konkret
specifically 75 ausdrücklich; 96 eigens, speziell
specifications *pl* 11T Technische Daten, Spezifikationen
to **specify** 72 angeben
speech bubble 16 Sprechblase
spelling 42 Rechtschreibung; 120 Schreibweise
sphere 40 Kugel
spike 62 Zacke
to **spill** 77 *(Flüssigkeit:)* laufen, auslaufen
spindle 29 Spindel
to **splash** 104T spritzen
splashing water 106 Spritzwasser
to **split** 117 reißen, springen
split-ring commutator 102 Stromwender mit Stromwenderlamellen
spontaneous 104 spontan
sporadic 53T gelegentlich, vereinzelt
to **spray** 106 sprühen
spraying water 106 Sprühwasser
to **spread** 76 sich ausbreiten
square 70F Feld

squirrel cage motor *104* Käfigläufermotor
stability *96* Stabilität
to **stabilize** *70* stabilisieren
stabilizer, integrated voltage ~ *70* integrierter Spannungsstabilisator
to **stack** *100* stapeln
stackable *100* stapelbar
stacking system *85* Stapeleinheit
staff, expert ~ *18* Fachpersonal; **~ entrance** *11T* Personaleingang
stainless steel *96* Edelstahl
stand *32* (Messe-)Stand
standard, environmental ~ *73* Umweltnorm; to **set up ~s** *79* Normen aufstellen
standardization *79* Normung
standardized *123* genormt
standby *17* Bereitschaft
starting salary *124* Einstiegsgehalt
to **state** *32* angeben, erklären, sagen
statement *76* Aussage, Schilderung
stationary *92* ortsfest, stationär
stator *102* Ständer, Stator
status, marital ~ *128* Familienstand
steel, stainless ~ *96* Edelstahl
stepper motor *95* Schrittmotor
stock, in ~ *33* auf Lager, verfügbar
to **stomp** *76* trampeln, treten
stone *27* Stein
storage *58* Lagerung, Aufbewahrung; **cloud ~** *69T* Datenspeicherung in der Cloud; **cold ~** *58* Kühllager, Kühlhaus
storeroom *11* Lagerraum
storey *50* Geschoss, Etage
strange *126* seltsam
strength *52* Stärke
to **stress** *126F* betonen
stress *34* Betonung; **compressive ~** *35* Druckbelastung, Druckspannung
strict *80* streng
string *117* Faden
stringing *117* Fadenzug
to **strip** *27* abisolieren
strip *40* Leiste, Streifen; **~ door** *58* Streifenvorhangtor
strippers *pl*, **wire ~** *26* Abisolierzange
to **structure** *7* aufbauen, strukturieren
structure *6* Aufbau, Struktur
study *112* Untersuchung, Studie
stuff *14T* Sachen, Zeug
sub type *72* Untertyp, Subtyp
subject line *32* Betreffzeile
subsidiary *20* Niederlassung
substance *113T* Stoff, Substanz; **hazardous ~** *38T* Gefahrstoff
substation *17* Umspannwerk, Transformatorenstation
to **suck in** *85* ansaugen
sudden *118* plötzlich
to **suffer from** *118* unter etw leiden
to **suit: to suit sth** *73* für etw passen
suitable *13* geeignet, passend
to **sum up** *91* zusammenfassen
sunlight *56T* Sonnenlicht
superior *120T* Vorgesetzte/r
to **supervise** *8T* überwachen, beaufsichtigen
supervised *19* unter Aufsicht
supervisor *12* Ausbildungsleiterer/in, Abteilungsleiter/in, Vorgesetzte/r
supplement *123* Zusatz, Ergänzung
supplier *9* Zulieferer, Lieferant/in
to **supply sth** *90T* etw zur Verfügung stellen, etw liefern
supply, power ~ (unit) *37* Stromversorgung, Netzteil
to **support** *29* tragen, halten, stützen; *43 (Argumentation)* untermauern
support *31* Träger, Halter; *90* Unterstützung
supposed, to **be ~ to do sth** *53T* etw tun sollen
surface *30* Oberfläche, Fläche; **clamping ~** *97F* Aufspannfläche; **~ finish** *30* Oberfläche(nbeschaffenheit); **~ roughness** *92* Oberflächenrauigkeit; **~ water** *112* Oberflächenwasser
surface-mounted *36* oberflächenmontiert; **~ device (SMD)** *36* SMD-Bauelement
surge: ~ current loading *72* Stoßstrom-Grenzwert; **peak forward ~ current** *72* Spitzendurchlassstrom
surgery/surgical light *98* Operationslampe, -leuchte
surrounding area *112* Umgebung
surroundings *112* Umgebung
survey *68* Umfrage
to **swallow** *126* schlucken
swimming pool: ~ attendant *56* Bademeister/in; **~ complex** *56T* Bäderlandschaft, Schwimmbadanlage
swing door *58* Schwenktür, Pendeltür
to **switch** *10* schalten; **~ on/off** *14* ein-/ausschalten
switch, emergency cut out ~ *14T* Not-Aus-Schalter; **end ~** *85* Endschalter; **~ contact** *49* Schaltkontakt
switchgear *10* Schaltgerät(e), Schaltanlage
switching *49* Schaltung; **~ device** *10* Schaltgerät, Schaltelement; **~ gear** *21F* Schaltanlage
to **swivel** *29* schwenken
swivelling head *30* Schwenkkopf
syllable *34* Silbe
symmetrical *41* symmetrisch
to **synchronize** *69T* abgleichen, synchronisieren
synchronously *104* gleichzeitig
system-guided *96* systemgeführt

T

tab *118* Reiter
tag *51* Anhänger, Etikett
to **tag** *53T* markieren, etikettieren, kennzeichnen
tailstock *30* Reitstock
to **take: ~ on sb** *18* jdn einstellen; **~ over sth** *79* etw übernehmen; **~ up time** *69T* Zeit beanspruchen; **~ care of sth** *32* sich um etw kümmern, etw bearbeiten, etw erledigen; **~ delivery** *114* Ware entgegennehmen, eine Lieferung in Empfang nehmen; **~ it in turns** *11* sich abwechseln
taken, Is this seat ~ ? *87* Ist hier besetzt?
talk *14* Vortrag
to **talk sb through sth** *39T* etw mit jdm durchgehen
taper *30* Kegel
target group *7* Zielgruppe
tear, wear and ~ *103* Verschleiß, Abnutzung
telecommunication *6* Fernmeldetechnik, Telekommunikation
temperature, ambient ~ *73* Umgebungstemperatur; **operating ~** *73* Betriebstemperatur; **~ detection** *74* Temperaturmessung, -erfassung
terms *pl*, **delivery ~** *56T* Lieferbedingungen; **~ of payment** *98* Zahlungsbedingungen
terrible *119T* furchtbar, fürchterlich
test run *62* Probelauf; **~ technician** *8* Prüftechniker/in
tester, voltage ~ *26* Spannungsprüfer
testing *11* Prüfung, Prüf-; **vibration ~** *24* Schwingprüfung, Vibrationsprüfung
theatre, operating ~ *98* Operationssaal
theme *51* Thema
thermal: ~ cutoff *73* thermische Abschaltung; **~ fuse** *73* Thermosicherung; **~ pellet** *73* thermisch geschütztes Gehäuse
thermoplastic *pl* *96* Thermoplaste
thickness *24* Stärke, Dicke
third party *112* Dritte/r
to **thread** *30* Gewinde schneiden
three-phase current *59T* Drehstrom
through-hole device *36* THT-Bauelement
throughout the company *52* in der ganzen Firma
thumb *102* Daumen
tight *58* dicht

to **tighten** *9* *(Schraube)* anziehen, festziehen
time, in good ~ *107T* rechtzeitig; **on ~** *74T* rechtzeitig, pünktlich; to **take up ~** *69T* Zeit beanspruchen; **waste of ~** *69T* Zeitverschwendung; **~ lag** *84* Zeitverzögerung
timetable *64* Programm, Fahrplan, Flugplan
tin *38* Zinn
tingle *52* Kribbeln
tip *24* Spitze; **nozzle ~** *117* Düsenspitze
titanium *34* Titan
tolerance *9* Toleranz; **out of ~** *9* außerhalb der Toleranz
tomorrow, by ~ *64* bis morgen
tone, signal ~ *50* Signalton
tool *14* Werkzeug; **cutting ~** *29* Schneidwerkzeug; **hand ~** *25* Handwerkzeug; **machine ~** *29* Werkzeugmaschine; **measuring ~** *24* Messwerkzeug; **~ holder** *31* Werkzeughalter
toolbox *25* Werkzeugkasten
top-heavy *14T* kopflastig
torque *105* Drehmoment
total price *115* Gesamtpreis
touch, to **get in ~ with sb** *64* sich mit jdm in Verbindung setzen
tough *11T* hart; *35* zäh
toxic *38* giftig, toxisch
to **trace** *71* ausfindig machen, aufspüren
traces *pl*, **copper ~** *36* Leiterbahnen
track, linear ~ profile *96* Linearachsprofil
trade *18* Gewerbe, Branche; **~ fair** *34* (Branchen-, Handels-)Messe; **~ magazine** *98* Fachzeitschrift
traffic *54* Verkehr
to **train sb** *83* jdn schulen
train, gear ~ *30* Getriebe
trainee *6* Auszubildende/r, Praktikant/in
trainer *14* Ausbilder/in, Dozent/in
training *7T* Ausbildung; **~ company** *11* Ausbildungsbetrieb; **~ course** *14* Lehrgang, Schulung
transcript *121* Mitschrift
transformer *73* Transformator
transistor *24* Transistor
transit *58* Durchgangsverkehr
transition *38T* Übergang, Umstellung
to **transmit** *16* übertragen
transmitter *122T* Sender
to **transport** *80* befördern, transportieren
transportation *10* Transport, Verkehr; *74T* Beförderung
traveller *54* Fahrgast
tray, floor ~ *83* Bodenwanne; **~ work** *10* Installation in Kabelpritschen
trial *90* Test, Probe
trial order *98* Probebestellung
triangle *40* Dreieck
to **trickle** *77* rinnen, (in einem Rinnsal) laufen
to **trip** *53T* auslösen
trolley *46* Wagen; **platform ~** *46* Plattformwagen, Flachtransportwagen
troubleshooting *17T* Fehlersuche
trough *62* Wellental
trunk, cable ~ *74* Kabelkanal
trunking *10* Leitungsführung
tube *40* Rohr; *AE* *70* (Elektronen-)Röhre; **X-ray ~** *57* Röntgenröhre
tumble dryer *53* Wäschetrockner
tuning, power ~ *62* Leistungsabstimmung
to **turn** *29* drehen; **~ sth on/off** *52* etw ein-/ausschalten
turn *102* Umdrehung; **in ~** *29* wiederum, seiner-/ihrerseits; to **be one's ~** *17* an der Reihe sein; to **take it in ~s** *11* sich abwechseln
turner *8* Dreher/in
type plate *115T* Typenschild
typically *118* normalerweise, üblicherweise

U

ultrasonic sensor *83* Ultraschallsensor
unavailable, to **be ~** *20* *(Telefon:)* nicht zu sprechen sein
uncommon *53T* selten, ungewöhnlich
uncoordinated *52* unkoordiniert
underground *51* unterirdisch; **~ cable** *17* Erdleitung
underscore *32* Unterstrich
understanding *9* Verständnis
uninterested *126* uninteressiert
union *54* Gewerkschaft; **~ representative** *54* Gewerkschaftsvertreter/in
unique *50* einzigartig
unit *11T* Gerät, Einheit; **control ~** *31* Steuergerät, Steuerung; **drive ~** *93* Antriebseinheit, -aggregat
unknown *33* unbekannt
unlimited *96* unbegrenzt
to **unload** *104* entladen
to **unpack** *74T* auspacken
unpleasant *52* unangenehm
unsatisfactory *119* unzureichend, unbefriedigend
unwanted *36* unerwünscht
up and running *74T* betriebsbereit; to **be ~** *115T* laufen, im Einsatz sein
update (on sth) *32* aktuelle Informationen (zu etw)
to **upgrade** *125* höherstufen, (sich) verbessern
upwards *81* aufwärts, nach oben
urban environment *112* städtischer Raum
usage *84* Verwendung
use, continuous ~ *103* Dauerbetrieb; **intermittent ~** *107* Kurzzeitbetrieb; **ease of ~** *60* Bedienungskomfort

V

vacancy *125* freie/offene Stelle
vacuum cleaner *103* Staubsauger
valuable *125* wertvoll
valve *84* Ventil
variable *104T* variabel, regelbar; **~ frequency drive** *104T* frequenzgeregelter Antrieb
variety *17* Abwechslung, Vielfalt
various *36* verschieden
to **vary** *104T* variieren, regeln; *107T* sich ändern, unterschiedlich sein
vehicle *48* Fahrzeug
ventilated, non-~ *106* unbelüftet
ventilation *14T* Belüftung; **~ fan** *73* Ventilator
ventilator *14T* Abzug, Ventilator
ventricular fibrillation *52* Herzkammerflimmern
venue *32* Veranstaltungsort
vernier callipers *pl* *24* Messschieber
versatile *92* vielseitig verwendbar
version *73* Ausführung, Modell
vertical *106* senkrecht, vertikal
via *36* Durchkontaktierung, Durchsteiger
vibration *118* Vibration; **~ testing** *24* Schwingprüfung, Vibrationsprüfung
vibration-cushioned *85* schwingungsgedämpft
video conferencing *90* Videokonferenz
view *13* Aussicht
virtually *96* praktisch
visibility *58* Sicht
visible *118* sichtbar
visualization, process ~ *10* Prozessvisualisierung
vital *10* essenziell, lebenswichtig, entscheidend
vocational: ~ college *18* Berufsschule, Berufskolleg; **~ school** *125F* Berufsschule; **~ training** *6* Berufsausbildung
voice-over *16* aus dem Off
voicemail *20* Mailbox
void *27T* unwirksam, ungültig
volatile, non-~ *59* nichtflüchtig

voltage, high ~ *15* Hochspannung; **mains ~** *49* Netzspannung; **operating ~** *62* Betriebsspannung; **repetitive peak reverse ~** *72* wiederkehrende Spitzensperrspannung; **integrated ~ stabilizer** *70* integrierter Spannungsstabilisator; **~ tester** *26* Spannungsprüfer
volume *55T* Volumen

W

to **wait:** to **keep sb waiting** *13* jdn warten lassen
wall chaser *27T* Mauerfräser
to **wander** *24* wandern
warning sign *51* Hinweisschild, Warnhinweis
warranty *27T* Garantie
to **wash: ~ down sth** *80T* etw abwaschen; **~ off sth** *80* etw abwaschen
washer *27* Unterlegscheibe
washing: ~ machine *80T* Waschmaschine; **~ system** *80* Waschanlage
to **waste** *84* verschwenden, vergeuden
waste: ~ dump *112* Müllhalde; **~ of time** *69T* Zeitverschwendung; **~ water** *64* Abwasser
water jet *106* Strahlwasser
water-heater *17* Warmwasserbereiter, Boiler
waterproof *56T* wasserdicht
waveform *62* Kurve
wave soldering *36* Wellenlöten
wavy *118* wellenförmig
way, by the ~ *11T* übrigens, à propos; **this ~** *11T* hier entlang
weakness *126* Schwäche
to **wear out** *103* sich abnutzen, verschleißen
wear and tear *103* Verschleiß, Abnutzung
to **weigh** *56T* wiegen
weight *9* Gewicht
welcome, You're ~. *71T* Bitte. Gern geschehen.
welder *76* Schweißer/in
welding *11T* Schweißen; **arc ~** *114* Lichtbogenschweißen; **~ bay** *11T* Schweißplatz
well-equipped *16* gut ausgestattet
well known *7* bekannt
wheelchair *86T* Rollstuhl
white collar workers *pl* *55* Angestellte
widely used *38* weit verbreitet
widespread *114* verbreitet
wilderness *112* Wildnis
wildlife *112* Tier- und Pflanzenwelt, Natur
willingness *124* Bereitschaft
window panel *58* Fenster, Scheibe
wire *26* Draht, Kabel; **~ strippers** *pl* *26* Abisolierzange
wireless *10* drahtlos, Funk-
wirer, control panel ~ *125F* Schaltschrankverdrahter/in
wiring *10* Verkabelung, Verdrahtung; **~ harness** *27* Kabelbaum
wish, Best ~es *33* Mit freundlichen Grüßen
to **withstand sth** *35* etw aushalten, einer Sache widerstehen
wobble *118* Wackeln
wooden *98* Holz-
work file *96* Arbeitsdatei
worker, blue collar ~s *pl* *55* Arbeiter/innen; **skilled ~** *8* Facharbeiter/in; **white collar ~s** *pl* *55* Angestellte
working: ~ envelope *114* Arbeitsraum; **~ hours** *pl* *16* Arbeitszeiten; **~ life** *107T* Lebensdauer; **~ space** *97F* Arbeitsraum
workmate *52* Arbeitskollege/-in
works *7* Fabrik, Werk
workshop *11* Werkstatt; **~ manager** *18* Werkstattleiter/in
worry: No ~ies. *71T* Keine Sorge.
worth, to **be ~ it** *27T* sich lohnen
wrench *14T* Schraubenschlüssel
to **write up sth** *19* etw *(Text)* ausarbeiten
writing, in ~ *69T* schriftlich

XYZ

X-ray *56* Röntgen; **~ machine** *120* Röntgengerät; **~ tube** *57* Röntgenröhre
yours: Y~ faithfully *33* ... und verbleiben mit freundlichen Grüßen; **Y~ sincerely** *33* Mit freundlichen Grüßen
zinc *34* Zink

Basic technical vocabulary (German–English)

Berufe – jobs

Ausbilder/in	training supervisor
Auszubildende/r	apprentice
Dreher/in	turner
Elektriker/in	electrician, electrical engineer
Elektroingenieur/in, -techniker/in	electrical engineer
Elektromeister/in	master electrician
Facharbeiter/in	skilled worker
Feinwerkmechaniker/in	precision mechanic
Konstruktionsmechaniker/in	construction mechanic
Maschinenbauer/in	machine builder
Mechatroniker/in	mechatronics technician
Meister/in	foreman/-woman
Schaltanlagenbauer/in	panel builder
Servicetechniker/in, -monteur/in	service technician
Techniker/in	state-certified engineer
Technische/r Zeichner/in	CAD engineer
Werkstattleiter/in	workshop manager
Werkzeugmacher/in	toolmaker

Handwerkzeuge – hand tools

Abisolierzange	wire strippers *pl*
Bügelsäge	hacksaw
Elektrobohrmaschine	electric drill
Feile	file
Flachrundzange	snipe-nose pliers *pl*
Hammer	hammer
Inbuss-, Innensechskant-schlüssel	Allen key
Kabelschuh-, Crimpzange	crimping pliers *pl*
Kombizange	combination pliers *pl*
Körner	centre punch
Lötkolben	soldering iron
Maulschlüssel	open ended spanner
Ringschlüssel	ring spanner
Schraubendreher, -zieher	screwdriver
Schraubenschlüssel	spanner
Winkel-, Trennschleifer	angle grinder

Werkzeugmaschinen – machine tools

Bandsäge	bandsaw
Bohrmaschine	drilling machine
Drehmaschine	lathe
Fräsmaschine	milling machine
Maschinenbügelsäge	power hacksaw
Schleifmaschine	grinding machine

Messinstrumente – measuring instruments

Gewinde-Grenzlehrdorn	thread plug gauge
Grenzlehrdorn	plug gauge
Grenzrachenlehre	snap gauge
Lineal	rule
Messgerät, Lehre	gauge
Messschieber	vernier callipers *pl*
Multimeter	multimeter
Oszilloskop, Oszillograph	oscilloscope
Spannungsprüfer	voltage tester
Tiefenmessgerät	depth gauge

Geräte und Komponenten – equipment and components

Brückengleichrichter	bridge rectifier
FI-Schalter, Fehlerstrom-schutzschalter	residual current device (RCD)
Kabelkanal	conduit
Kabeltüllle, -muffe	(cable) sleeve
Kondensator	capacitor
Ladegerät	charger
Ladekabel	charging cable
Leistungsschutzschalter	circuit breaker
Leiterplatte, Platine	circuit board
Leitungsführung	trunking
Magnetspule	solenoid
Netzkabel	mains lead
Potentiometer, Drehwiderstand	potentiometer
Schaltanlage, -tafel	(electrical) panel
Schaltanlagen	switching gear
Schaltbild, -plan	schematic, wiring diagram
Schalter	switch
Sensorspule	sensing coil
Sicherung	fuse
Sicherungsautomat	circuit breaker
Sicherungskasten	fuse box
Spannungsregler	voltage regulator
Spule	coil
Steckdose	socket
Stromzähler	electricity meter
Transformator, Trafo	transformer
Trennschalter	isolator, disconnector
Umspannwerk, Transformatorenstation	substation
Verkabelung, Verdrahtung	wiring
Verlängerungskabel	extension reel
Wechselrichter, Inverter	inverter
Widerstand	resistor

Spannung und Strom – voltage and current

Drehstrom	three-phase current
(elektrische) Ladung	(electric) charge
Erde	ground
Erdschluss	ground fault
Fehlerstrom	fault current, residual current
Gleichstrom	direct current (DC)
Hochstrom	high current
Laststrom	load current
Leckstrom	current leakage
Leistung, Nennleistung	power rating
Leistung, Stromverbrauch	wattage
Nennstrom	nominal current
Netz(strom), Stromnetz	mains, line current
Netzausfall	mains failure
Netzspannung	mains voltage
Neutralleiter(strom)	neutral (current)
Spannung	voltage
Spitzenspannung	peak voltage (PV)
Stoßstrom	surge current
Strom	current
Stromversorgung, Netzteil	power supply
Überlast(ung)	overload
Wechselstrom	alternating current (AC)

Leiterplatten – PCBs

Anschluss	connector
Bauelement	component
(Bauelemente-)Gehäuse	package
Beschichtung	coating
bestücken	to populate
Bestückungsaufdruck	silkscreen
Bestückungsplan	component mounting diagram
Bestückungsseite	component side
Chipsatz	chipset
Einplatinencomputer	single board computer
Flussmittel	soldering flux
integrierter Schaltkreis	integrated circuit (IC)
isolieren	to insulate
Isolierschicht	insulating layer
leiten	to conduct
Lot	solder
löten	to solder
Lötseite	copper side
Lötstopmaske	solder mask
Mikrocontroller, Einchipmikrorechner	microcontroller
Multilayerplatine	multilayer PCB (printed circuit board)
Schaltplan	schematic
Schnittstelle	interface
Schutzschicht	conformal coating
Vergussmasse	potting material

Tätigkeiten – actions

abschalten	to disconnect
(ab)schleifen	to grind
anbringen, montieren	to mount
aufladen, laden	to charge
auslösen	to trigger
befestigen	to fasten, fix
biegen	to bend
bohren	to drill, bore
drehen	to turn
entladen	to discharge
ersetzen	to replace
erzeugen	to generate
fräsen	to mill
hartlöten	to braze
kurzschließen	to short-circuit
lösen	to loosen
markieren, kennzeichnen	to tag
montieren	to assemble
ölen	to oil
reparieren	to repair
schmieren	to grease
schweißen	to weld
sperren	to lock
überbrücken, umgehen	to bypass
unterbrechen,	to disconnect
verstärken	to amplify
(vom Stromnetz) trennen	to disconnect
(weich)löten	to solder

Talking about numbers

Cardinal numbers / Ordinal numbers

0	oh/nought/null (*AE*) zero		
1	one	1st	first
2	two	2nd	second
3	three	3rd	third
4	four	4th	fourth
5	five	5th	fifth
6	six	6th	sixth
7	seven	7th	seventh
8	eight	8th	eighth
9	nine	9th	ninth
10	ten	10th	tenth
11	eleven	11th	eleventh
12	twelve	12th	twelfth
13	thirteen	13th	thirteenth
14	fourteen	14th	fourteenth
15	fifteen	15th	fifteenth
16	sixteen	16th	sixteenth
17	seventeen	17th	seventeenth
18	eighteen	18th	eighteenth
19	nineteen	19th	nineteenth
20	twenty	20th	twentieth
21	twenty-one	21st	twenty-first
22	twenty-two	22nd	twenty-second
23	twenty-three	23rd	twenty-third
24	twenty-four	24th	twenty-fourth
30	thirty	30th	thirtieth
40	forty	40th	fortieth
50	fifty	50th	fiftieth
60	sixty	60th	sixtieth
70	seventy	70th	seventieth
80	eighty	80th	eightieth
90	ninety	90th	ninetieth
100	one hundred	100th	one hundredth

In English you say:

101	one hundred **and** one
235	two hundred **and** thirty-five
1,563,765 1 563 765	one million, five hundred **and** sixty-three thousand, seven hundred **and** sixty-five

You use commas or spaces (and not a point) after the thousands (or millions) in large numbers.

Decimals

In English, you write decimals with a point, not a comma.

0.25	oh/nought point two five (*BE*) zero point two five (*AE*)
3.76	three point seven six
55.37	fifty-five point three seven
1.585	one point five eight five

Fractions

¼	a/one quarter
⅓	a/one third
½	a/one half
⅔	two-thirds
¾	three-quarters
5⁄16	five sixteenths
1½	one and a half

1 m^2	one **square** metre
1 m^3	one **cubic** metre
5^2	five **squared**
10^4	ten **to the power** of four

Symbols

+	plus/and
–	minus
±	plus or minus
×	multiplied by/times by (6 mm × 2 mm)
÷	divided by
=	is equal to/equals
≠	isn't equal to/doesn't equal
≈	is approximately equal to
<	is less than
>	is greater/more than
µ	micro- (one millionth)
%	per cent (*auch:* percent)
°	degree

Conversion tables

Area

English to metric	1 square inch (in^2)	= 6.452 square centimetres
	1 square foot (ft^2)	= 0.0929 square metres
	1 acre (ac)	= 4,047 square metres
	1 square mile (m^2)	= 2.59 square kilometres
Metric to English	1 square centimetre	= 0.155 square inches
	1 square metre	= 10.764 square feet
	1 square kilometre	= 0.3861 square miles
English to English	1 square foot	= 144 square inches
	1 acre	= 43,560 square feet
	1 square mile	= 640 acres

Distance

English to metric	1 inch (in)	= 2.54 centimetres
	1 foot (ft)	= 30.48 centimetres
	1 yard (yd)	= 0.9144 metres
	1 mile (mi)	= 1.609 kilometres
Metric to English	1 centimetre	= 0.3937 inches (3/8 inch)
	1 metre	= 39.37 inches (3 feet, 3 3/8 inches)
	1 kilometre	= 0.62137 miles
English to English	1 foot	= 12 inches
	1 yard	= 3 feet
	1 mile	= 5,280 feet

Energy/Force

English to metric	1 horsepower (hp)	= 0.746 kilowatts
	1 ounce-force	= 0.278 newtons
	1 pound-force (lbf)	= 4.448 newtons
	1 foot pounds (ft-lb)	= 1.355 newtons-metres/joules
	1 inch pounds	= 0.112 newtons-metres
	1 pounds per foot	= 14.59 newtons-metres
	1 British thermal unit (BTU)	= 1055 joules
Metric to English	1 kilowatt	= 1.341 horsepower
	1 newton	= 3.597 ounce-force
	1 newton	= 0.224 pound-force
	1 newtons-metres / 1 joule	= 0.738 foot pounds
	1 kilojoule	= 0.948 British thermal units

Mass/Weight

English to metric	1 ounce (oz)	= 28.35 grams
	1 pound (lb)	= 0.453 kilograms
	1 UK ton ('long ton')	= 1,016 kilograms
	1 US ton ('short ton')	= 907 kilograms
Metric to English	1 gram	= 0.035 ounces
	1 kilogram	= 2 pounds, 3.3 ounces
English to English	1 pound	= 16 ounces
	1 UK ton ('long ton')	= 2,240 pounds
	1 US ton ('short ton')	= 2,000 pounds
Metric to metric	1 metric tonne (t)	= 1,000 kilograms

Temperature

Fahrenheit (F) to Celsius: subtract 32, then multiply by 5, then divide by 9
Celsius to Fahrenheit: multiply by 9, then divide by 5, then add 32

Volume

English to metric	1 fluid UK ounce (fl oz)	= 28.41 millilitres
	1 UK pint (pt)	= 0.568 litres
	1 UK quart (qt)	= 1.137 litres
	1 UK gallon (gal)	= 4.546 litres
	1 fluid US ounce	= 29.57 millilitres
	1 US pint	= 0.473 litres
	1 US quart	= 0.946 litres
	1 US gallon	= 3.785 litres
	1 cubic inch (in^3)	= 16 cubic centimetres
	1 cubic foot (ft^3)	= 0.03 cubic metres
Metric to English	1 litre	= 0.568 UK pints
	1 litre	= 0.473 US pints

Terms, units and abbreviations

Term		Unit	
English	**German**	**English**	**German**
apparent admittance (*Y*)	Scheinleitwert (*Y*)	siemens (S)	Siemens (S)
capacitance (*C*)	Kapazität (*C*)	farad (F)	Farad (F)
charge (*Q*)	Ladung	coulomb (C) or ampere-seconds (As)	Coulomb (C) Amperesekunden (As)
conductance (*G*)	Leitwert	siemens (S)	Siemens (S)
current (*I*)	Strom	ampere (A)	Ampere (A)
electric field strength (*E*)	Elektrische Feldstärke	volt per metre (V/m)	Volt pro Meter (V/m)
electromotive force (*E*)	Spannung, Elektromotorische Kraft (*U*)	volt (V)	Volt (V)
frequency (*f*)	Frequenz (*f*)	cycles per second (cps)	Hertz (Hz)
frequency (*f*)	Frequenz (*f*)	hertz (Hz),	Hertz (Hz)
angular frequency (ω)	Kreisfrequenz (ω)	radian per second (rad/s)	1/s
resonant frequency (*fr*)	Resonanzfrequenz	hertz (Hz)	Hertz (Hz)
gain (*G*)	Verstärkung, Gewinn	decibel (dB)	Dezibel (dB)
inductance (*L*)	Induktivität (*L*)	henry (H)	Henry (H)
magnetic field strength (*H*)	Magnetische Feldstärke (*H*)	ampere turn per metre (At/m)	Ampere pro meter (A/m)
magnetic flux density (*B*)	Magnetische Flußdichte (*B*)	tesla (T)	Tesla (T)
phase angle (φ)	Phasenwinkel (φ)	degree	Grad
power (*P*)	Leistung (*P*)	watt (W)	Watt (W)
apparent power (*S*)	Scheinleistung (*S*)	volt-ampere (VA)	Voltampere (VA)
reactive power (*Q*)	Blindleistung (*Q*)	volt-ampere-reactive (var)	Var
reactance (*X*)	Blindwiderstand (*X*)	ohm (Ω)	Ohm (Ω)
capacitive reactance (X_C)	Kapazitiver Blindwiderstand (X_C)	ohm (Ω)	Ohm (Ω)
inductive reactance (X_L)	Induktiver Blindwiderstand (X_L)	ohm (Ω)	Ohm (Ω)
resistance (*R*)	Widerstand	ohm (Ω)	Ohm (Ω)
rotational speed	Drehzahl	revolutions per minute (rpm)	1/min or 1/s
susceptance (*B*)	Blindleitwert (*B*)	siemens (S)	Siemens (S)
voltage (*V*)	Spannung (*U*)	volt (V)	Volt (V)

Irregular verbs

be – was/were – been	sein
become – became – become	werden
begin – began – begun	anfangen, beginnen
break – broke – broken	brechen
bring – brought – brought	bringen
build – built – built	bauen
burn – burnt/burned – burnt/burned	(ver)brennen
buy – bought – bought	kaufen
catch – caught – caught	fangen
choose – chose – chosen	wählen
come – came – come	kommen
cost – cost – cost	kosten
cut – cut – cut	schneiden
do – did – done	tun, machen, erledigen
draw – drew – drawn	zeichnen
dream – dreamt – dreamt	träumen
drink – drank – drunk	trinken
drive – drove – driven	fahren
eat – ate – eaten	essen
fall – fell – fallen	fallen
feed – fed – fed	füttern, ernähren
feel – felt – felt	(sich) fühlen, empfinden
fight – fought – fought	kämpfen
find – found – found	finden
fit – fit/fitted – fit/fitted	passen
fly – flew – flown	fliegen
forget – forgot – for- gotten	vergessen
get – got – got (AE gotten)	bekommen, erhalten
give – gave – given	geben
go – went – gone	gehen, fahren
grow – grew – grown	wachsen
hang – hung – hung	hängen
have – had – had	haben
hear – heard – heard	hören
hide – hid – hidden	(sich) verstecken
hit – hit – hit	schlagen, aufprallen auf
hold – held – held	halten, festhalten
keep – kept – kept	behalten
know – knew – known	kennen, wissen
lay – laid – laid	legen
lead – led – led	führen, leiten
learn – learnt/learned – learnt/learned	lernen
leave – left – left	abfahren, verlassen, weggehen
let – let – let	lassen
lose – lost – lost	verlieren
make – made – made	machen
mean – meant – meant	meinen, bedeuten
meet – met – met	treffen
pay – paid – paid	bezahlen
put – put – put	setzen, stellen, legen
read – read – read	lesen
ride – rode – ridden	reiten, fahren
ring – rang – rung	klingeln, anrufen
rise – rose – risen	(an)steigen
run – ran – run	laufen, rennen
say – said – said	sagen
see – saw – seen	sehen
sell – sold – sold	verkaufen
send – sent – sent	senden, schicken
shake – shook – shaken	schütteln
set – set – set	setzen, stellen
show – showed – shown	zeigen
shut – shut – shut	schließen
sing – sang – sung	singen
sit – sat – sat	sitzen
sleep – slept – slept	schlafen
smell – smelt/smelled – smelt/smelled	riechen
speak – spoke – spoken	sprechen
spell – spelt/spelled – spelt/spelled	buchstabieren
spend – spent – spent	ausgeben, verbringen
stand – stood – stood	stehen
steal – stole – stolen	stehlen
swim – swam – swum	schwimmen
take – took – taken	nehmen
teach – taught – taught	unterrichten, beibringen
tear – tore – torn	(zer)reißen
tell – told – told	sagen, erzählen
think – thought – thought	denken
throw – threw – thrown	werfen
understand – understood – understood	verstehen
wake – woke – woken	wecken
wear – wore – worn	tragen (Kleidung)
win – won – won	gewinnen
write – wrote – written	schreiben

Acknowledgements

S. 7: Shutterstock/OPOLJA; **S. 10.1:** Shutterstock Creative/Dmitry Kalinovsky; **S. 10/2–4:** Ritter Starkstromtechnik GmbH & Co. KG, Dortmund/Michael Benford; **S. 12/1:** Shutterstock/Djomas; **S. 12/2:** Fotolia/Vadim Zaitsev; **S. 12/3:** Shutterstock/Monkey Business Images; **S. 12/4:** Shutterstock/Firma V; **S. 12/5:** Shutterstock/UncleOles; **S. 12/6:** Fotolia/ajr_images; **S. 14:** Shutterstock/ESB Professional; **S. 16/1:** Shutterstock/Matee Nuserm; **S. 16/2:** Shutterstock/science photo; **S. 16/3:** Shutterstock/michaeljung; **S. 16/4:** Shutterstock/Lighthunter; **S. 16/5:** Shutterstock/Dmitri Kalinovsky; **S. 17/1:** Shutterstock/Phovoir; **S. 17/2:** Shutterstock/Kekyalyaynen; **S. 17/3:** Shutterstock/Phovoir; **S. 18:** Fotolia/industrieblick; **S. 22/1:** Fotolia/Besler; **S. 22/2:** Fotolia/xmentoys; **S. 24/1:** Fotolia/bruno135_406; **S. 24/2:** Shutterstock/Minerva Studio; **S. 24/3:** Shutterstock/kurhan; **S. 25/1:** Fotolia/J.M.; **S. 25/2:** Fotolia/naruedom; **S. 25/3:** Fotolia/krasyuk; **S. 25/4:** Fotolia/photobalance; **S. 25/5:** Fotolia/PhotographyByMK; **S. 25/6:** Fotolia/Shahril KHMD; **S. 26/1:** Shutterstock/Volodymyr Krasyuk; **S. 26/2:** Shutterstock/5; **S. 26/3:** Fotolia/ALEXEY FILATOV; **S. 26/4:** Shutterstock/Eduardo Rivero; **S. 26/5:** Shutterstock/Volodymyr Krasyuk; **S. 26/6+7:** Shutterstock/Carlos Romero; **S. 26/8:** Shutterstock/vdimage; **S. 26/9:** Shutterstock/vvoe; **S. 26/10:** Shutterstock/ND700; **S. 26/11:** Fotolia/Vladimir Zhupanenko; **S. 26/12:** Shutterstock/Yanas; **S. 26/13:** Shutterstock/PhotoProRo; **S. 26/14:** Shutterstock/exopixel; **S. 26/15:** Fotolia/ivansmuk; **S. 26/16:** Shutterstock/Wongtanarek; **S. 26/17:** Shutterstock/Origination Nes; **S. 26/18:** Shutterstock/Winai Tepsuttinun; **S. 26/19:** Shutterstock/nito; **S. 26/20:** Shutterstock/a_v_d; **S. 27/2:** Shutterstock/AlexLMX; **S. 27/3:** Shutterstock/Natan86; **S. 28:** Shutterstock/Phovoir; **S. 29/1:** Fotolia/Kalinovsky Dmitry; **S. 29/2:** Fotolia/tm-photo; **S. 29/3:** Fotolia/Kzenon; **S. 29/4:** Fotolia/Fotolia RAW; **S. 29/5:** Georg Aigner, Landshut; **S. 29/6:** Fotolia/isaac74; **S. 29/7:** Fotolia/Andrey Armyagov; **S. 30:** Shutterstock/Vereshchagin Dmitry; **S. 34/1:** Shutterstock/Thanakorn Hongphan; **S. 34/2:** Shutterstock/Scanrail1; **S. 34/3:** Shutterstock/gualtiero boffi; **S. 36:** Rainer Knäpper, Lizenz Freie Kunst; Unna; **S. 37/1–5:** Jan Richter, Freiberg; **S. 40/1–5u.:** Georg Aigner, Landshut; **S. 41/2:** Jan Richter, Freiberg; **S. 42:** Shutterstock/ESB Professional; **S. 45:** Jan Richter, Freiberg; **S. 48/49:** OSRAM Licht AG, München; **S. 50:** Fotolia/mipan; **S. 53:** Shutterstock/Rawi Rochanavipart; **S. 56:** Shutterstock/FabrikaSimf; **S. 57:** Fotolia/sudok1; **S. 62/1:** ADF/Comsys Schweden; **S. 63/2:** ADF/Comsys Schweden; **S. 64:** Shutterstock/Rawpixel.com; **S. 67:** Siemens AG Bereich Automation and Drives, Industrial Automation Systems, Nürnberg **S. 68/1u.:** Shutterstock/ESB Professional; **S. 68/2u.:** Shutterstock/mimagephotography; **S. 68/3u.:** Shutterstock/racorn; **S. 70/1–10:** Wolf-Rainer Windisch; **S. 71:** Jan Richter, Freiberg; **S. 74:** Shutterstock/Mila Supinskaya Glashchenko; **S. 77:** Shutterstock/ChiccoDodiFC; **S. 78/1:** Fotolia/alice_photo; **S. 78/2:** Fotolia/Björn Wylezich; **S. 78/3:** Fotolia/ake1150; **S. 78/4:** Fotolia/Avantgarde; **S. 79/1:** Shutterstock/Oleg Golovnev; **S. 79/2:** Shutterstock/AJR_photo; **S. 80/1+2:** Klaus Hilmer/Carina Rauscher/Andreas Nachtwey; **S. 80u.re.:** Shutterstock/Andrey Burmakin; **S. 82/1:** Klaus Hilmer/Carina Rauscher/Andreas Nachtwey; **S. 82/2u.:** Shutterstock/abimages; **S. 82/3u.:** Fotolia/Alexander; **S. 82/4u.:** Shutterstock/Africa Studio; **S. 83–85:** Klaus Hilmer/Carina Rauscher/Andreas Nachtwey; **S. 86/1:** Shutterstock/leungchopan; **S. 86/2:** Shutterstock/Lisa F. Young; **S.86/3:** Shutterstock/Rehan Qureshi; **S. 86/4:** Shutterstock/SnowWhiteimages; **S. 89:** Shutterstock/maksimee; **S. 92:** Fotolia/Phuchit; **S. 95:** Georg Aigner, Landshut; **S. 96:** Stepcraft GmbH &Co. KG, Menden; **S. 100:** Shutterstock/TaraPatta; **S. 102/2:** Shutterstock/photoiconix; **S. 112:** Shutterstock/Jason Benz Bennee; **S. 114/1:** Fotolia/zapp2photo; **S. 114/2:** Fotolia/xiaoliangge; **S. 117:** Copyright © 2017 Simplify3D; **S. 119:** Jan Richter, Freiberg; **S. 120:** Shutterstock/Daniel M Ernst; **S. 122/1:** Shutterstock/Monkey Business Images; **S. 122/2:** Shutterstock/racorn; **S. 122/3:** Shutterstock/SpeedKingz; **S. 127:** Shutterstock/Michal Kowalski; **S. 136/File6:** Jan Richter, Freiberg; **S. 140:** Jan Richter, Freiberg; **S. 148:** Shutterstock/johnbraid

The British Isles